The Arab
Avant-Garde

THOMAS BURKHALTER, KAY DICKINSON,

AND BENJAMIN J. HARBERT, EDITORS

*The Arab
Avant-Garde*

MUSIC, POLITICS, MODERNITY

WESLEYAN UNIVERSITY PRESS

Middletown, Connecticut

Wesleyan University Press
Middletown CT 06459
www.wesleyan.edu/wespress
© 2013 Wesleyan University Press
Manufactured in the United States of America
Typeset in 10/13 point Galliard

Wesleyan University Press is a member of the Green Press Initiative.
The paper used in this book meets their minimum
requirement for recycled paper.

The Arab avant-garde: music, politics, modernity / Thomas Burkhalter,
Kay Dickinson, and Benjamin J. Harbert, editors.
       pages   cm. — (Music/culture)
              Includes index.
ISBN 978-0-8195-7385-8 (cloth: alk. paper) — ISBN 978-0-8195-7386-5
       (pbk.: alk. paper) — ISBN 978-0-8195-7387-2 (ebook)
              1. Avant-garde (Music) — Middle East.
     2. Music — Middle East — 20th century — History and criticism.
     3. Music — Middle East — 21st century — History and criticism.
       4. Popular music — Middle East — History and criticism.
              5. Music — Political aspects — Middle East.
        I. Burkhalter, Thomas, 1973– II. Dickinson, Kay, 1972–
                    III. Harbert, Benjamin J.
                       ML348.A73 2013
              780.956'0905 — dc23   2013017387

                       5   4   3   2   1

Contents

⌁

A Note on Transliteration

The Arab Avant-Garde adopts the transliteration system of the *International Journal of Middle East Studies* (*IJMES*), electing to omit indicators for long vowels and diacritical markings to signify emphatic letters. An ع ('ayn) becomes a ', and a ء (hamza) a '. For proper nouns, we have stuck to the most familiar Roman script versions, which frequently do not conform to the *IJMES* format. Transliterating Arabic, particularly in its varied spoken forms, can never be an exact science. We hope the reader will be patient with any seeming irregularities that arise from the many possible options produced by this process of conversion.

Introduction

"Arab" + "Avant-Garde"

⌒

KAY DICKINSON

From Alexandrian female heavy metallers and Beiruti jazz trumpeters who sample the noises of warfare to migrants into the avant-garde enclaves of Europe and North America, Arab culture has long offered up a wealth of exciting, challenging, and varied musics. Theirs is not a singular scene, a coherent body of interconnected performers. Rather, the sheer breadth of vanguardism in the Arab world and its diasporas—as well as the experimental work from elsewhere that is in its debt—spans history and geography too expansively to warrant any such classification. The range of compositional and improvisational techniques, performance styles, generic engagements, professional educations, inspirations, and intercontinental collaborations that have inherited the mantle of "innovation" within Arab music are vast. With the objective of honoring this multifariousness (although in no way encyclopedically encapsulating it), our anthology collects together studies of radical experimentalism within genres and modes as diverse as musical theater, improvisation, hip-hop, folk-inflected art music, and electronica. Its writers, too, hail from a complementary plethora of countries and disciplinary trainings: practicing musicians, Arab area studies specialists, ethnomusicologists, and scholars of popular culture and media, all dedicated, like their research subjects, to disturbing the Eurocentric resonances of monikers like *the avant-garde*. All are keen to imbibe, expand, and even challenge the growing body of literature on alternative, non-Western, and postcolonial modernities.

As such, our emphasis on comprehensively hybrid and globally dialectic practices purposefully undermines the focus on regionally specific genres and staid notions of tradition that consumes most books on Middle Eastern music-making. Given the dense spatial and temporal negotiations this book unfolds, the tired binary of tradition versus modernity that preoccupies so much of the scholarly literature about the region dissolves. Such dualistic assertions belie a protracted history of exchange, one that complicates contentions of "otherness" and sequestered "local expression" through its sustained cosmopolitanism. No longer can areas of the world be so easily isolated from one another, often to the tactical disadvantage of (an understanding of) the Arab world. Instead, we explore the many ways in which "tradition" and "innovation" are relationally defined and in dialogue. We posit crucial lineages of invention that often displace presumptions about mimicry or geographical belatedness, and which therefore insist upon shared global projects of cultural rejuvenation. Influence is polyvalent here, and ownership claims on "the avant-garde" are exposed as deeply conservative political gestures.

All that said, this volume fully acknowledges the boundaries that have been set up to establish exclusivity within the avant-garde. It is not without reason that the term has been seen as fraught, inauthentic, and tainted with imperialist agendas. And yet the musicians who have inspired our book still adhere to this label, and therefore its introduction is dedicated to recognizing their reasons for doing so. Understanding the contracts that enable musical experimentalism to interact globally is impossible without first exposing these tendencies within the avant-garde.

The Oppressive Etymologies, Histories, and Scholarships of the Avant-Garde

In the early nineteenth century, the term *avant-garde* began to capture greater semantic territory. Once purely a military phrase used to distinguish crack troops, it then assumed a high-ranking position within cultural expression, marking out art work that forged ahead and broke new ground. What can it mean to conjoin this French phrase, redolent with bellicose intent, to the word "Arab"? French forces, along with other imperial intruders, are no strangers to Arab terrain. Likewise, foreign intervention, and the Arab world's response to it, has shaped how the avant-garde has behaved over the years, and not just in this region. The sense of "progress," so crucial for stimulating avant-garde ambience, frequently (often unwittingly) stems from these actions of plunder and subordination, in the artistic field as well as others.

Plunder first. The colonization of Algeria, Tunisia, Morocco, and Greater Syria came in the wake of the brief Napoleonic "mission" to Egypt between 1798 and 1801. It was during these reconnaissance surveys that some of modern Europe's most expansive data on Egyptian music was collected, information that filled two whole volumes of Guillaume André Villoteau's *Description de l'Egypte*. The Napoleonic campaign thus gathered not only military but also cultural intelligence, if the two can be so easily separated. Findings like these and an augmented contact with the Middle East inspired new expression within Europe: Rimsky-Korsakov's *Scheherazade* suite, for example; Saint-Saëns's opera *Samson and Delilah*; and, in the visual arts, Matisse's paintings of "odalisques." European and American adventures to a highly phantasmagoric and partial "East" were also pivotal to the development of Western avant-gardes, as Kamran Rastegar's interview with Amir Elsaffar (chapter 2 in this anthology) testifies. In the hands of composers as diverse as the early Arnold Schoenberg or Sun Ra, modernism has fundamentally defined itself through an expansion of tonality beyond the typical Western scales. Certain figures, drawn to alternative modes and microtones, have wandered from their home traditions toward the Arab world for fresh outlooks. Highly prized booty here is the transcendental, something promised by the ecstatic potential of the Arab genre of *tarab*.

By naming, extracting, fetishizing, and leitmotifing "the East's" musical heritage, these citations can simultaneously fix and dehistoricize Arab music in detrimental ways. To start with, they might obscure a restless and complementary current of reinvention that is just as inquisitive as they are. As will become apparent, the flow of ideas is almost always read as the European-American avant-garde arming itself with fresh weapons for combating its own culture's stagnancy. Western assumptions of Arab form can hence catalyze what African American studies scholar Fred Moten exposes as "enforced hermeticisms," which—counter to intention, perhaps—rematerialize an implausibly closed and "solipsistic space of bourgeois aesthetic production" (Moten 2003, 40). As exotica, Arab creativity is put to work on a project of revitalization, its "strangeness" a primary attraction that all the while closes doors between its own practices and the avant-garde heartlands it has helped shape.

Furthermore, these Western iterations of Middle Eastern form are scored by a fine line that divides simple curiosity and eclecticism from a looting or corruption of Arab intellectual property. What differentiates the two is acknowledgment—most pressingly, acknowledgment that seeks not to expurgate colonial legacy. Although individual artists certainly pay their dues, the canon of Western literature that describes the avant-garde's inception distressingly lacks reference to contributions from the Arab world. We would do well here to heed the foundational proposition of Mike Sell's excellent monograph, *Avant-Garde Performance and the Limits of Criticism*: that scholarship and pedagogy dedicated to the avant-garde can be startlingly complicit with conservative, militaristic, and imperialist ideologies. Here is how. Matei Calinescu's *Five Faces of Modernity*, Renato Poggioli's *Theory of the Avant-Garde*, David Cope's *New Directions in Music*, Peter Bürger's book (also called *Theory of the Avant-Garde*), Daniel Herwitz's *Making Theory/*

Constructing Art: On the Authority of the Avant-Garde, Alastair Williams's *New Music and the Claims of Modernity*, Michael Nyman's *Experimental Music: Cage and Beyond*, Richard Kostelanetz's *Dictionary of the Avant-Gardes*, and Bill Martin's *Avant Rock: Experimental Music from the Beatles to Björk* are all considered classic tomes, text or reference books that peg out the boundaries of their subject. Yet none of them volunteers even the briefest mention of Arab art. Fleeting nods, sidelines, and footnotes, this is where the Arab avant-garde is lodged in English-language literature, pressed into the service of European-American inventiveness but with little concession granted to its own autonomy. In Jonathan D. Kramer and Larry Sitsky's *Music of the Twentieth Century Avant-Garde*, William Doering notes that "[Elliott] Carter even spent a summer transcribing Arab music . . . in Tunisia," although he neglects to distinguish the type of music or its provenance (Kramer and Sitsky 2002, 104). Of the seventy-plus featured composers in this volume, none hail from the Middle East. Bernard Günter, we hear in *The Ashgate Research Companion to Experimental Music*, has been saving up for an 'ud and learning Arabic *maqamat*, but he is never asked why (Saunders 2009, 281). In *Avant-Garde Jazz Musicians Performing "Out There,"* David Such remarks that Sun Ra once performed in Egypt, then fails to elaborate on why he did so, or to explore how profoundly influenced Sun Ra was by the country's culture (Such 1993, 117). After fruitless trawling for even the slightest acknowledgment of an Arab avant-garde, one might happen across Christoph Cox and Daniel Warner's collection, *Audio Culture: Readings in Modern Music*, which merely lists Halim El-Dabh (the subject of Michael Khoury's chapter in this book) as one of many contributors to the Columbia-Princeton Electronic Music Center (Cox and Warner 2004, 367). No contextualization or analysis ensues.

These omissions would be more excusable if their authors admitted their modest, localized ambits, which, save for the odd excursion to Japan, barricade their studies squarely within the borders of Europe and North America. But the titles itemized just now declare a universalism. Their capacious cast lists of largely Western (and male) heroes contrive still further a bounded designation for avant-garde genius. As a combined result, these writings insinuate that avant-garde uptake has confined itself solely to Western quarters. In his two foundational books, *Modern Music: The Avant-Garde since 1945* and *Modern Music and After: Directions since 1945*, Paul Griffith explicitly maps the journeys of the avant-garde: they rebound between Europe and North America exclusively and, while there are sporadic allusions to "African" and "Asian" colors and textures, their histories and inheritances, their passages along colonial trade routes, are never plotted out. In *The New Music: The Avant-Garde since 1945*, Reginald Smith Brindle goes so far as to prejudicially aver, "Avant-garde art only flourishes in the softer, sophisticated airs of the Western Democracies, or in the socialist states where artistic individualism is tolerated (such as Poland or Yugoslavia)" (Brindle 1987, 182).

Scholarly lacunae like these collude with other more territorially invasive dismissals of Middle Eastern agency. In 1869, the opening of the Suez Canal—that direct, European imperial-financial intrusion onto Arab soil—was celebrated by the building of the Cairo Opera House. Its first performance was not a local work, but Verdi's *Rigoletto*. This choice, along with various Western critics' election to ignore Arab avant-gardism, amounts to what cultural theorist Gayatri Spivak terms "epistemic violence": the deliberate imposition of Western models as the norm, the only, the paramount, at the expense of voices that might critique them or speak otherwise. Perpetuating a silence about the Arab avant-garde (however ignorant or innocent) has collectively connived to diminish its potency, clearing space, in this supposed vacuum of articulation, for narratives that drown out what the Arab world has to say about these injustices (Spivak 1988, 271–313). In an effort to *not* replicate such an agenda, this introduction will henceforth deliberately downplay certain currently dominant (in English-language discourse) explanations of the avant-garde in favor of debates that have preoccupied the Arab world and frequently been stifled outside it.

Yet while the historical eras and figures this chapter details refuse to adopt the Western conceptions of the avant-garde as the measure for judging global experimentalism, this is not to say they have quietly lived at a remove from these notions. Colonization put pay to that. For one, Arab music has transmogrified enormously in response to its absorption of European educational models and notational strictures (see Saed Muhssin's chapter for further details). The Moroccan thinker Abdelkebir Khatibi observes how techniques, models, and applications from afar can serve "a dominating and imperial will to power," particularly if they are judged to be imported. At the same time, he acknowledges their appeal for instituting "a certain rapport between man and fellow creatures, man and being" (Khatibi 1983, 36–37).

How might we engage with these ambivalences that have nevertheless enthralled many a composer and performer? This anthology, after all, elects to spend time with artists who openly invoke the term *avant-garde* in their self-descriptions, rather than those hoping to regain some pure, extinguished precolonial condition. Despite the occlusions, the partiality paraded as universality, the constrictive pigeonholing, the take without give, the violent colonial-linguistic overtones, the chronologies that salute only Europeans and Americans, despite all this, value and potential still remain. Each artist rationalizes her or his affinities differently, and a good deal of the hows and whys will be unfurled contextually in the chapters to come. Before then, a few words on why we, as researchers, continue to see merit in using the avant-garde as a lens for analyzing Middle Eastern music.

Firstly, thinking about the conjunction of "Arab" and "avant-garde" demands that we beam a searchlight on the forms of expansionism just detailed. Focusing on the Arab avant-garde lays bare how engagements with and imaginative counterpoints to Western practices give birth to a heterogeneity that is deeply incised by land and resource grabs. The blatant European etymology of the term *avant-garde* flags its own foreignness, even in English, and this is something that can be usefully hung on to. Other adjectival genre monikers, such as "experimental," rarely arouse such scrutiny, cannot trumpet an asymmetrical and unjust association with "the new," or help quash as effectively the paradoxically conservative insinuations of a dominating European or American claim on vanguardism.

The fertilization is never one-way. An Arab persistence splays open the multivalent, multidirectional, multisited, and multiply resourced makeup of the avant-garde, if not to liberate proliferating pathways to its freedoms, then surely to reveal its foundations in globalized accumulation and exploitation. The very existence of an Arab avant-garde helps defeat the well-worn imperialist tactic of falsely claiming cultures under occupation to be a tabula rasa, where nothing exists to challenge acquisitive ambitions. This is far from the case, as a succinct retelling of Arab history will prove.

The Past Certain Books Forsook

The mid-nineteenth to early twentieth century witnessed many assertions that discredit the idea of an Arab "blank slate" during what is now known as the *nahda* (renaissance) period. The movement can partially be read as a response to the arrival of the French and other forces in the Middle East: a reawakening prompted by urgency for self-affirmation in the face of annexation. Most of the following chapters make necessary reference to the *nahda*, and unsurprisingly so, considering that its impact was felt in many areas of life, from the arts and politics to translation and religious practices. Not only did the *nahda* era overlap with the birth of a clearly enunciated avant-garde sensibility around the world, it also precipitated many involved workings-out of how the Arab regions might absorb overseas—particularly European—influence. As its name suggests, the *nahda* was intrigued by what could be mined from the Arab and Islamic past, yet it was simultaneously fueled by energetic new dealings with other regions of the world, set in motion by the decline of the Ottoman Empire and its replacement by European domination. Many of its protagonists were dispatched on study missions to the West or dedicated time to translating its leading political, educational, and cultural tracts. Profiting from these expanded perspectives, *nahda* thinkers like Jamal al-Din al-Afghani (a religious activist deeply critical of Western ascendancy), Rifa'a al-Tahtawi (a translator, educator, and proponent of Islamic modernity), and Qasim Amin (an advocate of women's rights) formulated a productive paradox. It was one that cautiously derived lessons, often at close quarters, about statehood from Europe—including its concepts of nationalism—in order to forge a unique anticolonial regionalism. As prominent Egyptian *nahda* writer Taha Hussein put it, "I am pleading for a selective approach to European culture, not wholesale and indiscriminate borrowing. . . . [T]he preservatives of defense, religion, language, art, and history can be strengthened by the adoption of Western techniques and ideas" (Hussein 1954, 17–20).

These arbitrations took their musical form most concretely in the debates initiated by Cairo's 1932 Congress of Arab Music (for a full account, see Racy 1993). One of the many objectives of this event was to rationalize Arab music according to certain standardized, European means of measurement and notation, thereby establishing a more cohesive, transportable sensibility. In order to churn around how this might be achieved, composers from Europe such as Béla Bartók and Paul Hindemith were invited, figures well versed in documenting local folk forms but also in melding them with what we might consider to be proto-avant-garde art music. The ensuing formulae for the Arabic *maqam* systems have been hotly debated ever since. Likewise, the concomitant influx into the conservatories in Arab countries of European teaching methods is regularly defamed as devaluing, perhaps even deskilling, local expertise. Whatever the damage it did, there is no denying how the Congress mainstreamed international dialogue. This, in turn, helped launch some hugely popular twentieth-century artists, including Farid al-Atrash, Muhammad 'Abd al-Wahhab, and Munir Bashir, as well as the fascinating liaisons between *maqamat* and European avant-garde atonal and twelve-tone composition promulgated by the likes of Nouri Iskandar. Ultimately, the Cairo Congress was central to congealing an opposition between the self-proclaimed guardians of purist Arab musical parameters and those wanting to acknowledge or experiment with ideas from outside.

But the latter camp, as this anthology attests throughout, is peopled by musicians who anything but mimic Western trailblazers. All of them dialectically engage "Arab" with "avant-garde" to complicate trite yet damaging binaries such as East-West, South-North, traditional-modern, backward-advanced, rooting out the motivations that can pinion certain performers and populations to the less empowered enclaves of either side of these dichotomies. They regularly achieve this by reinstating obfuscated histories, speaking back to, inflecting, deterritorializing, and, crucially, expanding the exclusive canons of the avant-garde, while pointing out its origins in conflict.

Let us take, for example, the compositions of Aida Nadeem, a contemporary Iraqi performer currently living in exile in Denmark. In "Risala" (which can be translated as message, letter, dispatch, or treatise), acid "stabs" reminiscent of synthetic computer game gunshots, perhaps space invader weaponry, pierce the soundscape. The piece's vocal track is tightly compressed and dryly recorded but, at the same time, expansive, thanks to Nadeem's melodic range and the enduring studio-produced reverberation that trails it. Confined yet diffusive, conjuring up a bombed-out city but also disassembling such easy connotations, the piece's disruptive constitution speaks of its writer-performer's history within conflict: one that started in highly cosmopolitan Baghdad and has encompassed musical training in Europe. The forward thrust of avant-gardism in the work of this experimental artist draws not only on the Iraqi musical archive (a heavy casualty, in its recorded forms, in the latest U.S.-led invasion) but also on influences, ranging from Karlheinz Stockhausen to Talvin Singh, accumulated on her many fugitive journeys beyond her homeland. More than simplistic eclecticism, her music registers the diverse stimuli present at the politically charged flash points where the avant-garde meets military intervention.

For these reasons and more besides, Aida Nadeem's oeuvre will supply this initial chapter with material through which to test its principal theoretical suggestions. Nor is she alone in recruiting conflict into her work. To name but a few other examples, there are Halim El-Dabh's *It Is Dark and Damp at the Front* (detailed in Michael Khoury's chapter) and Mazen Kerbaj's *Starry Night* (see Thomas Burkhalter's and Marina Peterson's contributions). Compositions like these respond to the avant-garde's uneasy proximity to militarism, as well as to how noise has been conscripted as a ground-clearing and disorienting tactic in urban conflict at various sites during the "war on terror." These pieces can also function as an avant-gardist counter to the sustained musical and sonic torture inflicted upon detainees within American prison camps in Iraq and Guantánamo Bay, which, to date, does not contradict international law (see Cusick 2006 for a fuller account).

This Anthology's Structure

To best allow readers to experience and learn from such compositions, the authors in this collection have followed cues on how to order their thinking from conspicuously ongoing concerns within Arab music-making and the region's critical thinking more generally. These themes we are titling "Alternative Modernities: Norms and Innovations," "Roots and Routes," and "Political Deployments of the Avant-Garde." What the rest of this chapter unfolds is something of a ground plan for where we are heading collectively with this book. It is not, however, a summary of future essays, but more a subjective response to the urgent call to reduce, unmask, and reverse "epistemic violence," arranged so as to support later chapters' immersions into these three prevalent subject areas. The introduction's composition is unavoidably quixotic in the face of two characteristics: a profusion of dialogue on these issues across many planes within the Arab world and the lack of any precedents in the form of collected, systematic, establishing literature on the Arab avant-garde in English. For political reasons, it declines the tidy templates designed for the Western tradition, listening out, instead, for what resounds through a host of different Middle Eastern discourses on originality and experimentalism.

Part 1 of this book—and also its introduction—we have called "Alternative Modernities: Norms and Innovations." Here we establish how, stylistically, the avant-garde articulates its novelty and what it casts out as its opposite: the material it considers stale. Within these actions, newness, inspired by conceits often read as European in origin, resonates amidst forceful and reiterative incarnations of "Arab tradition." This discussion has to be prefaced by an acknowledgment that, when one types "Arab + music" into an academic search engine, it is rare not to find the results also clumped under the heading "traditional," so closely do the terms cohabit, at least in English-language debate. Does the inclination toward "tradition" encourage conservative, limiting, liberationist, or authentic discourse in relation to a "newness" that is just as complicated in its hermeneutics and sites of inspiration? "Tradition" might foster local pride and anti-imperialist nationalism or, alternatively, facilitate a projection of the region that is quaint, underdeveloped, and ripe for invasions of culture, as well as military hardware. The next part of the introduction will look into how various thinkers have addressed these questions, while the subsequent contributions of Shayna Silverstein, Kamran Rastegar, and Thomas Burkhalter examine particular musicians' and composers' responses to these problematics.

Kamran Rastegar and his Iraqi-American interview subject, Amir Elsaffar, interrogate the supposed standoff between modernity and tradition, exposing its bias toward Western-universalist models of the avant-garde that are convincingly undone by postcolonial and diasporic realities. Before heading into the transcription of his interview, Rastegar calls for a refiguring of modernity that correctly admits its limitations and contingencies. Elsaffar proves an ideal embodiment of all these aims, coalescing as he does the quest for innovation with a sincere and respectful urge to conserve time-honored modes of music-making. Bicultural by birth, Elsaffar leads us autobiographically through his diverse influences and educational travels. Through these, his work exemplifies not just a fluent integration of regional particularities but also a disintegration that radically questions and reformulates cultural specificity.

By converging on self-declaredly contemporary music from Syria (known there as *musiqa mu'asira*), and with a precise musicological attention to its formal qualities, Shayna Silverstein reveals how this movement formulates its vanguardism through thoughtful, politicized, and worldly engagements with history. *Musiqa mu'asira* is forged through an indexing of repertoires that existed before the modern era (frequently framed as local or folk) among a thoroughly institutionalized commitment to European art music, particularly, although not exclusively, that of the former Warsaw Pact states. What constitutes "the contemporary" in Syria is thus both political and spatial. Each musical constituent engages, unpacks, and transforms the others to reformulate how "the old" and "the new" might materialize, to stop either from freezing over. Silverstein's readings ultimately point out how uneven, and often contradictory, the social relations that shape creativity will always be.

An investigation of Beirut's experimental music scene and its placement within the global(ized) avant-garde allows Thomas Burkhalter to probe the "World Music 2.0" market's expectations of norms and innovations from Arab material. The long-standing hybridities of Beiruti culture and the mobility of its protagonists collide, today, with the profound alteration of the landscape of innovation, where cheaply produced digital audio files and video clips circulate and are commodified through web-oriented technologies. Here both the "Arab" and the "avant-garde" reconstitute themselves through newly available influences as well as the economic dynamics and (frequently Orientalizing) demands of these markets. While musical novelty now thrives amid a comprehensively globalized infrastructure, this is not to say that old dependencies and inequalities have ceased to haunt it.

Such geopolitical inquiry is furthered within part 2, "Roots and Routes," which takes on the avant-garde's interactions with space (the new cultural frontiers upon which it lays claim) and time (the *avant*, or before, as it translates from the French). How is the avant-garde localized and relocalized? Newness is frequently pinpointed on the map, creating subcategories and pecking orders within how innovation and its imitation are understood. Consequently, the central segment of the rest of this introduction observes how the avant-garde forces particular schisms between past, present, and future. It then inquires into some of the political and financial motivations for doing so. This overview lays the groundwork for the three detailed essays in part 2, all of which home in on individual composers so as to best grapple, through specificities, with the impact of roots and routes on the avant-garde.

Saed Muhssin's subject is the early-twentieth-century Egyptian pioneer Sayyed Darwish, highly rewarding as a historicist case study on the development of an Arab avant-garde. Amid a context of Ottoman, French, and British colonization, Darwish's inventiveness emerges inseparably from social revolution and anti-imperial struggle. His oeuvre as a whole legitimizes intermittent innovation by enfolding pleasingly conformist compositions and by speaking directly to and for the oppressed minorities of which Darwish, himself a day laborer, was also one. Through scrutiny of musical form, Muhssin's chapter disentangles how Darwish masterfully extended preconceptions about correct idioms to simultaneously become the forefather of the Arab avant-garde and "the people's artist."

Sami Asmar similarly engrosses himself in music that is at once populist and vanguardist. His focus, Ziad Rahbani, is the son of Lebanese superstars Fairuz and 'Assi Rahbani, and is an artist thus ripe for a survey of how roots (in both the national and the familial sense) can nourish experimentalism. While beholden in some senses to his legacy, Rahbani just as easily ridiculed musical traditionalism, which he saw as variously facile, conservative, and factional within the destructive politics of his Lebanese civil war setting. Here ingenuity and novelty function to critique and surpass warring and warmongering ideologies.

The creative constitution of Egypt's Halim El-Dabh and its emergence through the composer's travels around his homeland and to the United States are the concerns of Michael Khoury's essay. Before fully dedicating his life to music, El-Dabh earned his living as an agricultural engineer, a career that facilitated contact with the rich indigenous musics of Egypt and allowed him to experiment with recording technologies outwardly developed to aid farming productivity. As a result, folk traditions and manipulated wire recordings cohabit within his work in a manner that renders him a prime candidate for the avant-garde canon. And yet El-Dabh is rarely celebrated as a forerunner in these circles, an oversight that sees Khoury questioning how the composer's roots and routes preclude his entry into the pantheon while also laying out exactly how deserving he is of this accolade.

To round out this book, part 3, "Political Deployments of the Avant-Garde," investigates how Arab incarnations address some of these concerns through specifically politicized actions; how complex artistic expression can coincide with and reimagine anticolonial or antigovernmental rhetoric. Setting these priorities in motion, this volume's final portion begins with Marina Peterson's evaluations of the U.S. State Department's investment in the Tabadol Project, wherein Lebanese avant-garde performers were brought over to America, as an act of cultural diplomacy, to improvise musically with U.S. citizens. In navigating the requirements for recognition and participation, the musicians drew upon certain sonic cross-border cosmopolitanisms that might, potentially, act to dissolve difference. Yet Peterson also demonstrates how, in the post-9/11 environment, the democracy and harmony engendered within Tabadol's improvisations weathered the distinct traces of U.S. hegemony, territorialism, and state building.

Following on, Caroline Rooney assesses the potency of Palestinian hip-hop within that country's revolutionary and resistance movements, turning her attention to how solidarity might be generated by its musicians' decisions to work within this particular genre. With a set of references as eclectic and dialectic as hip-hop itself, Rooney sets about explaining how applicable this genre of protest, realism, validation, resistance, and resourcefulness in the face of scarcity proves to Palestinian struggle. However, crews such as DAM are not solely inspired by African American performers like Tupac Shakur and Chuck D because of their commitments to fighting for equality. They are concurrently recasting what some might read as the globalization of hip-hop into a broad internationalism that understands the Palestinian cause as just one of its nodes.

Likewise, Benjamin Harbert's topic is another subcultural category with global span: heavy metal as performed and appreciated by Egyptians. Via in-depth ethnography, Harbert reveals how this music at once alarmed the ruling regime through its "foreignness" and connected its scenesters to a protective network outside their nation's borders. Extreme metal has proven succor and inspiration for certain Egyptians drawn to its compelling expressions of rebellion, alienation, and transgression. By adopting and adapting its ico-nographies and musical practices, the scene unwittingly left itself vulnerable to the very state it frequently saw as the cause of its ills. These same symbols of transnational affinity became, in the hands of the police, justification for mass arrests of metallers under the suspicion of Satanism. To justify these actions, the regime insinuated that the incarcerated youths had surely sur-rendered to Western corruption and even Zionist infiltration, thus shoring up the government's weak affinities with an ever-strengthening Islamic bloc.

As has hopefully already become apparent, these debates and struggles are frequently fought on the battlegrounds of aesthetics and so it is toward matters of style that this introduction will head next, paying specific notice to how "newness" and "oldness" are politically figured within Arab music and the international avant-garde.

Alternative Modernities: Norms and Innovations

It has already been noted how Western discourse on the avant-garde snubs Arab exponents. For very different reasons, many scholars and artists working in or affiliated with the region are equally keen to uncouple experimentalism from local music-making. In order to appreciate the arguments about norms and innovations in the three chapters that follow this one, it is essential to understand the interplay between these concepts within the sites of Arab avant-garde production.

The term *asala* is never far from any conversation about culture in the Arab world. With a core meaning of "authenticity," *asala* is etymologically linked to words having to do with pedigree but also to *asal*, which means "root." Continuity is held firm, encased in the earth, an invocation of territory that is regularly played out, as Shayna Silverstein's chapter will soon illuminate, through reference to musical space. According to this line of thinking, the cross-border exchanges enjoyed by the avant-garde are corruptions. For Habib Hassan Touma, a principal historian of Arab music and author of the definitive text *The Music of the Arabs*, they represent "a monstrous distortion [that] has irresponsibly compromised the essence of Arabian music" (Touma 1996, 143). Touma ventures little other analysis beyond this dismissal, refusing to countenance hybrid forms within his purportedly scrupulous taxonomy of music from the region.

One wonders what he would make of Aida Nadeem's "Baghdad," a track that happily bundles together older Arabic modal violin flourishes with computer-programmed beats and Indian and Persian instrumental inflections. Nadeem is, surely, just as much an Arab as any of the composers and forms Touma elaborates. Unlike Touma's, Nadeem's work, and also the title chosen for our book, opens up the definition of "Arab" to a space beyond its usual geographical or stereotyping cordons. It acknowledges that the classification Arab bears a complicated history: always contested within the region by those feeling that it does not describe them (even if Arabic is their first language); central to twentieth-century independence movements, especially pan-Arab nationalism; saturated with the racist interpellations of the contemporary "war on terror"; and a force for unity once more amidst the highly divergent uprisings that cluster together as "the Arab Spring." Tellingly, the one record label that has perhaps most supported the hip-hop scene's rapid response to the 2011 insurgencies—housing artists such as Arabian Knightz and M.C. Amin—humorously appropriates the name of that most bureaucratic of international(ist) organizations, the Arab League. The label's motto: "It's not just hip-hop, it's a movement."

Unsurprisingly, then, the classification Arab is a fraught one and predilections for authenticity like Touma's can be seen to stem from a socially specific configuration of history that simultaneously shapes what the avant-garde might stand for within the region. What can be grouped together as the identifying characteristics of Arab culture and why? What notions of tradition buttress it? For Muslims, there is a deep-seated imperative to look to the days of the Prophet for model modes of governance and behavior, for guidance on the most contemporary of dilemmas. The later one is born with respect to this exemplary era, the harder it can be to maintain purity of thought and deed. The currency of *bid'a* within Islamic doctrine also vigorously intercedes here in that it not only connotes sin, heresy, and misguided transgression from the true path but also novelty.[1] It features in the moralistic assertions of the Egyptian government, Benjamin Harbert's chapter points out, which vilified heavy metal for infecting the country with, purportedly, harmful Western and Israeli influences.

Newness, however, is framed in many ways within the Arab world other than through Islamic semantics. There is the undeniable tendency, as Andrea Flores Khalil notes, to indulge "a precolonial past, linguistic origin, or unchanged tradition [which] is a mythification that emerged as a response to cultural marginalization" (Khalil 2003, 133). A similar impulse powers Aida Nadeem to avow: "You might force us to leave the country, you might set up a dictatorship, you might destroy the country, but our Iraqi heritage, the memories from my city, won't die and I'll keep singing about it. Maybe in a different colour or different style, but it will always be there and that will keep it for generations on. This is my resistance" (Nadeem 2010).

In the "Alternative Modernities: Norms and Innovations" section to come, Shayna Silverstein identifies parallel nation-building aspirations in how her Syrian case studies draw upon established regional musical vernaculars. To indulge the qualities that modernity sweeps aside—such as folklore, or even most religion—is to expose just how restricted modernity can be. Anticolonial rhetoric the world over, be it the *authenticité* of the Mobutu regime in Zaire or the Taliban's traditionalist inscriptions of everyday life, is quick to wield "tradition" as a defensive tactic. No wonder, if we are to heed Khatibi's comments about the "imperial will to power" or take seriously what postcolonial literature scholar Réda Bensmaïa portrays as "the great fear of having been body-snatched, so to speak, by European modes of thought and transformed into a simple cog in the system of reproduction of Western ideology" (Bensmaïa 2003, 160). Within such readings, the modern almost always arrives from elsewhere, exploitative, dominating, universalizing in its claims. To withdraw into an idealized past is to seek flight from these impositions. Morocco's Mohammed 'Abed al-Jabri concurs, noting that modernity is all too frequently figured as something that "can only engage Arab culture from the outside [and] it thus pushes its adversary into withdrawal and confinement" ('Abed al-Jabri 1999, 2). From this standpoint, modernity is less a right everyone can access equally (albeit, perhaps, belatedly) and more a globalizing endeavor spearheaded from elsewhere.[2] Boxed in by such muscular assertions of tradition, the Arab avant-garde not only suffers the generalized ostracism heaped onto artistic experimentation the world over, but its typical adversaries—complacency, conservatism, and reactionary sentiment—also hold exceptionally high social status within local anticolonial activity.

Analogously preferential treatments are restaged, to a certain degree, in how particular definitions of Arab music become illustrative of the totality within book-length studies on the topic published in English. Here, the canonical English-language texts, such as Henry George Farmer's *Historical Facts for the Arabian Musical Influence*, Habib Hassan Touma's *The Music of the Arabs*, and Ali Jihad Racy's *Making Music in the Arab World: The Culture and Artistry of Tarab*, allege coverage of the entirety of the field (save the last title) yet delve exclusively into the "traditional" and never the avant-garde.[3] Tellingly, in her *History of Arabic Music Theory*, Shireen Maalouf's conception of "Arabic music theory" ends, but for a nine-page afterthought on the Cairo Congress, in the nineteenth century and her central figures of analysis hail largely from the medieval period. Her book fixes Arabic modes and tonalities rather than discerning their historical and geographical mobility. Whatever the impulses behind this move, such incremental intellectual gestures cement "Arab life" (and music) as suspicious of modernity and what lies beyond, creating, through reiterative partiality, a representation of the region's musical output that has sadly become normative.

It is now surely time to examine this "tradition"—this strategic sanctuary, weapon, marker of self-determination, and forthright evasion of influence from dubious sources and forces—with circumspection. The Syrian-born, Lebanon-dwelling Arab nationalist poet Adonis holds it at arm's length because of the vigor it lent the Islamic Caliphate's lengthy stranglehold on the region. So hell-bent was the Caliphate on maintaining the clarity of hereditary line that meanings, practices, and values that conveniently and potently privileged their rule were embalmed as true to the Prophet's vision (Adonis 1985, 75). The journalist and critic Ghali Shukri joins the fray: "No matter how much the cultural heritage contradicts our daily life it is always right and we are always wrong" (Ghali Shukri, *Shi'una al-Hadith: ila ayn?* (*Our Modern Poetry: Whither?*), Cairo: Dar al-Ma'arif, 1968: 19–20; cited and translated in Noorani 2007, 79). For these thinkers, sloughing away convention can bring to light fresh techniques not simply for interacting with culture but also for simply existing in the world. Caution accelerates into out-and-out disdain in the work of the German theorist Theodor Adorno: "The return to peasant and folk art in a country that is in the midst of the industrialization process leads to costumings and concealments of all kinds, but never to compelling production" (Adorno, "Why Is the New Art So Hard to Understand?"; in Leppert 2002, 127–34, 129). To Adorno's mind, this type of "tradition" is deceptive, never openly admitting the marked variance between older incarnations of music-making and traditionalist forms that dominate in the present day. As an ethnomusicologist, Jonathan Holt Shannon strives to particularize such accusations by thoughtfully and persuasively plotting out how "authenticity" is designated. His book-length study of Syrian music-making, *Among the Jasmine Trees*, unravels tradition's presiding logics, convincingly arguing that the purity of form claimed by certain musical heritages comes with distinctly post-*nahda* priorities and political agendas (Shannon 2006, 60).

Variously, Adonis, 'Abed al-Jabri, and the Moroccan historian Abdallah Laroui all posit tradition as mobile and adaptive, the urge to stall it as ideologically driven, forever colored by the age in which this standstill is executed. Colonial archives, never the most neutral of sources, might also provide much of its character. Worse still, for Marxian thinkers like Adorno, traditional music suffers equally from the fate of all commodified music: it is just as alienated and alienating because there are vast, disjunctive chasms between production and consumption settings. From Adorno's perspective, only the new (read: avant-garde) can confront, perhaps even upend, these estranging industrial processes.

Yet traditional and avant-garde Arab music, despite the polarizations, share many of these pockmarks of estrangement, and such concurrences warrant scholarly attention. After all, both practices take advantage of similar (if not the same) technologies of amplification and recording, similar global networks of promotion and distribution. Seen from this vantage point, tradition is a commodity fetish, as well as a social bond and sometime servant of certain master narratives that hold court via control and stagnation. The avant-garde is steered by hegemonic and capitalistic flows too, although progress is more the name of its game. For Argentinian theorist Néstor García Canclini in his *Hybrid Cultures*, binaries like these collapse within a market economy, although such labels are extremely efficacious for negotiating the commercial placement of one's cultural production. As Thomas Burkhalter's chapter will reveal, Arab avant-garde musicians must play a careful, often contradictory, game of box-checking across these definitions if they are to garner success on the international market.

While their actions may sound pragmatic, even cynical and opportunistic, many members of the Arab experimental community still hold dear the license to strike up a genuine relationship with earlier musical iterations. The Arab avant-garde is as mercurial and crossbred as "tradition" is, its very *in*authenticity affirmed by the foreign taint this French term exposes. Adonis, Laroui, and 'Abed al-Jabri alike envision the benefits of a dialectical, rather than oppositional, rendezvous between tradition and modernity, as does Aida

Nadeem. Classical Iraqi poetry, for instance, assumes a leading role in her album *Out of Baghdad*, asserting a legacy endangered by war and displacement amidst other geopolitical signifiers that nourish rather than annihilate it. The historical fluctuations of "tradition" certainly cause Adonis to be wary of hegemonic alignments to it, but, like Nadeem, he is also quick to endorse a vibrant commitment to one's forebears. For him, "authenticity is not a fixed point in the past to which we must return in order to establish our identity. It is rather a constant capacity for movement and for going beyond existing limits towards a world which, while assimilating the past and its knowledge, looks ahead to a better future" (Adonis 1985, 90). Mohammed 'Abed al-Jabri sees history as continuity rather than rupture too. Approach and incentive are everything in the search for "a workable method to assume our relationship to *tradition*." He continues matter-of-factly: "The type of understanding of tradition that we construct will directly determine the type of investment that we will make of it. Similarly, the function that we would want to ascribe to it will in turn affect the way we construct our conception" ('Abed al-Jabri 1999, 120).

Adonis's and 'Abed al-Jabri's insights read well amidst the sound tracks to the 2011 uprisings. Taxi stereos and impromptu concerts were awash with work made familiar by twentieth-century protest singers, particularly Sheikh Imam and Mohamed Munir, or Arab nationalists like Muhammad 'Abd al-Wahhab and Umm Kulthum. All four drew extensively on tradition (classical as well as folk) to craft a grounded and persuasive liberationist discourse, roused once more in these recent reincarnations. As 'Abed al-Jabri continues, this is how heritage solicits contemporary commitment in order "to serve modernity and to give it a foundation within our 'authenticity,'" a process in which the Arab avant-garde also involves itself ('Abed al Jabri 1999, 7).

Just as specific politics course through each statement of tradition, so too is the Arab avant-garde's quarrying from musical history motivated. In the next chapter, Shayna Silverstein unravels how Shafi Badreddin's *Quintete*'s prominent folkloric references insist upon an ancient multiculturalism within Syria that other, perhaps dominant, traditionalisms might wish to obscure. Later, Sami Asmar details how Ziad Rahbani conspicuously interweaves familiar, local figurings into his more challenging pieces as a way of ensnaring a broader audience. For Caroline Rooney, authenticity encompasses the elements that resist comfortable familiarity elsewhere. They are then recast precisely as signifiers that *can* enter transnational debate, redolent with all the political potency of their primary sites.

But balancing the values and significations of "tradition" and "modernity" can prove extremely tricky, as the work of *nahda* predecessors corroborates. A celebration of diversity should never discredit how difficult it is for musicians to blend their styles, to override the deep imprints of their trainings.[4] 'Abed al-Jabri, leery of the bumpy ride initiated by global projects of "progress" and "development," cautions that "there are limits beyond which we cannot go in this investment process. What we can invest in today's intellectual activity is not tradition as a whole but rather tradition as survival" ('Abed al-Jabri 1999, 120). With this insight, 'Abed al-Jabri admits how partial, desperate, and pragmatic the adoptions of tradition and, by implication, modernity actually are. He reminds us of the lopsided access to "the modern" around the world and tradition's ready, but not necessarily wholly logical, placement as an opposite and therefore (even less plausibly) as a foil to it. The Arab avant-garde short-circuits the more debilitating outcomes of this routing. For all their promises, notions of "progress" over the last two hundred years have largely been, as any student of postcolonial thought or protester in Tahrir Square would point out, exploitative, determined by unjust and imperial divisions of labor, an excuse for further neocolonial policy making (including, in particular, those of organs like the International Monetary Fund and World Bank, which stalwartly implement the rhetoric of development). Progress also becomes another name for increased commodification, igniting the allure of novelty to diversify the market. These are factors to consider when weighing how the spread of the avant-garde can be classified as a globalizing endeavor, a topic that part 2, "Roots and Routes," takes up in its investigations of how space and time have been politically circumscribed. Where is artistic expression seen to stem from, and under what conditions does it travel?

Roots and Routes

As with all music, that which is filed under the category "Arab" is an intricate mix of other similarly complex labels: Persian, Kurdish, Turkish, Andalusian, Greek, Western. These terms, quite clearly, are also historically amorphous, hegemonic, and subject to abrupt change. Various empires, both invading and expanding Arab territory, have added voices to this repertoire and, as early as such things were recorded, there are mentions of an international trade in musical ideas. Minglings and mergings like these are rarely smooth, necessitating multiple acts of *translation* of one order or another, translation itself being a political action and one that is never entirely simple, translucent, or fully successful for all involved. Notably, the Arabic term for translation, *tarjima*, also encompasses what, in English, we would call musical interpretation. And, just as artistic coloring and improvisation spring from cross-fertilizing established repertoires, varied habits, and social structures, so too does Arab music. One of the most influential theoretical postulations on the subject is Abu Nasir al-Farabi's tenth-century *Great Book of Music*, which details the permeation of Persian and Greek forms and was later of significant influence to southern European music-making in the Middle Ages. The enactment and investigation of exchange to which this book contributes cannot therefore be proclaimed a modern phenomenon. Nor can the singular logics of local cultural contamination or delight in a presumed, effortless cosmopolitan hybridity lead particularly far along the path of comprehension. Amir Elsaffar, interviewed by Kamran Rastegar in chapter 2, exposes the inadequacy of any such simplistic conceptions of source or assimilation. Drawing cogently on examples from his own training and family history of migration, he renders "influence" a fluctuating and multivalent force. To appreciate the *processes* promulgating artistic and intellectual transactions (ones often highly bound up in commerce) is, we would argue, a much more revealing and fruitful aim.

As has been pointed out, philosophers like Mohammed ʿAbed al-Jabri have turned their attentions to such eclecticism, grappling with the political quandaries of refusing to quarantine any isolated notion of "the Arab past." Such propositions also benefit from considerations of the spatial; how both metaphorical and actual evasions of borders are conducted. In his *Contemporary Arab Thought: Studies in Post-1967 Arab Intellectual History*, Ibrahim Abu-Rabiʿ dubs the thinkers who live these hybridities and contradictions "migrating intelligentsia," observing how they waft "from one plane of thought to an antithetical; from the rational to the irrational, from the scientific to the metaphysical, and from the mystical to the philosophical" (Abu-Rabiʿ 2004, 266). The outcomes of these peregrinations are, to his mind, dislocation and alienation.

Yet are not dislocation and alienation, at one and the same time, two of the most profoundly affecting qualities associated with the historical avant-garde? In Arab hands, neither of these sentiments can be deemed idle mimicry of Eurocentric form; these modernist preoccupations are also intrinsic to and differentiated in Middle Eastern experience, with disenfranchisement, along with migration, war, and exile, sharply sensed across the region. Aida Nadeem's album *Out of Baghdad* details forced flight from her country of birth. Citations of genres from classical *maqamat* to European underground dance recount a highly politicized experimentalism, one that speaks of displacement but also insists on the principle of (creative) freedom. "Identity can't be a barrier," she asserts, linking territorial concerns straight back to the military-industrial complex: "I'm not nationalist, not at all; we've been a mixture in Iraq for thousands of years. . . . After the fall of Saddam, they started talking about federalization. It won't work, we used to live together; we need to keep living together tomorrow. Small countries and many borders make more money for the weapons industry, more troops to guard them" (Nadeem 2010). And so solid signifiers of location are ripped apart and reorganized, organically fused, muddling geopolitical certainties and national boundary lines. To consider Iraqi music is frequently to find it in the diaspora. Nadeem's reverberating vocal lines haunt all these spaces, returning to mark territory but also to lose it. An otherworldly quality persists, reminding the listener of *tarab*'s sought outcomes, with the emphasis here on asking the question of where, exactly, one might be transported? Movement shapes the bulk of the music discussed in this volume, for example Halim El-Dabh's journeys around Egypt and then to America, as presented in Michael Khoury's chapter.

Thorny cultural geography also distinguishes many of the experimental musical responses to the 2011 protests, with tracks like Omar Offendum et al.'s "#Jan 25 Egypt" and the Arabian Knightz's "Prisoner" (which samples Martin Luther King Jr.) conceding the potency of English as a global language and American history as an activist touchstone. Such connections are not always effortless, uninterrupted, or entirely determined by the artists' whims. As Marina Peterson's essay in this volume elaborates, with reference to a tour of America by Lebanese avant-gardists, the strong currents of border policing, nation-state security, colonial cartographies, and anti-imperialist aspiration exert considerable force within these circuits of culture. This instance, along with many others detailed in this book, exposes the unevenness of access to the avant-garde.

What can an account of the mobility, prejudicial rerouting, and door policies governing avant-garde people and their principles reveal? The acceptance of particular styles into the inner sanctum of the avant-garde is similarly policed and shuts out various aesthetic formulations. In a discussion of the difficult transposition of modernities outside the European ambit, one that bears equal applicability to the Arab avant-garde, postcolonial and subaltern studies thinker Dipesh Chakrabarty argues that "seeming 'incommensurabilities' [produce] . . . neither an absence of relationship between dominant and dominating forms of knowledge nor equivalents that successfully mediate between differences, but precisely the partly opaque relationship we call 'difference.' . . . [We should] write narratives and analyses that produce this translucence—and not transparency—in the relation between non-Western histories" (2000, 17). Here Chakrabarty urges an investigation of how and why local enactments of global trends exhibit similarities and divergences. This is exactly the work carried out in Saed Muhssin's chapter, where he dissects what, precisely, made Sayyed Darwish's compositions innovative within the specific context of twentieth-century Egypt. Complementary arguments are to be heard in Sami Asmar's reading of the Rahbani family lineage and their negotiations of the tides of twentieth-century Lebanese politics. All three of the chapters in part 2 concentrate on single figures, allowing for in-depth investigations of specific spatial and historical currents. What conclusions can then be drawn from mapping out these patterns? If a musical style appears to concord with another elsewhere in the world, the imperative is to look into the webs of power that can, variously, classify it as inextricable planetary hybridity, theft, compliance, degraded copy, solidarity, or happenstance. Each outcome bears its own value. As has already been noted of European and American appropriations of Arab cultural conventions, *ownership* claims render such overlaps distinctly political. And, when the "avant" within the avant-garde makes its presence felt, negotiations of artistic globalization, origin, and imitation are readily warranted.

Cultural echoes can be interpreted in all manner of ways. One perspective propounded by many Arab thinkers, as has been elaborated, is that phenomena like the avant-garde, alongside other modernizing tendencies, were born outside the region and have then been latterly refashioned within it. The threat to notions of tradition has been assessed, and it now makes sense to ponder how Arabs have also interpreted the flows of influence in an almost apologetic manner. Within the realms of cultural analysis, this view is elegantly explored by Adonis. He identifies the trait of "double dependency" as endemic to Arab expression: a bolstering, conservative, and retrogressive cleaving to the past that also locks itself to incompatible models of Western imperial modernity (Adonis 1990, 80). Shayna Silverstein expands further upon the impact of double dependency in her contribution, adding nuance and critique by examining music's placement amid isolationist and liberalizing currents within Syria. Adonis's pessimistic conclusion, it would appear, is only the tip of a particularly enduring iceberg. Writing around six hundred years earlier, in disparagement of the impulse for derivative behavior, the famous North African medieval proto-sociologist Ibn Khaldun pronounced: "The vanquished always seek to imitate their victors in their dress, insignia, belief, and other customs and usages. This is because men are always inclined to attribute perfection to those who have defeated and subjugated them. . . . Hence, arises the further belief that such an imitation will remove the causes of defeat" (1958, 53). The Congress of Arab Music pivoted on similarly deprecating principles, argues Jihad Racy, with the Arabs understanding themselves as long past their zenith and speeding to catch up after centuries of decline. The important lessons were to be learned from Europe (Racy 1993).

Arabs decrying their own backwardness? This is but one position, an assertion that, arguably, reaffirms geopolitical dualisms and a somewhat facile time line of "progress." Consolidating this take on belatedness, however well intended, can also undermine the very sorts of dialectical possibilities kicked up by the traffic between "Arab" and "avant-garde." Backwardness, after all, is the timeworn reasoning of many agents of (neo)colonial expansion. By concentrating on "underdevelopment" alone, the economic exploitation and the effaced labor that imperialism has undertaken to fund its own supposed advancement can be obscured. It is not hard to read how the European avant-garde has toyed with "the primitive Other" to generate its shocking novelty as, ultimately, playing by similar rules to those of colonialism's historical imperatives, whether or not this was its aim. For anthropologist Lisa Rofel, writing about modernity within China but with clear relevance to the formations of the European and American avant-garde, "These endeavors both encompass and abandon the subalterns they create, leaving them to maneuver along the boundaries of inclusion and exclusion" (Rofel 1999, 13). Something like the avant-garde, for Rofel, can never be an evenly spread universal practice, nor a locally self-contained one; instead, it is an interaction with emphatic designations of dominance and subordination. In the sharpest of terms, Marina Peterson's and Thomas Burkhalter's chapters expose how the European–North American matrix is still largely the border authority for entry to the global avant-garde, controlling, as it often does, the most compelling and powerful means of dissemination via, for example, record labels or concert bookings.

Geographically related forces also direct how time is framed and prioritized. The avant-garde's forward-thrusting teleology finds its inspiration nowhere more strongly than in a conception of time that rose to prominence relatively recently, in sixteenth-century Europe (Gray 2003, 101). With this temporality came a political perspective, an understanding of the self, a set of priorities, a social hierarchy, a belief that those not signed up for it must hurry along obediently in its wake or submit to its superiority. Johannes Fabian famously labels this overdetermination of time chronopolitics (Fabian 1983, 144). For sure, astute thinkers such as Georgina Born and David Hesmondhalgh have taken to task the European avant-garde's "fantasy that one could invent a new musical language without reference to other musics, without recourse to syncretism, stripped of representational intent, and through a process of pure conceptual invention" (Born and Hesmondhalgh 2000, 16–17). Yet the magnetism of originality, the erasure of outside aid in achieving it, and the arrangements of domination and subordination it weaves through history are potent. Nevertheless, through its own situated drive for novelty, the Arab avant-garde refuses a consignment of its homelands to backwardness, confounding a narrow European chronopolitical genealogy via its divergent investments in futurity. By charting out how, within Egypt,

Sayyed Darwish might have been "ahead of his time," Saed Muhsin's chapter gives life to all these issues.

Highlighting the inequitable rights of admission to "the new" tells only a fragment of the story. There is an urgent obligation to investigate the economics of modernization in the Arab world. Initiatives such as those unveiled by Muhammad ʿAli Basha in Egypt in the nineteenth century looked to Europe to create infrastructures of transportation (including the Suez Canal), communication, education, industrialization, and urbanization, all the while running the country into insurmountable debt to those selfsame quarters of the world that had been holding aloft the enticing beacon of (their) modernity. Unpaid loans soon became the excuse for a permanent British military presence in the country, making "progress" a high-stakes game in Egyptian history—an unfinished narrative when we take into account the role IMF structural-adjustment programs have played in the discontent prompting the Tahrir Square demonstrations. Analogous gaps between capitalist and aesthetic modernities like these are explored by way of Syrian experimental composition in Shayna Silverstein's chapter.

The Arab avant-garde places a different, more critical accent on the "not quite there yet." As Caroline Rooney's chapter reveals, Palestinian hip-hop artists pin their progress on the contingent dissolution of the Israeli occupation. Just as a recently revitalized state formation has hindered Palestinian self-determination, so too have Palestinians been failed by the supposedly modern infrastructures of international law, justice, and human rights. At one and the same time, Rooney contends, Palestinians are "at the forefront of the very question of our repressed, denied and ignored human connectedness," which positions them centrally in negotiations about our planet's future.

Another tactic for interrogating prevailing first-past-the-post appreciations of history is to shuffle that history's established order. This is exactly the type of work Michael Khoury's chapter undertakes with its detailing of how Halim El-Dabh experimented with tape composition in advance of Pierre Schaeffer's supposed invention of the technique. In both *The Permanent and the Changeable* and *An Introduction to Arab Poetics*, Adonis nudges this imperative further, painstakingly itemizing instances of Arab innovation in the early Islamic period that predate European equivalents. Artistic invention, he stresses, has always responded to historical change, where "the articulation of 'content,' therefore, calls for a modification in 'form'" (Adonis 1978, 3:40) Writing in the mid-twentieth century, Sayid Qutb, the leading theorist of the Muslim Brotherhood, spoke of an "Islamic vanguard" that would proceed toward a pure and total Islam, beyond the ignorant, underdeveloped state of secularism and the ill-conceived faith in which it then, for him, resided.

Such entreaties to reach forward into an unsullied future recur within the discussions about what a new, post-uprising Arab world should be.

Yet, like other thinkers, Sayid Qutb also respectfully bows down to the weighty pervasiveness of "tradition," which, as has already been argued, beats out a particular rhythm upon the experience of time in many Arab social milieux. If one reads tradition from within the rubrics of chronopolitics, as sustained cultural achievement, then asserting a rich, documented history in the region also acts as a rejoinder to the European avant-garde's simplistic insinuation of its geopolitical and colonial Others' primitivity. Take, for example, Behiga Hafez's piano composition "Karnak," specially written for and published as sheet music in the February 1929 edition of the nationalist-feminist (and French language) journal *L'Egyptienne*. Here, reference to a pharaonic temple conjures up the glory days of Egyptian dominance, lionizing a pre-Abrahamic past and deliberately sidestepping the factional religious affinities of more contemporary figurings. In these ways, the Arab avant-garde compels an alternative evaluation of temporality, one that stands alongside Andreas Huyssen's aspiration that "rather than privilege the radically new in Western avant-gardist fashion, we may want to focus on the complexity of repetition and rewriting, *bricolage* and translation, thus expanding our understanding of innovation" (Huyssen 2005, 15).

Political Deployments of the Avant-Garde

As is apparent from how avant-garde compositions like "Karnak" represent the past, present, and future, this is a body of music carrying aloft a strong political agenda, frequently in collaboration with larger postcolonial or liberation movements. Consequently, many of these artists are under direct threat for the work they produce or, like Aida Nadeem, have had to flee their countries of origin. Musicians were at the forefront of the 2011 uprisings, from M.C.Deeb in Tahrir Square to Tunisia's El Général, who released "Rais LeBled"—a direct-address indictment of the president and his mismanagement of the country—in the first days of the protests and who was immediately incarcerated by the then-ruling regime. The sound artist Ahmed Basiony tragically became one of eight hundred–plus victims of counterrevolutionary retaliations in Cairo, losing his life to a sniper bullet on the 28th of February 2011. Anti-imperialism, asymmetrical access to resources, political independence, state corruption, community solidarity, and outright revolution (be that through pan-Arabism, pan-Islamism, or other groupings) have been regular concerns, as the chapters in this book's final section will attest, and calls such as Aida Nadeem's to foster "contra-globalisation struggle, an international front . . . to create a different world"

(Nadeem 2010) are commonplace. With these convictions, the Arab avant-garde espouses the shared directive of its overseas relatives: to question authority and to rebel.

However, Arab avant-gardists more readily assert that revolution should be plotted through social, rather than aesthetic, means than their counterparts outside the region. European avant-garde dissent has primarily agitated against the conservative bourgeoisie by promoting radical formalism and railing against the institutions of art and culture themselves. Observations about these tactics form the core of respected texts on the subject, such as those mentioned earlier by Renato Poggioli, Matei Calinescu, and Peter Bürger. As noted previously, these works never explicitly state having definitional boundaries around Europe as they neglect to mention experimentation within Asia or Africa, an unfortunate universalizing act typical of the contributions to this subject available in English. Given the situation, Arab cultural activists are well practiced at tripping up and catching inadequacies within the dominant European avant-garde paradigms, charging them, ultimately, with restricted de facto elitism. Certainly, members of Egypt's Art and Freedom Movement of the late 1930s unequivocally declared, in their first manifesto, their solidarity with European artists fighting against fascism, but they were just as quick to expose what they perceived as the bourgeois complacency of their Western counterparts (Khalil 2003, 84). In doing so, they exemplify an inclination Yaseen Noorani attributes to Arabic modernism more generally, one that transfers "moral investment from a practice deemed to uphold social domination (aesthetic contemplation), to one envisioned as resisting domination (creative perception). [In turn] Arabic modernism casts its art as a practice of freedom that redefines a range of social relations as manifestations of tyranny" (Noorani 2007, 77).

Material conditions are preponderant here. Although avant-garde musicians rarely attract a large paying audience wherever they perform, the impact of income precarity varies enormously from location to location. If musicians cannot rely upon certain structures of support like a national welfare system or family wealth, large swaths of the population are easily excluded. The rise of the avant-garde in Europe must be situated amid a drastic decrease in secure patronage for the arts brought about by a decline in aristocratic and church influence. Rapid industrialization, urban migration, and the rise of the middle class must also be factored in, as should later developments in state support for those on low incomes. The Arab world does not share an entirely analogous legacy. True, Adonis notes a similar social rift in Arab history from the seventh to the thirteenth centuries, this time between the caliphate, hungry to shore up its power base through bloodlines to the Prophet, and artists, often of mixed parentage and therefore not considered fully "Arab" (Adonis 1978, 3: 9–11). But a comparably pervasive divorce from religious faith has not happened. What, then, of the deeply felt schism from the past, of the implied post-Christian secularism, of Europe's canonical avant-garde hegemony? The Western figuration of art's autonomy (and, from there, the preoccupation with formalism) is highly dependent on such circumstances, as are the frequent rejections of commercialism (such as those famously articulated in Clement Greenberg's essay "Avant-Garde and Kitsch").

When the avant-garde politicizes itself, it does so in relation to coordinates such as these, and never less so than when it stakes its claims of rebellion. In the West, the loudest of iterations have predominantly been the preserve of the loner or outcast figure. The ascendancy of a European brand of committed musicians often emerges out of disdain for or prolonged removal from all manner of apparati of the greater social body. Frequent victims are family and kinship ties, which are of enormous significance within the Arab world, not simply to one's social standing and sense of belonging but also one's ethics. To sacrifice these on the altar of individualism is, arguably, an easier action within more Eurocentric formations of the self. It is from within this crucially important context that Sami Asmar's analysis of the Rahbanis *as a family* within the avant-garde springs. Just as the lone mutineer loses ground to a more socially interconnected ideal, so too does the Arab avant-garde outsider frequently stand against enemies less familiar to his or her Western counterparts: namely, despotic leadership, contemporary G-8 foreign policy, racism, and the various "wars on terror" where Arabs truly are dangerously marginalized. The myth of bohemian Otherness is thus reacquainted with the realities of whether or not certain artists can or cannot elect to live at a remove from the social mainstream; the palpable mobilities of alienation are plotted out geopolitically.

In response, the Arab avant-garde can be seen to move away from seclusion toward group affiliation. Even throughout the *nahda* period, when art began to claim most vociferously a status separate from craft, social praxis, collectively lived out by the community, if not the nation, was central (Shannon 2006, 60). Within the thrust of current dissent in the Arab world, collectivity, rather than individualism, reigns. Before his untimely death (many would say martyrdom), Ahmed Basiony had dedicated years to group-created art works. Collaboration was a driving force, manifest in interactive reception environments and compositions like "City People" and "Cairo Sound," which refract found noise. Ultimately, such pieces were multiply authored by a metropolis in which Basiony was merely a single citizen. Methods like these deliberately dissolve the myth of the solo artist's unique capabilities, sharing ownership with larger public assemblages. One of the earliest and most potent documents of the 2011 uprisings is the *Khalas Volume One Mix Tape*, subtitled *Mish B3eed* (translation: *Not Far*), which features material from Tunisia, Algeria, Libya, and Egypt. The very format of the compilation stresses the commonality of revolutionary experience, the exigency to come together in joint struggle. The socio-historical particularities that brought about these musics have also encouraged populisms that other experimental artists might view askance. Ahmed Basiony's own recourse to the *sha'bi* genre, Ziad Rahbani's enjoyment of comedy, or Halim El-Dabh's harnessing of widespread pro-Palestinian sentiment (upon which Michael Khoury extrapolates) represent a few instances.

Such inclusive appeals to community cohesion are riven with a politics of how "Arabness" might be expressed. As has been noted, the *nahda* period set into play a localized polishing of (often European) nationalist precepts so that they might better serve the liberationist ideals of the day. It was at this juncture that *musiqa 'arabiyya* (Arab music) overtook *musiqa sharqiyya* (Eastern music) as an organizing label within the region, asserting the category "Arab," which was to become a central rallying ground for revolutionary and postrevolutionary action throughout the twentieth century and now, again, beyond the 2011 revolts. The registers used to convey "Arabness" are also up for debate. As Sami Asmar notes, performers like Ziad Rahbani have elected to compose lyrics in informal lexis, eschewing the elitist connotations of high Arabic for a populist pull. And nationalism draws circles of varying sizes within Middle Eastern avant-garde history. Unity and empowerment systematized under Palestinian emblems have been common within the musical avant-garde, as will become apparent (and then be expanded) throughout Caroline Rooney's chapter. Then there is Aida Nadeem's choice to sing in Turkmenelian, an often suppressed minority language within Iraq. One wonders what the music following the revolutions in Tunisia and Libya, whose emphasis on "ethnic minority" rights is strong, will bring.

There are also other cross-border allusions to consider, affiliations to subcultures with a more global reach. When Egyptian heavy metallers and Palestinian hip-hop artists latch themselves into previously established musical genres, can we, for example, think in idealist internationalist terms, applauding a networked fraternity that allows for fruitful exchange? Such are the aspirations of the artists featured in Caroline Rooney's, Benjamin Harbert's, and Thomas Burkhalter's chapters. These musicians certainly establish transnational camaraderie and exploit smoothly functioning distribution circuits. They also cannot help goading the genres they adopt into more fully accepting Arab struggles for freedom into their definitions of "rebellion" and "activism." This final injunction is similarly encouraged when overtly "Arabic" musical or linguistic inflections are welcomed into styles felt to belong outside the region. In moments of convergence and translation like these, the Arab avant-garde can simultaneously speak the same broad language as parallel avant-gardes while also clarifying and specifying through its own vernaculars. With the stress on global solidarity, the chain of influence that sees Arab creativity as following in the wake of music from elsewhere is downplayed in favor of the common ground that Aida Nadeem summons when she declares: "I don't believe in local change, it needs to be international" (Nadeem 2010).

The extent to which this internationalism might succeed as a politics of equality lies at the mercy of unrelenting colonial-capitalist continuities. That very same cosmopolitanism that spreads experimental tenets around the world owes its existence to channels of exploitation that have exposed some to geographical stasis, some to violent dispersal, and others to the privilege of international travel, often for expensive educations overseas. Within the Arab avant-garde, most fall into the latter category and, with that, comes a multilingualism that can be both enabling and protective. The publicity machinery of the cosmopolitan avant-garde, as Benjamin Harbert's chapter will reveal, can provide a trans- or postnational awareness about how oppressive local governments threaten musicians but those speaking particular languages have greater access to security than others. At the same time, Marina Peterson's chapter persuasively contends, cosmopolitanism can also be co-opted, with the U.S. State Department utilizing the concept to promote a particularly American hegemony of freedom and democracy in its funding of improvisational performances by Arab and American lineups. What happens when these institutions deploy the "freedom" of avant-garde improvisation for the purposes of state building, international diplomacy, and foreign policy justification?

Such internationalizing ventures are strong sites from which to perform what Abdelkebir Khatibi, in *Maghreb Pluriel*, calls a "double critique." Simultaneously inhabiting two or more subjectivities (the lived vocabularies of the oppressed and the oppressor), these musicians can point out the impossibility of fully encaging anything in such a binary, all the while revealing the damage that the effort to instigate such divisions enforces. By refusing to come down on one side or another and to unencumber such a divorce, by extending the parameters at either extreme, these musicians take part in what Khatibi identifies as "an other thinking." This is a politicized rhetoric that is painfully aware and condemning of oppressive governance yet can move beyond without forsaking what is useful from these pasts (Khatibi 1983, 47–111). Ultimately, a movement toward an altered, hopefully ameliorated future is implied here, a goal compatible with vanguardism. In these musical double critiques, stylistic colonization might one minute stand center stage, then the next weather critique, irony, absorption, the dubious property rights held over it presented for scrutiny. At other times, eclecticism asserts the diversity of oppositional voices worldwide, binding them together and working to dissolve the impact of difference in an imagined future. In articulations like these, Otherness is revealed as bearing a more complicated geographical ancestry than is often presumed. For instance, Aida Nadeem's concurrent insistence on Iraqi identity and lost subjecthood through ecstatic rendition offers a means not unfamiliar to the transnational avant-garde of complicating debilitating designations of history and geography. In these ways, her music's content and mode of delivery intertwine in order to advocate and embody a particular political imagination.

A Conclusion, A Hint of Things to Come

Within all this, the struggle for meaning, its erasure, and its overwriting positively trouble the stability of the Arab avant-garde, and the present volume cannot exempt itself from these machinations. Nor does it wish to. All its contributors hope to maintain the open-mindedness and generosity also implicit in a double critique in order to reenergize and focus with more historical complexity on music-as-institution. The various essays in this book will go into the greater details of training, status, organs of support, distribution, audiences, and the like, all the while proffering certain broader proposals about how musical aesthetics are tied to social formation—not to fix a single, stultifying definition but to imaginatively proliferate feasible understandings. They do so from a wealth of different positions (geographical and political), divergent disciplinary perspectives (from critical theory to ethnography to musicology), and disparate registers (including biographies and an interview). In this way, the eclecticism and dialectical prerogatives of the Arab avant-garde are honored, and unresolved diversity creates an ungovernable excess. Hassan Khan, a contemporary visual and sonic artist, sees promise in the very Otherness and obliqueness of experimentalism, an attitude that can be transported to the polysemy of a book like this one: "What I find interesting in art is the fact that there is always a 'surplus of the unexplainable' that is absolutely necessary for it to function in the first place, in a sense the market itself needs to become something that is not 100% commodifiable. To resist total commodification, it is necessary to never make the claim of resistance and instead just allow a condition to occur in spite of itself" (Khan in Fattouh, 2011). Accordingly, often brutal, largely capitalist-motivated urges are undone, although through tactics that more abrasively activist musicians would reject. Whatever one's feelings by the end of this anthology about the many quandaries set down within its introduction, the placement of "Arab" next to "avant-garde," we would all strongly argue, involves clearing space for some crucial debates on how values, knowledge, creativity, and cultural economies circulate through our world.

Notes

Many thanks to Lee Grieveson and Andy McGraw, along with my coeditors and contributors, for their helpful suggestions on how to improve this essay.

1. Adonis recasts this in damning sociocultural terms: "Arabs, influenced by the prevailing cultural structure, understand everything in light of their heritage—what it fails to illuminate becomes valueless. They feel that the unknown threatens both their capacity to understand and their inheritance, which represents perfection and infallibility in their eyes. What lies beyond the limits of their acquired perception, particularly as regards religion, concerns and confuses them, leading them, so they believe, astray" (Adonis 1978, 1:59) (translation my own).

2. Fredric Jameson is mindful of these distinctions in the uneven and biased assumptions of modernity around the world (Jameson 2002, 12–13).

3. Welcome rejoinder texts like the anthology *Colors of Enchantment: Theater, Dance, Music, and the Visual Arts in the Middle East* or Walter Armbrust's *Mass Culture and Modernism in Egypt* offer a respite from this blinkering, but they do so by spotlighting the popular, rather than the avant-garde.

4. Aida Nadeem talks about how hard it can be, in the Arab world, to find musicians with suitable experience of all these different approaches to musical structure and performance. The same is very much true of European and North Americans, who find the *maqamat* challenging to absorb.

References

'Abed al-Jabri, Mohammed. 1999. *Arab-Islamic Philosophy: A Contemporary Critique*. Translated by Aziz Abbassi. Austin: University of Texas Press.

Abu-Rabi', Ibrahim. 2004. *Contemporary Arab Thought: Studies in Post-1967 Arab Intellectual History*. London: Pluto Press.

Adonis ('Ali Ahmed S'aid). 1978. *al-Thabit w al-Mutahawwal (The Permanent and the Changeable)*. Beirut: Dar al-Awda.

———. 1990. *An Introduction to Arab Poetics*. Translated by Catherine Cobham. London: Saqi Books.

Adorno, Theodor W. 2002. *Essays on Music*. Edited by Richard Leppert. New translations by Susan H. Gillespie. Berkeley: University of California Press.

Aksikas, Jaafar. 2009. *Arab Modernities: Islam, Nationalism, and Liberalism in the Post-Colonial Arab World*. New York: Peter Lang.

Bensmaïa, Réda. 2003. *Experimental Nations: Or, The Invention of the Maghreb*. Princeton, NJ: Princeton University Press.

Born, Georgina, and David Hesmondhalgh, eds. 2000. *Western Music and Its Others: Difference, Representation and Appropriation in Music*. Berkeley: University of California Press.

Bürger, Peter. *Theory of the Avant-Garde*. 1984. Translated by Michael Shaw. Minneapolis: University of Minnesota Press.

Calinescu, Matei. 1977. *Faces of Modernity: Avant-Garde, Decadence, Kitsch*. Bloomington: Indiana University Press.

Chakrabarty, Dipesh. 2000. *Provincializing Europe: Postcolonial Thought and Historical Difference*. Princeton, NJ: Princeton University Press.

Cope, David. 1984. *New Directions in Music*. Dubuque, IA: W. C. Brown.

Cusick, Susan. 2006. "Music as Torture/Music as Weapon," *Transcultural Music Review* 10. Accessed November 27, 2010, http://www.sibetrans.com/trans /trans10/cusick_eng.htm.

Eisenstadt, S. N. 2000. "Multiple Modernities." *Daedalus* 129/1: 1–29.

Fabian, Johannes. 1983. *Time and the Other: How Anthropology Makes Its Object*. New York: Columbia University Press.

Farmer, Henry George. 1930. *Historical Facts for the Arabian Musical Influence*. London: New Temple Press.

Fattouh, Mayssa. 2011. "Interview with Hassan Khan." In *Art Territories*. Accessed August 14, 2011, http://www.artterritories.net/?page_id=1577.

Gaonkar, Dilip Parameshwar, ed. 2001. *Alternative Modernities*. Durham, NC: Duke University Press.

García Canclini, Néstor. 1995. *Hybrid Cultures: Strategies for Entering and Leaving Modernity*. Translated by Christopher L. Chiappari and Silvia L. López. Minneapolis: University of Minnesota Press.

Gray, John. 2003. *Al Qaeda and What It Means to Be Modern*. London: Faber and Faber.

Griffith, Paul. 1981. *Modern Music: The Avant-Garde since 1945*. London: J. M. Dent and Sons Ltd.

———. 1995. *Modern Music and After: Directions since 1945*. Oxford: Oxford University Press.

Harding, James M., and John Rouse, eds. 2006. *Not the Other Avant-Garde: The Transnational Foundations of Avant-Garde Performance*. Ann Arbor: University of Michigan Press.

Herwitz, Daniel. 1994. *Making Theory/Constructing Art: On the Authority of the Avant-Garde*. Chicago: University of Chicago Press.

Hussein, Taha. 1954. *The Future of Culture in Egypt*. Translated by Sidney Glazer. Washington, DC: American Council of Learned Societies.

Huyssen, Andreas. 2005. "Geographies of Modernism in a Globalizing World." In *Geographies of Modernism: Literatures, Cultures, Spaces*, edited by Peter Brooker and Andrew Thacker, 6–18. London: Routledge.

Ibn Khaldun. 1958. *An Arab Philosophy of History: Selections from the Prolegomena of Ibn Khaldun of Tunis (1332–1406)*. Translated by Charles Issawi. London: John Murray.

Jameson, Fredric. 2002. *A Singular Modernity: Essay on the Ontology of the Present*. London: Verso.

Jusdanis, Gregory. 1991. *Belated Modernity and Aesthetic Culture: Inventing National Literature*. Minneapolis: University of Minnesota Press.

Laroui, Abdallah. 1976. *The Crisis of the Arab Intellectual: Traditionalism or Historicism?* Translated by Diarmid Cammell. Berkeley: University of California Press.

Kendall, Elisabeth. 2006. *Literature, Journalism and the Avant-Garde: Intersection in Egypt*. London: Routledge.

Khalil, Andrea Flores. 2003. *The Arab Avant-Garde: Experiments in North African Art and Literature*. Westport, CT: Praeger.

Khatibi, Abdelkebir. 1983. *Maghreb Pluriel*. Paris: Denoël.

Knauft, Bruce M., ed. 2002. *Critically Modern: Alternatives, Alterities, Anthropologies*. Bloomington: Indiana University Press.

Kostelanetz, Richard. 2000. *Dictionary of the Avant-Gardes*. New York: Schirmer Books.

Kramer, Jonathan D., and Larry Sitsky, eds. 2002. *Music of the Twentieth Century Avant-Garde: A Biocritical Sourcebook*. Westport, CT: Greenwood Press.

Maalouf, Shireen. 2002. *History of Arabic Music Theory: Change and Continuity in the Tone Systems, Genres, and Scales*. Kaslik, Lebanon: Université Saint-Esprit.

Martin, Bill. 2002. *Avant Rock: Experimental Music from the Beatles to Björk*. Chicago: Open Court Publishing Company.

Masud, Muhammad Khalid, Armando Salvatore, and Martin van Bruinessen, eds. 2009. *Islam and Modernity: Key Issues and Debates*. Edinburgh: Edinburgh University Press.

Mernissi, Fatima. 1994. *Islam and Democracy: Fear of the Modern World*. London: Virago.

Meyer, Stefan G. 2001. *The Experimental Arabic Novel: Postcolonial Literary Modernism in the Levant*. Albany: State University of New York Press.

Moten, Fred. 2003. *In the Break: The Aesthetics of the Black Radical Tradition*. Minneapolis: University of Minnesota Press.

Nadeem, Aida. 2010. Interview by author. Digital recording via Skype, August, 10.

Noorani, Yaseen. 2007. "Redefining Resistance: Counterhegemony, the Repressive Hypothesis and the Case of Arabic Modernism." In *Counterhegemony in the Colony Postcolony*, edited by John Chalcraft and Yaseen Noorani, 75–99. New York: Palgrave Macmillan.

Nyman, Michael. 1999. *Experimental Music: Cage and Beyond*. Cambridge: Cambridge University Press.

Poggioli, Renato. 1981. *Theory of the Avant-Garde*. Cambridge, MA: The Belknap Press of Harvard University.

Racy, Ali Jihad. 1993. "Historical Worldviews of Early Ethnomusicologists: An East-West Encounter in Cairo, 1932." In *Ethnomusicology and Modern Music History*, edited by Stephen Blum, Philip V. Bohlman, and Daniel M. Neuman, 68–91. Urbana: University of Illinois Press.

———. 2003. *Making Music in the Arab World: The Culture and Artistry of Tarab*. Cambridge: Cambridge University Press.

Rofel, Lisa. 1999. *Other Modernities: Gendered Yearnings in China after Socialism*. Berkeley: University of California Press.

Safi, Louay. 1994. *The Challenge of Modernity: The Quest for Authenticity in the Arab World*. New York: University Press of America.

Saunders, James, ed. 2009. *The Ashgate Research Companion to Experimental Music*. Farnham: Ashgate.

Sell, Mike. 2005. *Avant-Garde Performance and the Limits of Criticism: Approaching the Living Theatre, Happenings/Fluxus, and the Black Arts Movement*. Ann Arbor: University of Michigan Press.

Shannon, Jonathan Holt. 2006. *Among the Jasmine Trees: Music and Modernity in Contemporary Syria*. Middletown, CT: Wesleyan University Press.

Spivak, Gayatri Chakravorty. 1988. "Can the Subaltern Speak?" In *Marxism and the Interpretation of Culture*, edited by Cary Nelson and Lawrence Grossberg, 271–313. Urbana: University of Illinois Press.

Such, David C. 1993. *Avant-Garde Jazz Musicians Performing "Out There."* Iowa City: University of Iowa Press.

Tibi, Bassam. 2009. *Islam's Predicament with Modernity: Religious Reform and Cultural Change*. London: Routledge.

Touma, Habib Hassan. 1996. *The Music of the Arabs*. Translated by Laurie Schwartz. Portland, OR: Amadeus Press.

Williams, Alastair. 1997. *New Music and the Claims of Modernity*. Aldershot: Ashgate.

Zuhur, Sherifa, ed. 2001. *Colors of Enchantment: Theater, Dance, Music, and the Visual Arts in the Middle East*. Cairo: American University Press.

PART I

*Alternative
Modernities*

Norms and Innovations

CHAPTER ONE

Transforming Space

The Production of
Contemporary Syrian Art Music

⌒

SHAYNA SILVERSTEIN

In the summers Solhi [al-Wadi] used to return to Damascus
and he soon mixed with the fledgling classical music enthusiasts and other
members of a revolutionary movement with a love for the fine arts, people
like Sadek Faroun and Rafah Qasawat. . . . Sadek and Rafah played the violin
while Solhi played the viola and conducted. They persevered and eventually, with
3 instruments, played the Introduction to Boieldieu's "Calif of Bagdad" and the
2nd movement of Schubert's Unfinished Symphony at the Ommayad Hotel
in front of an astonished public. In the late 1940s this quartet started the
serious classical music movement in Syria.
—Samar al-Wadi (2009)

Decades after this vanguard performance of "serious" music in the "the oldest
continually inhabited city in the world,"[1] the risks taken in pursuit of a space
for contemporary Syrian art music continue to push the boundaries of musical creativity and expressive culture in Damascus. In Syria and elsewhere in
the Middle East, composers who are invested in experimental approaches to
musical structures and processes develop their work in a musical culture that
tends to bestow aesthetic appeal and social prestige to modern Arab music
or to classical, romantic, and early modern periods of European art music.
Historically, the institutionalization of European art music in Syria has been
attributed to Dr. Solhi al-Wadi, a visionary committed to the musical life of
his nation. After graduating from the Royal Academy of Music in London
in 1960, he returned to Damascus and established the inaugural children's

music school in 1962. From the late 1960s onward, he invited educators from the Soviet Union to Damascus for residencies in piano, strings, and music theory, and likewise sponsored study opportunities in Moscow for Syrian students. He established the Higher Institute for Music and Drama in 1990 to provide domestic opportunities for higher education in the performing arts and conducted the Syrian National Symphony Orchestra until his sudden collapse onstage and subsequent death in 2007. His legacy continues to be honored today through commemorative concerts, commissions, and the dedicated efforts of those who were guided by his stern yet profoundly personal approach to tutelage.[2]

The post–World War Two era in which Solhi al-Wadi came of age was a period when Syria strove to determine an autonomous sense of nationhood. Symbolic resources such as folk music and dance were harnessed by various factions that competed for sovereignty over the nascent state of Syria in alignment with political ideologies of Arabism, Islamism, secular liberalism, and socialism (Wieland 2006). As suggested by al-Wadi's efforts, collaborations with institutions in Western Europe and the Soviet Union shaped the establishment of musical programs and activities in Syria. The founding of a Syrian conservatory for *musiqa klasikiyya*, or classical music, was predicated on these interactions that more broadly indicate historically contingent patterns of mobility. As music students pursued opportunities for training abroad that perpetuated aesthetic models of European modernism or Soviet socialist realism, respectively, their choices were situated within larger discourses of social progress and cultural modernity that Edward Soja (1989) has termed "geographies of imperialism."

In the first decade of the twenty-first century, a young generation of Syrian experimental composers has conceived a space for *musiqa mu'asira*, or contemporary art music. Informed by debates on critical aesthetics, modernity, and subjectivity in the Arab world and beyond, composers affiliated with *musiqa mu'asira* draw on particular compositional devices and techniques in ways that mediate global discourses of avant-gardism. In what follows, I will discuss how their work transforms aesthetic concepts of musical space and situate *musiqa mu'asira* in the context of contemporary Syria. In particular, this essay focuses on selected compositions by three composers—Zaid Jabri, Shafi Badreddin, and Hassan Taha—who collectively articulate the possibilities for transforming modern Arab music into a contemporary space for experimentation.[3]

This essay draws on a series of conversations, exchanges, and debates that I was privileged to join during a period of fieldwork in Damascus in 2007–2008. As an ethnographer of musical practices, I regularly visited the Higher Institute for Music to take private instrumental lessons, visit informally with students and faculty, and attend workshops, conferences, programs, and events that reflect the bustling pace of musical life in Damascus. In particular, the contributions of Jabri, Badreddin, and Taha stood out as emblems for a new generation of Syrian artists striving to suggest alternative creative visions of and for their society. In this essay, their embrace of cultural alternatives and experimentalism will be framed within the geographical contexts and institutional spaces in which they emerge. By situating this art world within the discursive and artistic practices by which composers, performers, and audiences become subjects of their own histories and experiences, I hope to demonstrate how expressive forms and musical performance are shaped by social spaces and spatialized practices. *Musiqa mu'asira* seeks to intervene with physical space in ways that articulate the very contemporaneity of music in Syria today. In other words, I will link the particularities of contemporary Syrian art music to the historical conditions, social structures, and discursive spaces from which it arises and which it may yet transform.

Spatializing Music History:
The Emergence of Musiqa Mu'asira

Contemporary Syrian art music has emerged in the past decade amidst a significant growth in entrepreneurship and economic liberalization in the Bashar al-Assad era.[4] Like his father, Hafez al-Assad, Bashar and First Lady Asma al-Assad institutionalized high and traditional arts as part of their economic reform policies. They expanded Syria's capacity to participate in global networks of cultural production by investing in arts training, infrastructure, and international collaborations.[5] At the time of this writing in summer 2011, the arts and culture sector is divided, like many Syrians, between support for and opposition to Bashar al-Assad's regime. Some arts leaders perceive antiregime Islamist factions as a potential threat to the musical arts and voice support for a secular state under Assad, whereas others condemn the regime for its violation of human dignity. Like most sectors of the Syrian economy, cultural production has declined during the conflict and, consequently, many artists have left the country. Though art music is no longer centered in Damascus, it is nonetheless sustained by Syrian composers and performers who continue their work abroad.

The main artery for music education and performance in Damascus is the Higher Institute for Music and Drama (hereafter referred to as the Higher Institute). The Higher Institute is adjacent to the world-class opera house, Dar al-Assad for Culture and Arts, which has served as the primary incubator for artistic collaboration and international exchange in Syria since its inauguration in 2004. The arts complex skirts Al-Umawyeen Square, a heavily trafficked area in central Damascus near the embassies and consulates of the Abu Roumanneh neighborhood. The complex is encircled by educational and cultural institutions including al-Assad National Library and the Department for Radio and Television. This zone bustles with motor traffic, arts students, and state clerks by day and with arts audiences by night in ways that dynamically texture the spatial experience of urban modernity in Damascus.

The Higher Institute is the entry point for those who aspire to participate in serious musical life and pursue Western art music. The majority of formal student programs and activities focus on classical Western art music or modern Arab music, the latter made possible by the 2003 establishment of an orchestra devoted to classical and modern Arab music and the recent expansion of performance studies to include Arab instruments such as *buzuq*, *nay*, *'ud*, and *qanun*. Following Solhi al-Wadi's retirement from public life in 2002, a young and energetic artistic director, Missak Baghboudarian, was appointed to lead the Higher Institute and the Syrian National Symphony Orchestra. Trained in Italy, Baghboudarian has facilitated numerous educational programs and artistic residencies that are supported by the state and by government-operated nongovernmental organizations (GONGOs) for the arts, such as the SADA (Echo) Musical Cultural Association and Rawafed, the cultural arm of the Syrian Trust for Development.[6]

Despite new levels of commitment to cultural expression and contemporary arts production spurred by economic reform, usually though not always through commissions administered by Syrian and European GONGOs,[7] *musiqa mu'asira* remains at the institutional periphery of art music practices in Syria.[8] Opportunities linked to *musiqa mu'asira* are furthermore dependent on transnational arts networks that are entangled with postcolonial geographies and histories. Not unlike other skilled workers situated at the periphery of globalized political economies, Syrian composers and musicians often undertake training abroad and return to Damascus with an expanded set of social and musical resources. The compelling effects of these histories, or what Henri Lefebvre terms "spatial actions" (1991, 222), can be traced according to the following profiles of three artists whose cosmopolitan visions have shaped the emergence of *musiqa mu'asira*. These three narratives illustrate the ways in which the subjects' pathways reveal or contradict certain logics in the geographies of spatial modernities—that is, the economic and political dependencies that contextualize the production of contemporary Syrian art music.

Shafi Badreddin, based in Luxembourg at the time of this writing, has pursued pathways in Francophone spheres of contemporary art music. After receiving a bachelor's degree in electrical engineering from Damascus University, he graduated in *'ud* performance from the Higher Institute (Badreddin, pers. correspondence). Prior to his relocation in early 2011, he taught music theory, orchestration, composition, and chamber music at the Higher Institute. His numerous compositions and arrangements are frequently presented by the Syrian National Symphony Orchestra and chamber ensembles, including the Damascus Festival Chamber Players. Badreddin has received several distinguished prizes for solo 'ud performance, including at a 2001 international competition affiliated with the Arab League of Nations, and has appeared as a solo 'ud player and composer at the Autumn Festival in Paris. In 2005, Badreddin received a diploma in composition from the National Conservatoire in Lyon, France, where he studied spectral music with Christophe Maudot, Serge Borel, and Delphine Gaude.[9] Badreddin also frequently works in Italy, where he has served as a member of the jury for the Valentino Bucci International Composers Competition held in Rome and received a special juror's mention at the 2 Agosto International Composing Competition in Italy in 2010. Badreddin's opportunities in Western Europe may be partially indebted to Syria's strong and enduring trade relations with France, Germany, and Italy. The last has served as Syria's foremost trading partner in Europe since the late 1990s and sustains these alliances through opportunities for economic growth and renewed commitments to tourism and cultural diplomacy.[10]

In contradistinction to these journeys across Western Europe and the United States, Zaid Jabri is currently completing his doctorate in composition under the supervision of Krzysztof Penderecki at the Krakow Academy of Music. Jabri's introduction to Lutosławski's *Cello Concerto* (1970) during early studies in music theory with Solhi al-Wadi is what inspired him to pursue composition studies in Poland. His first composition, *Two Songs for Soprano and String Orchestra*, won first prize at the 1997 Adam Didur Composers Competition in Sanok, Poland, after which he began studying with Zbigniew Bujarski at the Krakow Academy of Music. Jabri's choice to pursue studies in Poland may echo the pathways of earlier generations of Syrian music students who received training courtesy of scholarships available through the Warsaw Pact accords. Syria, which is a former non-Soviet Warsaw Pact country, displays aesthetic forms of socialist realism in ways that bear further consideration for a better understanding of twentieth-century intellectual histories in the Arab world.[11] Yet Jabri's long-term residency in Krakow does not circumscribe his work as a nostalgic retention of a shared socialist heritage that links Syria with Poland. Rather, his work is commissioned and promoted as a signifier of musical modernism by which Syrian cultural production circulates through contemporary arts institutions across Western and Eastern Europe, as well as Cairo, Dubai, and Damascus. The inclusion of his work in these networks extends the visibility of contemporary Syrian art music to venues that include the Warsaw Autumn Festival, "The Days of Polish Music" at Istanbul Bilgi University, the International Musikwerkstatt Buckow and Morgenland Festival Osnabrück in Germany, and an ongoing roster of commissions from Dar al-Assad in Damascus.[12]

Hassan Taha has taken a strikingly different approach to music education that is perhaps more typical of Syrian musical life than those of his colleagues in *musiqa mu'asira*. Raised in the central Syrian region of Homs, Taha began playing *'ud* and composing at an early age as a result of the influence of his uncle, the distinguished *'ud* player Samih Taha (Taha, pers. correspondence). He pursued performance studies on French horn at the Higher Institute and upon graduation secured a position with the Syrian National Symphony Orchestra. Due to the absence of a formal program in composition at the Higher Institute, he taught himself methods of orchestration based on works couriered from Europe by colleagues. While his resourceful strategies helped him informally circumvent political and economic barriers to the flow of goods, they also indicate Taha's relative lack of access to educational resources in comparison to his various colleagues. Nonetheless, he composes actively for chamber ensemble, symphony orchestra, and theater, and his work received national recognition at a February 2008 gala concert at Dar al-Assad that was dedicated solely to his oeuvre.

Taha has also played a critical role in launching collaborations with European cultural foundations and figures, one of which resulted in *Cadmus and Europe: East and West*, an instrumental suite commissioned by the European Commission and the Syrian Renaissance Association and premiered at Dar al-Assad in late 2009. Other recent works include an adaptation of Henrik Ibsen's *An Enemy of the People* (2008), commissioned by the Damascus Capital of Arab Culture Festival, and two musical theater works premiered in Germany, *The Bathroom* (2011) and *The Speech* (2011). Influenced by experimentalist composers such as Boulez, Xenakis, Ligeti, Penderecki, and Lutosławski, Taha recently completed artist residencies at the Maastricht Conservatory in the Netherlands and the Bern University of the Arts (BUA) in Switzerland. In the fall of 2010, Taha began pursuing a master's degree in music composition and theater at BUA to develop his longtime interest in musical theater.

These artists began their musical careers at the Higher Institute during the 1990s and pursued instrumental performance in Western art music under the supervision of Solhi al-Wadi. Generally, though not always, they left Syria to pursue opportunities for professional growth in Europe and North America and returned to Damascus to integrate their studies of Western art music with musical life in Syria. Part of what distinguishes their artistic pursuits from those of their peers at the Higher Institute is the geopolitical and cultural spaces that are conjoined through their work. It is precisely because of how these musical histories are imbricated in the material and discursive space of the Higher Institute that these projects may be coalesced into a sense of Syrianness; that is, this art world has become representative of the contemporaneity of Syrian life.

Representations and Transformations of Modal Space

Spatial relations in music have arguably indexed the very modernity of Arab identity since the category of *musiqa ʿarabiyya*, or Arab music, was formulated during an historical encounter between reformers, musicians, and scholars from Europe and the Middle East in 1932.[13] As suggested in the introduction to this volume, the conference in Cairo wrestled with ways to place Arab music on a "path towards progress" using "modern" and "scientific" methods and musical techniques from Europe (Racy 1991, 75). Participants tried to codify the relative tuning of the Arab musical system into a "master scale consisting of 24 equally-tempered quarter-tones. . . . Reformers were attempting to formulate a universal model to be re-universalized in practice" (Thomas 2007, 5). While these reform efforts arguably failed in their attempt to systematize Arab music, I would suggest that they point to the significance of pitch relations and the role of musical space in negotiating processes of modernization. .

Composers working today are heirs to these discourses that set an "aesthetics of authenticity" (Shannon 2006) in relation to concepts of heritage (*turath*) and modernity (*hadatha*).[14] For musicians in Syria, a sense of authenticity (*asala*) is expressed through the traditions of *musiqa sharqiyya*, or Oriental music, which refers to a genre of art music typified by improvised instrumental and vocal performances and a classicized body of repertoire from before the modern era. Vital to these creative practices is the production of what musicians and audiences term "Oriental spirit" (*ruh sharqiyya*). This affective quality emerges from how a musician articulates a sensitivity to the performance principles and musical grammar (*qawaʿid musiqiyya*) of Oriental music through the local dynamics of improvised performance.

Musiqa muʿasira is articulated through compositional strategies that interrogate the formation of aesthetic media and potentially transform the localization of musical meaning. In framings similar to those that inform the global configuration of avant-gardism elsewhere,[15] composers associated with *musiqa muʿasira* challenge these discursive relations by drawing on *maqamat*, or modal structures, as the main set of organizing principles that produce musical meaning in the performance of *musiqa sharqiyya*.[16] In this performance genre, musical space is organized as modal units.[17] Pathways emerge through the perceived distance between relative pitches that constitute a tetrachord (*jins*, pl. *ajnas*), the primary organizational unit of Arab *maqamat*. The transformation of modal space depends on how a performer negotiates pathways between tetrachords. Referred to as *sayr*, these pathways typically emerge through embellishments, timbral effects, and other stylistic techniques that are embedded in performance practices of solo instrumental improvisations (*taqsim*, pl. *taqasim*).

In the following sections, I will provide formal analyses of recent works by Jabri, Badreddin, and Taha in order to establish a conceptual framework for *musiqa mu'asira*. I draw extensively on interviews with the composers, in which they explain each work in terms of analytic methods, musical materials, and compositional processes. In particular, these analyses focus on how these three composers transform concepts of musical space by deconstructing *sayr*, exploring *jins*, and resignifying musical embellishments through experimental techniques. These interpretive analyses suggest that the aesthetic qualities of *musiqa mu'asira* emerge from the intertextual relations between discourses of European experimentalism and *musiqa sharqiyya*.

Zaid Jabri: Modal Representations

Zaid Jabri experiments with musical space through the mediation and representation of tonal, atonal, and modal structures.[18] According to Jabri, *Glyptos* (2005), a commission by the Warsaw Autumn Festival written for flutist Mario Caroli and the Krakow Percussion Group, is one of the first compositions in which he departs from Romantic-era conventions and experiments with classical form, orchestration, and tonality.[19] Rather than subscribe to hierarchical figure-ground relations between soloist and ensemble in concertino form, Jabri facilitates harmonic interaction between percussion ensemble and solo flute. In the opening of *Glyptos*, Jabri presents a rapid succession of polyrhythmic, pitched flourishes in the tubular bells and tom-toms with a sustained flute drone in the background. These opening gestures establish rhythmic subdivisions of triplets, quintuplets, and septuplets that he recalls in the second section with a metric imprecision that allows the rhythm, as Jabri depicts, "to swim in a relaxed 6/8 dance meter."[20] In this piece, Jabri shifts the role of percussion away from traditional accompaniment by experimenting with parameters of duration, intensity, pitch class, and timbre.

Jabri experiments with tonal conventions of tempered pitch space in several ways. He scores acoustic variables local to the timpani and subjects these to continuous retuning in concert performance. Atonal figures in the flute part are transformed through serial techniques of repetition, transposition, and retrograde. Melodic motion favors descent by semitones with frequent registral shifts and leaps by a seventh or ninth; this activity inverts constrained intervallic space, such as a minor second, in ways that generate tension and relaxation. Semitonal pitch relations are also destabilized by microtonalities in the flute (E half-flat and B half-flat in measures 24 and 27).[21] Glissando techniques are frequently used not only as embellishments but also as a means to equivocate the alignment of pitch space in diatonicism. Finally, Jabri employs extended instrumental techniques in all parts, most remarkably in an exchange between crotales and flute in the closing section. The crotales part moves dynamically through pitch space by means of arco technique—here by drawing a string bow along the brass surface. This produces a continuous series of sustained pitches that ascend stepwise by semi- and whole-tone intervals (G–C^3) and exchange registers with the flute part, which mimics percussive attacks by means of sixteenth-note slaps and descends by semitones (B–B flat–A) in the final phrase of the work.

The techniques employed in *Glyptos* signify less the production of sonic difference itself, such as arco techniques or microtonalities, and more the transformation of meaning in the process of composing polysemic figures. One way in which Jabri integrates discrete events into a narrative structure is through his concept of "modulation." In a 2010 interview, Jabri clarified that the concept of modulation refers not only to *musiqa sharqiyya* but also to diatonic shifts in Western harmonic progression, rhythmic and metric shifts in temporal processes, and sonorous shifts in timbre, texture, and registral space.[22] Jabri reflexively connects aesthetics and cultural representation of *maqamat* through his explanation of modulation. He distinguishes between traditional and contemporary music as distinct modes of cultural expression. Jabri shared that he "forbids" himself from attempting to render improvisational performance practices into composition. Improvisation, for Jabri, is a traditional practice that cannot be rendered by compositional texts into an authorial discourse of the composer. Moreover, he insists that improvisation is an art form that produces authentic values of cultural heritage which must be preserved through performance rather than through alteration by composition.

With regard to *Glyptos*, modulations gradually occur in the contrapuntal expansion from a fifth (A-E) to an octave (G-G^1) and through semitones in the timpani line in measures 43–65. This spatial expansion is complemented by a gradual intensification from fortepiano to fortissimo and a deceptive cadence in measure 65 that transitions into a dancelike section. Modulation may also occur through serial transformation of distinct figures, such as the inversion of a minor second into a leap by a seventh or retrograde Bach technique. Modulation, in *Glyptos* and more generally across Jabri's oeuvre, depends on multiple voices interacting with one another in ways that I suggest are heteroglossic, or capable of referring to several orders of representation within the same authorial voice. Heteroglossia, according to Bakhtin (1991), is constituted of dialogic interaction between voices in ways that open up the possibilities for multiple and subjective interpretations as potential meanings reinforce, overlap, and at times contradict one another. In this context, modulation may arguably be framed as a technique used by Jabri to either intimate or defamiliarize sonic events based on specific sets of relations constructed within the compositional narrative of his works.

This framework offers a conceptual apparatus for *Song without Words III* (2009), a work commissioned for the first Musahat Sharqiyya (Oriental Landscapes) Festival held at Dar al-Assad in Damascus.[23] The third of a series under the same title, the premiere featured Kinan Abo Afash, a cellist who performs with classical, jazz, fusion, and world music projects in Syria and the United States.[24] *Song without Words III* (solo cello, strings, and percussion) explores harmonics, perception, and resonating bodies and is inspired by the frequencies produced by moving a sound source, namely a metallic bowl, within greater or lesser proximity to the listening body. These sonorities are reimagined by Jabri in relation to *maqam bayati* as a creative response to the stipulation by festival curators that the commission be "inspired by *maqam*" (Jabri 2010, 49). This curatorial stipulation can be interpreted as an insistence that figures of *maqam* articulate links to classical Syrian musical heritage, that is, between tradition and modernity. Composers may negotiate this overdetermined and paradoxical operation by refuting it, as will be discussed with regard to Hassan Taha's work, or, as demonstrated here by Jabri, by participating in these operational practices of representation.

In *Song without Words III*, Jabri approaches *maqam* as a fixed set of intervals that constitute a compositional topic rather than a mutable set of tetrachords that emerge during a *taqsim* by modulation through other tetrachords. In other words, he represents *maqam* as a scalar figure rather than as a dynamic field organized by modes (Marcus 2002). *Song without Words III* thus explores the tetrachords associated with *bayati* as idiomatic spaces that can be modified by atonalist approaches to timbre, pitch design, and textural micropolyphonies. For example, Jabri extracts the lower tetrachord of *bayati* and performs a retrograde transformation in the first violin part. Figure 1.1a presents the lower and upper tetrachords of *bayati* according to standard *maqam* conventions, and Figure 1.1b represents the aleatoric transformation. By altering the lower tetrachord of *bayati*, Jabri maintains his aesthetic distinctions between, on the one hand, traditional musical practices of improvisation through *maqamat* and, on the other, contemporary compositional practices that decontextualize tetrachords and modes as fixed stylistic figures.

Fig. 1.1a. Lower and upper tetrachords in *maqam bayati*.

Fig. 1.1b. Jabri, *Song without Words III*, retrograde of lower tetrachord in *maqam bayati* in first violin, m. 30.

Song without Words III opens with an acoustic simulation of the resonances produced by striking a metallic bowl. These atmospheric conditions are mimicked by artificial harmonics and glissandi in the upper strings, which produce a background effect. The stillness of the sustained harmonics suggests a drone, as conventionally occurs at the beginning of a solo *taqsim* in *bayati*, and establishes the modal center (D). Though nonmetered, the opening is temporally differentiated by staggered entrances and heavy accents in the strings, which are individuated in the musical score by stand. This increases the textural depth of the work in ways that broadly suggest heterophonic qualities of modern Arab orchestration. The primary modal space of the work, the lower tetrachord of *bayati* (D–E half-flat–F-G), is introduced not by stepwise motion as would occur in a *taqsim* but rather as a vertically stacked sound cluster enmeshed among the sliding and partitioned string parts (Fig. 1.2).[25]

In the opening measures, the second violins iterate a motif that is similar to the Doppler effect by alternations between minor third and semitonal intervals, as depicted in Figure 1.3 (Jabri 2010, 49). This figure emerges in different voices and constructs a narrative through its transformation in the work. Jabri transforms musical material by means of aleatoric and serial techniques including Bach fugal sequences, inversion, repetition, retrograde, as well as registral shifts and transposition by a quarter tone in the solo cello part. Accents and bowing techniques in the strings also transform this motif

Fig. 1.2. Jabri, *Song without Words III*, vertically stacked realization
of lower tetrachord in *maqam bayati*, mm. 15–29.

Figure 1.3. Zaid Jabri, *Song without Words III*, "Doppler effect" motif in second violin, mm. 10–13

by dynamic shifts in timbre and intensity. The concomitant effect of these motivic transformations is to oscillate between tension and resolution, anticipation and peak, proximity and distance. In addition, the compositional design of harmonic effects structures the work as an oscillation between sheer and lush timbres. Sonorities are produced in the strings through a variety of techniques that include artificial harmonics, glissandi, double stops, pizzicato, tremolo, sul tasto, and molto lento vibrato. The intermittent use of bells intones other sonorities. By means of harmonic effects and explorations in sound, the overall structure is a dynamic alternation that swells and recedes between sections of heightened intensity and dampened stillness.

In addition, aesthetic qualities emerge through Jabri's assimilation of stylistic ornamentation associated with *musiqa sharqiyya*.[26] In *Song without Words III*, embellishments are not ancillary to the main melodic line but are constituent of that line itself in ways that resemble *musiqa sharqiyya*. Referred to as *zakhrafa* (plural: *zakhrafat*), embellishments generally consist of trills, tremolos, glissandi, grace notes, and the repetition of idiomatic figures. *Zakhrafat* are represented as compositional topoi through phrase structures that are incongruent with their stylistic referents. Jabri's modernist appropriation of formal stylistic devices creates an aesthetic effect that can be likened to, but does not directly mimic, conventional idioms of *musiqa sharqiyya*. For example, the background drone of artificial harmonics is produced in the strings by sustained whole notes that repeatedly ascend by semitone through lower neighbor figures (F#–G, G#–A). The background texture is punctuated by staggered entrances. In the foreground, the solo cello generates a sense of anticipation by gradual melodic ascension composed of octave leaps, sixteenth notes, and glissandi that shift registers by tenths (E-G^1) or octaves. This ascension peaks in measures 79–80 by means of a suspension that gives way to descending *sospiro* figures staggered in the strings. The lamentative character of this section is glossed by a reiteration of the Doppler effect motif in the solo cello as a retrograde set in the lower tetrachord of *bayati*, dampened by artificial harmonics.

Jabri eschews adherence to any given system of composition or stylistic period in favor of self-informed historical critique. As he himself explains, he draws upon stylistic devices, atonal techniques, and experimental approaches and refers to historical periods of Western art music, such as serialism, or to specific composers, such as Ravel and Ligeti. In ways perhaps comparable to his advisor Penderecki, he also distances his aesthetic framework from that of European avant-gardism, which he regards as an overtly formalistic approach. Jabri espouses a musical sense of cosmopolitanism that is expressed through his capacity to naturalize a broad range of effects, from single pitch-classes and clusters to heterogeneous sound shapes and canonic writing. In self-reflection, he recognizes a proclivity for particular features, such as a "relatively narrow" ambitus of a fifth, but suggests that while this "is probably due to my heritage . . . it is not something that I try to stick with" (Jabri, pers. correspondence). This statement registers a sense of cultural intimacy to structures of Arab music in ways that arguably Orientalize his subjectivity; however, Jabri disavows such intimacy by claiming to transcend the signifying capacity of music. Moreover, he internalizes processes of representation and projects subjectivity in ways that are embedded within the subjective conditions of autonomous art music. For Jabri, the musical meaning of his work arguably emerges from a social space that privileges European cultural imaginaries and projects Romantic conceptions of organicism and universalism that have been historically situated by scholars who seek to provincialize European art music.

Hassan Taha: Distending Modal Space

The German literary critic Peter Bürger situates the Western avant-garde within the historical development of institutions in capitalist society (1984). From this perspective, Hassan Taha's work serves as an apparatus for the social critique of mass culture and consumption practices in modern Syrian society. Taha is dedicated to developing new possibilities for contemporary music in Syria as a response to what he views as the degradation of modern Arab music by those who produce *taqlid* (lit: imitation), or the appropriation of musical conventions and folkloric idioms that are overtly "sweet and pleasing to the ear."[27] For example, he criticizes the burgeoning popularity of Oriental improvisation among fusion groups that assimilate the practice of *maqamat* and threaten to banalize it through their copycat efforts. Addressing this anxiety, Taha preserves an authenticity of modern Arab music by inscribing the structural dynamics of improvisation within his compositions. Taha also frames his projects as a means for social reform that will cultivate new audiences for contemporary music. In a televised interview with *Sharq wa Gharb* ("East and West" 2009), a talk show aired by the state-sponsored satellite television channel, he laments the decline of serious listening practices among contemporary audiences. Rather than providing music that stimulates bourgeois desire for modern Arab music, he argues that audience development is key to the modernization of society and seeks to promote new ways of listening through the production of critical aestheticism in contemporary Syrian music. He suggests that audiences should expand their capacity to appreciate and distinguish among contemporary art music, Oriental music, Arab music, and folkloric forms, among other categories of taste.

One way in which Taha integrates critical aestheticism into his composition projects is his critique of linearity in Arab music. Taha claims that linearity imposes constraints on musical texture through certain forms and structures (Taha, pers. correspondence). For instance, linearity might emerge melodically from an ambitus of a fifth, structurally by modal expansion through stepwise motion (as compared to vertical harmonic progression in Western tonal music), and orchestrally by homophonic relations among multiple parts that either double the melodic phrase or embellish the principal line through idiomatic fills, or *lazim*. To transform the linearity of Arab music, Taha proposes the concept of *tajsim*, or embodiment.[28] A spatial metaphor, the concept of *tajsim* shapes volume and depth into a three-dimensional sound texture by experimentation with harmonic effects, pitch space, polyrhythms, metric dissonance, and orchestration.

In *Sama'i Chromatic* (2006), written for clarinet, lute, cello, piano, and horn, Taha engages with *maqamat* as a discursive structure that he "destroys" through encounter with dodecaphonic and other experimental techniques (Taha, pers. correspondence). This approach constructs an antinarrative to the organizing principles that structure modal progression in *maqamat* as well as to parameters of rhythm, meter, and form. While Taha employs dodecaphonicism to expand the boundaries of form, he does not sustain a systematic treatment of aleatoric techniques such as repetition, retrograde, inversion, and retrograde-inversion transformations of pitch class series. Rather, he intermittently uses these techniques as expedients that reconfigure tropes of *maqamat* practice and potentialize "a new language" for Arab music. This approach offers an alternative to creative projects and prevents *maqamat* from "becoming frozen in a tourist museum" (ibid.). Taha celebrates aesthetic critique as a social intervention that preserves *maqamat* through the dynamics of performance and approaches cultural memory work as a creative and adaptive process.

According to conventions of modern Arab music, particularly those of the *muwashshah* genre associated with Aleppo, *sama'i* compositions are canonized as expositions in a given *maqam* that articulate and extend the aesthetic possibilities of that *maqam*. *Sama'i* is typically performed at a moderate tempo in a metric cycle known as *sama'i thaqil*. Subdivided into clusters of

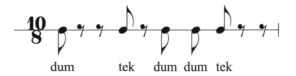

dum   tek   dum dum tek

Fig. 1.4a. *Samaʿi Thaqil*, standard rhythmic pattern.

Fig. 1.4b. Hassan Taha, *Samaʿi Chromatic*, cello, mm. 5–6.

3 + 2 + 2 + 3, *samaʿi* rhythms are typically performed by *riqq*, or tambourine, in a conventionalized pattern of higher and lower percussive attacks and rests (Fig. 1.4a). In *Samaʿi Chromatic*, Taha adapts these rhythmic figures to the cello part and displaces the third beat of the metrical pattern with a rhythmic accent rather than an *iss*, or rest (Fig. 1.4b). He also chromatically expands the pitch series from a diminished fifth (G-C#) to a full fifth (G-D) in measure 11 in ways that may be associated with his concept of *tajsim*. Further experimentation occurs in the clarinet by means of a repeated anacrusis that anticipates rhythmic subdivisions by an eighth note and by the production of minor-second intervals that are not local to the host *maqam* of the composition, *hijaz*. This activity constitutes compositional interventions of conventional *samaʿi* form by means of displaced figures, aleatoric techniques, and nonconventional orchestration. The instrumentation itself materializes new possibilities in timbral aesthetics insofar as *samaʿi* is typically performed by a *takht*, or a chamber ensemble comprising *nay*, *ʿud*, *qanun*, *kiman* (violin), and *riqq*.

In *musiqa sharqiyya*, *samaʿi* compositions traditionally develop through four sections, or *khanat*: the first *khana* introduces the primary *maqam* of the composition; the second *khana* establishes this *maqam* through a compositional statement that serves as a reprise between each section as a reprise between every section; the third *khana* destabilizes modal relations by modulating to a related *maqam*; and the fourth *khana* typically switches to a dancelike ternary meter in the primary *maqam* before a recapitulation to the melodic line of the second *khana*. In contrast to this traditional alternating sequence, Taha evokes sonata form in his narrative development of *hijaz* as the main topos of *Samaʿi Chromatic*. In the first section, Taja aestheticizes the modal space of *hijaz* through dodecaphonic techniques, the second section emerges through a distinct clarinet melody in a light duple meter, and the final recapitulation refers back to the initial chromatic development of *hijaz*.

Sama'i Chromatic generates the modal space of *hijaz* in ways that both depend on and equivocate the principles of modulation in *musiqa sharqiyya*. To illustrate his approach to modulation in the context of another *maqam*, Taha elaborates on the conventional pathways, or *sayr*, of *maqam rast*: "You have to pass through the intervals of *maqam rast* in order to make *rast* clear. Then you modulate, such as moving from G for *maqam hijaz*, or scale degree 3 to make [*maqam*] *sigah*, or 5 to make *bayati* [*sic*] from *sol*. You may use scale degree 3 or 7 to bridge between *maqam* [*sic*]. You finish the cycle by returning to *rast*—what 'Abd al-Wahhab called a 'happy finish'—as the center or the primary pitch" (Taha, personal correspondence).[29] In *Sama'i Chromatic*, however, pitch material neither "passes through" the intervals of *hijaz* nor modulates to related *maqamat*. The work opens with a drone on the French horn, accompanied by the cello and piano, that establishes G as the modal center of *hijaz*. Yet in the first section, Taha equivocates the pathways by which audiences typically anticipate and recognize the host *maqam* of *hijaz*.

The introduction critiques *maqam* practice in two additional ways. A traditional improvisation of *hijaz* on G introduces the *maqam* on a starting pitch (*mabda'*) of C, explores the upper tetrachord (C-D-E flat–F-G), descends by stepwise motion and repeating motivic patterns to the *qarar* (tonic) of G, and after a medial pause (*markaz*), states the primary melodic material in the lower tetrachord of *hijaz* (G–A flat–B-C). By contrast, in *Sama'i Chromatic* Taha outlines the lower tetrachord of *hijaz* through stepwise ascension in the lute part, which is then doubled by the clarinet line in the repetition of the statement. The scalar ascension through the lower tetrachord, rather than descending-ascending movement through both lower and upper tetrachords, departs from conventional pathways of *hijaz* (Fig. 1.5).

Second, Taha introduces chromatic intervals and pitches that are foreign to the modal space of *hijaz* in *musiqa sharqiyya*. The significance of chromaticism in *Sama'i Chromatic* is not that accidentals occur beyond the modal horizon of *hijaz* but rather that these pitches do not construct a narrative that is consensually agreed upon within the norms and expectations of general audiences of modern Arab music. Chromatic figures are typically a stylistic technique that anticipates modulations into related *maqamat*; these modulations develop a specific narrative curve through shifts between different tonal spaces. The individual events by which composers and performers aestheticize this narrative curve are recognized by connoisseurs in ways that display specific dispositions of taste. In measure 10 of *Sama'i Chromatic*, the clarinet, lute, and piano begin to exchange a sixteenth-note melodic figure

Fig. 1.5. Hassan Taha, *Sama'i Chromatic*, mm. 1–2.

based on a diminished fifth that segues into the second section of the sonata form. Deconstruction of the narrative discourse of *musiqa sharqiyya* by
means of encounters with dodecaphonicism and aleatoric techniques offers
new pathways through modal space. For Taha, these creative interventions
express his concept of *tajsim* by expanding beyond the linear relations of
musical space that he associates with *musiqa sharqiyya*.[30]

For *String Quartet* (2008), Taha establishes serialism, form, and modal
space as distinct compositional devices that he sets in dialogical relation to
one another. The first movement is a ternary sonata form that begins with a
serial pitch class set in the first violin (C sharp–G–F sharp–C-natural). Serialism is disrupted by repetition as well as the omission and inclusion of pitches
outside the established set. The first section segues into the next by means
of serial and aleatoric techniques. These consist of metric dissonance and a
canon in descending motion in the viola and cello parts in measures 12–15. The
conventional *sama'i* form is adapted by setting the rhythm in the cello part
and by increasing the density of pitch in ways that evoke percussive embellishments characteristic to *sama'i thaqil* in measures 25–29. A recapitulation
of the original melody in measure 30 resolves the ternary form and segues
into a dance section. This section is characterized by metric dissonance and

Fig. 1.6. Hassan Taha, *String Quartet No. 1*, melodic figure in *saba*
with dissonant cluster in upper strings, mm. 67–69.

polyrhythms in the viola and cello parts in measures 48–65 that adapt rhythmic patterns associated with the *tabl* drum of Syrian wedding dance music.

This section also features a lively melody set in the modal space of *saba*,
which Taha employs to signify the *muzaj* (atmosphere) of somberness typically associated with this *maqam*. As with modes used in his other compositions, *saba* is not used conventionally. Rather, Taha subjects the *maqam* to
aleatoric techniques including a dissonant cluster (C-D-F) in the upper strings
that marks arrival to this modal space. *Saba* is sustained by the repetition
of a melodic figure in the lower tetrachord of *saba* (D–E half-flat–F–G flat)
in the cello (Fig. 1.6) and by repeating triplet figures in measures 74–81. Yet
the sobriety of the atmosphere is juxtaposed with a lively dance meter that
alternates between 5/8 and 7/8 and sustains its brilliance through the final
measures of the movement.

The second movement of *String Quartet* playfully juxtaposes text-based
practices. Taha ciphers signature motifs through sequences that depict his and
his wife's given name, Najat, in historical reference to musical cryptograms
such as Schoenberg's *Suite for Piano* and Berg's *Lyric Suite*. For instance, a
pizzicato indicates the closed consonant of his name, Hassan, as would be
transcribed into Arabic text by a diacritical *sukun* over the letter *nun*. Live
performances of this movement use large-screen projectors to render these
texts as *khatati*, calligraphy associated with the decorative arts and cultural
heritage of Ottoman-era urban Damascus.

Taha positions his work in relation to a critical discourse that assesses
cultural innovation as either *taqlid* (imitation of form) or *tajdid* (creative

adaptation). This discourse can be traced to debates on social progress and reform associated with the Arab cultural renaissance, or *nahda*, that took inspiration from European forms and systems and catalyzed a search for cultural alternatives. Intellectuals favored works that offered new aesthetic constructs through processes of interpretation and adaptation and thereby articulated a modern Arab identity. Postcolonial critiques of expressive culture subsequently revisited the relation between a source and its interpretation and asked whether political and cultural dependencies are produced in the act of interpretation itself. For instance, Syrian literary critic George Tarabishi argues that conditions of modern Arab subjectivity are constituted by the initial "collision" in 1798 between Europe and the Arab world, with Napoleon's arrival in Egypt (1991). This encounter precipitated a shock (*sadma*) that conditions the ways in which a "shocked object" (the Arab world) reacts passively to the "shocking entity" (Europe). Adapting this metaphor of collision and shock to *Sama'i Chromatic* and *String Quartet* raises the question of whether an aesthetic critique of modern Arab music depends on the European intervention of aleatoric technique and dodecaphonicism. Does this ultimately reproduce dependency on European cultural forms and substantiate claims for European hegemony in contemporary art music?[31]

In the process of composing an alternative approach to modal space and the linearity of Arab music, Taha may be critiqued for a dependence on European forms of cultural modernity that not only imitates these forms but also reifies *maqamat* practices. I suggest, however, that Taha's work is not an effect of structural Orientalism. Rather than approaching experimentalism as a hegemonic force that collides with and expands a static field of modern Arab music, Taha engages with each field through "dynamic aesthetic choices" (Shannon 2006, 73). His strategic representation of these aethetic fields establishes a contiguous and mutually constitutive relationship between techniques and subverts subscription to any exclusive compositional system.

Planes of Modality

Composed by Shafi Badreddin and commissioned by Kinan Azmeh's Damascus Festival Chamber Players and the Syrian Trust for Development, *Quintete* (2008) is a chamber piece written for clarinet, violin, viola, cello and piano. In *Quintete,* Badreddin sets spectralism, *musiqa sharqiyya,* and popular folk music in dialogic relation with each other. He explores sonorities through the harmonic effects of microtonalities and micropolyphonies at the same time that he develops a musical narrative through conventional pathways of *maqamat* and the adaptation of musical idioms from Syrian folk music.[32] To explain his compositional strategies, Badreddin evokes the metaphor of a "mosaic" in which diverse parts are assembled into a collective whole (Badreddin, pers. correspondence). The symbol of a mosaic is often deployed in state discourses on cultural heritage and the arts to represent the nation's cultural and ethnic diversity.[33] In drawing an analogy between a cultural mosaic and his composition, Badreddin proposes that new forms of cultural meaning are generated when disparate elements are set in relation to each other. His work is, on the one hand, a musical narrative that emerges through the intertextual relations of *maqamat*, serialism, spectralism, and folk music. On the other hand, he conceptualizes sound within compositional parameters of timbre, intensity, duration, and density, in order to experiment with narrative form through the conceptual approach of spectral music.

The formal apparatus of the work suggests how Badreddin manipulates narrative conventions. The first movement, "Istihlal" (lit: introduction), is in sonata form and weaves between spectralism and *musiqa sharqiyya*. The modal space of *bayati* (D–E half-flat–F-G and G-A–B flat–C-D) is explored as pitch spectra through microtonalities, textural development, extended instrumental techniques, and aleatoric gestures. Badreddin conceptualizes the first movement as a metaphoric leading tone, or *zahir*, to the second movement, which is named "Dokah" (also the Arabic term for scale degree 2). Accordingly, the first movement recapitulates with a tonic of C that itself anticipates the modal center of *bayati* on D, which, in turn, is developed in the second movement. In the finale, Badreddin adapts folk music idioms from wedding dance music, usually played in *maqam bayati* or *sigah*, and concludes with ecstatic cadential flourishes that echo a Syrian wedding.

The following details the dialogic relations between these musical systems—spectral music, *musiqa sharqiyya,* and popular folk music—in order to better understand these distinct yet interrelated aesthetic spaces as representative of specific cultural contexts. According to Badreddin, pitch spectra are circumscribed within closed tonal systems. He gradually establishes a twelve-tone series through the introduction of pitches in the opening measures of "Istihlal," in which a tritone chord unfolds as an arpeggiated, contrapuntal figure in the piano (Fig. 1.7). As a constrained and spatially dense set of microtonalities, the tritone quivers with a tension that is maximized by tessitura of the string trio and the B flat clarinet. Dissonance among semitones evokes the paradigmatic relations of partial overtone series explored in spectral analysis. The dissonance emerges from a chromatic sequence (E flat, A, A half-flat, C, and D), arpeggiated in contrary motion by the piano hands.

Badreddin positions the intervals of the tritone as the set of pitch relations by which all consequent pitches are spatially related, whether by proximity, distance, or in absentia. Movement occurs by degrees of proximity or distance to the tritone in ways that are developed by the discursive interplay of

Fig. 1.7. Shafi Badreddin, *Quintete*, tritone arpeggiation in piano, m. 1.

spectralism and the structuring principles of *maqamat*. For example, a brief stasis in measure 6 emerges from the absence of dynamic movement among tritone intervals. When these intervals are subsequently recalled as descending flourishes in the piano in measure 7, their quick successive repetition increases instrumental texture. Hierarchical relations of tritone intervals to other pitch spectra are thus reinforced by reiteration.

This series is abruptly interrupted in the bass register of the piano by a sound cluster in measure 9 that signifies departure from the tritone through an unanticipated chromatic (F sharp). Similarly, Badreddin articulates both chromatic dissonance and timbral contrasts between instruments by means of the transfer of a raised fourth (G–C sharp) between the viola and piano parts in measure 10 (Fig. 1.8). The shock of chromatic dissonance is somewhat displaced by glissandi in the string trio, which lower and raise tritone pitches by a semitone, and by the clarinet, which vibrates altissimo on D.

The incorporation of glissandi in the strings evokes the embellishing gestures commonly performed in solo improvisational *taqasim* on *'ud* and violin. In the practice of *musiqa sharqiyya*, a performer will typically establish the *qarar* (modal center), then gradually modulate away from the center by means of embellishments, stepwise motion, and sequential motivic patterns.[34] Badreddin uses glissandi to establish and develop micropolyphonies, texture, and timbre through both spectralism and *musiqa sharqiyya*. In *Quintete*, glissandi are embellishing figures that anticipate but do not resolve expectations for the dynamic expansion of modal space. The dialogic relations between glissandi and tritonal space arguably destabilize the second section of this movement by manipulating stylistic conventions associated with these musical systems. *Quintete* opens with glissandi in the strings that build texture rather than develop the lower tetrachord of *maqam bayati*. Texture is intensified by staggered entrances between string parts and by double-voicing in the clarinet line. This orchestration also foregrounds the piano and establishes a hierarchy among instrumental parts. Finally, glissandi explore tritonal space

Fig. 1.8. Shafi Badreddin, *Quintete*, transfer of raised fourth
between viola and piano, mm. 9–10.

within close, yet imprecise, proximity to the pitches and help to sustain the tritone by repeating the tritone pitches.

Badreddin equivocates pitch structures of *bayati* in this composition through dialogic encounters between *musiqa sharqiyya*, spectralism, and atonalism. Whereas the overall development of the work is generally in accordance with the codified *sayr* of *bayati*, Badreddin defies conventional treatment of *bayati* by introducing pitch spectra that lie beyond the set pitches of the *maqam*. For instance, in the second section of this movement, he introduces *hijaz* into the modal horizon through an accidental enharmonic (A flat/G sharp) in the piano.[35] Rather than develop *hijaz* conventionally, Badreddin displaces pitch relations chromatically to suspend development of the *maqam*. For example, he raises the pitch class of the *qarar* (G) by a semitone (G sharp). Rather than directly outline the modal spaces of *hijaz*, he alludes to this *maqam* by means of a disjunctive melodic line and chromatic dissonance in the piano and clarinet (Fig. 1.9).

Spectral and aleatoric techniques shape the ambivalent pathways of this section. After a sense of resolution arrives in measure 20, microrhythmic activity and extended instrumental techniques increase density and texture.

Fig. 1.9. Shafi Badreddin, *Quintete*, ambiguation of modal center of *maqam hijaz* between G and G# in piano, mm. 24–26.

Techniques include col legno and saltando in the strings, the use of half an embouchure and altissimo in the clarinet, and an open pedal tone in the piano. Melodic lines in all parts explore the descending-ascending direction characteristic of *hijaz* yet in an interrupted and nonlinear pathway. Oscillation (G-C) in the strings suggests both spectral effects and the anticipation of a secondary *qarar* (C) by way of a *ghammaz*, or dominant (G).[36] A staccato sound cluster in the piano followed by a caesura brings a sense of closure to this section.

In the final four bars of the movement, Badreddin provides a formal reprise of the opening material. Piano arpeggiations resolve from the tritone to a C major chord and segue, by means of recall, into the second movement of *Quintete*. This transition is part of a larger modal progression in which C functions as a leading tone to the modal center of *bayati* in D. To summarize this movement, the narrative development begins with a tritone that expands into a twelve-tone system. The modal space of *hijaz* on G sharp emerges only to be interrupted by a reprise of the tritone, which resolves into C major. The noncadential resolution on C acts as a pivot point for the introduction of *bayati* in the second movement. In conclusion, the resolution of the tritone chord to C major, by means of the relative dominant of G indirectly suggested by *hijaz*, establishes *bayati* on D. "Istihlal" anticipates *bayati* as the main modal space of the composition.

In the second movement, "Dokah," the first ten measures anticipate and suspend arrival to the modal center of D (in *bayati*), evoking expressive elements of *musiqa sharqiyya*. *Bayati* develops by means of a voice exchange between cello and clarinet (C sharp) and by a pitch that, when slightly lowered, becomes local to the *maqam* (E half-flat). Other compositional devices include a vertical stack of the upper and lower tetrachords of *bayati* in the cello and clarinet lines as well as artificial harmonics, pedal tones, metric dissonance, chromaticism, and atonalism. As the last section of this movement accelerates by means of frantic *pont metallique* in the strings, the clarinet figures prominently in a high register with a melodic line that descends through the lower tetrachord of *saba* (G-flat-F–E half-flat–D). Badreddin reduces musical space by shifting into *maqam saba,* whose modal space in the lower tetrachord is smaller than *bayati* by a semitone. He thus articulates creative constraints of *musiqa sharqiyya* while positioning these in relation to the avant-gardist discourse of extended instrumental techniques.

Much of the second movement is characterized by the representation of a third aesthetic space, *musiqa sha'biyya* (folk music). Melodic fragments are situated as cultural indices that refer to the diversity of ethnic and religious identities in Syria. For example, Badreddin adapts a melodic phrase from traditional Suriani melodies and orchestrates it for all parts in unison. This adaptation could be interpreted as an embrace of the cultural heritage of Syriac Christian traditions in ways that affirm a public space for religious minorities. Badreddin also draws on a sonic emblem that represents his Druze heritage. Melodic contours in the clarinet part imitate the lower pedal tones of the *mijwiz,* a reed instrument played at Druze weddings in the southern province of Suweida. Badreddin cautioned me in an interview that his work is metonymic of Suriani and Druze identities and not wholly representative of these religious-minority communities.

The final movement, "Khetam-Kar," reimagines melodies and rhythms associated with *dabka* and *choubi,* genres of wedding dance music that are widely practiced throughout Syria and Iraq, respectively. Badreddin simulates the polyrhythms of *dabka* and *choubi* through metric dissonance, prepared strings in the piano, and col legno in the strings. The work ends with two musical events that adapt sonic tropes of a Syrian wedding: metric dissonance captures polyrhythms of the *tabl* drum in *dabka* dance music, and *zagharit,* or high-pitched vocal ululations typically performed by women to honor bridal households, are evoked by the cadential flourish.[37]

In what ways does the convergence of disparate musical worlds in this work assert a broader claim on the power of musical representation? Badreddin suggests that "music does not take on political content but exists for music's sake" (2011). I would counter this perspective by suggesting that the integrity of a musical work may mask the uneven and contradictory social relations that shape and are shaped by creative processes. For instance, is musical difference marked as popular music by the adaptation of folk music from minority communities, as avant-garde through the use of extended instrumental techniques and tritones, or as *musiqa sharqiyya* by the narrative progression between compositional sections? As these instances show, the production of difference through cultural representation reinforces binary oppositions between, respectively, high and low or East and West, that construct a fetishized space of Otherness. Badreddin's work arguably produces an Arab subjectivity that is destabilized by internal Others and external intervention in ways that both literally and figuratively problematize the work of representation.

Further questions of interpretation may be gathered from these analyses of the creative works that constitute *musiqa mu'asira*. What meanings are attributed to compositional devices in these musical works? What are the cumulative effects of these discourses, and for whom do they acquire meaning? This soundworld of *musiqa mu'asira* is contingent on the "aesthetics of authenticity" (Shannon 2006) that govern how music connoisseurs experience feelings of ecstasy and enchantment in the performance of *musiqa sharqiyya*. Jabri, Taha, and Badreddin destabilize these expressive effects by constructing an uneasy relationship among *maqam* pathways, folk music idioms, spectral microtonalities, and aleatoric techniques. However, the extent to which these soundworlds signify meaning for individual listeners depends on particular distinctions of taste. An ethnography of reception would help situate these distinctions in relation to the relative accessibility of social and cultural resources.[38] Although this line of inquiry is beyond the scope of this essay, the interpretive variability of meaning in *musiqa mu'asira* will be further discussed through the broader theoretical approaches presented in the next section.

Conclusion: The Predicament of Musiqa Mu'asira

Critical approaches to the study of space as a practice, discourse, and cultural imaginary (Lefebvre 1991) have argued that representational spaces are "transformed through and on the basis of relations of power" (Rabinow 2003, 354). This claim raises the question of whether and how this art world is imbricated in larger spatial formations that are embedded in local, regional, national, and global relations of power.[39] In what ways does the early twenty-first-century emergence of *musiqa mu'asira* articulate transformations of power, and how can these shifts be grounded by broader historical understandings?

Syria became an independent nation-state in 1947, following centuries of Ottoman rule and French colonial occupation. Since then, artists and intellectuals have debated the effects of imperialism and colonialism in the modern arts. Does contemporary music in Syria depend on external discourses or privilege Western concepts of art music? The Syrian poet Adonis claims that cultural expression in the Arab world has been constrained by the question of "how to engage European culture successfully while presenting a link to the Arab past" (1992, 86; cf. Shannon 2006, 73). This "double dependency" on European forms of knowledge—at once aesthetic, historical, and political—reproduces European cultural hegemony and positions Syrian music as a signifier of non-Western difference within the modern world.[40] Others question whether these cultural politics engender a crisis of representation, or "representational paralysis" (Deeb 2010), in which cultural production stagnates in the absence or suppression of creative expression.[41]

Rather than perpetuate the teleologies embedded in these critical discourses on cultural modernity, art historian Gao Minglu (2008) stresses the emergent quality of cultural production. He suggests that conditions of production are embedded in "a network of forever changing relations among human subjectivity, living space, and experience" (Minglu 2008, 137). Contemporaneity is therefore situated within the flow of everyday life as the "permanent" condition of modernity.[42] This reformulation brings together "the jostling contingency of various cultural and social multiplicities, all thrown together in ways that embrace the contradictions and inequalities within and between the particularities of shifting lifeworlds" (Smith 2008, 8–9). Recapitulating to Syrian experiences of modernity, this perspective suggests that the social contradictions and historical contingencies of *musiqa mu'asira* are what shape its various meanings in contemporary contexts.

The composers and works described in this essay are, in many ways, constrained by the predicament of Syrian modernity. They struggle to define visions of cultural modernity and build audiences who are open to these visions. This position has been exacerbated by Syria's isolation from the global flow of ideas, resources, and populations ever since the Ba'ath Party assumed power in 1963. Despite the Ba'athist state's claims toward social progress and economic development, it has willingly faltered in integrating these agendas into the global political and economic order. The authoritarian regime has legitimated this policy by invoking Third Worldist sentiments of anti-imperialism and anticolonialism that support central Ba'athist tenets of Arab nationalism and socialism (Wieland 2006). Moreover, the state has actively suppressed alternative visions—political, cultural, or otherwise— through systems of coercion that perpetuate a culture of fear between and among citizens (Wedeen 1999, Cooke 2007).

Musiqa mu'asira is therefore situated in complex economic and political conditions that beg the following questions: What makes this musical world contemporary? What historical processes have shaped the encounters and opportunities pursued by these composers? Does their creative work offer a new vision for cultural modernity in Syria today? Prior to the onset of social unrest in Syria in 2011 linked to the broader "Arab Spring," it seemed possible to attribute the blossoming of musical culture, ideas, and creativity in the past decade to policies of economic liberalization and cultural development mandated by President Assad. As described earlier in this essay, patronage of the arts increased through the building of new cultural centers and performance venues, state sponsorship of international contemporary arts festivals, allocation of resources to programs and events, and funds for individual artists. It is not insignificant that the musical works and professional livelihoods discussed here were made possible by state support for the arts.

It is problematic, however, to situate *musiqa mu'asira* as an outcome of economic development and social progress. The developmentalist logic of the Ba'athist state is perpetuated by the assumption that *musiqa mu'asira* marks an unprecedented flourishing of avant-gardism and postmodernism in the musical arts as well as the attribution of this development to economic liberalization in the last decade. These hegemonic forces conceal economic and social disparities that have increased due to flawed policies of industrialization and modernization since the 1970s. Whereas economic liberalization policies in the past decade assured citizens of increased access, benefits, and provisions, in reality, these have been distributed unevenly. Liberalization has failed to reduce unemployment, curtail rising costs of living, or stabilize domestic security (Abboud 2009). In short, a "social market economy" selectively infused by privatization measures has not reformed society but rather reproduced the systematic contradictions and social grievances that triggered the Syrian uprising in 2011.[43]

The predicament of *musiqa mu'asira* is that it is at once contingent on liberalization and yet marginalized by its engagement with global soundworlds. This field indicates the increased importation of conceptual and material resources; however, its emergence does not herald the diffusion of such cultural capital into the musical lives of many Syrians. Perhaps due to decades of relative isolation from the global order, connoisseurs reject efforts to engage with spectralism and atonalism and privilege *musiqa sharqiyya* as the most distinguished modern Arab musical expression. These aesthetic distinctions occur in the context of a Ba'athist regime that legitimizes its authoritarian power through anti-Western and anti-imperialist rhetoric, which, in turn, service its ideological commitment to pan-Arabism.

At the time of this writing in late summer 2011, contacts based in Damascus suggest that civil unrest and popular protests in Syria have not disrupted musical life at Dar al-Assad. Though some students are not able to travel to Damascus from other regions due to anxieties over violence, the arts complex has maintained its active calendar of programs and events, which are attended by full-capacity audiences. This situation is gradually shifting, however, as international economic sanctions make a negative impact on the arts. It is possible to conjecture that the arts are relatively immune because urban elite have been least affected by civil unrest, for reasons that may be historically traced to Hafez al-Assad's economic policies of *infitah* (opening) in the 1980s that benefited urban mercantile elite (Perthes 1995). Each of the composers discussed in this essay has been based in Europe since before the Arab Spring in order to pursue professional opportunities, and all plan to remain abroad for the foreseeable future. Like many Syrians residing abroad, they are uncertain about what paths their brethren will pursue and how this may affect the conditions in which they produce artistic work.

Rather than assume that experimental composition developed in teleological alignment with discourses of progress and modernity, this essay embeds *musiqa mu'asira* in the jostling conditions of history from which it emerged. The works discussed here represent the crossings, exchanges, and mediations that composers experienced as they traversed musical routes and encountered disparate narratives of the global avant-garde. Uneven, paradoxical, and textured by overlapping discourses of modernity, contemporary Syrian art music is itself an expression of the contemporaneity of musical worlds.

Notes

1. This slogan appears throughout tourism sectors to invoke Syria's role in the historical epochs of world civilization, from Mesopotamia to today.

2. Throughout my residency in Damascus during 2007–2008, I observed frequent articulations of nostalgia for Solhi al-Wadi through these and other mediums.

3. I began meeting with composers Hassan Taha and Shafi Badreddin in 2008 while conducting research in Damascus on traditional Syrian music and dance. Along with Zaid Jabri, these two composers have emerged as leaders in the field of art music through their commitment to creative activity, music education, and audience development. Other major figures working today include Nouri Iskandar (b. 1938), recognized for his adaptation of folklore into classical composition, as well as Kareem Roustom and the late Dia Succari (1938–2010).

4. Scholarship on postsocialist transition and social market reform is just now emerging in the field of Syrian studies (Abboud 2009). Economic data can be found in the annual reports published by the Oxford Business Group, which also mentions the social value and material benefits associated with entrepreneurship and small to midsized businesses.

5. The built environment reflects relations of power embedded in the infrastructural resources of rehearsal and practice rooms, acoustic technology in recording studios, state-sponsored venues (Dar al-Assad, the Citadel), and independent performance spaces (Art House, Mustafa Ali Gallery, and Teatro). Intellectual, commercial, and political spheres shape a discursive space in satellite, radio, and print media that has expanded the field of arts marketing and management. For instance, the *Cultural Diary* was launched in 2004 as a monthly

event listing and is distributed to an English- and Arabic-language readership. By and large, Arab audiences are targeted by talk shows on satellite television that feature live interviews with public figures. One of these, *Sharq wa Gharb*, is the primary outlet for composers and musicians to discuss their projects and debate issues such as music education and the role of the arts in Syrian society.

6. See the organizational website at http://www.echo-sada.org for more information.

7. See Boeux (2010) for an exhaustive discussion of contemporary Syrian cinema and Silverstein (2008) for growth in world music production.

8. While I have not been able to fully trace the emergence of the categorical label *musiqa muʿasira*, the term is consistently used in interviews and on printed materials in reference to the creative work discussed in detail in the second part of this essay.

9. Spectral music refers to the exploration of the properties of sound itself and issues of musical perception. It is commonly associated with late twentieth-century French composers, particularly Grisey and Murail.

10. The architect of social market reform in Syria, Deputy Prime Minister of Economic Affairs Abdullah al-Dardari, visited Italy in 2008 in a successful effort to actualize 150 new Italian-Syrian business opportunities. Italy also supports cross-sector training and development for Syrians (see Oxford Business Group 2007, n.d.).

11. See Antoun (1991) and Freedman (2010) for political histories of Syria's alliances within the Warsaw Pact.

12. Biographical details and a full list of works can be found on Jabri's website, zaidjabri.com. It is worth noting that Jabri and Azmeh possess web domains as part of musical professionalization of resource capital whereas Badreddin and Taha have not acquired domains to date. All composers mentioned here maintain sites on social networking platforms such as Myspace and Facebook.

13. The category of *musiqa ʿarabiyya* emerged at the 1932 Cairo Congress on Arab music, which strove to distinguish Arab musical traditions from non-Arab practices, such as Turkish and Persian musics, and to develop scientific approaches through documentation, observation, and analysis. Prior to this conference, the label *musiqa sharqiyya* was in popular use and remains so today. See El-Shawan (1984) and Thomas (2007) for further discussion.

14. These debates can be traced to the late nineteenth-century intellectual renaissance in the Arab world known as *al-nahda* (lit: awakening), which is explicated at length in the introduction to this volume. The *nahda* flourished in the late nineteenth and early twentieth centuries due to the circulation of print and sound media among the urban centers of Baghdad, Cairo, Damascus, and Jerusalem (see Sheehi 2004). Though under debate, the *nahda* is more or less indicative of developments in governance and technology as well as social cleavages that are linked to the rise of modernity, which has been dated to 1798 in the Arab world (see Gran 1998, Mitchell 1991, Abu Lughod 2005). For ways in which

twentieth-century Arab cultural production is imbricated in these processes, see Armbrust (2000) and Shannon (2006), among others.

15. See the introduction to this volume for a full articulation of a "globally configured avant-garde" suggested by Kay Dickinson.

16. While it is beyond the scope of this essay to fully explain the complex pathways of *maqamat* practice, I will draw on specific examples in the course of interpretation and analysis. In the absence of a comprehensive English-language study of Arab *maqamat*, see the work of Scott Marcus (1993, 2002) for detailed discussions of particular *maqam* sets situated in Egyptian performance practice. For discussions of cultural meaning and modernity in a Syrian context, see Shannon (2006).

17. The work of music theorist Fred Lerdahl (2001) on space, pitch, and transformational theory suggests how spaces may signify polysemic relations between musical objects. He argues that the perceived distance between musical spaces, such as pitch class and region, shapes the pathways by which transformations become meaningful in particular contexts. For an extended discussion on pathways and pitch class, see Gollin (2000).

18. Under the supervision of Krzysztof Penderecki at the Krakow Academy of Music, Jabri is currently completing his doctorate in composition with a work that sets Aramaic text to cantata form. This project addresses the issue of whether music bears meaning through procedural systems or whether the multiplicity of compositional systems is itself a contradiction of systems theory. Jabri designs prescriptive rules to form valid musical sequences out of the total space of all possibilities and to postulate a system that expands the constraints of dodecaphonicism. Based on proportions of quarter tones, musical space is distributed through twenty-four pitch classes, which are organized by ratio and transformed by sequence and series. The empiricism embedded in this formalistic approach is itself subjected to critical inquiry by Jabri, who asks whether music may be expressive or representational of that which is beyond musical structures.

19. Jabri (2005). With regard to the acquisition of sources, all scores and sound recordings for the compositions discussed in this essay were received directly from the creator by means of electronic transfer or print reproduction. Due to the absence of intellectual property rights in Syria, none of this material is subject to copyright law. At the time of this writing, scores and sound recordings remain unpublished.

20. Jabri was inspired by Czech conductor Leos Svarovsky, who suggested in a workshop that rhythmic attack could be "calm, and even soft; one doesn't have to beat percussion" (Jabri, pers. correspondence).

21. In *Glyptos*, microtones are not indexical of tonal relations in Arab *maqamat*; rather, Jabri employs them to explore the micropolyphonic effects of sound clusters in spectral worlds.

22. Jabri differentiates the concept of modulation from David Lewin's transformational theory, which postulates a teleological operation rendered globally within a closed musical system. Here, modulation refers to contextual shifts among and between multiple systems, including but not limited to Western diatonicism, Arab *maqamat*, and rhythmic developments pace Lutosławski's *Music Fenebre* (Jabri, pers. correspondence).

23. Musahat Sharqiyya was launched in 2009 by Rawafed, the cultural initiative of the Syria Trust for Development, as an annual symposium that brings together composers, musicians, and scholars from around the world to promote Oriental music. This festival, and the Jazz Lives in Syria Festival, is now managed by Hannibal Saad. For details, see www.jazzlivesinsyria.com.

24. *Song without Words III* was commissioned for solo cello by Dean Athil Hamdon of the Higher Institute; *Song without Words II* premiered with Kinan Azmeh on solo clarinet; *Song without Words I* was written to "echo" an earlier work by Jabri, *Two Songs* (1999).

25. Conventional expositions in this *maqam* would be characterized by ascending-descending stepwise motion, exploration of *bayati* (lower) and *nahawand* (upper) tetrachords, with possible modulations to *maqam 'ajam* on F and B flat (as scale degrees 2 and 7, respectively). The pitches referred to here are D, E half-flat, F, and G.

26. The performance practice of Oriental music in present-day Syria may be categorically differentiated from Arab music in terms of the relative orthodoxy of systematic approach by which the latter is discursively linked to *'ilm al-musiqa*, or the science of music that dates to the Abbasid era.

27. In a televised interview, Taha (2009) refers to a long-standing debate within the arts on *taqlid* and positions its value in relation to *tajdid*—that is, on the efficacy of innovation (*tajdid*) over adaptation and borrowing, even if from traditional customs (*taqlid*). This may also refer to nineteenth-century debates on liberal reform and religion in society with regard to modes of interpretation of religious doctrine.

28. Though we had met several times for informal interviews in Damascus in 2008, Taha first introduced the concept of *tajsim* to me during personal correspondence conducted by Skype in 2010. I am not aware of the extent to which he has written about this concept or discussed it in televised or other interviews.

29. Note that *rast* classification may indicate either the *jins* (tetrachord) or the larger *maqam* family, depending on context.

30. The role of accidentals in modal progressions is discussed in Marcus (1993).

31. For an extensive critique of Tarabishi in relation to modern performance practice in Syria, see Shannon (2006, 61–63).

32. The "mosaic" may be traced to Carleton Coon, *Caravan: The Story of the Middle East* (New York: Holt, 1958), as a schematic for social organization. In

present-day Syria, it refers to a model of multiculturalism that supports diversity and dialogue between religious, sectarian, and national groups. It also bears associations of cosmopolitanism tied to the cultural heritage of the historical Silk Road, Phoenician, and Mesopotamian civilizations, among other historical claims. For critiques on the "mosaic" as a structural-functionalist approach to collective identity that maps social and political order onto discursive imaginaries, see Eickelman 1989.

33. Syria is ethnically and religiously diverse, with a Sunni Muslim majority of approximately 75 percent. Alawites and other Muslim sects account for 15 percent, and Christian communities total 10 percent. Ethnically, the country is 90 percent Arab and approximately 10 percent Kurdish and Armenian (CIA World Factbook).

34. For an extended discussion of the role of tonic (*qarar*) and dominant (*ghammaz*) within Aleppine *maqam* practice in historic relation to D'Erlanger's treatises, see Iino (2009).

35. *Hijaz* is conventionally spelled (D–E flat–F sharp–G) (G-A–B flat–C-D), though these tetrachords vary in performance practice.

36. Though not equivalent to tonic-dominant relations in Western diatonicism, the *ghammaz*, or dominant, is typically a fourth or fifth above the *qarar* and signals the climactic turning point of modal development, eventually leading back to resolution on the *qarar*. Badreddin emphasized that the dominant is reinforced (*mithabat*) through its doubled meaning. What occurs is "not itself the dominant but resembles the dominant (*laisa al*-dominant *bas tshbah al*-dominant)" (Badreddin, personal correspondence).

37. One could criticize these as a rehearsal of Orientalism itself—that is, as a representation of Suriani melody, Bedouin rhythms, and feminine voice that reinforces these tropes of cultural identity in Syrian society in ways that further marginalize the lived experiences of those represented.

38. Please see Silverstein (2012) for recent work that discusses the effects of class, power, and cultural capital on the contemporary arts in a Syrian context. For a discussion of consumption practices in Old Damascus and the transformation of urban space, see Salamandra (2004).

39. Arjun Appadurai (2003) argues that these power formations are constructed in relation to each other as a claim for the segmentation of sovereignty from territory. The localization of spatialized experiences also serves as a critique of Edward W. Soja's (1989) seminal work on the historicization of space in terms of geographies of imperialism.

40. The concept of double dependency is critiqued by Shannon for the ways in which it reinforces modernity as "a product of autochthonous European developments" (2006, 64). Rather than project forms of alternative modernity that perpetuate postcolonial relations of dependency, Shannon suggests that a

search for cultural alternatives might instead lead to multiple visions of cultural modernities.

41. Miriam Cooke (2007) provides a compelling description of the stifling conditions in which artists and writers produced in "Dissident Syria" under President Hafez al-Assad's regime.

42. Minglu responds to debates on social modernity that contest the historical causality implicit in the concept of modernity. Jameson (2002) distinguishes between aesthetic modernity and capitalist modes of late modernity by particularizing the Habermasian model (1987) to specific historical and political conditions. See also Smith et al. (2008) for an extended discussion of contemporaneity as a construct that disengages modernity from historicized modes of representation.

43. Since 2004, banking, insurance, and trade sectors have expanded significantly. Private regional banks opened in 2004, private insurance companies received permission to operate in 2005, and the Damascus Securities Exchange opened in March 2009 (Abboud 2009).

References

Abboud, Samer. 2009. "Syria's Economy and the Transition Paradigm." In *St. Andrews Papers on Contemporary Syria*. Boulder, CO: Lynne Rienner Publishers.

Abu-Lughod, Lila. 2005. *Dramas of Nationhood: The Politics of Television in Egypt*. Chicago: University of Chicago Press.

Antoun, Richard T., and Donald Quataert, eds. 1991. *Syria: Society, Culture, and Polity*. Albany: State University of New York Press.

Appadurai, Arjun. 2003. "Sovereignty without Territoriality: Notes for a Postnational Geography." In *The Anthropology of Space and Place: Locating Culture*. Edited by Setha M. Low and Denise Laurence-Zunigam, 337–50. Malden, MA: Blackwell Publishers.

Armbrust, Walter. 2000. *Mass Mediations: New Approaches to Popular Culture in the Middle East and Beyond*. Berkeley: University of California Press.

Badreddin, Shafi. 2008. *Quintete*. Unpublished score.

Bakhtin, Mikhail. 1991. *The Dialogic Imagination: Four Essays*. Edited by Michael Holquist. Austin: University of Texas Press.

Boeux, Cecile. 2010. "The End of the State Monopoly over Culture: Towards the Commodification of Cultural and Artistic Production?" Paper presented at *Bashar al-Asad's First Decade: A Period of Transition for Syria?* (conference), Lund, Sweden, October 7–9.

Born, Georgina. 1995. *Rationalizing Culture: The Institutionalization of the Musical Avant-Garde*. Berkeley: University of California Press.

Bürger, Peter. 1994. *Theory of the Avant-Garde*. Minneapolis: University of Minnesota Press.

Cooke, Miriam. 2007. *Dissident Syria: Making Oppositional Arts Official*. Durham, NC: Duke University Press.

Deeb, Lara. 2010. "On Representational Paralysis, or, Why I Don't Want to Write about Temporary Marriage," *Jadaliyya*, December 1. http://www.jadaliyya.com /pages/index/364/on-representational-paralysis-or-why-i-dont-want-to-write -about-temporary-marriage.

Eickelman, Dale. 1989. *The Middle East: An Anthropological Approach*. Englewood Cliffs, NJ: Prentice Hall.

El-Shawan, Salwa A. 1980. "Al-musika *al-'Arabiyyah*: A Category of Urban Music in Cairo, Egypt, 1927–1977." PhD diss., Columbia University.

Freedman, Robert Owen. 1991. *Moscow and the Middle East: Soviet Policy since the Invasion of Afghanistan*. New York: Cambridge University Press.

Gelvin, James L. 1998. *Divided Loyalties: Nationalism and Mass Politics in Syria at the Close of Empire*. Berkeley: University of California Press.

George, Alan. 2003. *Syria: Neither Bread nor Freedom*. London: Zed Books.

Gollin, Edward Henry. 2000. "Representations of Space and Conceptions of Distance in Transformational Music Theories." PhD diss., Harvard University.

Gran, Peter. 1998. *Islamic Roots of Capitalism: Egypt, 1760–1840*. Syracuse: Syracuse University Press.

Habermas, Jürgen. 1987. *The Philosophical Discourse of Modernity: Twelve Lectures*. Translated by Frederick Lawrence. Cambridge, MA: MIT Press.

Iino, Lisa. 2009. "Inheriting the Ghammaz-Oriented Tradition: D'Erlanger and Aleppine *Maqam* Practice Observed." *Ethnomusicology Forum* 18: 261–80.

Jabri, Zaid. 2005. *Glyptos*. Unpublished score.

——. 2009. *Song without Words III*. Unpublished score.

——. 2010. "Coexistence of Tradition and Modernity in Syrian Music." In *Musical Coexistence: Tradition Meets Contemporary* (conference proceedings). Krakow, Poland: Academy of Music in Krakow.

Jameson, Fredric. 2002. *A Single Modernity: Essay on the Ontology of the Present*. London: Verso.

Knauft, Bruce, ed. 2002. *Critically Modern: Alternatives, Alterities, Anthropologies*. Bloomington: Indiana University Press.

Lawson, Fred, ed. 2009. *Demystifying Syria*. London: Saqi Books.

Lefebvre, Henri. 1991. *The Production of Space*. Translated by Donald Nicholson-Smith. Cambridge, MA: Blackwell Publishers.

Lerdahl, Fred. 2001. *Tonal Pitch Space*. New York: Oxford University Press.

Marcus, Scott. 1993. "The Interface between Theory and Practice: Intonation in Arab Music," *Asian Music* 24.

——. 2002. "The Eastern Arab System of Melodic Modes in Theory and Practice: A Case Study of *Maqam Bayyati*." In *The Garland Encyclopedia of World Music:*

The Middle East. Edited by Virginia Danielson, Dwight Reynolds, and Scott Marcus, 33–46. New York: Routledge.

Minglu, Gao. 2008. "'Particular Time, Specific Space, My Truth': Total Modernity in Chinese Contemporary Art." In *Antinomies of Art and Culture: Modernity, Postmodernity and Contemporaneity*. Edited by Terry Smith, Okwui Enwezor, and Nancy Condeem, 133–64. Durham, NC: Duke University Press.

Mitchell, Timothy. 1991. *Colonising Egypt*. New York: Cambridge University Press.

Oxford Business Group. 2007. *The Report: Emerging Syria 2008*. Oxford Business Group.

———. n.d. *The Report: Syria 2009*. Oxford Business Group.

Perthes, Volker. 1995. *The Political Economy of Syria under Assad*. New York: I. B. Tauris.

Rabinow, Paul. 2003. "Ordonnance, Discipline, Regulation: Some Reflections on Urbanism." In *The Anthropology of Space and Place: Locating Culture*. Edited by Setha M. Low and Denise Laurence-Zuniga, 353–62. Malden, MA: Blackwell Publishers.

Racy, Ali Jihad. 1991. "Historical Worldviews of Early Ethnomusicologists: An East-West Encounter in Cairo, 1932–1991." In *Comparative Musicology and the Anthropology of Music: Essays on the History of Ethnomusicology*. Edited by Bruno Nettl and Philip V. Bohlman. Chicago: University of Chicago Press.

Salamandra, Christa. 2004. *A New Old Damascus: Authenticity and Distinction in Urban Syria*. Bloomington: Indiana University Press.

Salti, Rasha. 2006. *Insights into Syrian Cinema: Essays and Conversations with Contemporary Filmmakers*. New York: ArteEast.

Seale, Patrick. 1989. *Asad of Syria: The Struggle for the Middle East*. Berkeley: University of California Press.

Shannon, Jonathan. 2006. *Among the Jasmine Trees: Music and Modernity in Contemporary Syria*. Middletown, CT: Wesleyan University Press.

Sheehi, Stephen. 2004. *Foundations of Modern Arab Identity*. Gainesville: University Press of Florida.

Silverstein, Shayna. 2008. "Local Meets Global at 'World Music Nights' in Damascus." In *Syrian Studies Association Newsletter* XIV: 1.

———. 2010. "A Crisis of Representation? Secularism and the Critical Aesthetics of *Dabke* Performance." Paper presented at *Bashar al-Asad's First Decade: A Period of Transition for Syria?* (conference), Lund, Sweden, October 7–9.

———. 2012. "Mobilizing Bodies in Syria: *Dabke*, Popular Culture, and the Politics of Belonging." PhD diss. University of Chicago.

Smith, Terry, et al. 2008. "Introduction: The Contemporaneity Question." In *Antinomies of Art and Culture: Modernity, Postmodernity and Contemporaneity*. Edited by Terry Smith, Okwui Enwezor, and Nancy Condee, 1–22. Durham, NC: Duke University Press.

Soja, Edward W. 1989. *Postmodern Geographies: The Reassertion of Space in Critical Social Theory*. London: Verso Books.

Taha, Hassan. 2008. *Sama'i Chromatic*. Unpublished score.

——. 2008. *String Quartet*. Unpublished score.

——. 2009. Interview. *Sharq wa Gharb*. Damascus: Syrian Satellite Television (November).

Tarabishi, George. 1991. *Al-Muthaqqafun al-'Arab wa-al-turath* (*Arab Intellectuals and Their Heritage*). London: Riad El-Rayyes.

Thomas, Anne Elise. 2007. "Intervention and Reform of Arab Music in 1932 and Beyond." In *Conference on Music in the World of Islam*, Assilah, Morocco, August 8–13.

Thompson, Elizabeth. 2000. *Colonial Citizens: Republican Rights, Paternal Privilege, and Gender in French Syria and Lebanon*. New York: Columbia University Press.

al-Wadi, Sarmad. 2009. "My Father!" *Sarmad & Linda: A Journal of Two Multinationals in Lebanon* (blog), November 27, http://sarmadinbrummana .blogspot.com.

Wedeen, Lisa. 1999. *Ambiguities of Domination: Politics, Rhetoric, and Symbols in Contemporary Syria*. Chicago: University of Chicago Press.

Wieland, Carston. 2006. *Syria at Bay: Secularism, Islamism, and "Pax Americana."* London: Hurst & Co.

CHAPTER TWO

Balancing Integration
and Disintegration

Amir Elsaffar and the
Contingent Avant-Garde

KAMRAN RASTEGAR

The avant-garde is so constitutive to our notions of modernity and culture that rarely is this term subjected to systematic definition within academic discourse. In this, the avant-garde is a key paradigm of the notion of cultural modernity; to define it would require stepping outside the epistemic boundaries of modernity and postmodernity. This is not to say that attempts to define avant-garde practice are either futile or folly but rather to simply note that, as a concept, it is married to what are essentially the Eurocentric narratives of modernity, which are developed through a notion of sequential avant-garde movements that are eventually absorbed into the heart of the West's universalist high culture. As a constitutive narrative to cultural histories of modernity, the avant-garde is a story with a pleasing ending. It goes like this: the previously marginal artist is eventually feted by the arbiters of cultural legitimacy as a genius. (The tragic variant delays the celebration to a posthumous recognition—still essentially a happy ending.)

How does the modernist fetishization of avant-gardism relate to our understandings of modern or indeed contemporary musical practices adduced with the ethno-cultural descriptor "Arab"? Recent studies on colonial and postcolonial modernity have attempted to distinguish or deuniversalize modernity, positing resistant or regionally inflected modernities that speak a different language and embody different values, where the conception of the modern is concerned. In my own work, I have termed these *contingent modernities* (Rastegar, 14), a corollary to Julio Ramos's description of *divergent modernities* in Latin America (Ramos) or Jonathan Holt Shannon's suggestion of "alternative or counter modernities" in his study of Syrian contemporary music (Shannon, xix). What these and other idealized alternatives to the Eurocentrist narrative propose is that modernity's universal claims are in fact limited, requiring redefinitions of the modern with new parameters for its universal aspirations. One manner by which these limitations may be exhibited is within the narratives of the avant-garde (what Rosalind Krauss terms the *modernist myth* of the avant-garde) that purport a diametrical opposition between the poles of "tradition" and "modernity," with a wholesale celebration of the avant-garde's "disgust for the pieties of tradition" (Sweet, 151). This valuative system marks as reactionary the non-European modernities that have not adopted this antitradition stance as a basis for their conceptions of modernity. This is why, for example, many Euro-American scholars still often find the works of nineteenth-century Arab authors as somehow lesser exemplars of a universal modernity, imitative and unfulfilled in their articulation. This is why ethnomusicologists of the Arab world are still so often tied to the poles of tradition versus modernity as essential parameters for a lifetime of academic research.

A cursory view of Amir Elsaffar's work presents him as embodying a set of contradictions—in an oxymoron, he could be termed a conservational avant-gardist. He is, on one hand, an innovative jazz virtuoso improviser and composer whose primary instrument is the trumpet and whose original compositions make use of *maqam* theory within jazz and other new musical frameworks and, on the other, a stolidly traditional practitioner of the Iraqi *maqam* genre, as a singer and *santurist*.[1] However, Elsaffar evinces little concern with what observers may see as irreconcilable contradictions in approach between radical impulses for reinvention and conservative impulses to retain and reaffirm "traditions." Instead, he moves easily between modalities of traditionalism and antitraditionalism with seemingly little need to justify his embrace of both.

Here, I will briefly attempt to reconcile Elsaffar's balancing of these purportedly contradictory stances in a critical overview of his work. Then, in the interview that follows, Elsaffar himself articulates his journey from a solidly Western training in jazz and classical trumpet, to the adoption of *maqam* theory in his performance and compositions, to his study of and archival project involving the hermetic Iraqi *maqam* tradition.[2] In the text that precedes the interview, I will outline the way by which Elsaffar's esoteric accumulation of influences sets his work out as a move beyond the modernist (and Eurocentric) origins of the concept of the "avant-garde"—which Bourdieu traces as a juncture within the economy of "disinterestedness" by which the autonomous field of cultural production is characterized. This move beyond is also one that abandons as exhausted the conception of the avant-garde as a self-conscious appending of Western modernist traditions with often surface elements of exotic Others of the European interwar high-art experimentalists (as with the primitivist interwar works of Igor Stravinsky or the folk importations of Béla Bartók) to a much more fundamental reconsideration of the boundaries and inner workings of "traditions," both Euro-American and Arab.

Beyond his training in classical and jazz trumpet, Elsaffar's compositional work has been centered in a recent area of jazz innovation, that of expanding upon the African American core of the music through synthesis with other "world" musical traditions. While jazz has long been a home to a certain form of exotic experimentation—for example, as the once celebrated and now more often derided subset of the 1970s and 1980s "fusion" movement—Elsaffar should be seen within a newer and more complex expression of this impulse. The exotophilic fusion genre has brought in non-Western instrumentation and melodies within a fairly conservative jazz framework, exploring or exploiting the non-Western elements with little critical examination of the sociocultural implications of such appropriation. From the first recordings of his Two Rivers Ensemble, a New York City–based group comprising both jazz and traditional Arab *takht* instrumentation, Elsaffar has explored a more complex form of intercultural negotiation between the "jazz" and the *"maqam"* worlds he inhabits, a trajectory that has only developed and grown more abstracted in his later recordings and original compositions. The success of these projects has at times depended upon the emergence of a broader scene of musicians of Arab origin who have significant training and experience in jazz theory—including, in Elsaffar's ensemble, performers such as Tarek Abboushi, a Palestinian *buzuq* player who is trained as a jazz pianist and composer, and Zafer Tawil, who is also Palestinian and is a multi-instrumentalist and a stalwart of the New York *maqam* music world who, for many years, has gigged in diverse settings involving jazz, rock, and other genres. So Elsaffar's innovative endeavors need to be seen in the context of the emergence of a critical mass of practitioners and performers who also share a fluency and innate ability to "speak" in jazz and *maqam* terms.

In the end, however, Elsaffar's collaborations with Hafez Modirzadeh, Vijay Iyer, and Rudresh Mahanthapappa represent his most challenging and conceptually rich steps toward an avant-garde impulse to reevaluate the essential terms of both the jazz and *maqam* fields. The collaboration with Modirzadeh, an Iranian-American saxophonist based in the San Francisco Bay Area, involves a set of conceptually interrelated compositions using Persian *radif* as well as *maqam*. The project, recorded and released under the title *Radif Suite*, represents a deeply radical take on the challenge of approaching both jazz performance and *maqam/dastgah* (the modal system used in Persian classical and related Iranian musics) theory. As Elsaffar notes in the interview to follow, he has embraced Modirzadeh's project of cultural "disintegration"—but not the disintegration of tradition into the radically modern (which would echo the primitivist movement in the interwar avant-garde); rather, he espouses the disintegration of both "modern" (jazz) and "tradition" (*maqam/dastgah*) in a common gesture.

From the perspective of a Eurocentric avant-garde mythos, a paradox exists in Elsaffar's simultaneous identity as a devoted student and archivist of the *maqam* tradition. The Iraqi *maqam* has long been seen as a genre in decline, kept alive by a dwindling number of largely elderly practitioners. Elsaffar's efforts to engage with this genre have been fundamentally focused upon conservation. The Iraqi *maqam* is a formalized system that relates melodic content and lyrics within a proscribed-improvised structure. The learning of this music requires first a deep understanding of the range and limits of what is proscribed and what is acceptable in terms of improvisation. The genre is at core centered on vocals, both through performance and the interpretation of classical poetry. Despite the challenges this must pose to someone for whom the language in which the poetry was composed is not his mother tongue, Elsaffar has devoted himself to learning Iraqi *maqam* as both a lyricist and a *santurist*. In this aspect of his work, he has taken a strictly conservative approach—as suggested during the interview when he describes his study of the *maqam* as fitting the traditional master-student relationships of the past, for example.

This reconception of the value of traditional conservation by a practitioner of avant-garde "disintegration" is not contradictory. Arguably, it echoes the traces of the contingent modernities of the Arab *nahda*, of the now-hidden idealism of earlier generations of cultural innovators in the Arab world. However, what is radical and definitively avant-garde is the diasporic and bicultural dimension of the East-West encounter that Elsaffar and others represent, which has led to a new form of avant-garde, moving away from the ambivalent and melancholic modernity of primitivism to a critical position that disintegrates in two or more directions at once. Elsaffar brings a double fluency as both a New York–based contemporary musician steeped in the boundary-breaking countercultures of jazz and a committed preserver of a fading and devalued tradition, that of the Iraqi *maqam*. In this we see a challenge to the long-standing presumptions that have come with the category of the avant-garde, a challenge that also brings to the fore the idealism of the divergent modernities of the non-Euro-American world, which now emerge from the soil of the diasporic, the transnational, and the bicultural.

Interview

KR: Maybe it'd be good to begin with the usual questions—where you grew up, your early life and influences, how you started out as a musician . . .

AE: I was born and grew up in the suburbs immediately west of Chicago. My mother is American—that is, of British background—her family came not long after the *Mayflower*, in the middle of the seventeenth century. My father came from Baghdad; he left Iraq in 1953 to study in England and then was back and forth between England and Iraq, and then the United States and Iraq, from 1953 to 1967. My parents married in 1966 and moved to Iraq, and when the Six-Day War happened, my father decided he didn't want to stay in the region anymore. And that's when they settled in Chicago, the late 1960s. Apparently they got to Chicago during the riots . . . when was that, in 1968? The Black Panther riots? They were driving in and listening to the radio, saying, "What's going on here?" [laughs] So, that was their welcoming party.

So I grew up in a bicultural household, I'm the youngest of three, and while we didn't learn to speak Arabic growing up, we were exposed to all aspects of the culture while growing up. One [other Iraqi] family was just a block away, my father had cousins who lived a few towns over, and we had, every week, if not one then several gatherings of Iraqis that would certainly involve food and music in the background. But the main thing is that we didn't speak Arabic, probably because our . . . actually it could be any number of reasons; there were families where both parents were Iraqi whose kids didn't necessarily speak it, in fact most kids didn't.

I guess the first musical recordings I heard, that my father played when I was young, were Louis Armstrong and Ella Fitzgerald, particularly *Porgy and Bess*—that was an album he really loved. And then the *Blues Brothers*, that was another record I remember hearing when I was really young, and apparently when I was three I learned how to play the record player and I would play the same record—the *Blues Brothers* sound track—and it had a scratch and sounded terrible. I think my father finally got fed up hearing it and just smashed the record. [laughs] But that's another story.

Essentially my exposure to music was Western music, what was played in the house, it was jazz and classical and opera and so on. My mother was particularly into Renaissance culture—she was a Cervantes scholar, so she was really into that period of history. And interestingly, of course, Cervantes was in Spain just after the Moors left—probably there's a connection there. . . . So in the house there was also a lot of Spanish spoken; when I was growing up, I heard Arabic, Spanish, and English a lot. I don't speak Spanish very well, but I have a good accent. And then eventually when I learned to speak Arabic I was able to with almost an undetectable accent, having heard the language so much as a kid.

In terms of the music, the first music I really got into was the Beatles, when I was nine, and then solo Beatles after that, until I realized it was mostly trash. [laughs] I mean, Paul McCartney didn't have the most illustrious career . . .

KR: Wings . . .

AS: Yeah, and then after, in the '80s . . .

KR: *Pipes of Peace . . . [laughs]*

AS: Yeah . . . [laughs] but I really liked that sound, so I wanted to hear it all. But then I made my way to the Rolling Stones and found my way to the blues, through Hendrix and Clapton. Then I got into jazz, through a book about Hendrix called *Crosstown Traffic*, where I read about Miles Davis and Coltrane. I found *Kind of Blue* in my mother's CD collection and started listening to that in high school. I'd begun playing the trumpet at nine, but I wasn't into it. I started the guitar at ten, and that was my main instrument until I was fourteen or fifteen until I heard *Kind of Blue*. When I got into jazz, I mean, jazz guitar was cool but when I listened to the music, trumpet had a lot more appeal to me. Then I attended a summer seminar at the Berklee College of Music when I was fourteen, and that was really important for my education in jazz, theory, harmony, and so on, and I continued to study with people in Chicago after that. I went to college at DePaul University and got a degree in classical trumpet, but I was performing with jazz groups in town throughout those four years. And during that time my sister had started an ensemble . . . she had studied in Bloomington, Indiana, and studied ethnomusicology—actually, she got her degree in viola performance, but she was really interested in Arab music and got into it long before I did. She just had a few CDs and transcribed some tunes, and she found these mostly American musicians . . . you know, hippies, just like, "Let's play something in this cool mode." So when I was twenty years old, she played a recording for me of this instrument . . . and I didn't know what it was. I listened to the whole track, and I was really blown away. She asked me to guess what the instrument was, and my mind went to a flute, like some sort of *nay*, or maybe a violin . . . but then it turned out it was a trumpet. That was Sami El-Bably, who was a great Egyptian trumpet player, who unfortunately died in 2001. So while *Kind of Blue* changed my life at one point, that recording changed my life as well. He was playing these ornaments in a stylistic way that was purely from an Arab tradition . . . and he was playing quarter tones, on a trumpet. When earlier on my sister had shown me what Arab music was about, I'd thought, "Well, I play a chromatic instrument, it's too bad I don't play something else." So when I learned that it was possible to create those sounds on a trumpet, that really changed my perspective. And then later I was able to go to Egypt and I met him, on two different occasions. It wasn't exactly a lesson, but he played for me and sang for me, and I watched a rehearsal that he conducted. . . .

I moved to New York just after graduating from college, and in NY I was finding my way in the jazz scene, and I discovered that there are many different scenes that exist under the heading of jazz, and the kind that was most appealing to me was that of musicians who were exploiting their cultural heritage, so [these are musicians, like] Rudresh Mahanthapappa and Vijay Iyer, both of whom had been friends of mine from before, both of them are Indian, South Indian . . . and there are a bunch of others, incorporating African, Latin . . . but those sounds were attracting me more than some of the other trends, like jazz based on twelve-tone or even classical music.

KR: This scene that is, in your words, "exploiting cultural heritage," did it seem that this was a fairly minor part of the wider scene, or . . . ?

AE: Well, it was more marginal then. But now it's becoming much more central. For example, last year I won the Chamber Music America grant. When [the grants] were announced, I think they gave out a total of ten. One was to Rudresh. One was to Rez Abbasi, who is a Pakistani guitar player, plays a sort of fusion instrument between guitar and sitar, I forget what he calls it . . . he's a very good musician. And there were two others who were neither black nor white—actually that was surprising, that there were no African Americans—there was one Latino, and there was Adam Rudolph, who is working in different kinds of percussion. . . . So overall there were no musicians who were playing straight-ahead jazz, and more and more, the jazz scene is consisting of musicians who go beyond the African American tradition and the influences of twentieth-century classical or other Western music. That has been the paradigm for a long time. But now other cultures are really taking a more central role—I think Latin culture was probably the first, with Dizzy Gillespie and Machito and all the Afro-Cuban influences. Then in the '70s Indian music started coming into the fold, with Mahavishnu and others, and now it's really opened up to other things and it's become more integral to the scene.

KR: So do you see yourself within a sort of tradition then? You mentioned some of what was going on in the '60s and '70s, Gillespie and others. In terms of Arab influences, you can also go back to Coltrane, for example, and if I'm not mistaken one of his bass players, Ahmed Abdul-Malik, sometimes played the 'ud with him. And my former teacher Yusuf Lateef was experimenting with different non-Western instruments and elements in the '60s. But I think in those days these things were pretty marginal to the mainstream of the jazz scene. So if today it's becoming a much more central new direction, do you think there is a continuity there with what these earlier innovators were doing, or do you see this as a totally new phenomenon, with different roots?

AE: There is some degree of continuity between what we're doing now and some of what was happening then—I'm glad you mentioned Coltrane. . . .

But I wouldn't say that includes, for example, "Caravan"—you know, by Duke Ellington—because there was more of an exotic element to that, a Hollywood approach, to a lot of what was happening. And incidentally if you listen to "Caravan," it has a phrase that is almost identical to part of an Umm Kulthum song, "'Awidtu 'Ayni'"—you know that one? [sings melody, emphasizing chromatic descending phrase] It's just the same as "Caravan" [sings melody, emphasizing chromatic descending phrase]—it's almost the same, but it was composed after "Caravan" . . . so was [Riyadh] al-Sunbati influenced by Ellington? Because that also was part of what Egyptians were doing—you see it all the time in their films, the self-Orientalization. So, I think at a certain point an important shift took place, away from this ex-oticization of the music. That's why Coltrane was ahead of his time. Most of what was happening then was this exotic interest, or a sort of "fusion." But I think what's happening now—the notion of creating a fusion of "us" with "that exotic thing" is not at all where people are coming from. What's happening now is coming from within, especially when you find practitio-ners who are bicultural, or biracial, to begin with. In my case, I don't feel like I'm introducing anything exotic. Nothing is more natural to me: the *maqam* is as natural as bebop, or certain types of free jazz, or playing in symphony orchestras. So if I'm going to compose a piece that happens to have elements from these different traditions, it's just autobiographical, it's just what's coming out of my experience. And in my own compositions, if I have something that feels West African or so on, if I'm not intimate with it, then it's not me and I feel really cautious about using it. There's no quali-tative judgment you can apply, saying that "Ok, that's not true music and this is," but in my own experience, there's a certain quality when the music feels really integrated. . . . It just comes from who I am, and so now when I try to compose purely equal-tempered music, I find I can't. I had a project with Vijay Iyer, who plays piano, and at first I thought, "Great, here I can do one thing that's simple," but then when I sat down to write, nothing was coming out as equal tempered, and we had to just retune the piano to put the quarter tones into it. But I can appreciate the exotic thing too. I did an arrangement of a Dizzy Gillespie tune for David Sanchez and Danilo Perez and others, a song called "Kush," and I purposefully used self-exoticizing elements. I took the *maqam nawa athar*—which is made from two *hijaz* tetrachords—because that's the most Hollywood, blatant sound, and I said, "I'm going to harmonize in perfect fourths"—because that's another thing they do. But I just exaggerated it, I put two perfect fourths—a fourth over the main melody, and another fourth above it—just sort of making fun of it, and after a while I kind of embraced it, you know those records that are all about "the land where they have deserts and women . . ."

KR: Sounds of Araby . . .

AE: Yeah, sounds of Araby! I just was thinking, ok, that's someone's take, and some of it may be good. It may be lacking in terms of validity within a tradition. But sometimes it's done with great players and has a great composer, and so I've become more accepting of that type of thing. But to get back to your question, yes, I think there is a qualitative difference between what's happening now and most of what was happening in the '60s.

KR: So would you consider this new scene an avant-garde in jazz terms?

AE: I think so. Up until recently, these multicultural projects have been really clean-sounding—like playing a *maqam* with a different beat—often taking out quarter tones, to accommodate Western instruments, taste, and so on. It's become a kind of "Mediterranean jazz" . . . a certain sound that's become very well established, drawing from Turkish or Arab music, but in a sort of "modern" instrumentation or context. I wouldn't think of it as falling into any category of avant-garde. It's not pushing harmonic envelopes or breaking out of preestablished structures or forms. It's still within the form. But I see that changing. I think my own music is an example, where I'm using the intonation of *maqam* but—for example—making chords out of it. Especially with a new piece I just finished, where I've written a progression of sixty different chords that are all microtonal, but they're not based on Western classical theories of microtonal overtones, but rather using *maqam* as a basis for harmony. Some of them are jarring, some are pleasant. . . . I'd say it's simultaneously breaking out of conventions in jazz and using the melodic framework of *maqam* as a basis for this.

Look at someone like [saxophonist] Hafez [Modirzadeh], my collaborator on my last recording, who's studied with Ornette Coleman and Mahmud Zolfunun . . . do you know Zolfunun?

KR: I know of the Zolfunun family, with the father who's a violinist and his sons who all play different instruments.

AE: Mahmud plays violin, he's in California. I think Jalal plays *tar* or *setar*. And then there's a pianist, Ramin, who plays a Persian-tuned piano, it's really beautiful. They're really great musicians, they're rooted in a . . . there's kind of a standardization that happened with Persian music in the, maybe, '50s or '60s, and these guys have a little bit of an older approach. But so, for Hafez, Mahmud is his mentor—but so is Ornette Coleman, they're of equal importance in his life. He's spent a significant amount of time with both of them. By virtue of working with someone like Ornette, you're already going to be working with unconventional forms. So for a couple of decades he's been working on breaking free of the confines of *maqam* or *radif*, but using intonation in a Western approach of shifting tonics. Using George Russell's harmonic theoretical model, but with a microtonal system. Hafez was telling me that he was speaking to someone—[Dariush] Tala'? Is he the one who recorded the whole *radif*?

KR: *Yes, he recorded the entire* radif *on* tar, *I think.*

AE: Even he was saying to Hafez that "We need to break free of the *radif*, we need to break free of it," you know, as if feeling confined by a system that no doubt had a specific purpose at a specific time. So for Hafez, no half-steps and no bar lines are the first two rules. It really blew my mind when I began playing with him. You really have to have control over your instrument in order to not play a half-step, but melodically it does a very particular thing. And it's not just "no half-steps" and you're playing in [*dastgah*] *shour*, it's "no half-steps" and you're playing in *shour* in D, and then *sigah* in A flat, and so on . . . and it just opens up this whole new realm. And as for the no bar lines, he didn't want the music to look divided by measures, and didn't want the sound of it to be repetitive. And with that comes a whole notion of culture being more fluid, not being nation-states and cultural boundaries that divide. The bar line becomes metaphorical. And Rudresh and Vijay are the same, really pushing the musical boundaries of their own traditions. And Adam Rudolph as well, with his approach to South Indian percussion.

KR: *Could we just talk a little about your studies in the Arab world, where you picked up the* santur *and began to study the Iraqi* maqam?

AE: I won a competition [in 2002] that gave me money to travel, so I immediately decided to take a trip. I went to Morocco, Tunisia, and Egypt, but the main thing was to go to Iraq. I was planning to stay for a few weeks but ended up staying for three months, and then I came back again later and stayed for another three months. I showed up with the trumpet, and just as Sami El-Bably had introduced the trumpet to Egyptian music, I was convinced that I was going to do the same to Iraqi music—a somewhat delusional idea, because I didn't really have grounding in the music. I had some teachers who were really encouraging and excited about a new instrument in this music, but I also certainly had people telling me that it wasn't possible to play this music on trumpet and who told me I had to play it on a traditional instrument. I tried to argue that you could play it on trumpet, that it wasn't about the instrument but who was playing and how they played it. Thing was, I didn't want to have to learn a new instrument, knowing how much goes into learning one instrument—it takes years. But I soon realized that trumpet was going to limit my ability to get to the heart of the music, so I on my own decided to learn to sing because when you sing you really get the intonation integrated with yourself. And with the *santur*, I just really loved the instrument when I heard it when I was young, and it had a certain call to me. And of course the *santur* and *jawza* [stick fiddle] are really the only two instruments that accompany the singer in Iraqi *maqam* music. The *'ud*, the violin, the *qanun*, these are more modern—from the 1920s on—instruments that they started adding to the groups. So I wanted to learn a traditional instrument and chose the *santur*—also because it's a rhythmic instrument, and so I could address some of the questions I had. Not just in playing Iraqi *maqam* but more generally about the rhythmic approach in *taqsim*, and within the nonmetric forms. Because it's really distinct. And it was clear to me when I heard any Arab musician playing *taqsim* that there was a propulsion in the music that made the *qafla* [a cadential phrase that acts as a climax or end to the improvisation] work, that made the modulations make sense. And it's not really talked about, and I think it's only through practice that you can get to it. And as far as I know, no one has a theory for it—I don't know if you could even come up with one. And it's those rhythms that are the underpinning of a vocal approach. When you sing, even when it's free-metered there's a pulse; it can be very fast, or slow, depending on how you hear it. But it's there. So I started learning these two instruments [voice and *santur*], and I only started at the end of my time in Iraq, at the end of 2002, and I took a few lessons with one guy there. Then I was in Jordan and Syria, where I spent two months in Aleppo studying the *muwashshahat*, I was trying to learn a *muwashshah* each day—I think I've forgotten most of them by now, unfortunately. [laughs] I really have to review them.

But then my most significant period of study was first in England, and then in Holland and Germany, where I found expatriate Iraqis living as refugees. My main teacher was Hamid al-Saadi, who was in London, he had been there for seven years . . . he eventually went back to Iraq. He is the only living master who has memorized the entire Iraqi *maqam* tradition, at least the Baghdadi *maqam*—every city has its own. He taught me, out of the fifty-six *maqam*s that he knows, he taught me forty-two of them. Those I remember much better than the *muwashshahat,* because I go back and listen to them, and I perform about fifteen or so of them now. He was an incredibly detail-oriented teacher and would never let me get away with any deviation from the *maqam*—unless they were deviations that were acceptable within the framework. There were some occasions when I would sing something different but it would turn out to be equally acceptable. At times I was confused to begin with, when singing *maqam*, in knowing where the improvisation begins and where the composition begins. Unlike the *muwashshahat,* which are very composed pieces, or, for example, folk songs, where you have a core melody but then improvise on it, or with a *mawwal* or *layyali,* which is totally open and free—but that's clear too, although it can be a little nebulous, since improvisation is always based on some sort of known repertoire . . . but in comparison to all these, the Iraqi *maqam* is really specific. It's most like the *dastgah,* or the Azeri *muqam.* Those are the two traditions that are most similar. I found that people had transcribed the Iraqi *maqam*, but it only partially made sense, even following along with a recording. And it drove me crazy at first. My teacher would teach me a piece, I'd memorize it exactly as he taught it, then I'd be given his approval that we were ready to move on to another one. Then I'd listen to a recording of the same exact *maqam*, and it was unrecognizable to me. And I'd think, ok, this must be cataloged incorrectly on this recording. But then later I'd realize—yes, it's the same one, but there's so much flexibility in the domain of one *maqam*. So you have to learn the variations.

The Baghdadi *maqam* is this conglomeration of peoples who have passed through, either from different parts of Iraq, or Persia, or Turkey, or the Gulf . . . so with every single phrase, you can pretty much trace it to a specific tribe, or region. With Persian *radif* you can do the same, trace parts to a region or tribe or composer, but it seems to have happened more organically with Iraqi *maqam*, so that it's very fluid. It has been affected by who had more influence—for example, from the Turkish when they ruled or from the Persians. And it's very regional. Mosul has a very specific style, which actually has a lot in common with Aleppine music, given the historical connections there. And Kirkuk has another tradition, oriented more to Kurdish and Turkmen cultures, and that is very close to the Azerbaijani style—they sing in a higher register, and so on. And then Basra is a different thing altogether again. So sometimes you see the same names, but there are so many differences as well. It would be my dream to learn them all. But they all follow the same principle, of each *maqam* being a model of a melody that's specific enough to be recognizable. For example, how you end the melody is very important. But each melody is really just a bunch of possibilities, sung in a semi-improvised way.

Then I went to Holland to study *santur* with Wissam Azzawi (or Ayyub; he goes by both), who plays with Farida [Muhammad 'Ali]. Then I studied with Baher Rijab in Germany, in Munich. He had been a *santur* player, although he mostly plays *qanun* now. His father was the most important scholar, singer, and *santur* player in the Iraqi *maqam* tradition of the twentieth century. So I spent a couple of months with Baher, a couple of months in Holland, and then six months in London. That was the most important experience. Because it wasn't just lessons, it was a full teacher-student relationship. I'd come to his house at noon and spend all day with him until the evening, 'til seven or eight at night. Not just having a lesson with him, we'd eat together, I'd pray with him. I'd really try to live alongside [him] and walk in his footsteps in that time. There was much more to the experience than just getting some musical material and then going home. And he didn't have to let me stay so long with him, but he enjoyed having me around too. We had a really close friendship in that time, and that human connection is really important. Reading historical accounts, it's clear that's how the [Iraqi] *maqam* has been transmitted. It's not just through lessons, but it's more living with the master, in situations that can go on for years. I didn't have that luxury, unfortunately. And it wasn't so [clear] at the time, it wasn't until afterward when I would look back and realize that this was what we were doing. For me at the time it was just an experience, but later it became more apparent—and it's the same with other traditions; in India, for example, the apprentice lives with the master, cleans the house, does the laundry . . .

KR: Were there other younger musicians studying with these masters? For example, in London, were there other students, or was your teacher living a quiet life, as so many refugees do?

AE: Not in London. I didn't find or hear about any. Well, actually, among the refugees there, Hamid had one student who was living in Germany. He would call him on the phone and ask questions or sing stuff over the phone, and I think he's performing now. Baher had one student who was studying the Iraqi *maqam*. And all the guys in Holland teach, but I think they mostly have Dutch students—they're teaching at conservatories and so on, not Iraqi students. More recently I think they have some Iraqi students showing up, but it's not very widespread in Europe. And in Iraq they have the Ma'ad al-Dirasat al-Naghamiyya (Institute for Melodic Studies), which is supposed to be about [Iraqi] *maqam*, but when I was there they were mostly studying *sama'iyat*. It was supposed to be about the study of [Iraqi] *maqam*, but it sort of turned into a place to just study Arab/Turkish music more generally. About thirty to forty students graduated per year, but very few new faces were being added to the [Iraqi] *maqam* scene—in Baghdad that scene was mostly made up of older people who had been doing it for a long time. And with them, most of them had their two or three *maqamat* that they sang or performed really well, but didn't go very far beyond that. So it's only been a handful who have kept it going as a fuller tradition.

KR: Maybe we can move to the question of what you see your contribution might be—through your musical practice broadly speaking—to innovation within the mainstream of Arab music. Not just in terms of Iraqi maqam *but also with your original compositions and so on.*

AE: Well, I don't know. It's pretty clear to me in jazz what impact my work could have. I can see myself as part of a movement that I believe will have an impact in the long term—it has its place in the jazz tradition. Especially now that I feel I'm moving to find a musical language that does what Hafez [Modirzadeh] says is not just "integration" but "disintegration," stripping things of the specificity of cultural traditions in search of a more common human element. Having two musicians of two traditions playing together, without either one trying to mimic the other's tradition. That's often what "fusion" entails. But when each person maintains the strength of their own approach—and in the end there are so many different ways to do it.

But I don't know what my role is or will be in the Arab tradition. I can see the importance of what I do when I sing purely the [Iraqi] *maqam*. For example, when I'm playing to audiences from Iraqi communities, I have kids who come up to me afterward and who want to learn it. We perform not only for older people who have a nostalgic connection to this music, but I also see twenty- and thirty-year-olds dancing and singing along to the music. So I can see the value of what we're doing here in the Iraqi diaspora. And a couple of times they've reported on me for Iraqi news or TV in Iraq, and people will contact me to thank me. It seems to matter to them that an American, who could just live the extravagant life that we have here, has taken the time to learn the music, the songs. It somehow makes people consider the value of this music. So I see the potential for me—in fact, it's sort of a dream of mine, as well as being my duty, to bring this back to Iraq and to younger musicians. Because I do think the Iraqi *maqam* will go through a revival. I see my contribution down the line, teaching it in Iraq, or here, or wherever.

As for my own compositions, such as for the Two Rivers Ensemble, I expect they will resonate for some Arab musicians, but I really just haven't experienced that yet. In fact, I've not been to an Arab country since 2006, when really I began to do these compositions. I hope my work will find an audience there, but I'll just have to see where it eventually finds its place.[3]

Notes

1. The *santur* is a hammered dulcimer instrument found in various forms from Eastern Europe to East Asia. Typically, the *santur* comprises a trapezoidal resonating box with strings stretched across the top of the instrument. The strings, often in sets tuned to the same pitch, are played using handheld "hammers" (usually wooden sticks).

2. In this article I will be using the term *maqam* for two distinct but related concepts. In general I will employ the term in its common usage so as to discuss various musical genres based upon the network of *maqam* systems common in the Arab world and beyond (especially Turkey, parts of Eastern Europe, and Central Asia). However, the term *Iraqi maqam* will be used to describe a specific genre of music commonly identified by this name, found with different local variants solely in Iraq, which is seen as distinct from but still related to the broader *maqam* field.

For more on Iraqi *maqam*, see Tsuge (1972). For a discussion of broader *maqam* tradition, see Touma (1971).

3. Interview conducted in New York, October 2010.

References

Abu-Haidar, Farida. 1988. "The Poetic Content of the Iraqi *Maqam*." *Journal of Arabic Literature* 19 (2): 128–41.

Krauss, Rosalind. 1986. *The Originality of the Avant-Garde and Other Modernist Myths*. Cambridge, MA: MIT Press.

Ramos, Julio. 2001. *Divergent Modernities: Culture and Politics in Nineteenth-Century Latin America*. Durham, NC: Duke University Press.

Rastegar, Kamran. 2007. *Literary Modernity between the Middle East and Europe*. London: Routledge Press.

Shannon, Jonathan Holt. 2009. *Among the Jasmine Trees: Music and Modernity in Contemporary Syria*. Middletown, CT: Wesleyan University Press.

Sweet, David LeHardy. 2005. "Edward Said and the Avant-Garde." *Alif: Journal of Comparative Poetics* 25: 149–76.

Touma, Habib Hassan. 1971. "The *Maqam* Phenomenon: An Improvisation Technique in the Music of the Middle East." *Ethnomusicology* 15 (1): 38–48.

Tsuge, Gen'ichi. 1972. "A Note on the Iraqi *Maqam*," special issue on Near East–Turkestan, Asian Music 4 (1): 59–66.

CHAPTER THREE

Multisited Avant-Gardes or World Music 2.0?

Musicians from Beirut and Beyond between Local Production and Euro-American Reception

⌒

THOMAS BURKHALTER

The latest tracks, songs, sound montages, and noises from the Arab world, Asia, Africa, and Latin America seem to contain revolutionary meanings. On theoretical grounds, these musics suggest reconfigurations of "modernity." They are small but passionate attempts to reshape the world into a place where "modernity" is not "Euro-modernity" or "Euro-American modernity" but where possible new configurations of modernity exist next to each other (see Grossberg 2010). These musics seem to prove claims by various social and cultural scientists: they declare the one-sided theories of modernization to be inadequate (Randeria and Eckert 2009). In other words, the old model of center and periphery is less valid than ever before. We are living in a world of multiple, interwoven modernities (Eisenstadt 2000).

The "digital media-morphosis" (Smudits 2002) is often brought forward as *the* catalyst for this revolution. Throughout the world, musicians find new ways to produce music at low cost and to promote it globally. Ideally, they offer new musical positions, challenge "ethnocentric" perceptions of "place" and "locality" in music, and attack the focus on musical "difference" in Euro-American music and culture markets.

In this article, I discuss music and musicians from Beirut in particular but include music from other cities in the Arab world, Africa, and Latin America to strengthen my argument. The focus lies on music that today reaches Euro-American reception platforms—music that is being licensed on European or U.S. labels; musicians who perform in Amsterdam, Boston, or Stockholm; and audio files and video clips that are being played and discussed on peer-to-peer networks, blogs, newspapers, and radio stations in Canada, Switzerland, or Germany. The perspective is a Euro-American one (or, to be ethnographically correct, one from a thirty-nine-year-old Swiss male ethnomusicologist who has worked for many years as a music journalist, earned experience on the board of the Swiss funding body Pro Helvetia, organized various concerts and festivals, and runs the online magazine *Norient*). My goal is to determine whether the strong claims around challenging concepts of modernity and place have an empirical grounding or whether they are, rather, naïve expressions of "wishful thinking."

The main questions discussed are whether these musicians and musics from Beirut and beyond are able and allowed to create independent musical positions, and thus form new multisited musical avant-gardes of today, or whether they are caught up in the old political and economic power imbalances. Are they still struggling for equal "Third World" or "Black" representation and thus continuing to create musical pamphlets—or a twenty-first-century version of Afro-Futurism? Or are they still being forced to mainly fulfill the expectations and adapt to the worldview of their Euro-American producers and audiences, and thus offering what I wish to refer to as "World Music 2.0," an updated version of "world music," instead of new vanguard positions?

World music was created by British record producers in the 1980s with the goal of diversifying the Euro-American market in order to sell more music. Consequently, world music is based on "musical difference" and "Otherness" in its core idea. Due to this focus, the world music catalog for the Arab world contains mainly classical Arab ensemble music, popular *taqtuqa* songs of the 1930s–1970s, and folk music, but almost no psychedelic rock from the 1970s, punk, metal, electronic music, electro-acoustic experiments, or *musique concrète*. This is true despite the fact that this very music has been produced not only in Beirut but also in other Middle Eastern, African, Asian, and Latin American cities for many years. It is after a long period of nonrepresentation that musicians of these genres have started to perform successfully on various Euro-American reception platforms.

New Music from Asia, Africa, and Latin America

Before focusing on Beirut and the Arab world, a broader overview seems necessary. New music from Africa, Asia, and Latin America is progressively reaching Euro-American reception platforms, and is being discussed with increased interest by ethnomusicologists, popular music scholars, journalists, and bloggers. Not many years ago, small niche audiences, exclusively, listened to music from these continents, and many of its present-day supporters merely ignored the new sounds, rhythms, and noises emerging from these places. To them, music from Africa, Asia, and Latin America fell into the category of world music and was criticized as being "too cleanly produced," "too much of a middle class taste," "too boring," or "too cliché." Today, authors of blogs, DJs, and curators—the multipliers of the present—are considering a multitude of terms to categorize these upcoming styles—for example, global ghettotech, ghettopop, cosmopop, worldtronica, and World Music 2.0.

In terms of its style, the sample is broad: commercially successful styles of pop music like reggaeton (Marshall 2009) and *kwaito* (Steingo 2005; Swartz 2003) and electronic music styles like *kuduro* (Siegert 2009), *nortec* (Madrid 2008), *baile* funk (Stöcker 2009; Lanz 2008), *shangaan* electro, *cumbia electronica*, and *mahragan* (Swedenburg, 2012) form the popular end of the spectrum. The experimental end offers African, Asian, and Latin American *musique concrète*, free improvisation, noise music, and sound art (e.g., Wallach 2008). Despite the many differences among these musical styles, some commonalities can be clearly identified, which will be discussed in more detail in the "Beirut" section of this article. M.I.A., an artist of Sri Lankan origin from London, is one of *the* spearheads of this new musical development. Her hit "Paper Planes" from the sound track of the internationally renowned film *Slumdog Millionaire* (Daniel Boyle, 2008) typifies a lot of what these new musics often represent. In her multiple-modern world, as Beck would call it (Beck 2007, 108), many of the old opposites (or extremes) become nullified: mainstream culture versus counterculture, pop versus art music, fun versus activism—and First World versus Third World.

Updated Afro-Futurism?

One could adopt an activist stance and argue that these musicians from Africa and Latin America, along with their contemporaries in the diaspora in Europe and the United States, create a form of Afro-Futurism and thus follow a long line of academic and nonacademic discussions and struggles. Afro-Futurism is often regarded as a movement that intends to highlight the importance of the Afro-American heritage (Gilroy 2003) and Jamaican bass culture (Bradley 2003) for the constitution of modernity.[1] In my view, this link is less strong than the others that I propose later. Perhaps one could argue that these musicians are creating an updated version of Afro-Futurism: their music is accompanied neither by the science fiction aesthetics of classical Afro-Futurism nor by a clear political program but rather by a strong realism, or a performed realism. The videos and lyrics of Somali-Canadian rapper K'Naan are a strong example of this: they seem to overexcite our visual and acoustic nerves. We find Somali pirates next to cliché pirates from Walt Disney, lions and elephants next to pictures from the Somali civil war, and the Beatles next to the stars of African and African diaspora music history—Fela Kuti and Bob Marley, for example. The fact that K'aan has produced official clips for the FIFA World Cup in South Africa only demonstrates how successful and comfortable he and other such musicians are in switching between counterculture and mainstream. Their musics are contradictory and offer multiple meanings; while listening, I can drift into reverie: I hear the chaos of our world, the hectic rush of our daily lives, the anger of these musicians with world politics and economics, and their hope to secure their existence through music.

New Avant-Gardes?

Before arguing that these musicians have the potential of creating a new musical avant-garde, a short reconsideration of the term *avant-garde* is necessary. In current European music discussions, the term is often equated with "new music"—with composers like Karlheinz Stockhausen, Pierre Boulez, or John Cage. For the musicians mentioned in this article, a broader conception of avant-garde is used (based on definitions by Hegarty 2009; Jauk 2009; Van der Berg 2009). Accordingly, artists of the avant-garde are those who seek to break with a dominant musical canon. They want to reposition music (and art) within society. Moreover, they redefine the role of music cyclically: sometimes music depicts real life, sometimes it becomes a form of protest (either as shock treatment or through irony), or it can serve as an escape into imaginary worlds. Today, music often depicts real life. I have briefly illustrated this with rapper K'aan, and I will do so in more detail when discussing Beiruti musicians' sound treatment of the Lebanese civil war.

Avant-garde in this broad conception includes pop avant-garde. This includes art-pop musicians like John Lennon, Pete Townsend, or Bryan Ferry; that is, graduates from art school rather than conservatories (Jauk 2009, 73); however, "nonacademic" pop musicians also belong here, such as those playing rock 'n' roll, psychedelic rock, punk, or Krautrock, especially in their first experimental states. Pop avant-garde includes what is sometimes referred to as "Black sound," a continuum including blues, reggae, calypso, hip-hop, house, dubstep, grime, UK funky, and much more. In their article "Black Sound—White Cube," Dieter Lesage and Ina Wudtke claim that Black sound remained—and still remains—largely unconsidered in the avant-garde context (Lesage and Wudtke 2010). I keep observing that these present-day musicians from Africa, Asia, and Latin America help to change this: they perform not only in clubs and concert halls but also at art exhibitions and events, and here their work is more easily recognized as avant-garde. In my view, these musicians bring avant-garde, pop avant-garde, and Black sound together rather easily.

Case Study: Musicians and Music from Beirut

Between 2005 and 2011, I interviewed around ninety musicians of different generations and other cultural actors in Lebanon, with the intention of understanding as much as possible the lifeworlds and actions of six of the key musicians in particular (Schütz 1975; Berger and Luckmann 1966). The research led to a book and various articles that present a broader overview of the social makeup of the local music scene(s), focus on the interaction between these musicians' music and their traumatic childhood memories within the Lebanese civil war (1975–1990), and highlight their difficult position of trying to create art for art's sake, but being pushed to promote certain cultural and political values both actively and passively (e.g., Burkhalter 2013; Burkhalter 2011a).

Beirut, often associated with war, is an active urban and cosmopolitan center. It builds on a long tradition of cultural activities and exchanges with the Arab world, Europe, the former Soviet Union, the United States, and elsewhere. Beirut today hosts a rather lively music scene, with electro-acoustic musicians, free improvisers, rappers, rock and metal bands, Arab singers, and ʿud and qanun players (see detailed list, discography, and web links in Burkhalter 2013). All these musicians organize their own small concerts for "insider" audiences.

In summary, their sociopolitical setup is as follows: Most of these musicians were born in the early stages of the Lebanese civil war. Among them, one finds men and women, Sunnis and Shiʿa, Maronites, Druze, Christian Orthodox, Greek Orthodox, Armenians, Palestinians, and members of other groups. The majority belongs to upper-class families, and many were educated at international universities in Beirut or at art schools like l'Académie Libanaise des Beaux-Arts (ALBA). A good number hold master's degrees in theater, cinema, or fine arts. Within Lebanon, these musicians often become linked with the sector of civil society that opposes mainstream cultural, social, or political values. Most of them do not believe in any of the regional politicians and clan leaders. In a conservative, radicalized, and highly commercialized country like Lebanon, their political approach lies mainly in their focus on musical quality and value. Thus, these musicians can be considered "alternative" in relation to their surroundings and to the dominant "commercial" pan-Arab pop scene that is constantly reproduced by Saudi satellite TV stations (Hammond 2007; Frishkopf 2010; Burkhalter 2011c).

Their music is mainly self-produced in small (home) studios and released on small record labels often owned by the musicians themselves. One notable exception is the "Ruptured Sessions" hosted by journalist Ziad Nawfal of Radio Liban. Nawfal invites local musicians into the studio for long interviews and often allows them to record tracks. The musicians use a great variety of instruments and audio software. Many musicians possess laptops. They work with various programs to record, edit, manipulate, convert, repair, analyze, or mix audio files—for example, Pro Tools, Logic Pro, Cubase, Ableton Live, or MAX/MSP. It is thus not surprising that, at first listening, their music is replete with well-known principles from Euro-American avant-gardes and pop avant-gardes, and this is exactly what these musicians are often criticized for, by both local and international listeners.

At the annual conference of the Society for Ethnomusicology in Middletown, Connecticut, in 2008, Christopher Miller discussed this criticism with a focus on experimental-sounding music from Indonesia. In a panel discussion titled "Local Experiments: Decentering the Global Avant-Garde," he stressed that musicians in Indonesia might not know John Cage, but they deploy similar principles of creation. The case of the musicians in Beirut is different. Many of these musicians are very well informed about the transnational trends and the history of their specific genre: I found great collections ranging from free improvisation, free jazz, and electronic music to various subforms of metal on their CD shelves and laptops. Interviews with the musicians about their musical references and inspirations offered evidence of their detailed knowledge about musicians, composers, and aesthetics in their specific niche music—often past and present. These musicians are further influenced by postmodern aesthetics of other art disciplines and many nonmusical phenomena of the present.

Many musicians focus on sonic textures, similar to musicians of the historical avant-gardes and pop avant-gardes. They do not shy away from very harsh, noisy, trashy, distorted, and edged sounds and noises. Further, musicians from different genres like to prepare their instruments. They use different techniques and materials to work on the trumpet, the double bass, and the acoustic guitar. They record on old reel-to-reel tape machines, or they manipulate Arab pop music tapes. Fundamentally, most of these musicians celebrate what is often labeled as postmodern aesthetics (Manuel 1995). They switch back and forth between different genres such as rap and *musique concrète*. Some musicians clearly prefer the principle of randomization (aleatoric): Charbel Haber of the postpunk group Scrambled Eggs produces his recordings in endless procedures between computer music and tape music. The band sends live recordings of jam sessions, manipulated guitar sounds, and effects of the software program Reaktor back and forth between a computer and a reel-to-reel tape recorder up to five times. The goal, Haber says, is to "get these really deep and dirty sound textures that we love so much" (Haber 2006). The project *The Untuned Piano Concerto* by pianist Cynthia Zaven is based on one of her performances in New Delhi—chance also plays an important part here. Zaven had an old, untuned piano installed on a truck and rode on it through New Delhi. The result was an acoustic interaction of improvised piano passages with the honking of cars and other street noises. The project was realized within an art context—which is not unusual for this Beiruti scene.

Most of the musicians have turned toward an aesthetic of the daily and common, often stamped by real life experiences, as we will see. They would agree with the old Pop Art definition "Art = Life, Life = Art" (Jauk 2009, 48). They organize sound with an experimentalist approach, and they establish an art of everyday life. They use samplers (the instrument of the postmodern era par excellence) to include noises of their local environment and of the technologized, media-dominated, postindustrial world; the latter can be heard clearly in the approaches of laptop artist Tarek Atoui, which I have described in detail elsewhere (Burkhalter 2010). Atoui creates acoustic landscapes full of breaches and contrasts. He mixes glitch sounds with samples of political speeches, Chinese and Arab voices, war noises, and popular tunes. The music swings back and forth between the old categories of "serious" composition and pop music. In his performances, Atoui controls his laptop like a rock star would his guitar—it's a "hedonistic copy and paste," typical for the pop avant-gardes of today (Jauk 2009, 67).

Some of the musicians work in an interdisciplinary fashion, across the various branches of art (think of Fluxus): the audiovisual performances of Praed, the duo of Raed Yassin and Swiss clarinet and e-bass player Paed Conca, link videos from Grendizer (a Japanese manga hero for many Lebanese kids growing up in the 1980s), visual archive material, pop melodies, and free improvised music. The use of improvisation hints that clearly "local" and "regional" material (or sources) enters these Euro-American-inspired avant-garde tracks and sound bodies.

Not many musicians work, however, with the instruments, sounds, or principles of Arab music; almost none of them use the quarter tones of Arab *maqam* music—several singers state openly that they do offer "Arab flavors" yet do not master the techniques of Arab singing. Consequently, most musicians either work with tempered scales or with untempered noises and drones. Metal bands sometimes play within scales that resemble Arab ones: harmonic minor scales, pentatonic scales, and Locrian and Lydian modes; however, their idol bands in the United States and Europe do so too.

Again, both local and international listeners criticize the musicians for this absence of "Arab" music. A short explanation for this seems necessary. If we look at the historical facts, we see that today's musicians from Beirut follow a trend set by Arab modernists and intellectuals in the twentieth century.

These modernists started to criticize the main cultural forms of the Arab world, mainly after al-Nakba (literally, "the catastrophe" of the creation of the State of Israel in 1948) and al-Hazima (literally, "the defeat" in the Arab-Israeli war of 1967). According to some of them, Arab music is based on emotions only. They compare its endless repetitions, the circling around specific notes, to ineffectual Arab politics. In their search for modernity (hadatha), many musicians therefore looked toward the West exclusively, or they mixed singer-songwriter traditions with Arab instrumentation and languages (Racy 2003, 5, 92; Shannon 2006, 76ff.; Lagrange 2000, 98–99; Touma 1998, 180–88). The education system was and is based on Western teaching methods. Today, Arab music is often performed by big orchestras, and not anymore by small Arab *takht* ensembles. The music is rendered as well-tempered harmonies instead of wild heterophony. The situation is similar to Cairo and its opera house, which this book's introduction discusses as a relic of European imperialism.

In Lebanon, Bedouin and village music, too, was translated into an art and city music for elite audiences. From the 1950s onward, radio stations, festivals like the one in Baʿalbek, politicians, and the Ministry of Tourism supported the creation of a new and modern Lebanese music—a music well known through the many concerts and CDs of Fairuz and the Rahbani Brothers, Wadiʿ al-Safi, Zaki Nassif, Sabah, and others (for a detailed history of music in Beirut, see Burkhalter 2013). Instruments like the traditional *mijwiz* clarinet were replaced by the flute—the former were too harsh-sounding and disturbing.

From all my interviews conducted in Beirut, the consequences seem clear today: a lack of musicians who want to work around regional music, and a lack of musicians who learn Arab music in its whole aesthetical dimensions (Touma 1998, 180–88). Yet attacks by various critics against these musicians for being Westernized seem unfair. A source of blame may only be posited by examining a far more complex picture.

New Sounds from Other Arab Cities

In the Arab world beyond Beirut, a large number of musicians go in similar directions. On the CDs of the Egyptian label 100Copies and around the 100Copies performance space, we find musicians experimenting with the noises of Cairo and electronic music (e.g., Mahmoud Refat, Ramsi Lehner, Adham Hafez, Kareem Lotfy, and Omar Raafat). Hassan Khan has presented his multimedia works of sound, picture, and text at numerous exhibitions and festivals in the Near East, Europe, and the United States. Kareem Lofty and Omar Raafat (with Casio PT Mini keyboards) mix noise with distorted, psychedelic-sounding Egyptian melodies (for example, by the keyboardist Islam Chipsy) and the latest "autotune" sounds from *mahragan*—also called techno-*sha'bi* or electro-*sha'bi* (Swedenburg, 2012). Mohammed Ragab—alias Machine Eat Man—works with analog synthesizers. He defines his mixture of Arabic voice, flute samples, drums, psychedelic synthesizer movements, and electronics as "Egyptronica."

Further musicians range from pioneers like Halim El-Dabh to composers in Syria, rappers in Palestine, and metal musicians in Cairo (as covered by Michael Khoury, Shayna Silverstein, Caroline Rooney, and Benjamin Harbert, respectively, in this book). The list might also include pioneers like Nassim Maalouf, who created a trumpet with which he can play the Arab quarter tones, and many other contemporary musicians. In addition, there are musicians of Arab origin living outside the region who frequently network with musicians in the Arab world. Mahmoud Turkmani, a Lebanese musician and composer living in Switzerland, is one example. Turkmani experiments with Egyptian *takht* ensembles, video, and film. In his piece "Ya Sharr Mout" ("Son of a Bitch"), he harshly criticizes both the Europeanization of Arab music and the extreme commercialism of Lebanese postwar mainstream culture. On his CD *Zakira* (2004), he and an Egyptian *takht* ensemble perform *maqam*-based music that (to insiders) follows surprising paths. Turkmani's way of rendering Arab music is in "opposition" to contemporary Western art music that often just adds Arab melodies, rhythms, or sound textures—and remains contemporary Western art music to the core. Turkmani's experiment provoked negative reactions. Arab musicologists called him a traitor to Arab music. My assumption is this: changes from within a musical "culture" or "tradition" seem more threatening to conservative insiders than playing European classical music and just adding Arab-sounding melodies.

Similar approaches are sometimes tagged "alternative modernity" (Gaonkar 2001), referring to a modernity that does not work with Euro-American music structures but reformulates principles of "local" music "cultures." Theoretically, alternative modernity is a very delicate concept—for many reasons.[2] Musically, it offers a huge number of possibilities. Palestinian singer Kamilya Jubran and Swiss trumpet player and electronic musician Werner Hasler highlight where such an approach could lead: their track "Wanabni" builds on principles of *maqam*-based music: Jubran moves from section to section by small tonal steps into higher pitches, then comes down again at the end. Trumpet and electronics interact with her voice, following her and creating heterophonic moments. Jubran's singing voice is the focal point. She is singing in *maqam huzam*, a mode based on an eight-tone scale with untempered three-quarter pitches (see Burkhalter 2012 for detailed analysis).

Overall, these examples show that new renderings of Arab music are not excluded from what here are referred to as multisited avant-gardes.

The hope is that these musicians' struggle for more representation and against physical aggression and/or censorship will achieve success after the revolutions of 2011. During these uprisings in Tunisia, Egypt, Libya, Bahrain, Yemen, and Syria, many "alternative" musicians produced protest songs and video clips (see Burkhalter 2011b). The clip "Not Your Prisoner" by Egyptian rappers Arabian Knightz, Palestinian rapper Shadia Mansour, and producer Fredwreck mixed hip-hop beats and rap lyrics with film sequences and photographs from the demonstrations in Cairo's Tahrir Square. This YouTube clip is an example of a truly transnational product: while Arabian Knightz attended the demonstrations in Cairo, Shadia Mansour sent her vocal lines over the Internet, and Fredwreck, the producer of rap stars including Snoop Dogg, edited and mastered the track in Los Angeles. Other musicians opposed these protest songs. They preferred to demonstrate on the square, as citizens, and not promote their own work through what they call "superficial" protest music. I observed similar discussions in my fieldwork in Beirut during the 2006 war between Israel and Hezbollah. The different ways the musicians reacted to this war led to discussions about the artist's role in war and conflict. Some argued that the artist's duty is to create good art, and to be quiet when he or she is in turmoil emotionally. The artist should absorb as much as possible, establish an emotional distance from the events, and then make his or her artistic statement. Others stressed that an artist has to make him or herself heard, to stay active and help the community—and, if necessary, to stop working as an artist and help people on the streets (see Burkhalter 2011a). In Cairo, Mahmoud Refat, owner of the label 100Copies, told me that he found no time to produce music during the Egyptian revolution of 2011 (Refat 2011). In Tahrir Square, his colleague and the musician Ahmed Basiony were killed during the demonstrations—Basiony, again, was an important motivator for many students at the American University in Cairo to start experimenting with sound. Today, young female musicians like Ola Saad and Yara Mekawei perform concerts and produce installations around sound art. Saad told me that she and others do so "for the sake" of Ahmed Basiony: "We try to remember him in continuing what he taught us" (Saad 2013).

Internationality:
Distribution to Primary and Secondary Markets

The musicians and bands from Beirut are covered on their own websites, on platforms like Forward Music, Lebanese Underground, and the unofficial download site Pirate Beirut (for a long list, see Burkhalter 2013). Online distribution allows these musicians to sell their albums in small quantities in different countries. The local platforms for selling CDs or concert tickets are, however, small. Often, these musicians from Beirut and other Arab cities reach well-educated elites only.[3] The status quo will not change as long as the mainstream Arab media focuses on commercial products and local and regional cultural funding remains scarce—in 2013, some musicians and cultural actors have observed small changes: the Lebanese group Mashrou' Leila was invited to perform at big international festivals in Ba'albek and Byblos, and in Cairo—two years after the revolution—up-and-coming musicians and producers receive offers to compose sound tracks for new Egyptian films, jingles for TV, and radio ads. "Many people and firms are hungry for new and fresh sounds," Mahmoud Refat told me in an interview (Refat 2013).

International NGOs open an alternative market for these musicians. For example, they are asked to give workshops in the Palestinian refugee camps in Lebanon or to contribute to, for example, Israeli-Palestinian peace projects. While some musicians refuse to work in these secondary markets, others cannot afford not to take the opportunity.

To earn money with their music, these musicians need to focus on performing and selling mainly on Euro-American platforms. They thus remain largely dependent on festivals, arts funding, NGOs, and media in Europe and the United States. Regionally, the musicians' networks and the distribution of their music are almost nonexistent. With some exceptions, musicians from Beirut and Cairo, for example, meet at festivals in Europe and the United States—but *not* in Cairo or Beirut.

Organizers in Europe or the U.S. send official invitations to visa authorities to ensure that the musician can leave the Arab world and fly to Europe or the United States. Organizers also vouch for the musician to fly back home after the concert. The crucial point is the border between the nation-state and the global field (Derrida 2005, 57). Sounds and sound formations may travel worldwide, but for the musicians, national and political borders are still binding. The decision whether musicians from the Arab world can physically participate on Euro-American reception platforms or whether they just deliver sound samples is made in the visa and passport administration offices (see Marina Peterson's chapter). Hence, making transnational music is not quite so democratic. On my last trip to Cairo, in March 2013, Egyptian musicians told me that it is becoming increasingly difficult to get an exit visa to travel to festivals and concerts abroad—they all hope that this problem does not worsen in the near future.

Beyond NGOs, art councils, and event organizers, bloggers, DJs, and producers have become the main mediators and multipliers of this music. Again, most of them live and work in Europe and the United States. These multipliers are constantly in search of new, crazy, or bizarre sounds and videos, which they mediate for their niche audiences. In the best case, they open up possibilities for musicians from Beirut and beyond. In the worst, they stage mainly themselves and receive most of the profit. The blogosphere trend *shangaan* electro, the music of Tsonga musicians in Soweto, was pushed internationally by Honest Jon's Records in London. Now, Euro-American producers remix these tracks into more accessible versions for the Euro-American club scenes. In the *kuduro* video clips from Luanda, which were recorded with mobile phone cameras, scantily dressed women dance with men who have lost a leg in the Angolan civil war. The *kuduro*, clattering out of a parked minivan, is seen as the first African music made by purely electronic means. This cheaply produced music struggles to meet the aesthetic and technical demands of the transnational world market. The international *kuduro* trend is still mainly being produced in Portugal and France.

These structures of distribution to the Euro-American reception platforms have a great influence on what music is being heard and staged or not. Further, this has repercussions for the musical productions. Day by day, the musicians negotiate strategically between the local and the Euro-American platforms. At times, they offer different music, or different explanations and readings for the same music. I myself realized the strategic self-positioning of these musicians in one incident involving Tarek Atoui. Atoui is cited in a Lebanese book as saying that, during the 2006 war between Israel and Hezbollah, he hit the streets to collect sound recordings: "He was arrested and detained for three days, during which time he was whacked on the head and lost partial hearing in his left ear, permanently" (Wilson-Goldie 2010, 55). To me, Tarek Atoui told a different story: he said he did little more than watch TV. To a Lebanese scholar, Atoui seems to have felt it was important to stress his activism. To the Swiss ethnomusicologist, he stresses his neutrality, and his aim is to be recognized mainly as an artist. He creates art for art's sake, and not resistance or war music.

Reception: Resisting and Staging Exotica

A large portion of the musicians challenge our Euro-American perceptions of their home countries, and our ethnocentric ideas about "locality" and "place" in music. These musicians do not want to satisfy the preference for "cultural difference" of us Euro-Americans, ethnomusicologists, and music lovers. They want recognition for their catchy house beats, their powerful indie rock and punk, or their refined noise and sound collages—and not because they are from a foreign or even exotic place. They want to create individual musical identities, apart from self-exoticism, commercialization, and propaganda. Tarek Atoui refers to an international level when he reflects about his role as an artist in Lebanon: "I think that it is important that people in Europe hear and see that Lebanon offers a great variety of music. In producing experimental music I might help to open up minds in Europe and the United States and go against stereotypical views: Lebanon, the Middle East and Islam have much more to offer than fundamentalism, terrorism, and conservative crowds" (Atoui 2006).

Some musicians, however, have rediscovered the appeal of "exotic" and "psychedelic" sounds. They are cocreating an international trend in today's blogosphere (which is still dominated by Euro-American writers, DJs, and producers).[4] They know that exotica sells on foreign platforms: what is obscure, ironic, and exotic does, for example, benefit disproportionately from the avalanche effect of the virtual commendations on platforms like Facebook.[5]

From the point of view of postcolonial theorists, and of many musicians from Beirut, this new celebration of exotica might be remarkable or even sobering at first hearing. For many of them, this long tradition of looking for new, exotic sounds and rhythms by Western music creation has left a negative taste (see Locke 2009; Binas-Preisendörfer 2010; Taylor 2007; Born 2000). In European art music, composers like Claude Debussy (in Java), Béla Bartók (in Hungary), Leoš Janáček (Czechoslovakia), and many others experimented with folk music traditions; in the genre of world music (1.0), musicians and producers like Peter Gabriel, Ry Cooder, and Paul Simon performed with local musicians of other "cultures"; and from the 1980s, Indian and Pakistani music of the second generation in the UK mixed sitar melodies and *tabl* rhythms with club beats. They portrayed their home countries not in a folkloristic but in a "modern" way (see Hutnyk, Sharma, and Sharma 1996; Zuberi 2001; Burkhalter 2000). To my ear, however, they often reproduced old Indian music stereotypes, mixed them with drum 'n' bass beats, and thus celebrated an essentialist multicultural hybridity. Often, in these projects, the beat serves as the "modern" downbeat (and basis), while the singing—or the sitar playing—becomes no more than "pseudotraditional" ornamentation. Jonathan Shannon calls this principle "theme and variation," ultimately seeing in it a power imbalance: "Such an approach would merely reiterate in musical terms the idea that European modernity is a standard upon which other, alternative modernities are based" (Shannon 2006, 67). In Beirut, many musicians are very critical of this old formula. They try hard not to create "cheap fusion," they told me. The further aim is to invert the power structures one often finds in international projects: in "Wanabni," the Swiss musician Werner Hasler is following Kamilya Jubran in her singing, and not the other way around.

If these musicians stage exotica, they stage it in a different way. This I intend to show now in more detail with Beiruti musician and artist Raed Yassin.

Raed Yassin: Manipulating Biographical Material

Many of Raed Yassin's tracks show his aesthetic references and tastes clearly. His fascination with popular culture, especially what is often referred to as kitsch and trash, becomes obvious: for example, when he performs with local or international free improvisers, or when he manipulates popular music by past and present stars from Egypt, Syria, and Lebanon on turntables, or when he converts himself into a typical solo entertainer with a small keyboard, a drum computer, and a microphone. Raed Yassin searches out songs from the psychedelic rock music scene in Beirut and other Arab cities in 1960s and 1970s. Beirut, at the time, hosted up to two hundred psychedelic rock bands. They formed a network of musicians, clubs, and fans and thus prepared the ground on which local avant-garde musicians can now work on their careers (see Burkhalter 2013).[6] Yassin is further interested in the light entertainment music of the 1950s. Back then, the mix of calypso, samba, bossa nova, and belly dance rhythms became the sound track of the emerging mass tourism to the Arab World (Weinrich 2006, 178).[7] The music in these nightclubs "violated every boundary of authenticity," writes Rasmussen. It is this violation that Raed Yassin and many of his contemporaries thrive on: "The nightclub sound was a musical hybrid generated by the creative invention and innovation of second-generation and post–World War immigrants who were inspired by modernization and Orientalism. Reflecting the influence of American popular music and the modern trends of Cairo, Egypt, musical innovators Muhammad al-Bakkar, Eddie "The Sheik" Kochak, and Freddy Elias incorporated Western instruments and modern emergent styles into their performances during which a kind of musical caricature of the Orient was created" (Rasmussen 1992, 69).

The Egyptian musician Omar Khorshid is an idol for many. In the nightclubs of Beirut and Cairo, Khorshid set to music hits like "La Cumparasito" and "La Paloma." Critics call Khorshid the James Last of the Arab world.[8] Yassin regards him as a genius, though, because of his surf-guitar style and his brilliantly presented tremolo. Again, Yassin shares this passion with contemporaries worldwide, first and foremost with American-Lebanese guitarist Sir Richard Bishop, who released a tribute album to Khorshid titled *Freak of Araby*.[9] His brother Alan Bishop runs the U.S. indie label Sublime Frequencies, which produced albums with collages from rare, obscure, and psychedelic-sounding samples from all over the world, for example, the CD *1970s Algerian Proto-Rai Underground,* compiled by Hicham Chadly.

The regional scene of "new wave" *dabka* (Silverstein 2007, 2012) came into focus through the same label, and through Raed Yassin. "New wave" *dabka*, a genre of festive music, offers a somehow similar but contemporary sensation to the psychedelic music of the 1960s and 1970s. Contemporary *dabka* musicians control their synthesizers with small MIDI boxes. They create the typical Arab quarter tones and imitate the shrill sounds of the double pipe oboe *mijwiz*, the traditional *dabka* instrument (Rasmussen 1996). In 2010, this *dabka* scene found a fan community outside its informal market of cassette tapes and MP3s. One reason for this expansion was a CD and a world tour of Syrian *dabka* singer Omar Souleyman, which was produced and organized by Sublime Frequencies—with the help of Raed Yassin. This shows how tastes and trends are created across transnational communities.

Raed Yassin's other projects (like Praed, mentioned before) are primarily based on themes related to Beirut and the Arab world, especially to Arab cinema, comics and contemporary art, disasters, and archives. *The Adventures of Nabil Fawzi*, a dialogue project with the American bass clarinettist Gene Coleman, plays around the topic of Nabil Fawzi—the Arabic name of Superman. In his installation, Yassin offers a tribute to Sami Clark, one of the most successful pop singers during the Lebanese civil war. Yassin calls Clark his fictive mentor, and he contrives a genealogy linking Clark to the Yassin family. The installation features four turntables simultaneously playing a different Sami Clark LP. Alongside this, we see a series of manipulated photographs, in which Sami Clark appears to entertain the Yassin family during a birthday party. A text indicates that these objects are the only remains after an explosion that destroyed the Yassin family apartment during the war. Fiction and reality, fun and trauma find each other in this project.

Musicians like Raed Yassin do not work in the same way with "exotica" as did previous generations. These musicians actively reveal the "exotic" presentations of strangeness and put it onstage either as a colorful or a painful or even traumatic play. Ethnomusicologist Veit Erlmann brings the differences to light. He defines the intercultural modus of world music (1.0) with the term *pastiche*, which he defines as a form of parody that lacks the polemical or satirical aspect. World music (1.0) tries to highlight unspoiled musical forms and idioms. However, it mixes sounds of the completely commercialized present with the pseudohistorical patina of different places and times (Erlmann 1995, 14). Musicians like Raed Yassin have replaced pastiche with parody. They play joyfully with some of the Euro-American fetishizing and leitmotifing of the East. At the same time, they feel close to musicians and artists in the pop avant-garde who were for a long time fascinated by "primitive" people (Primitivism) and the perceived fetishes of primitive people (Van der Berg 2009, 98; Toop 1997) but were often far from the earnest "pastiche" observed in world music

(1.0). Some of the Beiruti musicians talked about their fascination with the beatniks in the 1950s and 1960s, and some of their forefathers (Paul Bowles, Alan Hovhaness, Jack Kerouac, William S. Burroughs, and Allen Ginsberg, to name a few), and with their literary and musical visions of East Asia and North Africa (Hieber 2009, 120–21). These visions were often developed in exchange between musicians from the West and the East.[10]

Today, Raed Yassin's taste for kitsch and trash can be seen as influenced by the new international trend for "exotica," but it goes far beyond that—it has a very biographical grounding too. Many of his works do draw heavily on acoustic source material from the Lebanese civil war. Yassin collected this material from political parties (or militias; for example, the Christian Lebanese Forces or the Shiite Amal party), radio stations, old recording studios, small record shops, cassette stands, and private people. His twenty-three-minute sound collage—or sound montage or "bricolage"—"CW Tapes" ("Civil War Tapes"), is packed with this archival material: propaganda songs from various right-wing militias to those of left-wing singers; political speeches from leaders of all the confessions; news jingles and ads (from Pepsi to Barilla) from around two hundred radio channels; melodies from children's programs—for example, the title melody of *Grendizer*; noises from bombs and rifles; the kitschy Franco-Arab pop music of singers like Sami Clark, Azar Habib, and Al Amir Al Saghir; and much more.

Here, I shall highlight only a few sections (for a longer description, see Burkhalter 2013). "CW Tapes" opens with the sounds of tuning a radio receiver. Then bombs explode (0:46)—not bombs of warfare but bombs of joy. "We hear detonations that exploded to celebrate the election of the Christian leader Amin Gemayel in 1982," Yassin explains (Yassin 2006). At 0:58, Gemayel praises the Lebanese resistance in a long speech. He argues that the Palestinians will never be able to throw the Lebanese into the sea, thus reflecting his people's worries that the Palestine Liberation Organization (PLO) could become too strong in Lebanon. At the same time, we hear Camille Chamoun far in the background; the former president, also an important Christian leader in the civil war, tells people how to get rid of the Palestinians. According to Yassin, "Chamoun in the background is saying openly what Gemayel in the foreground is actually saying, but not so clearly" (Yassin 2006). This is typical for the piece: within "CW Tapes," the acoustic source material often stays recognizable. For Lebanese listeners especially, the way Yassin plays with and contrasts politically loaded material thus clearly becomes a form of protest. At 8:10, we hear a dense mix: with a news jingle from Sawt el Shaab, the radio station of the communist party; a news ad for pizza and macaroni; and the news jingle from the Christian right-wing station Voice of Lebanon (8:22–8:35). This jingle was being aired during particularly catastrophic events for the Lebanese. "For many Lebanese it is still very traumatic to hear it," Yassin explains (Yassin 2006). The melody of the jingle is well known, as it was based on the sound track for the American film *Shaft*, written by Isaac Hayes in 1971. At 18:25, popular Lebanese singer Philemon Wehbe enters with his piece "Naku immak ya Lubnan" (Lebanon, They Fucked Your Mother). "This is probably the strongest direct statement against violence and war in the history of Lebanese music so far," Yassin claims (Yassin 2006). Philemon Wehbe recites the names of many Lebanese clan leaders who, according to him, "fucked" Lebanon. He gives them Armenian endings to ridicule them: Druze political leader Walid Jumblat becomes Jumblatian, Chamoun Chamounian, and so on. The song's features include numerous examples of typical Arab synthesizer sounds (see Rasmussen), hand drums, and the singer's voice over an overamplified microphone with a lot of reverb. At 20:20, Yassin uses an effect on the voice of a news presenter to imitate bombs and Kalashnikovs: "As children we would perform these fake guns and bombs with our mouth. The 'Bah' would be the bomb in our children's language." Then "CW Tapes" ends with a sudden stop: no fade-out.

Yassin is not solely interested in these "political" layers. In my interviews, he argues that he hears the piece aesthetically for the most part. "CW Tapes" uses quite a broad range of techniques of editing and sound manipulation, but we hear no red thread. The editing appears very rough: no slow fade-in or fade-out, but rather a lot of cuts and immediate changes. Yassin says that he borrowed this eclectic approach from the local radio stations and from popular Lebanese music in the 1980s. According to him, both were made with very rough mixes and underwent many abrupt changes: "I mixed my music exactly in the way the radio programs did during the civil war. They used to play songs, then put another on, stopped it, and talked nonsense. It was like a war between music and words, a real mess" (Yassin 2006). Shortly after this statement, Yassin goes one step further: "My work derives directly from my environment. I saw how close relatives got killed; I lived in Beirut when it was destroyed, and when it was reconstructed. I lived like a nomad, and had to move between many homes, between Beirut and the Lebanese mountains. In my artistic work, I love to deconstruct and reconstruct sound and media files. I feel at home when I work with the sonic material that surrounded me during my life. However, I organize this material in the way I want" (Yassin 2006).

Mazen Kerbaj: Staging War and Violence

To stage war and violence is another trend that arouses similar questions to those around "exoticism." M.I.A. is again the most known example here.

She illustrates this very clearly on her 2010 album *Maya*. In the video of the track "Born Free," she presents herself as an activist and shocks the viewer with radical violence. The video shows executions of many red-haired men—representative of prisoners in the Sri Lankan civil war, as M.I.A. argues. The acoustic horror trip mixes sirens, explosions, screaming people, and noise; the voice of M.I.A. is manipulated to create the effect of a shouting dictator.

Soon after the release of *Maya*, M.I.A. and her authenticity were criticized harshly. The daughter-in-law of Warner Music CEO Edgar Bronfman uses provocation to attract attention, and to sell more records. M.I.A. is only one among many examples. There is also the Jamaican singer Terry Lynn, who poses with a big gun on her album, the dancehall star Mavado, the *kuduro* video clips, *baile* funk from the favelas in Rio de Janeiro, and much more.[11]

My field research in Beirut shows clearly the appeal of incorporating violence in music. Lured into stressing cultural differences on the Euro-American platforms, many musicians strategically focus on war and violence, or they use this link to their biography occasionally. One could argue that from an international perspective, these musicians have replaced one exotic element with another: traditional-sounding music for images and noises of gunshots and rockets. My research shows, however, that judging this is very delicate.

The musician with whom I discussed these issues the longest was Mazen Kerbaj, a trumpet player and cartoonist. Kerbaj is a main musician of the very active free improvised music circle that he started in 1997 along with Paris-based Lebanese musicians Christine Abdelnour and Sharif Sehnaoui. The three formed a trio, attracted more musicians, and created Musique Improvisée Libre au Liban (MILLS), an organization for free improvisation in Lebanon. They organize the annual international festival Irtijal (Improvisation) and launched their own label, Al-Maslakh (The Slaughterhouse), with the goal "to publish the un-publishable in Lebanon" (Kerbaj 2005).

The album *brt vrt zrt krt t* showcases Mazen Kerbaj as a solo artist. He is experimenting with distinct trumpet techniques and sounds—and using no software to manipulate them. His trumpet blubbers, jars, and claps from the deepest to the highest frequencies. In the track "Blblb Flblb," his trumpet is filled with water and thus creates deep bubbling sounds; it whispers softly and airily and screams in a high pitch. In "Zrrrt," he plays the trumpet with a tube. He sits on a chair, the tube around his neck and the trumpet between his legs. In "Taga of Daga," he uses a longer tube that is five meters. In "Tagadagadaga," he works with rhythmic patterns. Within each of the different tracks, there is little change, but we hear that Kerbaj controls those sounds, and we hear his rhythmic precision. It was the Austrian trumpet player Franz Hautzinger who told Kerbaj after a concert that Kerbaj's trumpet in fact sounds very much like helicopters and rifles. This led Kerbaj to think about the relationship between the sounds of his childhood and youth and the sounds that he likes and creates now.

I had many debates on how the Lebanese civil war (or the current unstable situation) entered and continues to enter these musicians' music and musicality. During my interviews, it seemed that most of the musicians remember the war similarly. Their sonic memories are full of propaganda music and speeches from the various militias, radio ads, and jingles, plus the sounds of rifles and bombs. The musicians argue that they know all the weapons of war just by listening to their sounds, and that they can tell from where to where a rocket flies, and whether or not a weapon is of direct danger to them. As noted before, their ears were shaped by around two hundred radio stations that constantly informed listeners about who had been killed, and which streets were open to traffic and which were not. According to them, the ear played an important role in the war. In my many interviews, absurd and often very cynical questions full of black humor were raised: "Is war good ear training?" Or, "Can listening to the weapons of war replace musical solfège?"

Today, Kerbaj believes that his sonic memories determine, to a certain extent, which sounds he likes or dislikes. "I have, for example, a very special relationship to silence," he says. "I was always afraid of silence. In silent moments we were always afraid of something worse to come" (Kerbaj 2005). On the other hand, Kerbaj states clearly that his musical taste and perception keep changing, through listening, musical education, and practice. Kerbaj identifies, as his main influence, the free improvised music scene in Europe. It seems clear that his attention to silence has also been nurtured by music history—first and foremost through composer John Cage's discussions about silence and his silent piece *4'33"*. Other main influences, Kerbaj argues, are the pioneers of free jazz, for example, Peter Brötzmann and his album *Machine Gun—Automatic Gun for Fast, Continuous Firing* (Kerbaj 2006). Within and just after the 2006 Israel-Hezbollah war, many of the musicians showed a certain fascination with conflict (see Burkhalter 2011a), similar to Italian futurist Luigi Russolo and his 1913 manifesto *The Art of Noises* (Russolo 2005) and the futurist writers around Filippo Tommaso Marinetti. This fascination seemed nurtured, however, by the personal experience of civil war in the first fifteen years of their lives (Burkhalter 2011a) and not necessarily by a regard for war as an aesthetic and mythical phenomenon, as it was for the futurists (Witt-Stahl 1999). Thus, these are the questions to ask: What is "local" music? Do the trumpet sounds of Mazen Kerbaj, for example, derive from the surroundings where Kerbaj grew up? Or do we hear a "version" of free improvisation or avant-garde music only, similar to that from performers in Europe and the United States?

This and many other examples show the complexities of the interactions of local music production and Euro-American perception, and of the interactions between biographical experiences and transnational music knowledge.

Analyzing Music from Different Perspectives

If we want to understand the motives, possibilities, and struggles of these musicians, I believe we need to work with a complex (and maybe experimental) methodological setting. I worked with an accordingly experimental, multidisciplinary research layout. To stand the test of time, this analysis had to be close to the musicians, the music, and the daily realities of the international reception platforms. This methodological approach thus switches between close reading of music and broad overviews of contexts and trends. I conducted my research from three main perspectives: the musician as an actor, music-making as a process, and the music as a media product. I further organized an international reception test and analyzed and "read" music from Beirut from various perspectives (for a detailed analysis, see Burkhalter 2013).

If we analyze in this way, we arrive at complex answers. Take the issue of "war," for example. From a Euro-American perspective, these musicians from Beirut gain more interest when focusing on the Lebanese civil war. From a Lebanese perspective, however, they are breaking a taboo when discussing war in public (Khalaf 2002). From an artistic perspective, we can see them manipulating material with the techniques of avant-garde and pop avant-garde. From a political and historical perspective, we hear feedbacks from the conjunctions between music, warfare, and the Middle East. And from a biographical perspective, many of the musicians use music as self-therapy for dealing with their personal traumatic war memories (see Maus 2007; Sutton 2002). Many other perspectives can be added, and I believe that these diverse perspectives offer a more interesting and important picture than one clear end result.

How, for example, this interaction between war memories and musical output works in detail is almost impossible to analyze—and I have tried to do so around interviews with Mazen Kerbaj elsewhere (Burkhalter 2011a). Here is merely a short summary. The process is musical and extramusical, and it works consciously and unconsciously. Deeper forces can be traced in the psychological and sociological processes of musical socialization (Kleinen 2008; Dobberstein 1994; Nuber 2000). Important are processes of memorization: these always happen within a social group (Assmann 2007) and from the perspective of the present day (Schmidt 2006). This again leads to the phenomenological argument that all human actions are intentional. The translations from sonic memories to an acoustic output, therefore, function within complex interactions between psychology and strategic performing. One thing is important to state clearly: whether or not to introduce sounds of war is a hotly debated topic within these musicians' circles, their audiences, and their critics (see Burkhalter 2011a).

This kind of research suggests that the bundle of influences and forces that lead a musician to produce his or her piece of music is almost impossible to unwire—for the scholar, and for the musician as well. The musicians from Beirut are constantly influenced by a huge amount of musical and nonmusical forces: from psychological traumata to impact from the surrounding society, local and global politics, technology, transnational zeitgeist, and much more. At the same time, these musicians are actively trying to create their own and special music—by pushing a variety of limits and by using the possibilities offered by our digitalized and transnational world.

Outlook: Focusing on Knowledge

Some Lebanese musicians describe their transnational networks as "taste" communities but not always as "knowledge" communities. They share tastes for similar sounds and trends, but they do not have the same knowledge of the specific material with which they are working. They are critical of superficial renderings of war, violence, and exotica. Musician Serge Yared makes a typical argument: "The role of an artist is to offer critical depth and to see everyday issues from a different angle. So when we work with the topic of war, we try to show it from personal, maybe not so known, perspectives. I'm always a bit angry when I see these superficial references to war" (Yared 2012).

Matters are, however, far from black and white. Many Lebanese musicians experienced war from an elite position: some moved abroad during the civil war. And the 2006 war between Israel and Hezbollah they observed from the safe city center. This is not meant as judgment but rather to be taken into consideration. And one should never underestimate what elites themselves went through, especially during the civil war.

Manipulating popular "trash" and "street" culture with experimental music techniques, too, is at its core not that different from translating "village" music into "city" music—as Lebanese composers have done from the 1950s onward. In both cases, "elite" artists rendered "nonelite" music to meet the tastes of local and international elite audiences.

Whenever we as scholars focus on reference cultures and "sampling cultures," considering these questions, constellations, and contradictions can be very fruitful:

1. What is the material (musical styles, sounds, and noises) musicians use in their works?
2. How do the musicians know the material? And how knowledgeable are they in transforming it?

3. How is the material manipulated, transformed, and decoded? The new works are copies, covers, remixes, mash-ups, and so on—in some works, the references stay recognizable, in others they do not.
4. Of what importance is the material? (Are references credited? Are references discussed in titles, lyrics, images, interviews?)
5. How do the musicians position themselves toward the material? Possible renderings are homage, mockery, parody, persiflage; playing with double meanings; stating direct protest; shocking with radical realism; ignoring and escaping.

This research includes both interviews with musicians and analysis of their media products. It leads into what ethnomusicologist Veit Erlmann suggested years ago: "analysing the ways histories of cultural, social, or political contexts are inscribed into music" (1995, 10). It's not about judging one approach over the other: musicians do not necessarily need to have experience and knowledge of the material they use to transform it into great music. This analysis does, however, reveal what is at stake. It shows motivations and visions from musicians and recipients. It highlights diverse positions toward an idea, a musical style, a place, or the world.

Conclusion

Diverse forms of life have taken the place of the old-style cultures, which we have always imagined as types of national or regional culture. These life forms (in my opinion: today's cultures, cultures after the end of traditional cultures) do not stop at the boundaries of ancient cultures but cross through all these. Therefore, they can no longer be grasped with traditional cultural categories. "Transculturality" wishes to show both that we are situated beyond the condition of traditional culture and that the new forms of culture and life pass through these ancient formations as if they were self-evident. (Welsch 1994, 147–48)

The three subcategories of my research catalog offer the following temporary results. From the perspective of "musicians as actors," we often find elites, cosmopolitans who have the chance to travel. Less-privileged musicians remain deliverers of samples and ideas, as is the case with Angolan *kuduro*. On the level of "music making (in practice)," we hear that many of these musicians are very well informed about transnational trends and the history of their specific niche genres. They overcome the East-West, South-North, traditional-modern, and backward-advanced binaries (see this book's introduction) rather easily. Their music is full of well-known principles from Euro-American avant-gardes and pop avant-gardes. This does not at all mean that they just copy Euro-American musicians and artists.

Raed Yassin, Mazen Kerbaj, and others offer us a hint at the complexity of influences and strategies in music-making. The musicians are constantly negotiating between their own creative ideas and the potential of these ideas on the various reception platforms. To observe this struggle is one of the main tasks of researchers of music making in *today's* world. We learn about the position, knowledge, creativity, and craftsmanship of these musicians and about the possibilities and obstacles within our digitized, globalized media world. This analysis should be as precise as possible—and beyond any romanticism. Many, myself included, somehow wish that the "Global South" creates a zeitgeist. These musicians from Africa, Asia, and Latin America deserve a new avant-garde, and not a World Music 2.0 network.

If we look from the perspective of "music as a media product," we find that these musicians are still confronted with old power relations. Some of them work in two careers: they play indie rock or free improvisation within their transnational niche genres, in small clubs for little money; and they introduce new and old representations of exotica, war, or violence in big world music festivals or in art biennials. Often, only these big events hold the power to organize the necessary funding and visa clearances for traveling.[12]

All in all, I would, unfortunately, use the category World Music 2.0 for these new musics that cross from Africa, Asia, and Latin America to the Euro-American platforms. It is a theoretical category, and a provocative hint that there are still many boundaries to cross and stereotypes to break. A short definition of World Music 2.0 would run as follows: World Music 2.0 uses the possibilities of the growing digitalized music market for a more independent and manifold production of music. On the one hand, World Music 2.0 musicians construct confident past-colonial, transcultural positions and form (finally and distinctly) new multisited avant-gardes of the twenty-first century. On the other hand, these musicians are still caught in old postcolonial structures and dependencies, especially whenever they aim to reach international platforms. This becomes clear in their ongoing focus on war and violence, and exotica. The musicians do, however, replace the "pastiche" of world music (1.0) with "parody."

Notes

1. Steve Goodman (alias Kode 9) (Goodman 2010), for example, describes how Afro-American musicians in genres like reggae, dub, dancehall, jazz, rap, and house created worldwide musical trends, and also influenced through "audio viruses" the Euro-American mainstream—mainly in the bass structures of music and music making—with specific patterns (for example, rhythm patterns), artistic

approaches (improvisation), and techniques (sampling). Eric Davis, in his online essay "Roots and Wires" (Davis 1996), argues similarly when he links the writings of John Miller Chernoff (1979) on polyrhythms in African music to British styles of club music. He mentions the "Hardcore Continuum" (Reynolds, 2009) from ardcore (hardcore techno or hardcover rave) in 1990, jungle, drum 'n' bass, garage, two-step, grime, dubstep, and UK funky.

2. First, "alternative modernity" affirms that "Euro-modernity" is the standard. It underrates research claims that Euro-modernity was invented with or even in the "peripheries" of the world (e.g., James 1989), and it undercuts visions of multisited modernities. Second, "culture" and "tradition" cannot be defined in essentialist terms.

3. To sell CDs online is even more difficult than it is in Europe or the United States. Potential international customers often fear purchasing CDs in Arab online stores with their credit cards.

4. An increasing number of blogs (e.g., *waxpoetics*, *awesometapesfromafrica*), labels, and websites focus on non-Western popular music from the 1950s to the 1970s—for example, psychedelic music in Iran (Finders Keepers 2010), Nigeria (Soundway 2010), and other places around the world.

5. The South African art-pop collective Die Antwoord is probably the most successful example here. The group plays with the stereotype of the primitive, beer-drinking, white South African; the collective's most successful video clip has received seven million views on YouTube (accessed October 24, 2010).

6. The LP *Waking Up Scheherazade* (Grey Past Records 2007) covers psychedelic rock songs by Arab bands from the era, including the Lebanese bands The Sea-ders, Simon C. Edwards & His Soul Set, The Kool Kats, Tony Franks & The Hippin' Souls, and The News. The Sea-ders (later renamed The Ceaders) can probably be called the most successful Lebanese rock group of all time. In 1966, they released a single with the two tracks "Thanks a Lot" and "Undecidedly" on the Decca label in the UK. In 1967, the band released an EP with the same songs on the PAX label in Israel, just before the outbreak of the Six-Day War. After the war, it was discovered that PAX had represented a Lebanese band, and, according to an Israeli record collector, this became the "most funny and tragic error in the history of records in Israel" (www.mistovev.haoneg.com).

7. Bob Azzam, a Lebanese of Jewish origin born in Egypt, for example, became an idol. He performed the Arabic song "Mustapha" in the Maxim nightclub in Paris, and it became a global hit.

8. James Last (born 1929) is a German composer and big band leader whose arrangements and "party versions" of international hits (from a variety of genres) were enjoyed by audiences worldwide for their "catchiness."

9. Richard Bishop and his brother Alan Bishop are two of the main musicians

behind the band Sun City Girls, formed in Phoenix, Arizona, in 1979. In 2010, Raed Yassin invited the band to perform in Beirut.

10. Egyptian composer Halim El-Dabh (born 1921), for example, was in contact with members of the Beat Generation (Seachrist 2003).

11. Again, one big influence comes from gangsta rap and other popular music genres that have celebrated "being poor."

References

Assmann, Aleida. 2007. *Der lange Schatten der Vergangenheit. Erinnerungskultur und Geschichtspolitik*. Bonn: Bundeszentrale für politische Bildung.

Beck, Ulrich. 2007. *Risikogesellschaft: auf dem Weg in eine andere Moderne*. Frankfurt am Main: Suhrkamp.

Berger, Peter L., and Thomas Luckmann. 1966. *The Social Construction of Reality: A Treatise in the Sociology of Knowledge*. New York: Doubleday & Company.

Binas-Preisendörfer, Susanne. 2010. *Klänge im Zeitalter ihrer medialen Verfügbarkeit: Ein Beitrag zu Fragen von Popmusik und Globalisierung*. Bielefeld: Transcript.

Bradley, Lloyd. 2003. *Bass Culture: Der Siegeszug des Reggae*, Höfen: Hannibal.

Burkhalter, Thomas. 2000. "East Isn't East: Asiatische Musiker in England zwischen Tradition und neuer Identität." *Norient—Independent Network for Local and Global Soundscapes*. Accessed December 29, 2010, http://norient.com /stories/eastisnteast.

———. 2010. "Tarek Atoui—or: Reflections on the New Musical Avant-Gardes of the 21st Century." In *Indicated by Signs*. Edited by Aleya Hamza and Edit Molnar. Bonn and Cairo: Bonner Kunstverein and Goethe Institute Kairo.

———. 2011a. "Between Art for Art's Sake and Musical Protest: How Musicians from Beirut React to War and Conflict." *Popular Music and Society* 34 (2).

———. 2011b. "Im Rhythmus der Revolution." *Norient—Independent Network for Local and Global Soundscapes*. Accessed August 9, 2011, http://norient.com /stories/arabischerevolution2011.

——— 2011c. "Frauenrollen und Popmusik in der arabischen Welt: Von unantastbaren Starsängerinnen, Models in Unterwäsche und selbstbewussten Musikerinnen." In *Thema Nr. 1: Sex und Populäre Musik*. Edited by Dietrich Helms and Thomas Phleps, 189–200. Bielefeld: Transcript Verlag, Beiträge zur Popularmusikforschung.

——— (with Christoph Jacke and Sandra Passaro). 2012. "Das Stück 'Wanabni' der Palästinenserin Kamilya Jubran und des Schweizers Werner Hasler im multi-lokalen Hörtest: Eine multiperspektivische Analyse." In *Black Box Pop: Analysen populärer Musik*. Edited by Dietrich Helms, 227–56. Bielefeld: Transcript.

———. 2013. *Local Music Scenes and Globalization: Transnational Platforms in Beirut.* New York: Routledge.

Chernoff, John Miller. 1979. *African Rhythm and African Sensibility.* Chicago: University of Chicago Press.

Davis, Eric. 1996. "Roots and Wires: Polyrhythmic Cyberspace and the Black Electronic." Paper presented at the Fifth International Conference on Cyberspace, Madrid. http://www.techgnosis.com/cyberconf.html.

Davis, Mike. 2007. *Planet der Slums.* Berlin: Assoziation A.

Derrida, Jacques. 2005. *Paper Machine.* Palo Alto, CA: Stanford University Press.

Devereaux, Andrew. 2007. "'What Chew Know about Down the Hill?': Baltimore Club Music, Subgenre Crossover, and the New Subcultural Capital of Race and Space." *Journal of Popular Music Studies* 19 (4): 311–41.

Dobberstein, Marccl. 1994. *Die Psychologie der musikalischen Komposition.* Köln-Rheinkassel: Verlag Christoph Dohr.

Eisenstadt, Shmuel Noah. 2000. *Die Vielfalt der Moderne.* Weilerswist: Velbrück Wissenschaft.

Erlmann, Veit. 1995. "Ideologie der Differenz: Zur Ästhetik der World Music." *PopScriptum* 3: 6–29. Accessed December 29, 2010, http://www2.hu-berlin.de /fpm/popscrip/themen/psto3/psto3010.htm.

Fensterstock, Alison. 2010. "Sissy Bounce Rap from New Orleans." *Norient—Independent Network for Local and Global Soundscapes.* Accessed December 29, 2010, http://norient.com/stories/sissybounce.

Frishkopf, Michael, ed. 2010. *Music and Media in the Arab World.* Cairo: American University in Cairo Press.

Gaonkar, Dilip Parameshwar. 2001. *Alternative Modernities.* Durham, NC: Duke University Press.

Gilroy, Paul. 1993. *The Black Atlantic: Modernity and Double Consciousness.* Boston: Harvard University Press.

Goodman, Steve. 2010. *Sonic Warfare: Sound, Affect, and the Ecology of Fear.* Cambridge, MA: Massachusetts Institute of Technology.

Grossberg, Lawrence. 2010. *Cultural Studies in the Future Tense.* Durham, NC: Duke University Press.

Hammond, Andrew. 2007. "Saudi Arabia's Media Empire: Keeping the Masses at Home." *Arab Media & Society* (October).

Han, Byung-Chul. 2005. *Hyperkulturalität. Kultur und Globalisierung.* Berlin: Merve, 2005.

Hegarty, Paul. 2009. *Noise/Music.* New York: Continuum.

Hieber, Lutz. 2009. "Psychedelische Plakate in der Counter Culture der USA." In *Avantgarden und Politik: Künstlerischer Aktivismus von Dada bis Postmoderne.* Edited by Lutz Hieber and Stephan Moebius, 111–44. Bielefeld: Transcript.

Hutnyk, John, Sanjay Sharma, and Ashwani Sharma. 1996. *Dis-Orienting Rhythms: The Politics of the New Asian Dance Music*. London: Zed Books.

James, C. L. R. 1989. *The Black Jacobins*. New York: Vintage.

Jauk, Werner. 2009. *pop/music + medien/kunst: Der musikalisierte Alltag der digital culture*. Osnabrück: Electronic Publishing Osnabrück.

Khalaf, Samir. 2002. *Civil and Uncivil Violence in Lebanon: A History of the Internationalization of Communal Conflict*. New York: Columbia University Press.

Kleinen, Günter. 2008. "Musikalische Sozialisation." In *Musikpsychologie: Das neue Handbuch*. Edited by Herbert Bruhn. Hamburg: Rowohlt Verlag.

Kolland, Franz. 2010. "Grundlagen einer Soziologie der Globalisierung." In *Soziologie der globalen Gesellschaft*. Edited by Franz Kolland, 13–49. Vienna: Mandelbaum Verlag.

Lagrange, Frederic. 2000. *Al-Tarab: Die Musik Ägyptens*. Heidelberg: Palmyra.

Lanz, Stephan, et al., eds. 2008. *"Funk the City": Sounds und städtisches Handeln aus den Peripherien von Rio de Janeiro und Berlin*. Berlin: metroZones 9 and b_books.

Lesage, Dieter, and Ina Wudtke. 2010. *Black Sound—White Cube*. Vienna: Löcker Verlag.

Locke, Ralph P. 2009. *Musical Exoticism: Images and Reflections*. New York: Cambridge University Press.

Lull, James. 2000. *Media, Communication, Culture: A Global Approach*. New York: Columbia University Press.

—— 2002. "Superkultur." In *Grundlagentexte zur transkulturellen Kommunikation*. Edited by Andreas Hepp and Martin Löffelholz, 750–73. Konstanz: UVK/UTB.

Madian, Azza. 2010. Email message to author, August 7.

Madrid, Alejandro L. 2008. *Nor-Tec Rifa! Electronic Dance Music from Tijuana to the World*. Oxford: Oxford University Press.

Manuel Peter. 1995. "Music as Symbol, Music as Simulacrum: Postmodern, Pre-Modern, and Modern Aesthetics in Subcultural Popular Musics." *Popular Music* 14 (2): 227–39.

Marshall, Wayne, Raquel Z. Rivera, and Deborah Pacini Hernandez, eds. 2009. *Reggaeton*. Durham, NC: Duke University Press.

Maus, Fred Everett. 2007. "Music and Sexual Abuse." Paper presented at the Conference on Feminist Theory and Music—*Speaking Out of Place*, McGill University, Montreal.

Mueller, Gavin. 2007. "Straight Up Detroit Shit": Genre, Authenticity, and Appropriation in Detroit Ghettotech." MA thesis, Bowling Green State University. http://etd.ohiolink.edu/view.cgi?acc_num=bgsu1182534766.

Nuber, Ursula. 2000. *Der Mythos vom frühen Trauma: Über Macht und Einfluss der Kindheit*. Frankfurt am Main: Fischer Taschenbuch Verlag.

Prior, Nick. 2008. "Putting a Glitch in the Field: Bourdieu, Actor Network Theory and Contemporary Music." *Cultural Sociology* 3: 301–19.

Racy, Ali Jihad. 2003. *Making Music in the Arab World: The Culture and Artistry of Tarab*. Cambridge: Cambridge University Press.

Randeria, Shalini, and Andreas Eckert. 2009. "Geteilte Globalisierung." In *Vom Imperialismus zum Empire*. Edited by Shalini Randeria and Andreas Eckert, 9–31. Frankfurt am Main: Edition Suhrkamp.

Rasmussen, Anne K. 1992. "An Evening in the Orient: The Middle Eastern Nightclub in America." *Asian Music* 2: 63–88.

——. 1996. "Theory and Practice at the 'Arabic Org': Digital Technology in Contemporary Arab Music Performance." *Popular Music* 3:345–65.

Reynolds, Simon. 1999. "The Hardcore Continuum." *The Wire*. http://www
.thewire.co.uk/details/contributors/?contributor=51.

Rosengren, Karl Erik. 2002. "Internationale und interkulturelle Kommunikation." In *Grundlagentexte zur transkulturellen Kommunikation*. Edited by Andreas Hepp and Martin Löffelholz, 37–66. München: UVK/UTB.

Russolo, Luigi. 2005. *Die Kunst der Geräusche*. Mainz: Schott Musik International (Edition Neue Zeitschrift für Musik).

Schütz, Alfred. 1975. *On Phenomenology and Social Relations: Selected Writings*. Chicago: University of Chicago Press.

Seachrist, Denise A. 2003. *The Musical World of Halim El-Dabh*. Kent, OH: Kent State University Press.

Shannon, Jonathan Holt. 2006. *Among the Jasmine Trees: Music and Modernity in Contemporary Syria*. Middleton, CT: Wesleyan University Press.

Siegert, Nadine. 2008. "Kuduru—Musikmachen ohne Führerschein." *EthnoScripts* 10: 102–24.

Silverstein, Shayna. 2007. "'New Wave' Dabké: Popular Music and Media in Lebanon and Syria." Paper presented at the annual meeting of the British Forum for Ethnomusicology, Newcastle, April 19.

Silverstein, Shayna. 2012. "The Stars of *Musiqa Sha'biyya* in the Levant." In *Out of the Absurdity of Life: Globale Musik*. Edited by Theresa Beyer and Thomas Burkhalter, 62–69. Solothurn: Traversion.

Steingo, Gavin. 2005. "South African Music after Apartheid: Kwaito, the 'Party Politic,' and the Appropriation of Gold as a Sign of Success." *Popular Music and Society* 28 (3): 333–57.

Steinholt, Yngvar Bordewich. 2005. *Rock in the Reservation: Songs from the Leningrad Rock Club, 1981–86*. New York: Mass Media Music Scholars' Press.

Stöcker, Katharina. 2009. *Welche Rolle spielt der "Baile Funk" in Verbindung mit Gewalt? Zur Musik einer neuen Generation in den Favelas Brasiliens*. Munich: Grin Verlag.

Sutton, Julie P. 2002. *Music, Music Therapy and Trauma: International Perspectives.* London: Jessica Kingsley Publishers.

Swartz, Sharlene. 2008. "Is Kwaito South African Hip-Hop? Why the Answer Matters and Who It Matters To." *The World of Music* 50 (2): 15–33.

Swedenburg, Ted. 2012. "Egypt's Music of Protest: From Sayyid Darwish to DJ Haha." *Middle East Report* 42 (265). http://www.merip.org/mer/mer265 /egypts-music-protest.

Tagg, Philip, and Bob Clarida. 2003. *Ten Little Tunes: Towards a Musicology of the Mass Media.* New York: Mass Media Music Scholars' Press.

Terkessidis, Mark. 2010. *Interkultur.* Frankfurt am Main: Suhrkamp.

Toop, David. 1999. *Exotica: Fabricated Soundscapes in a Real World.* London: Serpentstail.

Touma, Habib Hassan. 1998. *Die Musik der Araber.* Wilhelmshafen: Noetzel, Heinrichshofen-Bücher.

Truax, Barry. 2002. "Genres and Techniques of Soundscape Composition as Developed at Simon Fraser University." *Organised Sound* 7 (1): 5–14.

Van der Berg, Hubert, and Walter Fähnders, eds. 2009. *Metzler Lexikon: Avantgarde.* Stuttgart: J. B. Metzler.

Wallach, Jeremy. 2008. *Modern Noise, Fluid Genres: Popular Music in Indonesia, 1997–2001.* Madison: University of Wisconsin Press.

Walser, Robert. 2003. "Popular Music Analysis: Ten Apothegms and Four Instances." In *Analyzing Popular Music.* Edited by A. F. Moore, 16–28. Cambridge: Cambridge University Press.

Weinrich, Ines. 2006. *Fairuz und die Brüder Rahbani: Musik, Moderne und Nation im Libanon.* Würzburg: Ergon Verlag.

Welsch, Wolfgang. 1994. "Transkulturalität. Lebensformen nach der Auflösung der Kulturen." In *Dialog der Kulturen. Die multikulturelle Gesellschaft und die Medien.* Edited by Kurt Luger and Rudi Renger, 147–69. Vienna: Österreichischer Kunst and Kulturverlag.

Westerkamp, Hildegard. 2002. "Linking Soundscape Composition and Acoustic Ecology." *Organised Sound* 7 (1).

Wilson-Goldie, Kaelen. 2010. "Adventures in Experimental Music." In *Untitled Tracks: On Alternative Music in Beirut.* Edited by Tanya Traboulsi, Ziad Nawfal, and Ghalya Saadawi. Photographs by Tanya Traboulsi. Beirut: Amers Editions.

Witt-Stahl, Susann. 1999. *But His Soul Goes Marching On: Musik zur Ästhetisierung und Inszenierung des Krieges.* Karben: Coda.

Zuberi, Nabeel. 2001. *Sounds English: Transnational Popular Music.* Champaign: University of Illinois Press.

Cited Interviews by the Author

Haber, Charbel 6/27/2006
Kerbaj, Mazen 9/25/2006
Kerbaj, Mazen 8/27/2005
Madian, Azza 8/5/2010
Rastegar, Kamran 7/31/2010
Refat, Mahmoud 3/8/2013
Refat, Mahmoud 4/20/2011
Saad, Ola 3/5/2013
Yared, Serge 6/15/2012
Yassin, Raed 9/18/2006

PART II

Roots and Routes

CHAPTER FOUR

The "People's Artist" and the Beginnings of the Twentieth-Century Arab Avant-Garde

SAED MUHSSIN

This chapter concerns a musician who lived a few months short of thirty-one years (1892–1923). Sayyed Darwish grew up in poverty and held a day job as a laborer. At the age of sixteen, he was "discovered" and, from there, went on to change the face, and some of the internal organs, of Arab music forever.

Darwish's life coincided with great social and political change in his homeland, Egypt, and he responded to this deeply through his music. As we will see in this chapter, he incorporated the politics of the era into the subject matter of his songs, yet, beyond this, he led a musical revolution, parallel to the social one, that challenged some of the very foundations of the Arab and Turkish musical traditions. We will see that Darwish's work was not only itself avant-garde but that it has also inspired later composers to explore unfamiliar forms and innovative ideas.

His accomplishments are truly multilayered. First, there are his tangible contributions, such as the invention of new song forms. Here, his phrasing deviates from the traditional aesthetic that had been in place for centuries. He introduced tonal elements that were unacceptable within the traditional *maqam* system, molded the melody and musical structure around the semantics of the lyrics, and created a new relationship between the singer and the listener. His subject matter was social in nature, aiming to raise awareness and trigger change. Much of this chapter will be dedicated to detailed musical analyses of these particular achievements.

Beyond these concrete and quantifiable musical innovations, Darwish has been influential in other, less calculable ways, which will also be touched on in the course of this chapter. Foremost of these is how he legitimized experimentation and the pursuit of musical visions that fall outside tradition. His broadening of the possibilities of what Egyptian music could be through a radical break from expectations and training is summarized by one of the scene's other great composers and singers, Muhammad 'Abd al-Wahhab. On hearing Sayyed Darwish perform for the first time, 'Abd al-Wahhab declared that Darwish had "ruined his life" ('Abd al-Wahhab, undated interview). Furthermore, Darwish set an example of innovation and individualism that captured the hearts of the masses, not just the appreciation of other musicians.

Indeed it is remarkable, and a bit unusual, for an avant-garde artist not to be obscure. Not to be only a musician's musician. To be sure, Sayyed Darwish had known failures and rejections early in his career (Sahhab 1987, 17–19). However, at this point, he was being judged for his performance abilities alone and compared with singers like Saleh Abdel-Hayy and Salama Higazi, for whom he was no match. Even then, his potential was not lost on these musicians. When, in 1917, Darwish sang in between acts during Salama Higazi's play *Ghaniyat al-Andalus* (*The Female Entertainer of Andalusia*), the audience complained to Higazi about his poor choice of a singer. To this Higazi responded, "But still, he is the future of music and singing in the east, and my successor" (Sahhab 1987, 20).

His early setbacks aside, Darwish was, on the whole, respected, especially as a composer and musical visionary. Never marginalized for his departure from the Arab and Turkish musical traditions, he has, to this day, enjoyed the popularity and respect of both other musicians and the general public. Four factors can be gleaned to explain this widespread acceptance. Firstly, it was to his advantage that he was a revolutionary musician during a time of social and political revolution and that many of his thematic preoccupations were social and political in nature. He wrote songs about longshoremen, day laborers, farmers, hashish smokers, bread kneaders, clerics, and waiters, to name just a sampling of his everyday-life-centered subjects. Many of his songs also foreground revolutionary-nationalistic proclivities, including Egypt's modern-day national anthem, "Biladi Biladi" ("My Country, My Country"). A second contributing factor is that, throughout his life, he composed numerous traditional works that enjoyed extensive popularity, such as his *adwar* and *muwashshahat*, two song forms that were well liked at the time. Third, many of his avant-garde compositions were meant for musical theater. Since these times marked the very beginnings of musical theater in Egypt, the novel context may have prepared the audience for the new music it incorporated. Finally, Darwish composed a number of songs that were heavily traditional in some respects but that seamlessly blended in experimental elements. Hearing those pieces has the effect of preparing the listener for the possibility of unusual elements in songs that are otherwise safely conventional. One example that comes to mind is "Ya Halawit Umm Ismail" (loosely translated as "Oh How Lovely Is Umm Isma'il"), from the 1919 musical play *Renn*. With gentle humor, the song's lyrics detail the work, family, and community of a female farmer, Umm Isma'il, all framed within a simple form and melody that retain many components of a basic folk tune. However, there are also experimental elements: piano accompaniment with harmony and a jumping bass line, as well as an unusual chromatic accidental that appears repeatedly throughout the song.

Darwish is discussed fairly widely in the literature on Arab music. Two informative and detailed writings about him are the well-researched and largely academic Darwish chapter in Victor Sahhab's *Al-Sab'a al-Kibar fi al-Musiqa al-'arabiyya al-Mu'asira* (*The Seven Greats of Contemporary Arab Music*) and the 1956 essay by Nezar Mrouhe, "Sayyed Darwish: A Major Arab Pioneer." However, close musical analysis of the composer's most revolutionary works is missing from the literature. The published descriptions of Darwish's accomplishments largely concentrate on personifying him as "the people's artist," utilizing music as a means of expressing their plight and aspirations instead of practicing it as a detached form of entertainment aimed at granting the listeners (and performers) a sensation of ecstasy (referred to as *tarab*). Darwish is also credited in this literature with adapting melody to reflect the meaning of the lyrics. Commentators briefly touch on musical dimensions when they note the new forms in which he wrote: his input into the development of Arab musical theater; his experiments with harmony; and his tonal innovations, including the invention of a new *maqam* (*zanjaran*), which combines the archetypical Western tetrachord (*'ajam*, major) and the archetypical Eastern tetrachord (*hijaz*).[1] These writings have provided a necessary overview of Darwish's imprint on Arab music in an accessible style for a general readership. However, as will become clear later in this chapter, there are limitations to these discussions that hide central characteristics of this composer's work, and thus the full magnitude of his innovations.

My impression in researching this chapter is that Sayyed Darwish's contributions are often generalized to the point where his true impact on Arab music is no longer clear. References to him as "the great innovator" or "the people's artist" sound almost meaningless given the ubiquity of floral language and exaggeration in ordinary discourse both today and in years past. After all, almost every singer who appears in the media is referred to as "the great artist," and many second-rate performers become "masters." To understand the depth and breadth of Darwish's influence, a musical discussion is necessary. To that end, many of the points I shall establish will be based on the analysis of a monologue (a song form) entitled "Wallahi Tistahil Ya Qalbi" ("My Heart, You Deserve It") (see Appendices 1 and 2 for a full transcription of this song and a translation of its lyrics). This was one of eighteen songs, sixteen of which were composed by Darwish, for the musical *Rahit 'Alayk* (*You've Lost Everything*), first performed in 1920. The song's lyrics are attributed to Amin Sidqi, a comedic playwright and poet with whom Darwish collaborated on a number of plays.[2] A large portion of this chapter will be dedicated to examining, analyzing, and contextualizing Darwish's innovations through this case study. I shall also discuss how, once Darwish had set the example, composers and performers who chose to do so enjoyed a large degree of liberation from the bounds of a centuries-old tradition, and equally deep-rooted preconceptions about aesthetics and the function of music.

This piece was chosen because, in it, Darwish clearly departs from convention in form, phrasing, and prosody, and, while the melody line is fairly simple and no modulations occur, the song reflects the composer's tonal innovation and experimentation. It demonstrates many of the compositional techniques that Darwish employed and, in the context of Arab music, invented to achieve emotional immediacy and convey specific sentiments to the listener, rather than arrive at *tarab*.

I do not wish to create the impression that all of Darwish's works were situated equally outside tradition. In fact, some were comfortably within it. As mentioned earlier, Darwish composed numerous pieces in standard forms and tonalities, most notably *muwashshahat* and *adwar*. He sang such works as well as those of other composers in coffee shops and at private events in order to make a living as an entertainer. It was not uncommon for composers to earn money in this fashion, at least in the early stages of their career. In fact, this was virtually the rule for the great Arab musical innovators of the twentieth century. The tension between the external pressure to entertain and remain safely within expectations and the internal desire to create a new music is a topic in and of itself—and not one covered in this chapter, given its general irrelevance to Darwish's career. His life and work indicate that he was capable of being both a traditionalist and an innovator. He was an accomplished composer in both worlds. In fact, it is not at all clear that Darwish wore different metaphorical hats when composing a typical *muwashshah* or *dawr* compared to when he was writing new music. It could well be argued that his compositions were solutions to different musical problems; in other words, he wrote in a groundbreaking fashion whenever he encountered new musical quandaries. In line with the themes of this anthology, this chapter will focus on his innovations and will not discuss at much length his traditional work.

This is a much-needed focus. Later tributes to Darwish and later versions of his works have tended to ignore much of his inventiveness in order to create the misleading impression that he was the composer of "pretty" tunes, which lend themselves readily to contemporary arrangement and singing styles. This is the case with "Wallahi Tistahil," one of his few avant-garde pieces of which there are modern recordings.[3] In these recordings, there is no use of polyphony, while the original version in Darwish's voice is rich in this. More recent renditions also make extensive use of instrumental interludes and fillers, something Darwish practically did without. Contemporary singing styles often accentuate the separation between phrases, whereas, in Darwish's recording, most of these phrases were tightly bound together to achieve a breathtaking continuity. The "lying by omission" of these versions essentially waters down the revolutionary aspects of Darwish's work and turns phrases like "the great innovator" into platitudes.

Such designations also sideline alternative narratives, ones that problematize the cultural and artistic identities of the colonized and examine how such identities have been nurtured by colonization to help ensure its own continuity. As we will see in this chapter, the Egyptian ruling class—which worked hand in glove with European governments and interest holders—brought European culture and its pedagogy into Egypt with the aim of modernizing and improving the country. A cultural and artistic hierarchy was thus established with European formations implied as superior. As such, the rejection of all things European was certainly a natural impulse for Egyptian nationalists. Darwish's reaction thus seemed counterintuitive in that not only did he not spurn European music, he also understood and deconstructed it, creating new tools with it to solve new musical problems and create a new language.

From Tarab to Revolution

Darwish was born into a time in which the silenced majority was about to make its voice heard and radically change the political and social order of Egypt. Several forces were at work: England and France wanted to further colonize the country using a puppet king and government and an army whose officer class was primarily Turkish. The land was concentrated in the hands of an upper class loyal to the king, and Egypt's working class was poor, without rights or hope for peaceful change. However, the musical milieu into which Sayyed Darwish was born seemed practically medieval, pretending that nothing unusual was happening. The following section, which presents a brief biography of Sayyed Darwish, aims to establish this context both historically and musically.

Sayyed Darwish al-Bahr was born into a working class neighborhood in the coastal city of Alexandria in March of 1892. His musical education began in primary school, where he memorized the Qur'an, trained as a cantor of religious texts, and performed traditional Arab songs. This was not unusual, as many of Egypt's musicians received their basic musical training reciting the Qur'an (*tajwid*) and other religious chants (*tartil*).

As a child, he soon put this instruction to use, as poverty and the absence of his father, who had died, necessitated that he help support the family. At first, he performed in religious ceremonies in private homes, and later as an entertainer in coffeehouses and bars. It was probably at the latter that he was first exposed to alcohol and drugs, which were to accompany him until the end of his journey and are generally considered the causes of his premature death. In addition to singing in the evenings, he worked during the day as a laborer on construction sites.

The first major milestone in Darwish's career took place in 1912 when he was asked to tour for a second time as a performer with the 'Atalla group (he had done so before in 1909). This time, his absence lasted two years, during which he not only performed but also studied music, acquired repertoire, and improved his *'ud* skills. Back in Alexandria, Darwish composed and performed, but personal circumstances drove him to leave town for Cairo in 1917, where he lived for the next six years until his death in 1923.

It was in those six years that his most innovative pieces were developed, with much of his avant-garde work being in musical theater. During this period, his output amounted to 233 songs for thirty musicals (Sahhab 1987, 32). His break into musical theater came from the actor and director Najib al-Rihani, who not only hired him to perform but was also one of the first to commission compositions from him. In his first year as a musical theater composer, Darwish wrote twenty-two tunes for two plays for Najib al-Rihani's troupe (Sahhab 1987, 32–33). Darwish's success as a composer was immediate, and, by 1919, he was writing not only for Rihani but for his competitors as well, and it is to Rihani's credit that he did not object to this (Sahhab 1987, 21). Darwish's most significant contribution to musical theater, as detailed later in this chapter, was the invention of musical forms that made it possible to tie the plot tightly to the singing.

Darwish's working class roots and his social and political consciousness were central in informing these creations. He looked for a music that would reflect the times and the new ideas that came with them. He also aspired toward a music that more immediately connected the singer to the audience. He wrote dozens of songs on subjects that were not traditionally handled in music of the time: the experiences of laborers in different vocations, the lamentable political realities of the country, humorous elements of everyday life, as well as nationalistic conjectures. The last are significant because they embody an engagement with larger questions about the future of the country, not just the well-being of a particular class.

More broadly, Egypt's music at the turn of the twentieth century was undergoing changes that were part of a larger social and political transformation. This was an era when several trends and developments that had started decades earlier were reaching their climax. While Racy establishes this period as taking place between the 1860s and 1920s, setting the context requires going back a few decades before this range (Racy 1997, 26).

Up until the late nineteenth century, music in Egypt was considered a popular form of entertainment. It played an essential role in a variety of activities, including religious rituals, private gatherings, and even in the workplaces of manual laborers. However, music had never been treated as a serious discipline, neither by its practitioners nor by its audience. Little theoretical work had been undertaken and little understanding was deemed necessary to perform music. Perhaps this explains why music as a profession was not regarded highly by the public (Racy 1997, 16–17). An often-heard anecdote is that, on the day of Darwish's wedding in 1919, the *ma'hun* (a religious cleric who records marriages and divorces) asked what Darwish's profession was—information required for his marriage forms. When Darwish responded that he was a musician, the *ma'hun* refused to record the wedding. He only yielded when Darwish changed his response to teacher.

The disregard for the profession notwithstanding, music played a well-established role in the lives of Egyptians. It did so in a number of frameworks, depending on the occasion and the setting. The most common of these frameworks, and the one most discussed, is the *wasla*, a musical set comprising a succession of songs, instrumental compositions, and instrumental and vocal improvisations lasting up to two hours or even longer (Sahhab 1997a, 13). At the tonal center of a *wasla* was a *maqam*, and, although modulation was common in most songs, at least in passing, and a central part of every *taqsim*,[4] *mawwal*, and *layali*,[5] the *wasla* aesthetic dictated that the *maqam* had to hold a prominent position within it and that, eventually, a *wasla* needed to resolve on that *maqam*. The most common instrumental configurations during that period were the *dulab, tahmila, bashraf, sama'i*, and *longa*.

Although a *wasla* contains instrumental segments, singing lies at its center. Several song forms were popular at the time, such as *mawawil* and *layali*, along with the *muwashshahat* and *adwar* forms discussed earlier. *Mawawil* and *layali* are nonmetric, the former usually precomposed and the latter typically improvised. *Muwashshahat* and *adwar* are two examples of metric compositions; the *dawr* (singular form of *adwar*) form also has a call-and-response section, where the call is improvised by the singer and the response is a repeated, precomposed phrase by the chorus. The subject matter is primarily romantic love and longing.

Accompanying the singer in a *wasla* is a small ensemble called a *takht*, usually consisting of an *'ud* (fretless short-necked Near Eastern lute), *qanun* (plucked Arab/Turkish zither), *nay* (hollow reed flute), violin, *riqq* (tambourine), possibly other percussion instruments, and sometimes a small chorus singing refrains and responses.

Not only is the structure of a *wasla* heavily regimented, so is the layout of its components. More specifically, all the precomposed forms just mentioned, both instrumental and vocal, have several elements in common: symmetry of phrasing, symmetry in length and rhythm, and regularity in form. For example, the typical pattern of a *muwashshah* is A-A-B-A, and for *sama'i*, *longa*, and *bashraf* it is A-R-B-R-C-R-D-R (with "R" referring to a recurring refrain).

In addition to the *wasla*, there were other musical formats, such as those used for religious occasions and mystical rituals, which utilized prescribed repertoire and instrumentation often dating back to medieval times. The musical needs of ethnic and religious minorities in Egypt were routinely serviced by musicians of the same groups, with their own unique repertoire and instrumentation. According to Racy, the music was largely compartmentalized and little cross-fertilization took place (Racy 1997, 21–22). In short, while music touched many aspects of day-to-day life and was practiced in a plethora of settings, including entertainment venues, celebrations, and religious occasions, it followed ancient rules, both in framework and in content. Darwish rebelled against these rigid musical prescriptions and their limited topical scope.

In contrast to music, which was largely in a state of dormancy, the political scene was well past the point of no return, witnessing a fundamental reshaping of the social order and a redistribution of power and wealth. Egypt was on the path to independence, casting off its Ottoman, British, and French colonizers.

Officially, Egypt was ruled by the Muhammad 'Ali dynasty on behalf of the Ottoman Empire. In reality, however, a puppet government controlled by England and France administered the country, protecting European colonizers' financial and strategic interests and ensuring that Egypt's social and political order remained unthreatening. The European powers maintained armies in Egypt and intervened militarily when necessary, such as in the crushing of Egyptian army general Ahmad 'Urabi's revolt of 1882. However, for the most part, the country was ruled by proxy.

The 1882 revolt is considered the point at which Egyptian nationalist consciousness began to accelerate, a trend that continued until Gamal Abdel Nasser's revolution in 1952. Egyptian nationalists were repressed, and clashes with government forces as well as the British Army took place regularly; demonstrations were dispersed with force, at times deadly force. Sayyed Darwish lived during a period when many Egyptians—working class, educated, and urban alike—begrudged how European control kept them poor and powerless. Yet for many of these Egyptian nationalists, the relationship with European culture was more complicated than simple resentment.

While the ruling class's affinity for European culture was only natural because they were tied to Europeans in business, and therefore social relations, even Egyptian nationalist scholars and artists were drawn to it. European culture was considered foundational to their ability to establish economic and military supremacy. A profound change was taking place in Egypt—nationalist certainly, but, in some cases, modeled on European culture. This was made possible by Egypt's rulers, who strived to bring European culture into Egypt, with, for instance, Muhammad 'Ali (r. 1805–1848) Westernizing the country's military, industrial, and educational systems (Racy 1997, 27). 'Ali's grandson Isma'il (r. 1863–1879) is renowned as the ruler under whom the most dramatic European cultural influence was absorbed. The increase of European cultural infiltration under Isma'il may have been largely circumstantial, explained by Isma'il's reckless national spending and the economic opportunities this presented for Europeans, leading, ultimately, through debts to France and Britain, to greater European intervention in Egypt's governance. The Westernization of the school system required Western-educated scholars, and so Egypt's government sent many Egyptians to Europe to study. They returned to teach in metropolitan Cairo, where Egypt's new universities were located and which was prospering because of the influx of Europeans and the many Egyptian peasants who had migrated there for work and education. Finally, to provide entertainment to the expats living in Cairo, European performers were regularly invited over and the Cairo Opera House was inaugurated in 1869. Consequently, Western music was readily available in Cairo, and Sayyed Darwish was fully exposed to it (Sahhab 1987, 15).

However, by the turn of the twentieth century, Egyptian music was still largely unchanged, with songs in traditional forms centered mostly, as they had been for centuries, on romantic love (except for devotional music, where the subject matter was religious), performed in traditional *waslas* as entertainment leading to *tarab*. Society, on the other hand, was on the verge of revolution. The music was clearly out of touch with the times.

New Forms

As discussed in the introduction to this chapter, Darwish created new forms and adopted and refined the innovations of his predecessors. Three song forms in particular became very popular in musical theater, musical films, and as stand-alone compositions independent of drama. However, their role in musical drama is central since, at least in two of the cases (the monologue and the *muhawara*), they made its development possible, first onstage and later on-screen.

THE MONOLOGUE

Arab monologue form first played a role in musical theater similar to that of the aria in opera. Sayyed Darwish pioneered the form. Although it is rumored that one monologue had appeared in 1911 in a musical play by Kamil al-Khula'i, no recording, lyrics, or any other information is available about that piece (Sahhab 1997b, 102–18). Regardless of whether or not that one monologue existed before Darwish's, it was Darwish's many such compositions that defined the form, and his vision for its dramatic effect that realized its potential as a cornerstone of musical theater in Egypt. Many later composers (including all the greatest Egyptian composers of the twentieth century, Muhammad 'Abd al-Wahhab, Zakariyya Ahmad, Riyadh al-Sunbati, and Mohammad al-Qasabgi) wrote dozens of monologues that were mostly freestanding, although a few were part of larger theatrical or film contexts. Darwish's monologues were songs of a narrational nature, often expressing and explaining the emotional state of the singer. They were forward-moving and had no refrains or musical repetition.

The piece at the center of this chapter, "Wallahi Tistahil," is one of Darwish's early works in the monologue form. In it, the composer showcases several of the techniques he honed to achieve specific emotional effects. For the purposes of this discussion, these techniques show that, while Darwish broke many conventions, he also replaced them with his own well-considered approach. He never mistook liberating himself from the rules of tradition for freedom from carefully crafting his compositions, but, rather, he was trying to achieve something that was impossible in the old forms. Accomplishing such a maneuver would require not just creative vision in an artist but also a deep connection with and understanding of the audience receiving the piece. This is so precisely because, when working outside tradition, the tools that produce a predictable reaction in the audience (such as falling back on beloved and familiar themes) are a lot less accessible.

THE *MUHAWARA* (EXCHANGE) OR DIALOGUE

The first known *muhawara* on record was written by Sayyed Darwish. The song, "'Ala Qadd al-Layl Ma Ytawwil" ("As Long as the Night Lasts"), was first performed in 1920 by Darwish and Hayat Sabri in the musical *Al-'Ashara al-Tayyiba (The Good Ten)*. While Darwish continued to compose *muhawara*, it was not until 1924 that another composer, Mahmud Rahmi, tried his hand at four such exchanges, which were then performed by Muhammad 'Abd al-Wahhab and Samha al-Masriyya (Sahhab 1997b, 119–23).

As the name suggests, the *muhawara* is a dialogue between two or more singers, devised for musicals, first onstage, then on-screen. Darwish laid the foundations of the form as a repetitive refrain and movements in which the singers alternate, by way of a conversation. Many of the greats of the twentieth century adopted the *muhawara*, including 'Abd al-Wahhab, Sunbati, and Zakariyya Ahmad, who included them frequently in the fifty-four musical plays he wrote between 1924 and 1930 (Sahhab 1997b, 124). The form was refined over the years, and later composers had their own personal take on it, but it remained a staple of musical theater and film well into the second half of the twentieth century.

THE *TAQTUQA*

Darwish cannot be credited with inventing this form, which emerged early in the twentieth century. The inventor, according to Egyptian music historians Kamal al-Najmi and Abdel-Aziz Anani, was an obscure musician by the name of Muhammad 'Ali Lu'a (Sahhab 1997b, 72). However, Darwish saw the potential in the form and used it for many of his compositions. The *taqtuqa*, a lighthearted song in colloquial Egyptian Arabic, made up of four episodes (couplets) and a refrain, enjoyed a rapid rise to popularity in Egypt that was sustained for decades.

The monologue and the *muhawara* became dramatic tools used to drive the plot in musical theater. In films, they tied together the drama and the singing and smoothed the transitions back and forth. In my view, Darwish's main contribution to both formats was to enlist these new forms to make the drama possible.

The *taqtuqa* thrived and, even in the 1980s and 1990s, when the general listenership shifted away from the elaborate, musically complex compositions of the earlier part of the century, many Egyptian pop songs remained essentially variations on the *taqtuqa* form.

"*Wallahi Tistahil*"

RECORDING

Given the political and social context, and Darwish's heightened awareness of it, the related symbolism in many of his pieces should be pointed out. "Wallahi Tistahil" was recorded according to the typical setup used in 1920s Cairo. A microphone of sorts was placed at front, with the singer closest to

Fig. 4.1. *Maqam shawq afza.*

it. The accompaniment was placed behind, in this case a piano and violin. As was customary at the time, the sound engineer then exclaims "Allah" once or twice, imitating listeners in the heat of a passionate *tarab*. Typically, the sound engineer would also name the lead performer; here this happens at the end of the song when he declares, "ahsantum ya Sheikh Sayyed" ("Well done, Sheikh Sayyed").

MAQAM AND TONALITIES

The piece is in *maqam shawq afza*. Figure 4.1 describes this scale, as well as its basic structure.

Maqam shawq afza, similar to *maqam zanjaran*, contains two tetrachords from two worlds. The first is ʿ*ajam*, an ancient Arabic word that means non-Arab, as well as to speak Arabic nonfluently, or with a foreign accent. The second is *hijaz*, the name of the region in Saudi Arabia where Mecca is located. The ʿ*ajam* tetrachord, as indicated earlier, is the equivalent of a Western major tetrachord.

The intonation of the major third in an ʿ*ajam* tetrachord/pentachord is slightly lower than an equal-tempered Western major third. The fourth (and the fifth, in the case of a pentachord) is a pure perfect fourth (or fifth), and the second is a pure perfect fourth below the fifth. In a *hijaz* tetrachord, the intonation of the root and the fourth are a pure perfect fourth. The second is a raised minor second, and the third is a lowered major third. As a result of these intonation differences, and although *shawq afza* contains no quarter tones, the piano is at times out of tune with the voice and the violin.

Darwish furthered such experimentation during the recording of another song, "Al-Bahr Byidhak Wallahi" (from a 1919 musical *Qululu* [*Tell Him*]).[6] The song contains quarter tones (*maqam bayati*), and the piano is played louder and closer to the foreground compared to the recording of "Wallahi Tistahil." The clash between the flat seconds in the piano accompaniment and the half-flat seconds of the singing produces a disturbing effect.[7] Whether or not there was a political message in this discord is pure speculation, especially in the absence of period reviews or commentary on the song. However, it is safe to say that Darwish was well aware of the dissonance and that he was experimenting with something that serious (for lack of a better word) Arab musicians avoided.

METER AND RHYTHMIC MODE (*IQAʿ*)

"Wallahi Tistahil" was recorded without rhythmic accompaniment. Traditionally, the piece is performed in 4/4, more specifically in the rhythmic mode of *wahidah*. I found no credible record of what rhythmic mode Darwish used in performances of the song that had percussionists present.

INSTRUMENTAL ACCOMPANIMENT

The first thing one notices about Sayyed Darwish's recording of this song is the instrumentation—namely, the use of piano accompaniment. While unusual in the context of Egyptian music of the period, the involvement of piano was an experiment that Darwish conducted repeatedly. A partial list, with all the examples involving polyphony, runs as follows: "Ya Marhaba Buh," "'Ala al-Niswan Ya Salam," "Ma Qulti Lak Inn al-Katra," "Shidd al-Hizam," "Lahn al-Muwazzafin," "Salma Ya Salama," "Yihawwin Allah," "Ya Wardi Ya Full," "Lahn al-'Arbagiyya," and "Al-Bahr Byidhak." The use of polyphony demonstrates a deconstruction of the Arab aesthetic in two ways. While others dabbled with Western instruments, they usually went for ones that allowed tone-bending to match Arab intonation. Darwish chose the piano. And while others had the Western instruments follow the melody line in the traditional monophonic fashion, Darwish made repeated use of polyphony.

It is worth mentioning here that, when these songs are rerecorded by other artists, even in the modern period, in which Western sounds are ubiquitous in Arab music, the piano is not present, nor is the polyphony from the original recording employed. The song is sterilized into a traditional Arab texture. As will be pointed out later, other elements are changed to make Darwish's songs sound more traditionally Arab.

Returning to "Wallahi Tistahil," the piano creates two types of polyphony scattered throughout the song: block chords and a melodic accompaniment in which the piano weaves its way between the song's melody line and harmonizes in thirds, mostly, but not completely, following the song's contour and rhythm. These techniques are familiar from his recordings of other songs too.

AN EXAMPLE DEMONSTRATING BLOCK CHORDS

In measure 10, the piano plays a C major chord, as the melody has a repeated C, and in measure 11, when the melody is a repeated B (scale degree 3), the piano carries three repeated G major chords (Fig. 4.2).

Fig. 4.2. Polyphony example 1, block chords.

Fig. 4.3. Polyphony example 2, counterpoint.

Another use of polyphony in the piece happens very soon after, when the piano harmonizes in thirds with the singing. Notice that, while the piano is following the contour of the melody, the rhythm is not exactly the same (Fig. 4.3).

Sayyed Darwish's use of polyphony—and polyphony, in general, in Arab music—is usually referred to as Western harmony by the literature on Arab music and is largely discarded by its theorists as out of place (Sahhab 1987, 46). Indeed, if the theorists' point is that it is not possible to produce effects like the ones facilitated by functional harmony and the equal-tempered twelve-pitch octave within Arab structure, then their argument is valid and Darwish's music is "wrong." But his work cannot be evaluated according to the overtone series and stacked thirds. If that was what he was aiming for, he would not have juxtaposed *maqam bayati*, with its half-flat second in voice and violin, against *kurd*, with its flat second on the piano (as he did in "Al-Bahr Byidhak"), in order to produce a strong dissonance that can be missed neither by a musician nor by many listeners.

The violin also featured in the recording follows the melody line, but draws on an uncommon (for the period) technique—pizzicato—which appears at the end of the piece at the final ritardando. Although the generations following Darwish made use of the pizzicato (especially in instrumental music), in listening to Arab music composed in the same period (1910s and early 1920s) or earlier, I have not encountered it.

Another unusual characteristic of the accompaniment, and one also found in other Darwish songs, is the near absence of melodic fillers between phrases. In "Wallahi Tistahil" there is only one interlude, and relatively short at that, lasting a mere single measure. In fact, there is hardly space between the phrases, as most of them are connected and the singing is virtually continuous.

Iman al-Bahr Darwish, the grandson of Sayyed Darwish, recorded "Wallahi Tistahil" in the 1980s. Although he is best known for resurrecting and repopularizing his grandfather's music, Iman al-Bahr Darwish's version of the song has a much more active melodic accompaniment than the original recording. He has added interludes and made the instrumental introduction a lot longer, as well as dropping the polyphony and the piano accompaniment altogether. He thus sterilizes the song and distills it into a fairly traditional (although still beautiful) melody line. Paradoxically, he has un-Darwished it, all in the name of reviving Darwish's music.

In my view, the desired effect of the continuous singing is to accentuate anxiety, distress, and immediacy. This touches on an issue discussed earlier: the traditional Arab song was just a song and the goal was enjoyment as such through *tarab*. Darwish's molding of the tune to convey the essence of the lyrics was one of the notable characteristics of his composition style. In an essay written for the (postrevolutionary) government-owned magazine *Al-Kawakib*, entitled "If Sayyed Darwish Lived On," Muhammad ʿAbd al-Wahhab points out: "It is undoubted that the late Sayyed Darwish laid the foundations for the first upsurge of Egyptian music. . . . Darwish was the first [composer] to turn the mind's attention to the semantics of the lyrics. He understood the connotations of the words and transformed them into sung words where the tune fits perfectly with the meaning. Before Sayyed Darwish, singing did not pay attention to their meanings. The singing we heard merely demonstrated the skills of the singer and his ability to control his voice. Nothing brought the meanings of the words to our attention" (ʿAbd al-Wahhab 1954).

Earlier singers concentrated on demonstrating vocal prowess rather than interacting with lyrics; melody was what served to produce *tarab* for the audience. Darwish seems to insist that a song can be something different: an expression of a human state. The composition, as well as its performance, has to be molded so that a song communicates this, fostering a new relationship between the singer and the listener. The singer no longer simply provides a service to the listener (*tarab*) but is essentially saying that, as human beings, both sides have something in common and something to talk about. In essence, "the people's artist" title is well deserved not just because Darwish's songs address subjects that are part of the plight of everyday life of the Egyptian working class but also because the relationship between the singer and the listener is a new one, a more intimate one. The singer was of the people.

FORM

"Wallahi Tistahil" falls neatly into the description of early monologues detailed earlier, which is only to be expected since Darwish invented the form. Structurally, "Wallahi Tistahil" begins with a short (two-measure) instrumental opening that introduces the *maqam* and many of the basic tonal ideas of the piece.

Following on, the piece drives forward without any repetition or even variation on earlier phrases. A few motifs do crop up, yet these are related conceptually and not fully duplicated. For example, several phrases begin by ascending from D to F sharp or G and then descending all the way to low G. To name a few examples, phrases A, B, and E fall into this category. Another motif is the long or repeated B notes in the melody. The dramatic effect is an enhancement of the monologue's narrational role. After all, this is a form that was born in musical plays. Although later monologues by other composers, such as some of the most memorable compositions of 'Abd al-Wahhab and Muhammad al-Qasabgi, were not written for musical plays, the form afforded these composers a constant forward movement that was simply not possible in refrain-based songs.

PROSODY AND PHRASING

On first encountering this piece, around 1995, I was struck by its phrasing. In fact, I heard it while driving and the quality of the recording and the road noise obscured the piano altogether. And yet, judging by the phrasing alone, it was clear that Darwish was doing something extremely unusual to Arab music. He was adapting the piece's structure to convey the mood and meaning that he envisioned. The three structural aspects I shall focus on here are extended syllables; asymmetric phrase lengths; and the repeated use of a specific rhythmic pattern.

As Figure 4.4. shows, the first syllable of the song extends a whole measure and covers eight notes. The second syllable is two and a half beats long. While

Fig. 4.4. Extended syllables.

elongating syllables was fairly conventional in vocal nonmetric improvisation forms, this was not the case in composed songs. The new aesthetic that Darwish introduced here is suggestive of wailing, enhanced by its particular placement in the musical *Rahit ʿAlayk* (*You Have Lost Everything*). It is sung when the protagonist has lost his beloved, his kingdom, and has wandered far from home. This practice has since been assimilated and stretched by composers such as Muhammad ʿAbd al-Wahhab—for instance, in his monologue "Ya Jarat al-Wadi," with its seven-measure "ya" syllable.

Even more striking is that "Wallahi Tistahil" does away with one of the architectural foundations of Arab music, symmetry of phrase lengths. The lengths of the first five phrases (in measures) are 3½, 2, 2, 4, 5, something that is not dictated by any asymmetry in the poem. In Appendix 1, the poem lines are broken down so that they correspond to the musical phrases, but, while the former are regular, they are not matched with musical consistency. This style was in no way dictated by a lack of knowledge about convention on Darwish's part; after all, he had composed many traditionally balanced pieces. Furthermore, he had spent the early years of his musical career performing songs by other composers that fell comfortably within these rules, suggesting that the decision to make phrase lengths asymmetrical was a deliberate one, free of external constraints stemming from the structure of the poem, and definitely not one reflecting ignorance of the long custom of symmetry. Darwish was aiming for a new aesthetic, a new architecture. Confronting his audiences with unpredictable phrase lengths further enhanced the dramatic effect of Darwish's compositions, building tension and delaying its resolution by playing with the expectations created by their stylistic literacy. In "Wallahi Tistahil," the resolution occurs in the second part of the song—in the seven phrases following the interlude, when the phrase lengths of the last seven phrases are 4, 4, 2, 2, 2, 2, 4. Again, these variations became widespread practice among later composers like Muhammad ʿAbd al-Wahhab.

A rhythm that occurs repeatedly in this piece is a dotted eighth followed by a sixteenth (Fig. 4.5).

One possible explanation for the repeated use of this rhythm is that the composer was thinking about the theatrical performance. Given that, at this

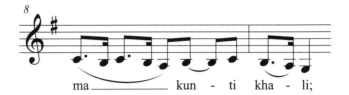

Fig. 4.5a. Dotted eighth + sixteenth.

Fig. 4.5b. Dotted eighth + sixteenth.

point in the musical, the performer's world seems to have collapsed and he has lost everything, this rhythm would work well with his staggered walk across the stage. However, since I found neither a script for the play nor a critique by an attendee, there is no evidence that the actor was actually walking in such a way. The explanation for the repeated use of this rhythm is just a plausible speculation.

Conclusion

My overarching objective in this chapter has been to address the question of whether or not the work of Sayyed Darwish can be considered avant-garde—indeed the beginning of avant-garde music of the modern period in Arab music—or whether it is just part of the continuity of a music that has evolved over millennia. Beyond this, I have sought to explore how his work has affected that of later composers.

The method that I felt would best illuminate the first objective was keeping the discussion as close to the music as possible, with other elements brought in to provide context. This type of analysis is missing in the many writings about Darwish, and the lack of detailed musical interpretation can render any writing on this great composer generic and unsubstantiated. Such additions to Darwish scholarship are especially needed because contemporary exposure to his oeuvre comes mostly through modern recordings or performances, not the ones he himself made. Indeed, not a year passes without a Darwish tribute concert or recording. (I myself am guilty of partaking of a few of these.) However, most modern recordings repeat the same thirty or so Darwish pieces, neglecting the majority of his works. Worse still, they ignore some of the more musically adventurous forays. Further, on the rare occasions when pieces like "Wallahi Tistahil" are revived, they are typically sterilized, stripped of the experimental elements for the sake of prettiness. Therefore, contemporary exposure to his music omits fundamental facts about this unique artist and the credit due him for making possible what is now considered the second golden age of Arab music, the twentieth century. (The first golden age occurred centuries earlier, during the middle Abbasid period.)

Using one piece, "Wallahi Tistahil," as the main musical example, and his large body of works as a reference, I have attempted to show that Darwish pursued a vision for music to convey emotional and dramatic content, and to nurture a new relationship among composer, musician, and audience. To fulfill this aim, which he felt could not be done using traditional forms, compositional techniques, and subject matter, Darwish introduced new formats, sounds, tonal structures, phrasings, prosody, and rhythms, often within a single piece, taking his music far beyond the natural evolutionary trajectory of tradition and well into what distinguishes the avant-garde at its best.

His music worked so effectively that most of the important twentieth-century Egyptian composers who came after Darwish were influenced by him. To name but a handful, there were Muhammad 'Abd al-Wahhab (who will have the last words in this chapter), Zakariyya Ahmad, who was so taken with Darwish that he was accused of stealing whole musical ideas from him (Sahhab 1987, 98), and Muhammad al-Qasabgi, who adopted Darwish's forms in his compositions, especially for musical drama, and followed in his footsteps by experimenting with polyphony (Sahhab 1987, 79). Like Darwish, none of these complex and sophisticated composers abused their liberty; they made the most of it to create new works that still felt deeply connected to tradition.

In a Voice of Cairo radio interview with Muhammad 'Abd al-Wahhab, which exists, undated, online, 'Abd al-Wahhab claims: "I had been eager to hear Sayyed Darwish about whom I had heard a lot. . . . Then one day I found out he was performing in Cairo. I attended his concert, heard him, and it ruined my life" ('Abd al-Wahhab, undated interview). The impact of Darwish's innovations was clearly a turning point within Arab musical history.

Appendix 1

"Wallahi Tistahil"
Arabic lyrics and their English translation
Lyrics by Amin Sidqi (ca. 1920)
The sentences are broken by musical phrases and
not as they appear in the original text of the poem.

و الله تســـــتاهل يا قلبى

By God you deserve the punishment, oh heart

ليه تميـــــل ما كنت خالى

Why love again after you have been vacant

انت أســـباب كل كربى

You are the cause of all my suffering

وانت أســـــباب ما جرالى

And all that has happened to me

إيه بقى اللى ح يواسينى

What is left to console me

بعد ما انهـــــدت آمـــالى

Now that all my hopes are ruined

اذا كان حظى ناســـينى مين اروح له اشكى له حالى

After my fortune has abandoned me, to whom do I complain

ان شكيت قلبى وحواسى يعمـــلوا مؤامـــرة علىّ

If I complained, my heart and senses would conspire against me

وان بكيت والحب قاسى تشـــتكى منـــى عينىّ

And if I cried, and love is cruel, my eyes would protest me

أعمل ايه واحنا ف غربة

What do I do, being in a foreign land

والأغراب دول زى اليتامى

Foreigners are like orphans

يا مين يواسيهم فى كربه

Who could comfort them in their times of need

يامـــا بيقاســـوا ويامـــا

And these occur frequently

يارب كل من له حبيـــب

God, for all those who have a beloved

طـــال بعـــاده وللا قريب

Who is away for a time long or short

ما تحـــرموش منه وهـــاته له بالســـلامة

Don't deprive them of their beloved ones and bring the departed back safely

Wallahi Tistahil

Sayyed Darwish

Notes

1. *Maqam zanjaran* in Western notation:

2. A recording of the song in Sayyed Darwish's voice is in circulation, though not easily available. Samples may be found online. Recordings by other performers do exist; however, I have not discovered one that is true to the original. The closest version I found was one by Iman al-Bahr Darwish, Darwish's grandson. Although the sung parts of the latter are fairly close to the original, notable distinctions exist. As the analysis later in this chapter discusses, the musical introduction is replaced with a longer one. The key of the original is G while the latter recording is in B flat. Iman al-Bahr's vocal abilities are better than his grandfather's, thus his ornaments are more sophisticated, and generally his singing is clearer. But the modern arrangement weakens the effect of the relentless singing in the original, which has hardly any breaks and only one instrumental interlude. The grandson's version also incorporates many short *lawazim* (instrumental fillers that separate phrases).

3. The most notable example is Iman al-Bahr Darwish's, mentioned in the previous note.

4. Refers to a nonmetered instrumental improvisation.

5. The *mawwal* (plural: *mawawil*) and *layali* are both nonmetered solo vocal forms. Many *mawawil* were composed, while most *layali* were at least in part improvised.

6. In researching this song, I found that it is often confused with another, "Al-Bahr Biyidhak Lih." The latter song is apparently by Sheikh Imam, although I did not find definitive proof of this.

7. The quality of the recording (and I have only found one, Darwish's original) may contribute to this particular effect.

References

'Abd al-Wahhab, Muhammad. Undated. Interview for Voice of Cairo Radio Station. Excerpt available at http://www.sama3y.net/forum/showthread .php?t=64634.

——. 1954. "If Sayyed Darwish Lived On," *Al-Kawakib* (Cairo).

Mrouhe, Nezar. 1956. "Sayyed Darwish: Major Arab Pioneer." Translated from the Arabic and edited by Sami Asmar. Published in *Al-Jadid* 5 (29), 1999.

Racy, Ali Jihad. 1997. "Musical Change and Commercial Recordings in Egypt: 1904–1932." PhD diss., University of Illinois at Urbana-Champaign.

Sahhab, Victor. 1987. *Al-Sab'a al-Kibar fi al-Musiqa al-'arabiyya al-Mu'asira*. Beirut: Dar al-'Ilm Lil-Malayeen.

———. 1997a. *The First Conference of Arabic Music, Cairo 1932*. Beirut: Al-Sharika al-'Alamiyya Lil-Kitab.

———. 1997b. *Arabic Musical Forms and Genres*. Beirut: Dar al-Hamra Press.

CHAPTER FIVE

Challenging the Status Quo in War-Torn Lebanon

Ziad Rahbani, the Avant-Garde Heir to Musical Tradition

‿‿

SAMI W. ASMAR

Sometimes music history evolves predictably, sometimes it takes unexpected paths. When one of the Arab World's most prominent composers, the late 'Assi[1] Rahbani of Lebanon, married the preeminent singer Fairuz,[2] it came as no surprise that their son, Ziad[3] Rahbani, would turn out to be a talented artist who would make a significant mark on the history of Arab arts. But when Ziad created his own music, it was startling that much of his subject matter was satirical parody of his parents' craft and his nation's state of affairs. The loving son had no personal axe to grind; he simply considered the work of his parents' generation, though pioneering in its time, to represent artistic elitism squarely out of touch with the social and political failures of the country.

Raised in a Christian community that tended to lean politically right of center in the complicated politics of Lebanon, the young Ziad Rahbani rebelled and adhered to socialist principles that were manifested in his life and music. During the fifteen-year period of this small nation's sectarian-civil war, Ziad Rahbani refused to seek shelter outside the country, as droves of his compatriots did, or even move out of his primarily Muslim neighborhood, where he supposedly did not fit in.[4] Instead, he was propelled to write and perform musical theater spoofing the futile system that had led to the brutal war. His pioneering work, often disguised as comic relief during a painful and violent era, was initially shocking to the conservative society but quickly earned him universal respect as a true nonpartisan patriot. His reputation spread like wildfire among young intellectuals throughout the Arab world, where he remains a tremendously popular role model. A critically acclaimed composer, songwriter, and playwright, the prodigal son of the prominent Rahbani family is an intellectual iconoclast in the context of the entire traditional Eastern Mediterranean Arab culture.

A strong indication that Ziad Rahbani is an avant-garde artist is that most music critics cannot slot him into a category or even find appropriate words to describe his work. In 2009, the literary journal *Al-Adab* dedicated a series of articles by Arab music experts to his career. Prominent music historian Elias Sahab's leading article describes him as an exceptional phenomenon who leaves historians "at a loss" because he expresses himself "strangely" and resembles "a wild plant defying the natural laws governing the lives of plants" (Sahab 2009, 34). Other authors in the volume describe him as a rebel, ever-changing, unfamiliar, contradictory, and a genius; terms indicative of the notorious characteristics of an avant-garde artist.

This chapter will examine the career of Ziad Rahbani, a prime exemplar of modernism in Arab music, against the background of the artistic norms of the time and his own upbringing in a history-making musical family. His personality, as well as his creative output, was shaped by two events: the serious illness of his father and the start of the Lebanese civil war. His unique lyrics, innovative orchestration, and holistic approach to the arts are the elements that ultimately identify him as an avant-garde artist who has broken new ground by courageously addressing taboo subjects head-on and forging what has become known as his own school of music. In his work and beyond, he persistently challenges the political and social structure of his local environment, amassing a large following from far beyond his own small country. This chapter will analyze examples of his works and interpret their surface and hidden meanings to uncover his intellectual depth, courage, and avant-garde experimentalism.

Unlike his famous mother, who rarely makes public statements, Ziad Rahbani welcomes interviews (see Rayess 2009, 96), writes editorials, and utilizes every opportunity to express his opinions on various subjects, making it possible to base the study of his work on his own public accounts.[5] A brief biography of his world-famous parents helps describe his musical background as well as the geographical, social, political, and cultural environment in which he grew up. This discussion will also sketch out the musical traditions of Lebanon and the rest of the Arab world that he challenged in order to leave his own mark, starting at a young age.

Imagery and Symbolism in the Lebanese Rahbani Musicals

A small country located on the eastern Mediterranean shore, Lebanon lacks exportable natural resources but has a beautiful and strategic geography suitable for an economy based on tourism, trade, and service industries, which add to the revenues from entrepreneurial Lebanese expatriates worldwide.[6] Openness to the West and widespread foreign-language skills dating back to the seafaring days of the Phoenicians have allowed Lebanese businesses to profitably link Western institutions with the rest of the Arab world. Unlike other countries of comparable size, Lebanon's four million residents are particularly diverse religiously, with nearly two dozen Muslim and Christian sects officially recognized in a complex and delicate system of alliances and quotas that determine government positions along with the military, civic, judicial, and educational dimensions of people's lives. As far as its recent history, Lebanon gained independence in 1943 from the French Mandate, which had replaced Ottoman rule after World War One. The French drew borders that intentionally enfranchised a large Christian population and created a political structure that seemed to purposely keep the nation fragile and susceptible to violent upheavals from civil wars and territorial violations. Despite this, Lebanon has experienced periods of high economic prosperity and intellectual strength that have made it a regional pioneer in cultural and political freedom of expression. As such, the country is home to numerous print publishers and broadcast media, as well as prosperous cosmopolitan entertainment, food, fashion, and arts industries.

Lebanese music at the time of the country's independence was derived from several sources including indigenous folk music and religious chants, especially among the Western-missionary-influenced Christians. The strongest influence, however, was the cosmopolitan music imported from Egypt. In the first half of the twentieth century, Cairo was the leading center of musical production in the Arab world, spreading its wares via successful broadcast, record, and film industries. Singers like Sayyed Darwish (see Saed Muhssin's chapter in this volume), Muhammad 'Abd al-Wahhab, Umm Kulthum, Farid al-Atrash (of Syrian origin), and many others were very popular in Lebanon. Lebanese musicians such as Sabah sought recognition by establishing residence in Cairo and performing with an Egyptian dialect. In the 1950s, the Lebanese government's plan to boost tourism included a project to formally sponsor artists from all over the world to perform in the town of Ba'albek, the site of Roman ruins and an occasional summer gathering point for poets and intellectuals of the *nahda* (renaissance) movement from the 1920s onward. Local musicians were sought to create uniquely Lebanese music for the festival, and the Rahbani family, among others, answered the call.

The key member of the Rahbani family is Fairuz, born Nuhad Haddad in 1935. She was discovered in high school for her singing voice, recruited into the National Conservatory, and later given a job at the national radio station as a chorus singer, where her supervisor, Halim al-Rumi, noticed her incredible ability to memorize long poems and correctly perform all the microtonal subtleties in the complex *maqam* system. He gave her the stage name Fairuz, meaning turquoise, and introduced her to an aspiring composer named 'Assi Rahbani. 'Assi and his younger brother Mansour worked together as composers and songwriters and signed their work only as the Rahbani Brothers, never revealing how they divided the writing and composing assignments (Asmar 2009).[7]

The Rahbani Brothers' first collaboration with Fairuz was "'Itab," a song that launched her to stardom practically overnight. 'Assi and Fairuz were married in 1954,[8] settled in the Beirut suburb of Antiliyas,[9] and, on the first day of 1956, had their son Ziad, the first of three children. Maintaining a long and prolific career, Fairuz became the most famous Lebanese singer of all time and was dubbed "ambassador to the stars." She never behaved as a spotlight-seeking celebrity, even at the peak of her career or when receiving awards and honors from organizations and heads of state; she remained shy and highly private, with a trademark rigid stage presence.[10] Ziad Rahbani was raised in this environment of frequent world travel and mingling with very important people, and these formative years distinctly shaped his personality.

For the Ba'albek festivals, the Rahbani Brothers and Fairuz created grand works called Lebanese Nights and collaborated with the singers Sabah, Wadi' al-Safi, and Nasri Shams al-Din and the composers Zaki Nassif, Tawfiq al-Basha, and Philemon Wehbe, among others. From 1957 until the early skirmishes of the civil war, the Rahbanis appeared in practically every season of the festival, introducing a musical play with a dozen songs that would resonate for the rest of the year, some for decades. Those compositions are currently viewed as part of the, or possibly *the*, essence of Lebanese music. The Rahbani Brothers derived their musical expression from four sources that they handily fused:[11] village folk music, mainstream urban music, Byzantine-era church chants, and Western music. They borrowed and arranged local village folk songs and learned to play folk instruments such as the *buzuq*. The musical nuances of the church liturgy strengthened their appreciation of the *maqam* melodic system. Training in Western music enabled them to utilize harmony, which is not native to Eastern music (for a discussion of the characteristics of the *maqam* system in Eastern music, see Touma 1996). The Rahbani work covered a spectrum of themes: from a somber patriotic oeuvre accompanied by brass sections (notably the epic song for Jerusalem titled "Zahrat al-Mada'n" ["Flower of Cities"]) to simple. lyrics in the local dialect, such as duels between Wadi' al-Safi and Fairuz in the *'ataba* and *mijana* genres (Asmar 2001) or the playful and percussive "Hanna al-Sakran" ("Drunk Johnny"), which accompanied *dabka* line dances.

The genius of the prolific Rahbani Brothers was in establishing a school of music distinct from the dominant Cairo style of lengthy songs centered on unrequited love[12] or the Aleppo style of traditional *waslat*, which grouped together precomposed and improvised vocal (*mawawil*) and instrumental (*taqasim*) pieces all sharing the same *maqam*.[13] The new textual and musical imagery of the Rahbani Brothers' songs typically featured a cheerful young woman (*sabiyya*) carrying a water jug (*jarra*) to the spring (*'ayn*) as an excuse to run into the special young man (*shabb*). The mayor (mukhtar) would settle the ensuing family disputes, typically via a *dabka* dance contest in the village square. The innovative Rahbani Brothers also created the character of the peacemaker among feuding tribes as a symbol of a much-needed unifying leader for the conflicted Arab regimes, many of which were fresh out of a revolution or coup. The intentionally happy endings gave people hope for a bright future. In the 1977 musical *Petra*, they addressed the futility of a colonial superpower trying to break the will of a small nation, a stand-in for the continued occupation of certain Arab lands. The wholesome description of village life and intended subtexts resonated for the sophisticated city folks who longed for the simplicity of their home villages and mother's homemade bread yet needed the sophistication of urban life. All this was skillfully presented via folk instruments along with a European symphonic string section, an accordion, and brass. By simplifying life down to a struggle between good and evil where good prevails, the Lebanese synthesis of folk and urban, Arab and European music gained tremendous popularity throughout the entire region, much of which was struggling to find its place or leave a mark in the twentieth century. The Rahbanis' entry into the history books was primarily due to their break from the Cairo or Aleppo schools of music, although both continued to thrive.

The handling of local and regional politics by the Rahbani family was also deft. The family could have been influenced by savvy politicians into eulogizing the leaders or factional warlords of the civil war. However, their own political senses led them to celebrate the glory of the land instead. They composed a series of songs for all the major Arab capitals. By singing for the Palestinian cause without politicizing it and by honoring Arab cultural centers without exalting their rulers, they earned more political respect for the small nation of Lebanon than the entire diplomatic corps had done. This approach was also clever given that their contemporaries in Egypt, such as Muhammad 'Abd al-Wahhab and Umm Kulthum, had sung for their leaders but were then forced to awkwardly face a change of regime from monarchy to republic (Sahab 2001, 211–14, 253–54).

This volume's introduction discusses the *nahda* movement, which had a deep impact on Lebanon's avant-garde intellectuals, composers, poets, and philosophers, and whose musical tenets were epitomized by the legacy of the Rahbani Brothers. They had fostered a new cultural language that eventually settled into its own signature imagery, seen by many as a favored alternative to the artistic vocabulary commonly manifested in the Cairo or Aleppo schools of music. This movement did not go unchallenged for long. None other than the supposed heir to the Rahbani throne, Fairuz's son, broke away down a different path.

The Rise of the Heir to the Throne

Ziad Rahbani grew up in the midst of a highly significant historical period for Arab music. As a boy, his daily routine included sitting through rehearsals with world-renowned musicians, listening to conversations between his mother and composer Muhammad 'Abd al-Wahhab,[14] or watching his father conduct the opening act of a new Lebanese musical presented in another capital or his uncle write lyrics that every Arab child came to memorize. He displayed his musical and lyrical talents at an early age and started offering opinions to his parents. After publishing a collection of poetic concepts as a teenager titled *Sadiqi Allah* (*God Is My Friend*), he was entrusted with some of the family's creative work, including minor acting roles and then a position as substitute piano player in the orchestra that backed his mother. In 1971, he composed a song for his aunt Huda. Two years later, at age fifteen, Ziad received his first spotlight, playing a detective in the musical *Al-Mahatta* (*The Station*) when his father developed health problems requiring hospitalization. Mansour Rahbani was so moved by his brother's absence that he wrote the lyrics of a song titled "Sa'louni al-Nas" ("People Asked about You") and collaborated with his young nephew Ziad, who composed the music.[15] The resulting work, sung by Fairuz, is still popular decades later, accruing critical acclaim for Ziad and, more important, paving the way to a new relationship with his mother in which he would later take over, virtually exclusively, as her songwriter. He quickly developed into a very prolific composer. As a member of the Rahbani Brothers staff, he was allocated several songs and theme music pieces. One key assignment was the composition of the brilliant instrumental introduction of the 1975 Rahbani Brothers musical *Mayys al-Reem* (*The Deer Meadow*), which turned out to be the group's last musical prior to the interruption of the civil war. Even at nineteen years of age, his compositions were described as forward-thinking (al-Amir 2000, 6), although his work was generally considered to fit the Rahbani style. Ziad later stressed the obvious, that he was greatly influenced by the Rahbani Brothers (Muruweh 1998, 303).

He then reached a crossroad and faced two options. He was qualified to follow in his father's footsteps as a songwriter and composer and inherit the family business of grand musicals, where the path was already paved and filled with welcoming producers and government officials who would grease the wheel for his future productions. He also had the opportunity to independently pursue new intellectual and creative challenges, especially given that the Rahbani Brothers' style had probably lost its novelty for a person who had grown up in its kitchen, figuratively and literally. Two back-to-back events, intimated earlier, guided him down the second path: the illness of his father, which made him more mature, and the start of the civil war, which made him more cynical. 'Assi Rahbani (b. 1923) suffered a brain hemorrhage in 1972, an event that shocked the family and the nation and resulted in gradual mental deterioration that slowed his productivity until his death in 1986.[16] His condition led Fairuz to separate from her husband in 1979 and ultimately team up with their son musically. The Lebanese civil war broke out in 1975,[17] revealing that Lebanese society was fraught with enormous problems, which Ziad Rahbani felt compelled to address in his own way. In a 1995 interview, he reflected that he considered himself lazy and unexpressive prior to the civil war but, with its outbreak, he became very sensitive, nervous, and angry, sentiments that motivated his art (Marshilian 1995, 12). He would not pretentiously claim to have made a difference in the country, but he reckoned that, if one was unable to change a bad system, one should at least prevent being changed by such a system. During the height of the civil war, when the homebound Lebanese population could not move around and listened to the radio extensively, he presented a very popular show with sketches and clips from his work; it was rumored that fighters declared temporary cease-fires in order not to miss it.

Still occasionally collaborating with the Rahbani Brothers (and always maintaining good familial relationships, often expressing his pride in his genetic heritage), Ziad Rahbani branched out and wrote his own theater productions. Although he had never studied theater, he achieved a prolific run within this format from *Sahriyya* in 1973 to *Lawla Fushat al-Amal* (*Were It Not for the Glimmer of Hope*) in 1994. This period closely paralleled the civil war. Ziad Rahbani was unusual for his increasingly prolific output at a time when fellow artists' productivity dropped in response to emigration. Interestingly, he never toured with his plays and refused to have any of them video-recorded; only audio recordings exist and they were broadcast on the radio and sold on cassette. It was in these works that his ideas reached the point where they clashed with the popular style of his parents. Ziad Rahbani rejected the static, happy storylines common to the plays of the Rahbani Brothers because they did not address the real challenges of a modern urban and multicultural nation where the acute economic divisions and political segmentation could not be swept under the proverbial carpet of a let's-all-get-along *dabka* near the '*ayn*. Ziad Rahbani felt that the Rahbani Brothers' musical theater, based on the romantic utopia of village life, was no longer appropriate in the era of a brutal civil war (Shaoul 1980, 7). New theater with courage to ridicule the insanity of the bloodshed was needed. He criticized the Rahbani Brothers for their shallow approach to the country's major political and social problems, and their oversimplifying of the world into good and evil, while real life and the real conflict were significantly more complex.

Thus, he broke completely new ground for Arab playwrights and songwriters; unlike many others, with the exception of Sayyed Darwish (who was active decades earlier), he wrote about poverty and the prevalent corruption. Even his romantic songs addressed the class differences between lovers. Caricaturing the very vocabulary his family popularized, in one play called *Shi Fashil* (*Failure*), which is about the staging of a play, the producer character tells the director to make sure not to leave out the obligatory mukhtar, the beautiful *sabiyya*, and, of course, the *jarra*. He asks if sex might be added to the plot because sex sells tickets, as does nationalism. In the musical *Nazl al-Surur* (*Happiness Hotel*), a struggling innkeeper daringly sings about sending his son to work peddling goods on the sidewalk. In *Bil-Nisba Libukra Shu?* (*What about Tomorrow?*), the wife of a waiter, the main character, offers other hospitality services to European tourists.

Such taboo social topics as prostitution, child labor, the prevalence of drugs, the corruption of officials, and prohibited marriage between the different sects and economic classes were fair game for Ziad Rahbani's songs and plays. Political topics were even more prone to be parodied. In *Film Amriki Tawil* (*Long American Film*), the setting is a psychological clinic or "hospital for the crazy" to show the insanity of the war. When the southern strip of Lebanon was under Israeli occupation and its liberation had become the rallying cry of politicians from all sides, he ridiculed them with a song called "Al-Janub" ("The South") sung by a child. "Their words were empty and they ran out of words to praise" the steadfastness of the people of the South, according to one lyric. They had exhausted all possible patriotic songs, but they had done nothing practical to help or find a solution that was of national interest and not simply concerned with sectarian or political gain.

Audiences knew these taboo topics sprang from real life, but no artist dared expose them before Ziad Rahbani, so they laughed at the dark humor sometimes even if the script was not intended to be funny. Fans walked away from Ziad Rahbani plays in admiration of his intellect and his courage; the number of his followers grew increasingly inside and outside Lebanon. His avant-garde approach was shocking because social commentary and political criticism had never before been so loud and explicit a part of the Lebanese musical culture. Artists' careers were at stake and they did not want to lose their livelihood, but Rahbani reveled in taking such risks. Community leaders rejected his criticism and implied that challenging cultural norms was bordering on unpatriotic behavior. The clergy accused him of blasphemy. As is often the case in conservative societies, when critics of an outspoken "philosopher" run out of weapons, they resort to religious accusation as the heavy artillery for a destructive battle. But Rahbani was not intimidated. His growing fan base, especially the young generation, came to view him as the voice of the voiceless. In order to address religious criticism in particular, he counterstruck with an album titled *Ana Mush Kafir* (*I Am Not an Infidel*), an escalated attack on the corrupt officials who became rich at the expense of the national treasury, a charge elaborated in the next section.

Lyrics, Orchestration: A Study of Three Albums

Three key Ziad Rahbani albums, *Bi-ma Innu* (*Seeing as That*), *Ana Mush Kafir*, and *Bilafrah* (or *Bi al-Afrah*) (*On Happy Occasions*), deserve examination as the works of an avant-garde musician. The first addresses what can be considered personal and social issues, the second looks at societal and political ones, and the third is judged to be a musical tour de force because it includes a purposeful cross section of musical skills in composition and orchestration.

BI-MA INNU

Since Ziad Rahbani is not a singer (although this did not stop him from recording songs in his own voice, often out of humor), he partnered with other artists, especially the singer and actor Joseph Saqr (d. 1996), who starred in many of his plays. This album, subtitled *Joseph Saqr Sings Ziad Rahbani*, is a compilation of such collaborations. The twelve songs include some of Rahbani's top hits, such as "Isma' Ya Rida" ("Listen, Rida"), "'Ayshi Wahda Balak" ("She Lives without You"), and "Halih Ta'bana Ya Layla" ("A Tired Situation, Layla"). One song intimately recounts Rahbani's own process of asking for the hand of his wife, Dalal. Its title, "Marba al-Dalal" ("The Rearing of Dalal" or "Rearing in Opulence"), is a play on words since her name means opulence. The song is so personal that he records the statement "This is such a true story that I will sing the first and last verses myself" and proceeds with his own delivery before handing the song to Joseph Saqr, at which point he pervades the track with giggles and comments.[18] He describes how a poor man meets his future father-in-law to formally propose and, when asked about his line of work, satirically answers that he is the local garbage collector but also the proud owner of his own sofa!

Typically in the Arab world, songs containing lyrically difficult concepts get shelved as purely intellectual work for academics to analyze or elite connoisseurs to appreciate. But, as further illustration of the musical genius and avant-garde approach of Ziad Rahbani, he intentionally makes lyrics with challenging messages accessible to wide audiences. The task was not only to write lines that address topics avoided by other artists but also to make sure the music was appealing at a popular level, like medicine in a candy shell. For this, he used either an Eastern *takht* (an ensemble of traditional instruments; see *Bilafrah*, which follows, for orchestration techniques) or Western instrumentation invariably centered on a piano. On the other hand, for songs that did not tackle taboo topics, he composed jazz, which was considered avant-garde for Arab audiences. All in all, he cleverly selects elements of his works for the highest dial-settings of shock and creativity. In this context, it has been noted that Ziad's rebellious personality and courageous messages are restricted to his lyrics (al-Ghadban 2009). His melodies are sophisticated yet fluid and accessible toe-tappers, in typical Rahbani style. His primary avant-garde touch is adding other tracks, in which he either sings along in parallel with the primary vocalist, laughs at the lyrics, or comments in a satirical narration. The intentional distraction created by this line is utilized on several recordings and intended to create the feeling of a free-form live recording session. On this album, Rahbani innovatively changes the *'ataba* and *mijana* folk genres by inventing his own refrain and he uses the new technique as a filler between songs.

A similar social-issue theme appears in "Halih Ta'bani Ya Layla," where Saqr sings Rahbani's lyrics for Layla: "We can't get engaged. . . . You are rich and I am but a dervish." And again in "'Ayshi Wahda Balak," where Saqr admonishes, "She is living without you and without your silly love / Enough talking romantically when you have become the joke of the town." Such sentiments were not the type a professional songwriter would use on the topic of romance; here Rahbani's collective works reflect tremendous creativity in his choice of lyrics. He writes strictly in the Lebanese dialect, never classical Arabic, thus coming across as an average person, not a pretentious poet. He humbly presents himself as a "garbageman," a "dervish," or the "joke of the town," not quite the descriptors of a proud Rahbani prince.

Ziad Rahbani has always stressed that he is neither a poet nor a *tarab* composer (Sweid 2001, 6). These two affirmations have liberated him from two primary traditional criteria for Arab artists. For example, Umm Kulthum sang *qasa'd* (singular *qasida*) by well-known poets that stood on their own as high-quality publishable verse, and she performed in the *tarab* style (for a discussion of *tarab*, see Racy 2003). Rahbani simply has not concerned himself with such standards, although his music is in many cases *tarab*-inducing, regardless of his intention to avoid that label. To shirk the label of a poet, he considers his lyrics simply "sung conversations" (Muruweh 1998).[19]

ANA MUSH KAFIR

Sung primarily by Sami Hawwat and a chorus, as well as Ziad Rahbani, this album reflects Ziad's political and artistic maturity more than his others. Accompanied in the title track by a *buzuq* and a *riqq* for simplicity, he delivers the song himself to personalize its issues and literally defend himself from the accusation of not believing in God (being a *kafir*) that many conservative critics tried to attach to him. He turns the tables on the rich "merchant who monopolized the price of essential food items out of greed" and wonders, "Who is the real *kafir* here?" The same fate is meted out to the politician who does not mind a civil war if it suits his agenda, and he again wonders, "Who is the real *kafir* here?"

Typically, the European and North American avant-garde has been characterized by a turn from religion. In some Arab nations, however, an accusation of public rejection of God is harshly punishable, so such an allegation is the nuclear weapon of desperate critics. Lebanon is a country that is particularly complicated when it comes to legal matters because certain issues are governed by religious law rather than civil law, with the process playing out through an awkward system of parallel religious courts.[20] Rahbani devised an artistic defense against religious indictment, though, in this case, it was not a charge taken to a court of law.[21]

Other unusual attributes of this album include him delivering a short, spoken humorous introduction warning audiences not to pay more than market price for the cassette. This gesture is noteworthy because avant-garde artists are typically viewed as serious or fighting for a serious cause. Humor breaks the ice and increases the appeal of the album, thereby leavening the serious matters being addressed as well as reflecting Rahbani's personality.

In another song, "Shu Hal Iyyam?" ("What Days Are upon Us?"), he ridicules old-fashioned romantic Egyptian songs when least expected. The track, introduced by a long piano solo prior to an Eastern *takht* accompanying Rahbani, describes his amazement that a rich man would aid a poor one. The song imagines money flying through the air and deciding deliberately to land on a man who then becomes rich—a creative reference to corruption. He ends the verses with definitive statements in Egyptian dialect such as "*la mush sahih al hawa ghallab*" ("no, it is not true that love conquers"), an allusion to the classic Umm Kulthum song "Huwwa Sahih al-Hawa Ghallab?"

("Is It True that Love Conquers?), as if to say, in the middle of a completely different subject, "and, by the way, let me answer the decades-old question while we're at it, once and for all." He also starts the songs by clearing his throat, an inside joke among musicians at the expense of Muhammad 'Abd al-Wahhab, who constantly did so in live concerts.

Just as he confronts religious accusations in one song, he challenges the corrupt rich in another and, for good measure, contradicts the late great Egyptian diva widely popular among Arabic speakers worldwide to show his courage in breaking icons. Rahbani was critical of the fact that, since the days of Umm Kulthum, Arab audiences have kept longing for that golden age, as if no current art warranted pride. Why should radio stations keep repeating "Huwwa Sahih al-Hawa Ghallab?" for decades when young artists deserved airtime? While picking a fight, though, the iconoclast Rahbani would get record-breaking sales of his critically acclaimed albums.

BILAFRAH

This album comprises one long track of a live session. Its musicians improvise in a party setting, reflecting the title's "Happy Occasions," with the voices of tipsy friends happily cheering them on. Despite its ambience of a living room jam, the album was recorded in a studio by professional musicians who had been booked to record with Fairuz, who, at the last minute, could not make it.[22] Rahbani decided not to waste the opportunity of the gathering, ordered 'araq (an alcoholic drink) and meze (appetizers), and led the *takht* in a series of instrumental pieces and improvisations. The resulting musically impressive album has become a favorite among his fans, especially musicians and music students. Prior to Rahbani's trendsetting, recording artists would not dare sound so informal: another musical taboo now broken. To compound the feeling of a living room visit, he named the album with the Arabic phrase used as a reply to an invitation to a friend's house.

At this point in his career, Rahbani had received seven extensive years of training with the prominent Armenian pianist Boghos Jalalian and had become a highly capable jazz pianist. Along with the piano,[23] he mastered the *buzuq*—these being two very different instruments, in line with his complex personality. The piano is an archetypical Western instrument on which he performed his jazz compositions, and the *buzuq*, also played by his father, is an archetypical folk instrument of the region. He made the piano his instrument of choice in public performances and kept a habit of performing in jazz nightclubs in Beirut throughout his career to keep in contact with the public. Furthermore, in the highly acclaimed 1979 album *Wahdun* (*Alone*), the tracks sung by Fairuz are divided between jazz—"A Hadir al-Busta" ("By the Roar of the Bus"), "Wahdun" ("Alone")—and Eastern traditional style—"Ana 'Indi Hanin" ("I Am Nostalgic"), "Ba'atillak" ("I Have Sent You"), "Habaytak Ta Nsit al-Nawm" ("I Have Loved You until I Forgot Sleep")—sending the message that Ziad and Fairuz capably straddle two worlds.

The Rahbani Brothers were masters of fusing Eastern and Western orchestration. For example, they used the recorder and the accordion with the Arab modal *maqam* structure, in addition to exploiting full Western-style orchestras. But they had minimized *taqasim* (improvisations) and deviated from the classical Arab style, heavy on *takht* instruments like *'ud*, *qanun*, *nay*, violin, and *riqq*. Ziad Rahbani inherited skills within the Arab tradition, and the highly upbeat *Bilafrah* album was his statement: I am not a fully Westernized musician. On the heels of his many works in the jazz idiom on the piano (accompanied by double bass and Western drums), *Bilafrah* was composed and performed in a strictly Eastern style, a complete contrast and as if to reject predictability. In it, the folk *buzuq* is the featured instrument with a prominent *nay* alongside *'ud*, *qanun*, and *riqq*; this unusual ensemble is what makes it avant-garde. With no vocals, other than the cheers, the instrumentalists play a selection of previous Ziad Rahbani compositions as well as standards going back to Egyptian folk songs—an unusually beautiful mix peppered with solo improvisations reminiscent of a traditional *wasla*.

The Prodigal Son Is Reunited

Throughout his own busy career, Ziad Rahbani continued collaborating with his mother, Fairuz. She was courageous enough to sing his work, especially after the 1979 separation from her husband, despite its stark divergence from the style of the Rahbani Brothers and her fans' expectations. She sang several jazz songs, to the delight of many and the disappointment of others. After her husband's death, Fairuz carried on performing her classic works in concerts but chose not to collaborate with Mansour Rahbani, who continued to work for a couple of decades with his own three sons. For new material, she joined with her son and produced a number of albums. Ziad Rahbani's choices of lyrics for his mother were so different from those of the Rahbani Brothers era that critics were divided, with some politely calling the "new" Fairuz a mature woman who had come back down to Earth, freed from her prison and singing as an individual. Ziad Rahbani clearly intended to change the image of Fairuz allegorically singing as a child, an angel, a savior, or a national spokesperson, perhaps surrendering her credentials as the "ambassador to the stars."

But her reunion with Ziad Rahbani was not always smooth. In the late 1990s, Fairuz agreed to sing at the revived Ba'albek festival in a concert reminiscent of the old days. The producers were concerned about the health of the now-older diva in the cool evening of the open-air theater and arranged for her to lip-synch a couple of songs in order to prevent vocal fatigue. The audience may not have even noticed the difference had it not been for Ziad Rahbani, who was to be featured on the piano. He protested the miming by not showing up. The piano was rolled away from the stage at the last minute when his absence was announced, but its sound could still be heard from the recording, embarrassing Fairuz's team and teaching them a lesson about dealing with the often-temperamental son.

A decade later, in the midst of a Rahbani family squabble after the death of Mansour in 2009, Ziad Rahbani acted as the adult in the family. Mansour's children demanded financial compensation from Fairuz's earnings as the heirs to half of the Rahbani Brothers team. A public outcry ensued, with crowds protesting in the streets in defense of Fairuz. Editorial pages were full of opinions on both sides; this murky legal case was without precedent. Ziad Rahbani, who upheld a respectful relationship with his late uncle and cousins, remained silent on the issue for weeks. He then surprised the world by releasing a new album for Fairuz titled *Eh Fi Amal* (*Yes, There Is Hope*). The uncharacteristically mature Ziad delivered a positive theme in response to a dark episode in the history of the family. By giving his mother a new voice when she needed it most, perhaps he had assumed the proverbial throne over what was left of the kingdom. But, as expected, he did it his way, in his style, and addressing the issues he cared about. The fact is that Fairuz came to Ziad.

In the introduction to this volume, Kay Dickinson traces the derivation of "the avant-garde" from its French military origins and proceeds to point out how particularly engaging "Arab" and "avant-garde" binaries are, such as East-West or traditional-modern. Rahbani was transformed from a bohemian artist from a rich and famous family into a crack fighter in reaction to the civil war and militarization of Lebanon who fought his own battles fiercely. During his talent's growth spurt, he navigated the East-West and traditional-modern binaries, whatever their complexities, with fluency. It came naturally to him to switch between jazz and *maqam*, piano and *buzuq*, French and Arabic.

In *Popular Culture and Nationalism in Lebanon: The Fairouz and Rahbani Nation*, Christopher Stone examines the transition in Fairuz's career from the Rahbani Brothers to Ziad Rahbani as her primary writer and composer. He points out that, rising to fame from the ashes of the civil war, Ziad Rahbani first appeared to be the cure to the damaged Rahbani trinity, but his work quickly revealed a contrarian side that attacked the premise of his family's artistic legacy. Stone claims, however, that, in the process of parodying his family's work, he pays them hidden homage. The horrible conflict created a national nostalgia for the good-old days before the war, especially the golden age of the Rahbani trinity that practically defined Lebanese music. At the end of the war, the Lebanese people looked to Fairuz to reemerge in festival concerts as a marker and celebration of this event. Although Ziad Rahbani's project disabused his audience of the notion of a golden prewar age full of miracles, even he could not help being seduced by the power of nostalgia. This became apparent in 2000 when he produced Fairuz's concert series at Beiteddine,[24] on his terms and conditions. He surprised everybody by ending every concert with a classic Rahbani Brothers song, as opposed to one of his own, but in his own arrangement. These tracks were mostly from his album honoring his father, *Ila 'Assi* (*To 'Assi*), in which he refashioned Rahbani Brothers repertoire. This is a clever but not a particularly surprising position for Ziad Rahbani to take. He has often expressed his pride in his family and, in any conflicts with relatives, he has made clear that his disagreement is strictly artistic. He even speculated that, if his father had lived longer, he too might have evolved artistically toward his son. Furthermore, although he parodied the Rahbani messages, Ziad never critiqued individual songs artistically. So, for him to rearrange and feature those songs in his own context and under his own terms was simply typical Ziad Rahbani at work.

In such fashion, Ziad Rahbani's work continues to push the boundaries. He tackles social and political issues in his lyrics and explores experimental compositions and arrangements. He displays tremendous intellectual sophistication in breaking taboos via his art. The now middle-age Ziad rarely travels outside Lebanon and lives somewhat reclusively, although he sometimes makes television appearances to discuss politics and the arts. His life and legacy may continue to bear testimony to the indivisible duality of the artist and his role in breaking new creative, social, and political grounds while being inspired by local tradition and modern musical models alike.

Appendix 1

Translation of "Ana Mush Kafir" ("I Am Not an Infidel")
Lyrics and Music by Ziad Rahbani
Translated by Sami Asmar

I am not *kafir* but hunger is *kafir*
I am not *kafir* but disease is *kafir*
I am not *kafir* but poverty is *kafir* and oppression is *kafir*
I am not really *kafir* but what can I do
If all the elements of *kafir* have gathered in me

The person who prays on Sunday
And the one who prays on Friday
But abuse us every day of the week
So now he is religious and I am the one considered *kafir*?
Review the holy books and look up the word of God the Capable

I am not *kafir*, perhaps the country is *kafir*
I am buried at home not able to emigrate
You are grabbing the food out of my mouth while you have plenty
And if I curse what happens, you call me *kafir*
I am listed at all checkpoints in Western countries
And all police stations

I am not *kafir* since we now see you are actually the *kafir*
We have revealed who is *kafir*
And now everybody knows
Like I told you, you are turning it on me
But you are the head of *kafirs*

Amen

Appendix 2

Translation of "Marba al-Dalal" ("The Rearing of Dalal")
Lyrics and Music by Ziad Rahbani
Translated by Sami Asmar

You were reared in opulence
And they suffered for you, Dalal

We went to speak to your father
I wish you were there to hear what he said

In any case, and under all conditions
I am thankful to your father for his hospitality

He asked, Son, how is your financial situation
I replied, Sir, not to worry, I am content with my life
He said an attorney already proposed to my daughter
And not every day an important lawyer would propose
But people like you are a dime a dozen

In any case, and under all conditions
I am thankful to your father for his hospitality

He asked about my wealth
I said, Uncle, my love is my capital
Here I am standing without even bringing a present
To be honest with you, my situation is not to be envied
I inherited a broom and became a garbage cleaner
If it came down to me or the lawyer
It is not much of a question

In any case, and under all conditions
I am thankful to your father for his hospitality

I mentioned I live behind the building; it is not quite a shack
I wash clothes manually and have no freezer either
I do have a small sofa that is multifunctional
Just where did this lawyer pop up from

In any case, and under all conditions
I am thankful to your father for his hospitality

You were raised spoiled
And they suffered for you, Dalal
We went to speak to your father
I wish you were there to hear what he said

In any case, and under all conditions
I am thankful to your father for his hospitality

Notes

The author thanks Professor A. J. Racy for his kind support and generous advice and feedback on this chapter. The author also thanks Kathleen Hood and Sami Maalouf for their reviews and assistance and Michel Mirhej Baklouk and Iyad Wehbe for their historical accounts based on personal experience with Ziad Rahbani.
  1. Alternative spelling: 'Asi.
  2. Alternative spelling: Fayruz.
  3. Alternative spelling: Ziyad.

4. Beirut was divided into East and West during the war, with East Beirut primarily Christian and West Beirut primarily Muslim. Ziad moved out of his parents' home in East Beirut and deliberately settled in West Beirut to signal his independence from them physically as well as artistically and to show that he did not identify himself according to the dominant sectarian divisions.

5. The most notable interview was in 1997 on a two-hour Lebanese Broadcasting Corporation (LBC) TV show called *Hiwar al-ʿumr (Dialogue of a Lifetime)*, with Giselle Khoury. The show was so popular and controversial that, in an unprecedented move by the producers, he was asked back for a second part.

6. See Shepherd et al., eds. (2005, 220–23).

7. Using the Rahbani Brothers designation reflected well on the loving closeness of ʿAssi and Mansour but caused a problem among their heirs, as will be detailed in this chapter. They also had a younger brother named Elias who became a professional composer, and the three brothers had five sons among them working in the field of music. When the Rahbani Brothers team ended with ʿAssi's death, Mansour collaborated with his own three sons, who followed a style he seemed to favor—grandiose musical productions of universal themes—in contrast with the seeming simplicity of Ziad Rahbani's production.

8. She converted from Maronite to Greek Orthodox Christianity in order to marry ʿAssi Rahbani, in a country that rigidly formalized the structure of religious sects.

9. The Rahbani family had moved to Antiliyas from their ancestral village of Rahba, from which their name is derived.

10. She developed the image of a sexless angel in the deliberately managed Rahbani institution.

11. These were passed on to Ziad, who grew up in this musical environment.

12. See the section on romanticism in Arab songs in Sahab (2009).

13. For a modern examination of Aleppo's music and Syrian arts, see Shannon (2006).

14. As told to the author in a 1999 interview with Michel Mirhej Baklouk, the percussion lead for the Rahbani orchestra for decades and a family friend who appears in numerous recordings and on the cover of the *Bilafrah* album.

15. Lebanese poet and historian Henry Zghaib gave an account on the television show *Naghmant al-Bal* in which Ziad composed a melody and played it to his uncle Mansour, who liked it and wrote the lyrics of "Saʾluni al-Nas" to the melody.

16. For his funeral procession through city checkpoints, the warring religious factions declared a temporary cease-fire.

17. The war lasted until 1990, causing as many as a quarter million fatalities, according to some estimates.

18. Ziad lived the life of a playboy and did not seem the marrying type, residing with various girlfriends including the famous actress Carmen Lubbos (as told to

the author by Iyad Wehbe, who directed student plays of Ziad's works with his permission). In 1979, he was briefly married to Dalal Karam, who came from an aristocratic family and demanded to be wedded for the social status it accorded. Dalal bore him a son whom Ziad named ʿAssi after his own father. When the boy had grown into young adulthood, Ziad claimed a DNA test showed that he was not the biological father.

19. He notably avoided actual sung conversations in his plays. Whereas the Rahbani musicals included songs as well as sung dialogue, Ziad's mingled songs with only spoken dialogue.

20. For example, there is no civil marriage, so a Muslim would marry a Muslim under Islamic law and a Christian would marry a Christian under the rules of their particular church; mixed marriages seem to take place outside the country.

21. Singer and composer Marcel Khalife suffered a similar accusation that was taken to court and eventually dropped with tremendous media attention; he was accused of blasphemy for setting to music a Mahmoud Darwish poem that quotes a phrase from the Qur'an.

22. As told to the author in a 1999 interview with Michel Mirhej Baklouk (see note 14).

23. Ziad Rahbani told Muruweh (1998, 304–6) that, according to his father, Ziad had played his own simple piano compositions with one finger at age four; he started formal lessons at age nine.

24. Even the change of venue from Baʿalbek to Beiteddine reflected Ziad's will to break from the past.

References

ʿAbd al-Amir, Ali. 2000. *al-Hayat* (London) (September 6).

al-Ghadban, Yara. 2009. *Al-Adab* 57 (11–12): 61–66.

Asmar, Sami. 2009. "Mansour Rahbani: Legacy of a Family and a Generation." *Al-Jadid* 15 (61).

———. 2001. Chapter on Wadiʿ al-Safi. In *Colors of Enchantment: Theater, Dance, Music, and the Visual Arts in the Middle East*. Edited by Sherifa Zuhur. Cairo: American University Press.

Marshilian, Silvana. 1995. *Al-Usbouʿ al-ʿArabi* (June 13).

Muruweh, Nizar. 1998. *Fi al-Musiqa al-Lubnaniya al-ʿArabiyya Wa al-Masrah al-Ghinaʾ al-Rahbani*. Beirut: Dar al-Farabi.

Racy, Ali Jihad. 2003. *Making Music in the Arab World: The Culture and Artistry of Tarab* Cambridge: Cambridge University Press.

Rayess, Akram. 2009. *Al-Adab* 57 (11–12): 34–37.

Sahab, Elias. 2009. *Al-Musiqa al-ʿArabiyya Fi al-Qarn al-ʿIshrin*. Beirut: Dar al-Farabi.

———. 2010. *Al-Adab* 58 (11–12): 96–101.

Sahab, Victor. 2001. *Al-Sab'a al-Kibar*. 2nd ed. Beirut: Dar al-'Ilm Lil-Malayin.

Shannon, Jonathan Holt. 2006. *Among the Jasmine Trees: Music and Modernity in Contemporary Syria*. Middletown, CT: Wesleyan University Press.

Shaoul, Paul. 1980. *Al-Mustaqbal* (Beirut) (January 26).

Shepherd, Horn, and David Laing, eds. 2005. *Africa and the Middle East*. Vol. VI of the *Continuum Encyclopedia of Popular Music of the World*. New York: Continuum.

Stone, Christopher. 2008. *Popular Culture and Nationalism in Lebanon: The Fairouz and Rahbani Nation*. New York: Routledge.

Sweid, Muhannad. 2001. *Al-Nahar* (Beirut) (April 6).

Touma, Habib Hassan. 1996. *The Music of the Arabs*. Translated by Laurie Schwartz. Portland, OR: Amadeus Press.

CHAPTER SIX

A Look at Lightning

The Life and Compositions
of Halim El-Dabh

~~

MICHAEL KHOURY

As an agricultural engineer, Halim El-Dabh met with physicists and engineers to find a way to use sound and light to divert the flight path of bees away from crops—sound as repellant. There must be a way to apply these techniques to music and composition, he thought. His explorations into sound and agriculture carried over into recording and processing the sounds of his environment. In so doing, he created the world's first piece in the style of *musique concrète*, "Ta'bir al-Zar."

Halim El-Dabh's career has taken him from his position as an agricultural engineer in Egypt to migrating to the United States to becoming the father of the Arab avant-garde. While El-Dabh does not define himself as an avant-gardist, he is regularly heralded as one of the first Arabs of the twentieth century to work in this Western context. Among his accomplishments, he has conducted ethnographic research into African and Afro-Brazilian music; served as Igor Stravinsky's assistant in 1950 at the first Aspen Music Festival; studied with Irving Fine, John Donald Robb, Luigi Dallapiccola, and Aaron Copland; composed for modern dance icon Martha Graham; and participated in some of the early experiments at the Columbia-Princeton Electronic Music Center. In terms of an archive, he has made several individual contributions to compilations, including "Symphonies in Sonic Vibration-Spectrum No. 1" for the 1957 collection *Sounds of New Music*, on Folkways Records, and "Leiyla and the Poet" on the 1964 album *Columbia-Princeton Electronic Music Center*, on Columbia Records.

While overlooked in part due to his ethnicity and his non-Western up-bringing, El-Dabh finds a way to produce challenging art on his own terms. In this chapter, the contents of which were gleaned mainly from phone interviews with the composer, I will relate El-Dabh's formative years to his establishment of an Arab avant-garde. I will also discuss his position as an Arab artist living in the United States with respect to his contributions to and the leeway given him by the American avant-garde.

Historically, movements in the avant-garde have driven wedges between the past, or a status quo, and the present and future. At the same time, divisions are also instituted upon avant-garde subjects themselves through canons, hierarchies, and cultural literacies. Whether self-appointed or categorized as such, Halim El-Dabh has experienced these value placements on several sometimes-paradoxical levels, ranging from Leopold Stokowski making changes to his score because of its complexity to his being "discovered" and invited by Otto Luening to participate in the prestigious experiments at the Columbia-Princeton Electronic Music Center. The conditions of his practice cannot escape the relationship between two constructs: "his" culture and the implied norms of the avant-garde. His very participation in the avant-garde draws attention to the borders of these constructs.

In his compositions, El-Dabh draws upon the varied music of the Arab peoples and the world around him for inspiration. As this chapter will elaborate, El-Dabh's cultural influences are not limited to his agricultural vocation and encompass noises from his environment as foundational elements. In this sense, his recourse to local Egyptian traditions is markedly different from how many Western composers incorporate "world" tropes into their music. His "Egyptian material" refuses to be ornamentation, approximation, or ethnic styling that adds tinge or color. His music is a rendering of his intimate experience with people making music on a local level—for instance, by manipulating audio recordings of daily Egyptian life and mixing those sounds with atonal piano chords, rather than playing harmonized "exotic" scales on a piano.

By way of contrast, consider some Western composers who have drawn from traditional musics. Béla Bartók transcribed folk tunes and reworked them in an orchestrated form. Claude Debussy used his impression of gamelan music as a compositional departure. Philip Glass employs ornamentation borrowed from Indian classical music. Many contemporaries of El-Dabh in the United States have used ethnic elements in a manner that Lou Harrison described as transethnicism. David Nicholls defines this as "the employment or evocation of musical styles and techniques other than the composer's own" (Nicholls 1996, 26).

Clearly, El-Dabh does not conform to the profile of those who reference traditional styles from the "outside." Unlike these other composers, El-Dabh experienced Egyptian music as a native, not as a witness to the unfamiliar or foreign. He feels that his experience with indigenous Egyptian forms has stimulated latent responses within himself and that he is an indigenous artist. From his agricultural engineering perspective, El-Dabh has examined the relationship between the work and the lives of people making music; although not himself a farmer by trade, he fully understands the correlation between the cultural, agricultural, and musical differences as they shift according to locality.

Where might this compositional approach fit with the American avant-garde movement? Nicholls suggests that composers incorporating non-Western structures as a basis for their work might not be received as well as those who adapt ethnic forms merely as surface decoration:

> The American musical establishment has been able to tolerate (and, indeed, in some cases encourage) the use of folk and ethnic materials by Beach, Farwell, Copland and others because those materials have been (imperially) appropriated simply in order to impose an "American" accent onto the existing European musical lingua franca. With transethnicism, the situation is fundamentally different: for a composer to employ materials from "elsewhere" not merely as coloring, but as the basis of a compositional method, and therefore to display an attitude of seriousness toward cultures lying beyond imperialism's zone of tolerance is to effectively condemn his music to rejection by the American Eurocentric establishment. The greater the degree of transethnic influence, the greater the likelihood of rejection. (Nicholls 1996, 26)

But what if the transethnic elements come from the artist's own local repertoire? The modern Egyptian composer Nahla Mattar characterizes such uses of cultural material as "inheritance" (Mattar 2007, 1). While Mattar describes inheritance in temporal terms, I would add that it bears a cross-sectional dimension too, given El-Dabh's experience with frequent changes in music across relatively slight modulations in place. Egyptian historical and geographical influences are prevalent in much of El-Dabh's work, especially in "Leiyla and the Poet." In contrast to the more mathematical compositions of his contemporaries, El-Dabh interlaced pure electronic sounds with traditional strings and percussion, both Arab and Native American.

As discussed in the introduction to this volume, an Arab tweaking of Arab musical convention inherently engages postcolonialism, whether to erode the political fixity of "the local" or to reinvent a dynamic selfhood that rejects the Arab musician's role as culture bearer. Predictably, and in line with Nicholls's observations, when El-Dabh wrote in this complex fashion, his oeuvre failed to achieve wide acceptance. The most striking rejection of his work in the West occurred in 1958, when Leopold Stokowski conducted El-Dabh's "Fantasia-Tahmeel: Concerto for Derabucca and Strings" and made several cuts to the score because of its intricate and challenging rhythms (Seachrist 2002, 23).

The fact that El-Dabh is not a Westerner begs questions about his relationship with the avant-garde, which is largely made up of composers of European descent. Some of El-Dabh's European contemporaries in the 1950s and 1960s, such as Pierre Boulez, were staking their claim in a provocative manner with a postserial approach. Others, like Pierre Schaeffer and his *musique concrète* circle, were defining their own school in which to work. El-Dabh had no such confrontational agenda. Instead, he hoped to bring together his compositional techniques, the influences of a life spent in agriculture, and his local ethnic experiences. But because of his iconoclasm, El-Dabh's output and presence could be perceived as unsettling to Western avant-garde circles. In addition, the composer's inability to fit into a school or generalized approach may have affected the credit and distinction, or lack thereof, that El-Dabh has experienced.

Despite the dismissive reaction of the European-American avant-garde, El-Dabh was, perhaps unwittingly, laying the foundations for something new: an Arab avant-garde. A particular incident resounds. In 1952, the Juilliard School presented a performance of El-Dabh's "Monotone, Bitone, and Polytone." In attendance were the composers Gian Carlo Menotti, William Schuman, and Vincent Ludwig Persichetti, who all chastised El-Dabh because his work did not follow the "norms" of modern composition. Ironically, El-Dabh disrupted avant-garde conventions. He asserts that "Yes, I could be a threat to the avant-garde," and continues to stress that he never thought of himself in these terms. Rather, he considered himself a composer working with his own language. In this manner, El-Dabh's formation and experiences differ from those of most modern composers of European descent. The following survey of El-Dabh's trajectory as an artist reveals that his cultural influences constitute both a method of composition and a new movement.

Early Development

Born Halim Abdel Messieh El-Dabh on March 4, 1921, El-Dabh grew up in an environment where education and achievement held a high value. The ancient Coptic and Eastern Orthodox Churches played a critical role in his early experiences, with chant and ritual functioning as cornerstones (Seachrist 2003, 2). Being relatively affluent, the El-Dabh family had servants, one of whom introduced the young El-Dabh to traditional songs from Nubia, Upper Egypt, and Central Egypt, and these constituted some of the first musical experiences for the impressionable child (Seachrist 2003, 4–5). Other early musical encounters included street puppet shows (Seachrist 2003, 5).

Music was a prevalent part of El-Dabh's early life. His family kept an old upright piano in their home, and all the siblings were encouraged to play. In particular, his older brothers nurtured his musical interest. One of them, Bushra, recognized El-Dabh's acumen on the piano and coaxed his younger brother into taking lessons in theory and harmony at the Szula Conservatory in downtown Cairo. El-Dabh furthered his passion for music at age eleven, when he entered middle school. That year, he attended the Congress of Arab Music organized by King Fouad I in Cairo (discussed in this anthology's introduction). There he would have encountered Western composers and musicologists such as Béla Bartók, Jaap Kunst, Henry Farmer, Baron Erlanger, and Paul Hindemith. Cairo's 1932 Congress of Arab Music set out to define Arab music using Western documentation methods so that Arabs and the West could better communicate and understand one another. As Kay Dickinson mentions in her introduction, the congress spurred two key outcomes. First, it helped establish the careers of some of the Middle East's most popular music artists of the century. Second, it further delineated the traditionalists as separate from the more forward-looking experimentalists. I would argue that it had a third key function, at least as it pertained to El-Dabh. The congress exposed Egypt to the new recording technology known as the wire recorder. Likewise, in many of the avant-garde movements of the twentieth century, technology has played a key role. El-Dabh actually met Hindemith and Bartók, but the experience was lost on him, being only eleven years old. However, exposure to the wire recorder made a deep impression on the young El-Dabh and proved pivotal to some of his early work.

As his schooling progressed, El-Dabh followed a scientific curriculum in the hope of studying agriculture and participating in the family business of agricultural commerce. He also joined an informal study group with twelve other young men. The early intellectual curiosity that led him to join this group would be critical in his musical experimentation and freethinking. By age fifteen, El-Dabh had begun to open his world to international and Egyptian modern thought. He was immersing himself in the works of Sigmund Freud, Georg Hegel, Immanuel Kant, Aldous Huxley, and Naguib Mahfouz. At certain junctures in his life, El-Dabh would also have contact with some of the more well-known Egyptian composers and performers of the time, including Umm Kulthum, Muhammad 'Abd al-Wahhab, and Abdel Halim Hafez. He pursued a different trajectory than the aforementioned artists, however. While their paths crossed at times, little if any artistic exchange took place between them.

As noted, the relationship between music and agriculture was of critical importance to El-Dabh. Seachrist elicits a sense of conflict between the two passions in the composer's life (Seachrist 2003, 11–12, 16), but I would argue that they were productively connected. El-Dabh describes agriculture and music as complementary influences. As a part of his agricultural studies, El-Dabh traveled to villages throughout Egypt, where locals invited him to attend and participate in festivities where musical ensembles consisting of double reed instruments (*argul*), clarinets, drums, and trumpets would accompany singers and dancers (Seachrist 2003, 11). According to El-Dabh, "Agriculture was my way to the people" (author interview, October 12, 2010). The ceremonies and celebrations served as a critical turning point for him in devoting his life to music. El-Dabh noticed a correlation between those working the land and the practice of music. According to Seachrist, "He experienced the cyclic rhythm of nature when he learned to plant the *berseem* to hold the nitrogen in the soil, then to plant beans and peas to make the land fertile enough for wheat or corn" (Seachrist 2003, 11). He firmly believed that musical diegesis functioned similarly, and this close correspondence between agriculture and music comforted the young composer. El-Dabh's exposure to folklore and local music would be of paramount consequence to his future in music.

While radio gained popularity in these regions from the 1920s through the 1940s, El-Dabh relates the importance of retaining local traditions as an expression of cultural distinctness from the somewhat popular and homogenized government-run broadcasts. Between 1924 and 1934, "the musical portions of radio broadcasts consisted primarily of commercial recordings. Broadcasting commercial recordings from the privately owned radio stations served the dual purpose of advertising the recordings and filling in program time" (El-Shawan 1980, 95). Or, as El-Dabh says, "The radio normalizes everything" (author interview, July 7, 2010). Radio broadcasting in the subsequent decades tended to focus on popular musical styles as opposed to the rich and diverse musical cultures of Egypt. While the penetration rate of radio receivers escaped documentation by the government or NGOs during the 1930s and 1940s, a study by the United Nations Educational, Scientific, and Cultural Organization (UNESCO) indicates that their numbers nearly doubled between 1950 and 1956 (El-Shawan 1980, 108). If this increase is any indication, state-controlled radio likely had a significant impact on the range of music experienced by Egyptians.

Early Experiments

In 1944, El-Dabh created his first wire recorder piece using sounds from his surroundings. The collection of source materials for this piece happened concurrently with the experiments of the French composer Pierre Schaeffer, who premiered his first composition termed *musique concrète* in 1948. El-Dabh and Schaeffer were not aware of each other; however, Schaeffer gets the credit for being the father of this movement. Thousands of miles away in Egypt, El-Dabh conducted related experiments and would later return to electronic composition upon his visit to the United States. According to El-Dabh, "I didn't think of it as electronic music, but just as an experience" (Young 2007, 26). Ironically, El-Dabh and Schaeffer later worked concurrently at Radiodiffusion-Télévision Française, the home of much of Schaeffer's research, but the two composers never met.

El-Dabh furthered his fascination with indigenous music and observances when he became interested in the *zar*, a women's only ceremony where healing occurs through contact with otherworldly spirits. The *zar* is also a type of folk music; it is "directly linked with areas outside of Cairo and less influenced by Cairo's central musical domain" (Racy 1981, 20). In 1944, El-Dabh and his close friend Kamal Iskander loaded up a wire recorder and dressed as women to infiltrate one such ceremony just outside Cairo. They were quickly discovered, but the women allowed them to stay and document and participate in the ceremony. They even conducted a healing on El-Dabh and Iskander. The resulting recordings would serve as source material for the world's first composition to use recorded and processed sounds. El-Dabh describes it in his own words: "They have big *darbukka* drums and sometimes use flutes. They do a lot of incantations and their voices almost change in the process, and it's like different languages coming into being, and you feel as though you're on a different dimension, and all of a sudden you're lifted" (Young 2007, 26). El-Dabh manipulated these sounds using the rudimentary equipment at a local radio station, applying the effects of reverb, echo, and tone controls. He built up the piece by playing the source material, treating it according to the capabilities of the radio station, and then recording it on another wire recorder. During the process, he brought certain tones to the fore, edited others out, and enhanced particular sounds. Specifically, he concentrated on two elements: foundational tones and vocal noises. El-Dabh attempted to "filter out vocal and instrumental sound" in order to isolate the sound remaining (author interview, August 13, 2010). His effort yielded "Ta'bir al-Zar" ("The Expression of *Zar*").[1]

The piece is simultaneously spiritual and frightening, with El-Dabh creating an abstract aural rendition of the ceremony. He eschews traditional rhythmic elements, allowing sounds to emerge and sometimes predominate through his treatments. The point of reference is that of an indigenous listener, as opposed to an ethnographic document or the recordings of the women as a cultural touchstone. The treated drums and voices retain their cultural context and indeed form the substance of the composition instead of being invoked as attributes or references. El-Dabh is able to convey a perspective of someone who is inside the experience. The piece is a landmark of electronic music in that it references recorded material yet is electronically modified using a rudimentary echo chamber and by bouncing the piece from one wire recorder to another. Such fare became more common with the innovation of magnetic tape and Schaeffer's experiments with recorded sound. Critics and the media have, until recently, failed to recognize "Ta'bir al-Zar" as part of the avant-garde because even El-Dabh had forgotten the piece and left it out of his portfolio of compositions. Shortly after its creation, he presented it in an installation-like setting at a YMCA in Cairo. Given the newness of the art form, it is unlikely those who experienced it made a connection to the similar emerging work in the West.

In 1945, El-Dabh had begun work as an agricultural engineer in Cairo. While he looked forward to a life in agriculture, he still eagerly responded any time his brother Bushra invited him to visit and compose or play on his grand piano (Seachrist 2003, 12). His travels around the country helped strengthen his sense of the relationship between local agricultural practices and musical customs. Farming traditions differed by region as did the terrain. Likewise, the music differed from place to place. According to El-Dabh, "The music in Egypt changes every twenty miles" (author interview, October 12, 2010). El-Dabh viewed the culture of Egypt as fair game in his new musical work. Some may have regarded the local traditions as needing to remain local or utilitarian in scope. For El-Dabh, they did not represent opportunities for transgression in the name of the avant-garde but were rather a rich amalgamation of ideas and realizations. These concepts could exist together. Because of this orientation, locality and regionally marked material became a great source of strength to El-Dabh, instead of remote ideas to be rationalized and reconciled.

Soon after launching his agricultural career, El-Dabh responded to an invitation to join a group of French, Syrian, and Lebanese men with common interests in music and music appreciation. El-Dabh and three of the other group members would become close, and these colleagues proved critical in encouraging him along the path of modern music. They introduced him to composers such as Schönberg, Stravinsky, and Milhaud and discussed emerging ideas in philosophy. Also, around 1945, El-Dabh became enamored of tone clusters, as well as playing the inside of the piano (Seachrist 2003, 12). Thus began an interest in experimentation in nontraditional piano technique for the young composer. This approach stood in contrast to a more conservative traditional, European one present in Cairo during this time. The European understanding of performance, composition, and theory taught in the conservatories responded both to Egyptian demand and the listening habits of a large Western presence in Cairo (El-Shawan 1985, 144).

Egypt's identity shifted drastically over the course of El-Dabh's early life. Though Egypt declared its independence in 1922, the British maintained a military presence until 1956. In the 1930s and 1940s, the activities of the city's many international embassies and cultural attachés helped foster an environment in which Western and Eastern culture coexisted and citizens could avail themselves of both. El-Dabh believes that Cairo of the 1930s and 1940s served as a hub for music from around the globe and describes it as a progressive city that embraced culture. "It was a time of incredible advancement," El-Dabh observes (author interview, July 7, 2010). As a result, a plethora of societies existed in the city, some with connections to European countries, and this is the environment in which El-Dabh continued to develop his work. These societies were not perceived as Orientalist in nature, as they were not exclusive in their membership. Nor did they carry an agenda that smacked of imperialism. Rather, they exemplified Cairo's status as a place of emerging ideas and a crossroads of Eastern and Western intellectual thought. Several of the leading composers of the time incorporated Western elements, but Egyptian artists and audiences alike viewed their music "as part of an 'international' musical language to which all cultures have equal access" (El-Shawan 1985, 146).

El-Dabh went on to write several pieces during the mid- and late 1940s. During one of these periods of productivity, a friend contacted him and implored him to consider an offer from a classical music society to perform his own compositions. While El-Dabh had confidence as a young professional, he did not possess the same resolve with regard to his music (Seachrist 2003, 12–13). He feared being viewed as a dilettante. It took some time for the friend to convince him, but El-Dabh eventually relented and premiered his work for solo piano entitled "It Is Dark and Damp on the Front" on February 11, 1949, at the Assembly Hall of All Saints' Cathedral in Cairo (Seachrist 2003, 17). In reflecting upon the work, El-Dabh says, "That piece changed my life" (author interview, July 7, 2010).

The Emotional Response

"It Is Dark and Damp on the Front" was written for solo piano with distinct sections and employs some repetition in its form, alternating between tone clusters and descending lines. It is unlike other piano pieces of its time and makes little reference to serialism or the Viennese School. The work runs for roughly six minutes, but the score allows the performer to vary the length at the end. The piece is about the mass immigration of European Jews into

Palestine and the subsequent war with the Arab states. In a discussion decades later, El-Dabh explained, "The war is dark and damp in the heart of human beings. There is something there that is going to haunt people for years and years and years and years. War truly begins in the heart of every human being" (Seachrist 2003, 17).

The Assembly Hall was filled to capacity on the evening of the performance, with a cross-section of Arabs and Westerners in attendance. They reacted with great feeling to the piece. It is crucial to recognize that al-Nakba ("the catastrophe," referring to the loss of Palestine) then touched the hearts of many in Egypt. Egyptian soldiers were fighting in the war, and soldiers and their sympathizers in the audience must surely have responded with charged emotions to the depth of the music and the current tragedy, both as fellow Arabs and as people backing their own nation's participation in a war. Egyptians of all classes attended the concert, demonstrating Arab solidarity across social strata and proving the growing appeal of original Arab art. Although the performance showcased avant-garde work, the immediacy of al-Nakba and a budding sense of pan-Arabism likely fueled the attendees' fascination. "Nineteen forty-eight, for me, was very disturbing," El-Dabh says. "The whole balance in the Middle East was falling down that year" (author interview, July 7, 2010). El-Dabh was more taken aback by the horror and tragedy of war and the emergent refugee problem than the politics of the situation.

The piece is jarring, with dynamic contrasts that give the feeling of restlessness and shock. The peppered tone clusters in the upper register wrangle with the listener, giving a sense of darkness. The score asks the performer to repeat chords as a way of finishing the piece and allows her to choose how long this should continue. The open-ended nature of the conclusion could give one a sense of hope but could also symbolize the perpetual nature of the horrors of war. It leaves something with the listener that she may be unable to shed. Prominent disjointed chords invoke a dreamlike surrealism, capturing the disorientation and disbelief felt by many Palestinians with respect to losing their homes and land as the world stood idly by. "It Is Dark and Damp on the Front" conjures images of despair and uncertainty at best and a devastating, unresolved, yet reiterated sense of finality at worst. It represented the confluence of El-Dabh's training as a musician with his deep feelings about war and conflict, against the backdrop of a sympathetic and shocked international community in Cairo. The work had a broad appeal to those in the region, the majority of whom were deeply affected by al-Nakba. While progressive and considered ahead of its time, the composition also contained figurative references in the descending lines, recalling falling mortars. "It Is Dark and

Damp on the Front" bore a timely appeal to those in Egypt who may have closely identified the avant-garde elements of the piece with the stunned and unthinkable plight of the Palestinian people. The dismay and disbelief at the state of the Palestinians may have prepared those hearing the piece for the more avant-garde elements therein. At the same time, the figurative elements may have fostered a sense of identification that either allowed the listener to embrace the avant-garde figurings or transcend them.

About "It Is Dark and Damp on the Front," El-Dabh states, "I came to the realization that the front is in every human being. You have to have a balance. A balance in power and relationships. As long as someone is sitting on top of somebody, you can't have a balance. Without balance, there is no rest. Conflict has affected everyone in this world. It's perpetuating this kind of negative energy. It has a fear dimension. It perpetuates other wars. It perpetuates suffering for humanity. It's a composition of what happened. I felt a horror feeling, but I felt hope" (author interview, July 7, 2010). He also felt that the piece should evoke the murkiness and sadness in the world, "a thin hazy layer covering the minds of people." El-Dabh explains, "I wrote that piece for myself. I had to play what I did. It had a power of its own and I couldn't control it." To this day, El-Dabh believes that "we're haunted by something that happened in 1948."

The cultural attaché of the American embassy asked El-Dabh to repeat the concert at Oriental Hall of the American University in Cairo. That evening, the venue filled to capacity, with word of mouth prompting quite some excitement. The response to the performance was, again, powerful. Following it, El-Dabh was invited to install a recording of the work in an isolation booth as part of a visual art opening at a Cairo gallery (Seachrist 2003, 12–17).

Technical Innovations

The composition and performance of "It Is Dark and Damp on the Front" marked a critical turning point in El-Dabh's career. Not only did the piece convey great emotional depth, it also incorporated technical complexity and experimental approaches that El-Dabh would continue to employ throughout his career. Among these are multiple superimposed chords and unorthodox pedal techniques. El-Dabh performed the work on a nine-foot piano, which was a rare treat in Egypt at that time, manufactured by the French firm Pleyel and equipped with three pedals, which El-Dabh exploited fully to enhance the tone and dynamics of the piece (see notes to the score; El-Dabh 2010a). The piece shies away from traditional form but generates a sense of structure through its distinct sections and literal repeats throughout. Notes, like sections, reappear with fair frequency. The lowest occurs at the beginning, setting an ominous tone, with the highest appearing in the second section, invoking a rending sense of loss and fatalism. El-Dabh employs varying dynamics, especially in the second and last sections, where these can vary within the measure to invoke the visual dimension of the chaos of war and sudden movement. While the piece contains atonal elements, there is no evidence of serialism.

The French critic A. J. Patry, who attended the Assembly Hall performance, noted, "El-Dabh touches the instrument in a fashion of his own; he molds and fuses the sonorities of the piano[,] producing sounds and feelings pertaining to a basic cult. He has exposed the European ear to a different way of playing. One must notice the way he uses the pedals, producing from simple elements, complex superpositions of harmonies" (Seachrist 2003, 17). Patry's observations were especially significant because of his reputation for bias against unknown composers. He demonstrated a genuine interest in El-Dabh's work, however, and sought him out to discuss his approaches. El-Dabh reluctantly agreed, not yet comfortable with his standing as a composer or performer. While generally confident in himself, El-Dabh lacked conviction about the risk and responsibility that lay ahead in a life in music. He had not yet thought about leaving his profession, which allowed him financial and professional success.

Patry's interview helped El-Dabh express his ideas on composition. During it, El-Dabh expounded how all sounds derive from a single pitch. He asserted the significance of sound traveling throughout the universe and through time, and the necessity of employing only a single tone (Seachrist 2003, 19).

When asked recently about his use of dissonance, El-Dabh staunchly rejects the term. In reference to the tone clusters he uses in "It Is Dark and Damp on the Front," he classifies them as "clashes that produce vibrations, not dissonance." El-Dabh describes his technique of composing as "heteroharmony," a term El-Dabh created to describe the combination of "heterophony and chordal harmony in an interaction of chords and clusters with the focus on the unison" (El-Dabh 2010b). This revision of terminology both identifies and broadens the geographic and cultural locus of the avant-garde by relocating the source of new sounds. These noises do not spring from a rejection of conventional Western harmony but, rather, from the goal of isolating and exploring elements particular to Arab music. El-Dabh states that "heteroharmony theory comes out in terms of sound relationships." He feels that traditional harmony can create an imbalance and "eats up the energy of the music." To El-Dabh, traditional harmony may not be optimal "in terms of the harmonic production." In his own words: "My chordal and melodic styles are based on a structure that I coined and named as 'heteroharmony.' It is an approach based on the friction of tones in a desire to achieve unison. Sometimes I can achieve the feelings of the quarter tone by executing tonal friction in tetrachords of augmented seconds. Occasionally these augmented seconds could be juxtaposed over an Egyptian Arabic *hijaz*, or simply over regular piano scales" (El-Dabh 2010a).

"It Is Dark and Damp on the Front" proved foundational for El-Dabh's subsequent compositions. The piece sparked in El-Dabh an attraction toward experimentation, through the use of tonal clashes and clusters. "It became part of my writing in orchestral works and electronic works," he says (author interview, July 2010). This is specifically evident in El-Dabh's heteroharmony approach, which relies more on the vibrations created from contrasting tones than on traditional harmony.

New Opportunities

The technical elements of "It Is Dark and Damp on the Front" garnered El-Dabh critical acclaim and attention from Patry and the American cultural attaché in Cairo. At a time when he did not have faith in his future as a composer, these responses were especially flattering. Says El-Dabh, "People grasped hold of the technical elements" (author interview, July 7, 2010). Subsequently, the American cultural attaché arranged for El-Dabh to study in the United States at the University of New Mexico.

Based upon the merit of "It Is Dark and Damp on the Front," Aaron Copland invited him to enroll as a private student at the Berkshire Music Center at Tanglewood in Lenox, Massachusetts. There, El-Dabh met Irving Fine, who helped open an opportunity for him at Brandeis University, a school with Jewish roots. Fine would become one of El-Dabh's most influential teachers. When asked if he felt his Arab heritage proved an obstacle at Brandeis, the composer said he did not face any prejudice there. In fact, Brandeis enlisted El-Dabh to recruit non-Jewish students to attend the university. "I don't think I ever thought of discrimination," he observes (author interview, July 7, 2010). El-Dabh's experience was likely consistent with that of other Arabs in the United States at that time. Prior to the Six-Day War of 1967, Arabs were often viewed as exotic and the modern stereotype of the terrorist had not yet been proliferated by the American media. Like some Egyptians, El-Dabh also identified himself as African and felt a connection with the varied people throughout that continent. Regardless, El-Dabh was certainly a minority among those studying at Brandeis. His identity was more that of a composer honing his craft under the tutelage of well-known musicians than that of an Arab trying to establish himself among those in the avant-garde.

After his schooling, El-Dabh attained several other positions of prominence throughout his career. With the end of each of these professional breaks, another would inevitably emerge. "Every time I thought about going home, something pulled me back," El-Dabh observes (author interview, July 7, 2010). El-Dabh missed Egypt and his family but felt enthusiastic about the serendipitous openings that continued to arise, sometimes during the final moments just before he was due to leave.

One of these opportunities allowed El-Dabh to further his experimentations with the piano. Between 1955 and 1956, he held a residency at the MacDowell Colony in New Hampshire. There, he tested out what he terms "sonic vibration," attaching wires from the piano to his room at the colony and tying a drum to the side of the piano. He also began to explore with magnetic tape. The up-and-coming electronic music composers Otto Luening and Vladimir Ussachevsky heard about this and visited him in his cabin. They experienced his raw-trialing firsthand and later encouraged him to work in the Columbia-Princeton Electronic Music Center in New York City. Luening and Ussachevsky likely saw El-Dabh as a bit eccentric but at the same time were intrigued by his approach. Arab contexts informed El-Dabh's musical research as he continued the work he had begun in Egypt. He eventually arrived at the Columbia-Princeton Electronic Music Center in 1958, a facility that afforded El-Dabh a dynamic set of associations. There, he and several other composers experimented with early synthesizers and magnetic tape, doing their best to avoid mimicking the sounds of acoustic instruments. In an interview, El-Dabh says, "At Columbia, we didn't imitate real music, as it might take jobs away" (author interview July 2010). Instead, the composers focused on more abstract noises and the slowing down and speeding up of recordings, as well as the layering of different sounds. El-Dabh also experimented with tape-looping to create new rhythms by varying the length of the loop and then layering those rhythms with other sounds. He compared his consideration of the sonic to how a visual artist might relate to her media; he believed that, like the creations of a sculptor, sound could be carved and shaped out of noise.

While at the Columbia-Princeton Electronic Music Center, El-Dabh wrote "Leiyla and the Poet," a landmark contribution to electronic music. Mike Hovancsek declares, in the notes to a compact disc of El-Dabh's electronic work, "While many composers of electronic music at the time worked with a calculated, mathematical approach, El-Dabh's work reflected his cultural background, his compositional skills, his studies of Native American musics, and his years of experience with manipulated sound recordings. The results were stunningly powerful and original" (Hovancsek 2000). "Leiyla and the Poet" incorporates recordings of Egyptian flutes and the Arab *dumbik* drum to tell the ancient story of forbidden love between the first cousins Leiyla (also spelled "Layla") and Majnun. In the recording, we hear these instrumental selections sped up and slowed down to create a surreal backdrop that retains its elemental Arab attributes while still feeling modern, in part due to El-Dabh's sculpting of sound through electronic processing.

El-Dabh believed each engagement would be his last in America, and he always prepared to go home to Egypt as an assignment neared its close. This is a radically different experience from that of many of his American contemporaries who jumped at stable academic careers and may have preferred a more planned approach. In the Arab world, there is something of a fatalist outlook, and El-Dabh's experiences are no exception. This is evidenced in the Arabic language by the word *Insh'llah*: if God wills it. Opportunities in the United States were certainly increasing as the country experienced prosperity, including more funding available to artists. In a manner consistent with Arab culture, El-Dabh allowed his career to take a natural path, while taking advantage of these opportunities. Without a doubt, El-Dabh worked diligently within these engagements and exhibited outstanding productivity. He demonstrated imagination and creativity, but was perhaps less aggressive or strategic in his approach than other composers who were born and raised in the United States during this time. As a result, El-Dabh's persona seems devoid of the recognizable feature of "genius," itself an idea that emerges from modernist rhetoric of authentic creativity. He has never performed this Eurocentric articulation of individualism and, while this may have been a disadvantage, it also reveals the ideological limitations of a European avant-garde, as discussed in this volume's introduction.

Today, in Cairo, El-Dabh is studied by the second generation of young Egyptian composers working with some European-based training; his piano pieces are the subject of a current dissertation (Rasha Tomoum, email message to author, November 23, 2010). Throughout his life, El-Dabh has returned to Egypt several times, in part to keep his link with his home intact. He also contributed to the music that accompanies the light show at the pyramids. Ultimately, El-Dabh is considered by academics as one of many Egyptian composers to make a significant contribution in the twentieth century. The majority of documentation of modern music in Egypt centers on Gamal Abdel-Rahim and his students (El-Kholy 2003, 3). Likely, because Abdel-Rahim stayed in Egypt and taught there, influencing subsequent generations of composers, as such, there exists a more complete archive of his work. The contrasting documentation of the two composers begs the question of what El-Dabh's impact on Egyptian modern music would have been had he stayed in his homeland, or if he had embarked on a career in music there. Unflinchingly, El-Dabh asserts, "I would have composed in the same way. The energy of composing is very powerful, and I wouldn't have been stopped. If I didn't travel from Egypt, I would have had a parallel realization. If I had stayed in Egypt, I would have been working with quarter tones and *maqam* art" (author interview, November 6, 2010).

El-Dabh does not apologize for how his work fits or does not fit into any particular framing of "tradition." In this respect, he can be considered destabilizing to the avant-garde, Arab or otherwise. He has not set out to be a traditionalist composer in the Arabic folk or classical idioms, nor has he deliberately attempted to shed his cultural background in his work. El-Dabh has created something entirely new based upon his experiences. His seamless oeuvre, which moves from documenting the music of Ethiopia, to writing for Martha Graham, to experimenting with modifying pianos to achieve new sonorities, is indicative of an incredibly flexible and intellectually curious mind that knows no boundaries. The idea of "double dependency," where the composer struggles with having one foot in tradition and the other in the unwelcoming camp of the progressive West, may very well apply to many among the Arab avant-garde.[2] I find no evidence of this in El-Dabh. He does not view tradition as an impediment. Rather, in both a cross-sectional and temporal sense, El-Dabh views the world around him as a source of material to be explored. One could view El-Dabh's approach as naïve or extremely challenging, or perhaps a combination of the two. However perceived, El-Dabh's take must be credited as chance-taking, new, and a challenge to the status quo. Specifically, when serialism was in vogue, El-Dabh's work made no reference to it. And, as I have argued, his electronic experiments at the Columbia-Princeton Electronic Music Center pushed the boundaries, as compared with his peers, who worked to strip out any aural references to musical instruments. El-Dabh not only embraced the sounds of instruments but made solid use of them.

When asked if he feels bitter about not being adequately acknowledged for being the pioneer he is in several cutting-edge art forms, El-Dabh humbly replies, "I'm just a simple guy who doesn't expect credit" (author interview, July 7, 2010). From creating the first recorded piece in *musique concrète* prior to the birth of the form, to using tone clusters and playing the inside of a piano in 1949, to experimenting with electronic music at the Columbia-Princeton center, El-Dabh has undoubtedly been a forerunner of the avant-garde in the twentieth century. This is all in addition to his work as a scholar, ethnomusicologist, and composer. El-Dabh's achievements have yet to be fully appreciated, but he is the first among Arabs and Western artists during the twentieth century to lead the way with work of such convincing breadth and depth.

To be an Arab means to live with contradictions or, indeed, to live *as* a contradiction. This can manifest itself in statelessness, or the concept of the *kafir* (referring here to an outsider) in one's own land. El-Dabh easily travels from the metaphysical to the theoretical, sometimes in the same conversation. His ideas about aesthetic and universal balance coexist with diverse cultural engagement. El-Dabh is simultaneously on the outside and deeply inside music. The coexistence of the sublime and metaphysical along with the practicality of focused and applied work are common themes of Arab existence and elements of avant-garde movements through history.

Notes

1. Pointless Music issued a surviving excerpt of the composition in 2000 (Young 2007, 26).

2. See Kay Dickinson's introduction to this volume for further elaboration.

References

El-Dabh, Halim. 2010a. "It Is Dark and Damp on the Front." Kent, OH: Halim-El-Dabh Music.

———. 2010b. "Piano Music of Halim El-Dabh." Accessed November 3, 2010. http://www.halimeldabh.com/cdsales.html.

El-Shawan, Salwa. 1980. "The Socio-Political Context of *al-Musika al-Arabiyyah* in Cairo, Egypt: Policies, Patronage, Institutions, and Musical Change (1927–77)." *Asian Music*, 12: 86–128.

———. 1985. "Western Music and Its Practitioners in Egypt (ca. 1825–1985): The Integration of a New Musical Tradition in a Changing Environment." *Asian Music*, 17: 143–53.

———. 2003. "Zwischen Selbstbehauptung und freiem Spiel der Fantisie Neue Music in Ägypten." *Neue Zeitschrift für Musik*, 38–43.

Hovancsek, Mike. 2001. Liner notes to *Crossing into the Electric Magnetic*. Cleveland: Without Fear Recordings.

Mattar, Nahla. 2007. "Contemporary Egyptian Music Compositions: Between Inheritance and Delineation." *Proceedings from the International Music Council's Second World Forum on Music*, 1–23.

Nicholls, David. 1996. "Transethnicism and the American Experimental Tradition." *Musical Quarterly* 80 (Winter): 569–94.

Racy, Ali Jihad. 1981. "Music in Contemporary Cairo: A Comparative Overview." *Asian Music*, 13: 4–26.

Seachrist, Denise. 2002. "This Building Is Going to Fly: Halim El-Dabh and the Columbia-Princeton Electronic Music Center." *Bananafish* 16: 21–28.

———. 2003. *The Musical World of Halim El-Dabh*. Kent, OH: Kent State University Press.

Young, Rob. 2007. "Once upon a Time in Cairo." *Wire* 277: 24–27.

PART III

*Political
Deployments
of the
Avant-Garde*

CHAPTER SEVEN

Sonic Cosmopolitanisms

Experimental Improvised Music and a Lebanese-American Cultural Exchange

⌒

MARINA PETERSON

In February 2007, five Lebanese musicians traveled to the United States to perform with American musicians and dancers as part of the Tabadol Project. With funding from the U.S. Department of State, the Tabadol Project was cultural diplomacy as cultural exchange, a project of international understanding through the arts. "Tabadol," the American organizer explained to audiences, means "exchange" in Arabic. The project was originally planned for July 2006, but the Israel-Hezbollah conflict broke out on July 12, a week before the scheduled dates. The project was rescheduled for February 2007, when five Lebanese musicians traveled to the United States to perform with American musicians and dancers in Chicago, Philadelphia, Baltimore, New York, and Washington, D.C. Four of the five musicians were experimental musicians, two of whom—Mazen Kerbaj and Raed Yassin—were based in Beirut and two—Sharif Sehnaoui and Christine Abdelnour—in Paris (see chapter 3 of this volume for further discussion of these artists). They played, respectively, trumpet, double bass and electronics, guitar, and saxophone. The fifth musician, Ziad El Ahmadié, played 'ud. American musicians who participated in the project included the organizer, Gene Coleman (bass clarinet), myself (cello), Jane Rigler (flute), Alex Waterman (cello), Evan Lipson (double bass), Carmel Raz (violin), and Alex Wing ('ud). Dancers included Asimina Chremos, Nicole Bindler, and Emily Sweeney.[1]

Organizing an exchange around experimental improvised music opens a space for cultural exchange that does not rely on a stereotyped national sound. With sound unmoored from a national "tradition," the "culture" required by cultural diplomacy and exchange is in the body of the musician, as the person, rather than a particular musical tradition or sound, signifies the nation. The inclusion of the 'ud player in the Tabadol Project, who bore the responsibility of sonically representing national culture, created disjunctures in this logic along with new opportunities for improvisation.

The possibility for this project lay in an intersection of cosmopolitanisms in the context of post-9/11 U.S. foreign policy. Cosmopolitanism is often invoked as an aspiration, deployed for its emphases on transcending particularities and openness to difference. Though its terms are debated, the aim, for the most part, is not. Kant's (1784/1991) iteration of cosmopolitanism as universal liberal democracy provides a bulwark with which discussions of cosmopolitanism have had to grapple. Recent scholars, while rejecting Kant's Eurocentrism and elitism, reengage cosmopolitanism as a means of navigating some of the tensions of globalization, to convey an ethos of located difference, and for articulating a project of social justice on a world scale (Appiah 1997; Breckenridge, Pollock, Bhabha, and Chakrabarty 2002; Cheah and Robbins 1998; Harvey 2000; Held 2010; Kant 1991; Vertovec and Cohen 2002). Cosmopolitanism, Cheah posits, "primarily designates an intellectual ethic, a universal humanism that transcends regional particularism" (Cheah 1998, 22). Yet the aspirations of cosmopolitanism toward openness, commonality, and harmony entail transcending the national while depending on the nation as the basis for that transcendence. In this way, the nation remains integral to cosmopolitanism, positioned variously as a maligned particularity of essentialized culture and an attitude of closedness (Breckenridge, Pollock, Bhabha, and Chakrabarty 2002), a scalar stepping-stone toward and component of an aspired-to universalism (Kant 1991), or a home for the cosmopolitan subject (Appiah 1997). These tensions lay at the core of the Tabadol Project.

In practice, cosmopolitanism takes on different shapes, satisfies divergent projects, and has a range of intended and unintended effects. In the Tabadol Project, diverse cosmopolitanisms emerged through a series of turns in the respective logics of cultural diplomacy, improvised music, and national origin. Reflecting cosmopolitanism's status as "a domain of contested politics" (Robbins 1998, 12), in the Tabadol Project the cosmopolitanisms of experimental improvised music and the State Department were distinct, each deployed for particular ends.[2] While the democratic and cosmopolitan aspirations of experimental improvised music support aims of cultural diplomacy to transcend national borders in order to promote understanding and social harmony, the State Department also uses the language of cosmopolitanism for a project of nation-state making that is grounded in territorial specificity.

As participants in the Tabadol Project, the Lebanese musicians were figured at once as national citizens and cosmopolitan subjects. Already cosmopolitan subjects as early twenty-first-century Lebanese and as improvisers, the musicians imbued experimental improvised music with an attitude of openness, articulated in relation to its sonic and social inclusiveness. In this way, their outlook aligned neatly with the cosmopolitan logic of cultural diplomacy. At the same time, in navigating the requirements for recognition and participation, the Lebanese musicians' "located and embodied" (Robbins 1998, 2–3) sonic cosmopolitanism revealed the stresses and margins of the national in a nation-state-making project. Ultimately, despite continual emphasis on territorial specificity, through the course of the Tabadol Project, outlines of a cosmopolitan history of experimental music in Lebanon emerged.

Moving Bodies

The Tabadol Project navigated between the cosmopolitan aspirations of cultural diplomacy and the territoriality of hard diplomacy, using experimental improvised music as an unlocated form that enabled musicians from different countries to play together, while drawing out a national specificity for the purpose of securing State Department funding for exchanges with the Muslim world. State-funded cultural projects remind us of the perdurance of "national culture." Though the nation-state—the context for the culture concept—is a modern phenomenon, an understanding of national culture in which culture is both people and expression is deeply ingrained (Radano and Bohlman 2000). Thus presumed, this notion of national culture is reinscribed in practice and theory, through empirical and intellectual investigation. With the Tabadol Project, the national characteristics of the music and musicians were emphasized by the organizer in order to secure State Department support. The inclusion of an ʿud player, who, in bringing the "sound" understood as signifying nation and culture, reminded everyone of the tenets of such a project. The improvisers bore the burden of the nation in their bodies. Bringing Lebanese musicians into the cosmopolitan fold via cultural exchange makes bodies synecdoches for nation. In the service of the nation, recognition focuses on the "national bodies" of the musicians, while the specificity of music, place, and identity recedes. Bodies are thus marked in themselves and serve as containers for potentially transformed "hearts and minds." Cultural diplomacy is built on the movement of bodies across borders and the affective movement of sentiment, for which music, as a medium that "moves" people, is well situated.

As cultural diplomacy, the Tabadol Project maintained a meaning of cosmopolitanism as an ethic of openness to the world. An idealism of cosmopolitan membership supports the basic goals of cultural diplomacy, insofar as it affirms the potential for culture to transcend the sticky constraints and

potential divisiveness of politics and economics. Yet cultural diplomacy ultimately plays a supporting role to hard diplomacy, using the arts to produce
the nation in relation to overlapping pillars of membership, territory, and
security. Supporting tactics of governmentality (Foucault 1991) employed by
foreign policy to protect and promote the nation and its citizens at home and
abroad, cultural diplomacy uses arts and culture to, as the DiploFoundation
explains, "pursue national interests in an unintrusive, intelligent, convincing
and cost-effective manner. Culture is utilised actively in bilateral and multilat-
eral diplomacy to foster intercultural understanding and meaningful dialogue
between nations" (2003).[3] The U.S. Department of State (n.d.) maintains
that cultural diplomacy supports "our nation's foreign policy." Moreover:
"The ability of cultural programs to promote mutual understanding and
create a platform for ongoing international relations makes them a critical
component of our public diplomacy efforts. Cultural diplomacy transcends
borders, languages and generations, demonstrates our common humanity,
and fosters an appreciation of other cultures while conveying the unique spirit
and values of America." Hence, while hard diplomacy emphasizes a modular
nation-state system (Anderson 2006), cultural diplomacy is framed in terms
of a cosmopolitan aspiration for global democracy and cultural understanding that transcends borders.

Cultural diplomacy, though cosmopolitan in aspiration, depends on national culture. As part of post-9/11 foreign policy, the State Department uses
cultural diplomacy to bring the Muslim world into the cosmopolitan order
of the United States. In February 2003, Andrew Kohut, an independent
pollster and president of the Pew Research Center, told the Senate Foreign
Relations Committee that "The most serious problem facing the U.S. abroad
is its very poor public image in the Muslim world" (2003). Diplomatic efforts
have focused on "winning hearts and minds" by disseminating information
about the benefits of democracy as a system of beliefs and values as well as a
framework for economic prosperity and social stability (Beers 2002; Wright
2004). The Cultural Visitors Program, which provided support for the Tabadol Project, puts into play a series of identifications that move from whole to
part. Each level, imbued by the whole, increasingly loses specificity, such that
the part need only represent the whole in theory. "Muslim world" becomes
"predominantly Muslim country," which becomes "men from the Middle
East." That three of the musicians were Christian, one female, and two lived
in Paris was ultimately insignificant. In *Regulating Aversion: Tolerance in the
Age of Identity and Empire*, Brown attributes this to the "culturalization of
politics," such that "the interchangeability of 'Arab American' and 'Muslim'
in American political discourse is as routine as is elision of the fact that many
Palestinians are Christians and some Israelis are Arabs" (2006, 19).

Cosmopolitanism is thus framed as a national ideology: opening borders in order to open minds. The Lebanese, coming from a country falling into the State Department's category of "predominantly Muslim," are usually not easily granted visas to travel to the United States. Central to the exchange program were the visas the musicians received. As one musician commented, he was not often given a visa; and though when younger he was not interested in traveling to the United States, now he comes "whenever they give me a visa."[4] The visa marks what Derrida (2005, 57) describes as the frontier between the national and the global, determining whether the national border is a barrier prohibiting movement or an invisibility that allows a person to move in a seemingly smooth global space. In international travel, this movement is performed at the immigration counter, where proper visas are shown and scrutinized, passports scanned, movement evaluated. A nation's sovereign authority and trade relations with other nations affect the potential for movement, and papers take on uneven weight at borders, where bodies are slowed in more and less phenomenal ways. For instance, American musicians participating in Irtijal, the Lebanese musicians' festival in Beirut, made sure to not have their passport stamped if they had traveled to Israel, or they would not be allowed into Lebanon. Granting visas to males from predominantly Muslim countries was intended to convey an image of the United States as generous and open—to support an image of cosmopolitanism. This is done carefully and selectively, making those few who are chosen into model citizens of both their nation and the world through the beneficence of the U.S. government. As security efforts are enacted by bringing categorically threatening subjects to the United States, territory and membership merge in the bodies of the Lebanese musicians. Their status as cosmopolitan subjects and citizens of a predominantly Muslim nation are coeval and inseparable, as being granted the former is grounded in the latter. Mobility and immobility are coterminous, enacted in and through the musicians' bodies.

Presenting opportunities for travel for men from predominantly Muslim countries who ordinarily have difficulty obtaining visas to travel to the United States, the State Department occludes its own agency with regard to policy. As Brown (2006) explores, an opposition between a cosmopolitan outlook and intolerance toward Muslims reflects both a tension of liberalism and the secular ethics of tolerance. The musicians' travel experience raised some of these tensions. At the outset, the project was delayed by winter weather, when flights from Paris were canceled. After the musicians arrived in New York a day late, connecting flights were also canceled. Three of the musicians got seats on a small plane to Ohio, but after sitting on the runway they were asked to leave due to weight considerations. They were then rerouted through Washington, D.C., and arrived in Ohio—boarding passes falling out of their pockets—just in time to connect to Chicago. Two days of events I had organized at Ohio University had already been canceled, including a panel discussion with Terry Anderson, a former hostage and then journalism professor at Ohio University. During the three days en route, the musicians left and reentered the airports every few hours to smoke. Every time they came back in, they had to go through security, where their bags and bodies were searched thoroughly because of the ssss on their boarding passes. (After traveling with the musicians from Ohio to Chicago and on to New York, my boarding passes for several subsequent trips were also marked with ssss.) "It was okay," the Lebanese musicians said. "We made friends with the guards, who were very friendly." The purported neutrality of the ssss mark falls under a sign of universality that complies with the cosmopolitan. The marking is said to be randomly assigned, and if it is not, the targeting via "watch lists" also becomes impersonal, as "Muslim world" glosses individual distinctions. Yet limits to cosmopolitan openness emerged around these tactics, as the piece of paper inscribed with the marks that designate and allow travel—name, date, flight number, gate, seat—in another space—airport security check—became a marker of differential ease of movement (Derrida 2005).

The border delineated by the security check begins with the identification of the person with the pass, an interpellation of identity as that of intent to travel and as an individual legitimately authorized by the state in the form of a valid or authentic identification card or passport. The barrier of airport security slows movement, channeling people into cordoned rows, snaking back and forth for orderliness. That first checkpoint authorizes identity through "a driving permit or a *passport* . . . that guarantees the 'self,' the juridical personality of 'here I am'" (Derrida 2005, 61). In the years after 9/11, the ticket, or paper sheet allowing passage, was shown again to the person at the metal detector arch, who identified the presence or absence of the signifying marks of "high security," directing the traveler, with her bags, to the special scanning aisle (in some airports), or to the table on the side, where bags were opened and searched. Returning from New York after the final performance of the Tabadol Project, I had Marx's *Capital, Volume 1* at the top of my bag, in preparation for that week's teaching. In a moment of temporal confusion, I feared the scrutiny of the book, as I thought of Sen. Joseph McCarthy's campaign against communism half a century ago. But the shift from "communist" to "terrorist" is in fact a qualitative shift, and though the language demanding that one deny one's association remains the same, the signifiers of membership are now different, structured, as people around the world are by now well aware, around physique and stereotyping.

The project was intended to create new opportunities and international connections for the Lebanese musicians.[5] The U.S. Department of State

Cultural Visitors Program, which provided support for the Tabadol Project, focuses on providing "opportunities for young performing artists, filmmakers, and arts managers (ages 19–30) from countries with significant Muslim populations to take part in training, mentoring and residency experiences in the United States. These programs offer young professional artists creative approaches in the development of the visitor's artistic talents or arts management skills while promoting an understanding of American society, culture and values."[6] The success of these aims was evaluated through exit interviews. "Why did you decide to come to the U.S., and how will this experience influence you as an artist?" was one of the questions posed by the Kennedy Center for its video interviews. One musician responded, "I met a lot of very nice people who were helpful and friendly and they just need to exchange and make music." Another expanded, saying that the experience is integral to being a musician: "Especially in the music we play, it's music made on exchange and dialog with other musicians. So just meeting other musicians, speaking with them, playing with them, is the only thing that can make you advance with this music. So this was great to meet all kinds of different musicians in all the cities. To be able to share the ideas, to be able to listen to their music, how do they play the same kind of music, how do they see it, why do they do it, it's always different. So it's very good to make this exchange with other musicians, other artists." And more than this, it "opens your mind" to travel to another country, and "changes your view on trivial things, on everyday life." Finally, there were social effects. Another said, "I have a feeling [that in the U.S.] it's really easy to communicate with people, and they don't judge you." Propaganda, to the extent there was any, was expressed by the State Department official's urging the Lebanese musicians, during their first meeting in Chicago, to "let your friends know the U.S. is a good place, that Americans are nice people." U.S. national security, therefore, was fostered at home.

The Art of Cultural Diplomacy

In cultural diplomacy projects, political ideologies are worked through and help produce meanings of "art" that are, in turn, autonomous or extra-artistic, as art is construed as outside of social concerns at the same time as it is used for particular social ends such as cross-cultural exchange and understanding. Music, perhaps especially, contains the tension between a prescribed autonomy and a social basis that can provide a means of knowing a self and an other, and a malleability of meaning that has cohered into a diverse set of attributions. Its ability to support cultural diplomacy is encapsulated in Erlmann's assertion that "music's meanings are not intrinsic to the work of art but are constituted in the social and cultural practices of individuals engaging with music in a variety of ways" (1999, 186). As music is imbued with both universal abstraction and cultural specificity in the context of cultural diplomacy, it constitutes broad sociabilities while "representing" particular and identifiable identities.

The State Department's cultural diplomacy work uses art to affirm a universality of the human experience, a cosmopolitan aspiration that is ultimately construed as nationally specific. Its deployment of a cosmopolitanism framed as specifically American was especially clear during the Cold War (Davenport 2009; Von Eschen 2004), when abstract expressionism, modern dance, and jazz were presented to posit individual creativity and freedom of expression as defining features of the United States. The title song of *The Real Ambassadors*, a jazz opera written by Dave and Iola Brubeck, describes their experience as cultural diplomats, articulating how music was used for diplomacy.

> Who's the real ambassador?
> It is evident we represent American society
> Noted for its etiquette, its manners and sobriety
> We have followed protocol with absolute propriety
> We're Yankees to the core.

On the recording (Brubeck 1962), Louis Armstrong continues, in his gravelly voice:

> I'm the real ambassador.
> It is evident I was sent by government to take your place
> All I do is play the blues and meet the people face-to-face
> I'll explain and make it plain, I represent the human race
> I don't pretend no more.

> Who's the real ambassador?
> Certain facts we can't ignore
> In my humble way I'm the USA
> Though I represent the government
> The government don't represent some policies I'm for.

> Oh we learned to be concerned about the constitutionality
> In our nation segregation isn't a legality
> Soon our only differences will be in personality
> That's what I stand for!
> Who's the real ambassador, yes, the real ambassador?

Musical expression glossed social policy, as Louis Armstrong became "The Real Ambassador" abroad, while segregation still existed in the South. As the song suggests, music supports aspirations for universality better than politics, though when used for State Department tours during the Cold War it ultimately promoted a national agenda. Today the State Department's cultural policy emphasizes classical music, popular music, and jazz, primarily sending musicians abroad as cultural ambassadors for the United States, rather than inviting international musicians here.

An axis of popular/unpopular underlies the choice of what music is used for cultural diplomacy, precisely because of popular music's tendency, as described by Adorno in his essay on jazz, to create a kind of unified massness in its audience by engaging individuals in a collective experience. As he writes, "Jazz must possess a 'mass basis,' the technique must link up with a moment in the subjects" (Adorno 1967, 129). Adorno points to the means by which popular music constitutes a community of listeners who identify with one another through music. "Jazz fans," he writes, "identify with the society they dread for having made them what they are. This gives the jazz ritual its affirmative character, that of being accepted into a community of unfree equals" (Adorno 1967, 126). The music of *The Real Ambassadors*, which reflects the style of jazz musicians who served as cultural ambassadors in the Cold War, invariably has listeners tapping their feet. The song "Cultural Exchange" addresses the motivation for using jazz for cultural diplomacy with the lines: "The State Department has discovered jazz / It reaches folks like nothing has / Like when they feel that jazzy rhythm / They know we're really with 'em / That's what they call cultural exchange." Jazz was used to strike a balance between the poles of universal and national, fine art and popular. The popularity of jazz in Europe at the time guaranteed an audience for the presentation of something distinctly American. The music should be popular enough to have its listeners tapping their feet in unison. However, it could not be *too* popular, as it would risk achieving a universalism (of a global audience) unhooked from the nation.

The music of the Tabadol Project, on the other hand, is an esoteric form that is not performed in major concert halls or other mainstream venues. Decidedly *un*popular, experimental improvisation does not effect a "massness." Its "'technology of articulation'" is not that of the popular, which, as Erlmann suggests, is particularly successful in linking "the materiality of sounds and the creation of affective meanings" (1999, 187). Rather, its form and content are positioned against not only popular genres but against the defining characteristics of "music" itself: melody, harmony, and rhythm. Against "standardization, commercialization, rigidification" (Adorno 1967, 122), experimental improvised music promises to satisfy Adorno's call for an improvised, spontaneous music that would move people outside the much-maligned massness.

While the Lebanese component of the Tabadol Project attracted audiences new to this genre, many among them asked, "What is this? I've never heard anything like this before," and walked out of the concerts. The State Department representative, after hearing the music for the first time in Chicago, said, "Gene [the organizer] will have to frame this well in Washington. The Kennedy Center audience is not used to this kind of music." I had asked the organizer repeatedly if the State Department representatives really knew what kind of music it was. "Yes," he said, "they know. They're open-minded." My impression upon seeing the response of the representative at the concert in Chicago, however, was that she was *not* prepared for the kind of music that was being performed. The Kennedy Center representative was one of the first who said, "I've never heard anything like this before." During the Chicago performance, many Lebanese audience members left at intermission. In Philadelphia, however, audience members unfamiliar with the style stayed until the end, afterward expressing interest in the stories of the musicians and the genre.

Subsequently, the performance at the Kennedy Center was a lesson in how to make experimental music accessible.[7] The free one-hour performance featured a video by one of the musicians, a solo set by the ʿud player, and an improvisation with music and dance. Thus, the audience saw visual images of people and places in Beirut, heard what was presented as "traditional" music, and finally listened to experimental improvised music while watching female dancers move across the stage. While the ʿud player had a transcendent experience performing in the space, one of the improvisers complained about the distance from the audience and the formality of the staging, marking the uneasy fit between experimental improvised music and the space of national cultural diplomacy. Indicating how cultural diplomacy also helps create "art," in being sponsored by the State Department experimental improvised music was imbued with an element of populism that was necessary for this project. The relative popularity of the music reflected a point of divergence between the logics of experimental improvised music and of the State Department. The effort to shape the music into what was required for cultural diplomacy indicates how tactics of governmentality are used to shape and frame their object, even if benignly. At the same time, the need to frame indicated the limits of experimental improvised music to serve as a medium for cultural diplomacy, such that something of the music also escaped the logic of the State Department.

Improvising Exchange

The first performance of the Tabadol Project was in Chicago. Because of the travel delays, this was also the first time we all played together, though most of the musicians had played with each other in various configurations prior to this evening. We started with a large ensemble piece with all the musicians there that night, which, along with the Lebanese, the organizer on bass clarinet, and myself on cello, included an Italian percussion player who was in Chicago at the time. We started off quietly. A recording of the performance preserves the sound, though not our interactions or often the actual instrument being played. Soft percussive tones are heard first, though these could be sounds from the audience. An object with ridges is dragged across the edge of an instrument or string. Something makes an air sound, and the clicks of the ridged object become louder. The sound of a cymbal being tapped with a mallet grows louder. The bass clarinet enters, played with short, repetitive air sounds. The texture becomes increasingly dense as repeating air sounds and soft pitches are heard from percussion, bass clarinet, and trumpet, some sustaining while others begin making patterns, moving into pitches. A high pitch alternates with a blown air sound as the texture is maintained.

The ensemble sinks into an improvisation organized largely around short gestures passed between players of either regular repetition of a sound or a sustained air sound, while others maintain a consistent sound—a high pitch, the texture of a drum being played consistently—that provides a base for these exchanges. After a few minutes, it moves into an ambient sound that is accented with the sound of a triangle. Over the twenty-one minutes of the improvisation, sonic sensibilities and textures emerge and decay. At times everyone will be playing, and then the energy created recedes and fewer players gently intervene in the space created in time, leaving silence between sounds that always remain soft. Halfway through, the group begins to sound like a group. The tentative exchanges created with brief gestures move into more sustained sounds that coalesce as a whole, sounds coming out of the texture and going back in, no single instrument dominating. The sound stops entirely around fifteen minutes. Is this a moment when someone has to decide whether it is the end or whether we continue, as often happens in a group improvisation? The bass clarinet begins again strongly, with pitches, taken up by bowed sounds on percussion instruments, fragments of a melody on the 'ud, repeated, rearranged, their rhythm echoed by the bass clarinet. Someone drags the notched object across an edge or string again as the music becomes more agitated, louder, the 'ud continuing with what its player described later as "Oriental" sounds. Never becoming very loud, as might sometimes be the case, the energy recedes, musicians stop playing. Now only a few play, softly, air sounds and a high pitch sound sustained and silenced, sustained, and silenced.

It is tempting to draw a musical-social analogy through the improvisation, to suggest that one can hear in the sound a process of getting to know one another; that the tentative gestures and lack of coherence in the beginning that move into something that sounds more solidified reflect a process of overcoming our differences, achieving the mandate of the exchange project and of cultural diplomacy in general. That in listening, and making decisions about what, how, and when to play—even when to start and stop—a sonic collective is created that is a metaphor for a social collective in which disagreements are worked out as individuals move toward a cohesion organized around individual expression. The possibility to draw such correlations is supported by the framework of cultural diplomacy and by participating musicians, who confirm such aspirations verbally in other contexts. Yet such a reading projects a desired outcome onto the music, avoiding the messiness of sound and experience and excluding other possible meanings. I want to avoid making claims about the signifying capacities of abstract music, or the generation of a social order from a musical encounter. Both risk generalizing, flattening the multidimensionality of musical practice and sonic production into a singularity of what we want to see.

The democratic qualities of experimental improvised music—whose other face is an abstract modernist universality—emerge in particular practices. In other words, musical and extramusical meanings are created and cohere in formal sonic qualities and musical dynamics. Genre conventions that make links between sonic and social formations possible are the allowable sounds, modes of listening, and temporalities, usually learned from recordings and other musicians. Attributions of democracy, freedom, and openness take shape in diverse musical ways, reflecting the broadness of these categories and the ways in which their identification with music emerges in specific moments and practices.

Form differs among improvised musicians' general practice, with some playing continuous sound, moving from one texture to another, while others use more silence or shorter patterns or phrases. Generally, some consensus is reached in playing, although at times musicians will determinedly follow their normal mode regardless of the sonic input they are receiving. The cohesiveness depends on a similarity of practice—a kind of microgenre—from which they are coming. Relatively strict genre conventions organized around the production of unconventional and often "scratchy" sounds are conveyed through practice as well as discussions of "good" and "bad" improvisers and sessions. Such conventions restrict a simple attribution of "freedom" to the music, though its uniqueness as a musical genre warrants an acknowledgment of the aspiration evoked by the use of the term. At the same time, the ever present notion of "freedom" means that many musicians will resist articulating rules, and insist on their interest in including melody, popular song, and so on.

An avant-garde, underground form, experimental improvisation aspires to achieve Deleuze and Guattari's (1987) call for a deterritorialization of institutional "milieus."[8] Musicians are guided by ear rather than eye, with listening providing the basis for musical ideas and changing sounds. Moreover, the social structure of the global network of improvisers follows another of Deleuze and Guattari's concepts insofar as it is rhizomatic, spreading in a nonrational mode, the shape of which emerges from social interactions and encounters. Experimental improvised music also largely exists outside the market, or culture industry, with many performances played without pay or for door money, for small, intent audiences. With neither composer nor leader, in improvising, the musicians are guided by sound rather than a socially hierarchical system that dictates through scores and conductors what and how they should play. Attali, finding a social order in improvisation that challenges the norms of industrial capitalism, posits that "Any noise, when two people decide to invest their imaginary and their desire in it, becomes a potential relationship, future order" (1985, 143). With experimental improvised music, an abstraction and generalizability of "sound" underlies a belief in the music to facilitate collective sociability (such as with the Chicago-based Association for the Advancement of Creative Musicians and St. Louis's Black Artists Group [Lewis 2008]) that might figure as ahistoricized aspirations for communism (as seen with Cornelius Cardew or the English improvisation group AMM) or liberal democracy (as in the Tabadol Project).

Edwin Prevost (1995), a founding member of AMM who espoused the potential for musical practice to support a utopian socialism, writes, in the prologue of *No Sound Is Innocent*:

Listen!
Follow the sound.
Do not let it escape.
Pursue it and not the spidery threads of allusion.
Wait.
Let the sound come.
Embrace its resonances.
Move
The bow across the strings
In time with your heart.
As if playing for the very first time.

It is not only sound as a defining feature of music, but an idea of "sound" as both abstract and accessible, taking the "sound" of anything played on an instrument or other object, that facilitates these meanings. Thus "sound" both defines and constitutes the meaning of this sonic practice as music at the same time as sound is authorized as music through the historic and institutional trajectories out of which the genre emerged. Capturing the idealism of experimental improvised music, the owner of a Vietnamese restaurant in Columbus, Ohio, asked me, after I described what I had been doing, "You mean musicians from different places are able to play together, even without any rehearsal?"

The Lebanese described the music as inherently democratic; "anyone can do it . . . pick up some objects and make sounds." One musician, an autodidact, described herself as a "plastician of sound, not a musician." She was most interested in something that would be experienced through senses and perception, through "the body instead of the brain," and that would "change the space we are in" such that a new reality emerges. The Lebanese musicians described the music they play as "free improvised music." While the veracity of the term *free* is debated, for many the attribution holds meaning, whether as an actuality or an aspiration. "Freedom," as discussed by the participants of the Tabadol Project, resided with the musical choices of the individual.

For the *'ud* player, who often combined "Oriental" music with flamenco, jazz, or Afro-Cuban music, this was his first experience playing experimental improvisation. He had listened to his friends' recordings and "was always asking a lot of questions about this kind of music—what is right, what is wrong, how can we do it, what is the aim, what is the philosophy behind it?" He professed, "I wanted to try speaking this language of music on my instrument, to see how I can find a way to go into this field with this kind of traditional instrument" and determine whether it is possible or not. As he said, "I am totally convinced I must learn all my life, to learn something new." When the *'ud* player asked the improvisers if he could play rhythm and melody in this music, one responded, "Yes. It's free!" The apparent tension raised by this exchange—a knowledge of the actual limiting conventions of the genre and a response that inscribed the (often protested) idealism of the genre's name—reflects how the musical language of experimental improvisation facilitates these real and imagined social formations.

Another of the Lebanese musicians characterized his playing by saying, "I mainly improvise, I freely improvise, with material I determine what I want to improvise with, not set scales or preexisting music that I improvise with. I improvise out of nothing, out of 'scraps.'" The American organizer interjected, "Out of the ether." "Well," the Lebanese musician continued, "of course, you probably know it is not like this in reality. But I do remember when I first got attracted to this music, what fascinated me was to go from nothing and make something out of it, preexisting material you are working with. This pure improvisation out of sound is what attracted me." Another described the music by saying, "I work with sounds, like the sounds you live [with] every day, mostly train or horns. Sound is wider than music." Extended techniques and the use of objects to alter the "normal" sound of an instrument are common. As the guitarist explained, "Extended techniques, prepared guitar techniques, extend the potential vocabulary of the guitar, generating sound activity that you couldn't possibly generate if you're not extending the guitar with these tools, like a percussionist using sticks and other types of gear to change the sound of the percussion; you can do the same thing with the guitar."

Categories such as cosmopolitanism might attach unevenly to improvised music, used, thus, to create distinctions between improvisational practice. Bolstering the project's potential to support cultural diplomacy efforts, the American organizer stated that it would highlight the fact that there is a similarity of approach in different parts of the world. "What we're doing is not blowing into the horn like Brötzman," the organizer said, referring to a German improviser. Rather, for the musicians involved in the Tabadol Project, emphasis is on an often quiet and extended exploration of sonic textures, with improvisers choosing to mimic the sounds they hear, to find something compatible, or to play against the existing sound. Yet would Peter Brötzman's approach, described as aggressive, loud, raucous, and implicitly self-absorbed, not allow him to be part of a State Department project or participate in cultural diplomacy? Brötzman, like most improvisers, does play with musicians from different countries, so, putting aside the falsifiability of such a question, what emerges is a sense that particular musical modalities and practices support cultural exchange better than others, identifying cultural exchange as something organized around a modicum of gentle consensus rather than aggression. Such discussions again draw extramusical meaning from musical style, correlating sound with social formations.

Evoking a global social formation that is both imagined and constituted in practice, experimental improvised music challenges a perduring requirement of the performance of a distinctly "national sound." The Lebanese musicians used the term *global village* to describe the international network of experimental musicians that facilitated this exchange; musical collaboration that transcended national borders made possible by the geographic spread of a particular genre was, they said, "a positive result of globalization." Music figures as the ground for and negotiation of social relations in the contemporary moment, supporting a range of dynamics as a cultural signifier of belonging in an era of globalization. One of the Lebanese musicians mused that the twentieth century was a time of a new openness to difference, a shift reflected best by artists, who, he said, express such things directly rather than reflecting on them after the fact. Bringing the history of European art to countries "outside the so-called civilized Western countries" would "open new ground and help to strengthen the art practices both in the country you are going to and also in Europe and in America, because then they wouldn't only be speaking to their neighboring cities but to the globe." Drawing conclusions about social relations from improvisation, he said, those working in new artistic fields will leave a legacy of "an open mind, accepting a wider area." Hence, a cosmopolitan outlook described as inherent to experimental improvisation supports a way of being in the world, as a musician who is open to a range of nonmusical sounds might also be open to social difference.

However, while its cosmopolitan qualities were the basis for the exchange, the music, in its role as a medium for cultural exchange as framed by the State Department, was also required to have a specificity of place. The American organizer used the local, particular, and national aspects of the music (or musicians) in order to secure State Department support, aligning music and culture and sublating the cosmopolitan aspirations of the music to the nation (with nation referring both to Lebanon as providing the content of culture and the political requirements of the U.S. via the State Department).[9] Deploying what George Lewis calls the "transcultural practice" (2004, 152) of improvised music for cultural diplomacy in the guise of cultural exchange subordinates the rhizomatic tendency of the music and its social network to governmental tactics. "Seeing like a state" (Scott 1999) draws out and fixes "cultural" aspects of performers with traditions and histories that have not necessarily emerged in these terms in order to meet government arts funding guidelines that use "culture" in part to defuse polarizing politics.

Cosmopolitan Locale

Organizing an exchange around experimental improvised music opens a different kind of space for cultural exchange and suggests what a theory of subjectivity and place in a cosmopolitan order might look like. Different from Appiah's rooted cosmopolitanism, in which a person moves between the particularity of the nation and the cosmopolitanism of the world, here the particularity of place emerges as cosmopolitan. An actual cosmopolitan history of experimental music in Lebanon was obscured by the State Department's co-optation of cosmopolitanism for a national project that stereotypes nations and by the cosmopolitan sensibility that frames improvised music, both of which facilitate sociabilities that are unhooked from place, person, or sound. Yet this local cosmopolitanism—and the Lebanese musicians' position as cosmopolitan national subjects—emerged in efforts to fix a territorial specificity made throughout the exchange. Interview questions posed by the Kennedy Center to the musicians aimed to draw out a national identity: "What do you like most about being an artist in Lebanon?" "What do you find most challenging about being an artist in Lebanon?" "Why is it important for you to stay and work in Lebanon?" In response to these questions, and in other contexts, musicians situated the specificity of Lebanese experimental music in the pre–civil war cosmopolitanism of Beirut, the "Paris of the Middle East." Self-professed as the only experimental improvisers in Lebanon today, these musicians connect their work to a longer history of free jazz and other experimental music coming to and emerging from the city before and during the civil war, which lasted from 1975 until 1990. As one said, "This city has a very great history, culture and art from the sixties, even early seventies, and it was all destroyed because of the madness, and when the civil war ends, no one was winning anything, we all lose with civil war. So I'm trying now also to build this new scene and new activity and new language of Beirut and all kinds of arts and also a center for arts in the Middle East." In opening a new scene, these musicians are also "beginning to open space for others."

Experimental music—in spite of or along with its cosmopolitan aspirations and tendencies—has emerged out of particular histories, such that the pockets of players in this "global village" have different reasons and conditions of possibility for their practice. Moving across a geography shaped by colonialism and war, the Lebanese improvisers involved in the Tabadol Project were exposed to improvised music in Paris: the guitarist began playing after moving to the former colonial metropole in college, where he met his wife, the autodidact saxophonist, who was born in Paris after her parents moved there at the beginning of the civil war. They shared the music with friends still in Lebanon and, together, started Beirut's experimental music festival, Irtijal.

Those musicians in the Tabadol Project who live in Beirut are committed to staying there. Part of their desire to stay in Lebanon is to bring the world there, fostering openness to new things. They feel experimental improvisation allows them to participate in the international world of contemporary art. Experimental practice provides them with a way of "fighting the ethnocentricity of art." Having had to go outside Lebanon to "get a grasp" of contemporary art, their crucial and most important work is "bringing it back to Lebanon so future generations might have a chance to be confronted with this." Such aspirations are congruent with State Department goals of fostering democracy around the world, whether through politics proper or with modes of "democratic" thinking that include openness to difference and a cosmopolitan outlook. These goals are based in an understanding of the world as divided between "warring figures of the free, the tolerant, and the civilized on one side, and the fundamentalist, the intolerant, and the barbaric on the other" (Brown 2006, 6). Insofar as experimental music is framed as aligning with and facilitating openness to and tolerance of difference generally, it supports such a project.

But doing this with experimental improvisation also reflects a particular cosmopolitanism of Beirut, rooted in childhoods of war. Their cosmopolitanism is grounded not only in their movement between Beirut and Paris, the Middle East and Europe, but in an international geography of war. The condition of war in which they grew up and that drove intercontinental movements continues to imbue the music. Those who lived in Lebanon during the civil war described their music as reflecting the sound of bombing that was the background of their childhoods. At the same time, they are ambivalent about this identification (Burkhalter 2010, 2011), uneasy about having their art defined by war, and even more uneasy about the international recognition gained by work that was made within and in response to war. During the 2006 conflict, Mazen Kerbaj posted his own comics on a blog that was read widely by an international audience. Though he had never made art about the civil war, he felt obliged to respond to this war, and was happy that his blog brought attention to the suffering in Lebanon. The blog was significant for facilitating relations between Israeli and Lebanese people, which was otherwise impossible. It also supported artists, pushing "more people to work more, and show their stuff, and resisting" in this way. Yet, rather than aiming to bring awareness to a cause, making art was a means of maintaining Kerbaj's sanity. War was a tragedy, with lasting human consequences of poverty and suffering, and the musicians understood why art would be a secondary concern within the country.

Along with his blog, Kerbaj's widely circulated improvisation with the sounds of bombing in summer 2006 is part of a wider tradition of Lebanese contemporary artists responding to war (Burkhalter 2009, 117–22; Cotter 2006; Kerbaj 2006). This improvisation is, undoubtedly, of a very particular place and time. "Starry Night" begins softly. Ambient sounds are heard, and overtones on the trumpet. He pauses, then blows harder, as a bomb explodes. The trumpet continues and another bomb explodes, this one setting off car alarms, which continue as Kerbaj scrapes and blows a bit, then pauses, coming back with forceful air sounds. A dog barks. Another bomb, followed by car alarms. Kerbaj plays softer than the street sounds, then comes in stronger, again with air sounds. He plays with and against the street and the city, the bombs, traffic, possibly blowing through the plastic tube he often attaches to his trumpet, making air sounds that in a painting would appear as short, forceful strokes. One hears an intensity of expression. He pauses. Another bomb. Playing again, the sounds shift to higher, sustained pitches, mixed with rough, repeating air sounds. "Starry Night" becomes "evidence" of a geographic—and by extension cultural—specificity expressed through music. Yet at the same time, turning the bombs into *sound* draws on the nonlocalized logic of the musical genre to turn this specificity into something general and abstract as part of an attempt to defuse a fear of the actual danger of the bombs. These bombs, while known to be in Beirut, also evoke a geopolitics of war, reflecting a global divide that creates a commonality among the parts of the world that might have such a soundscape—a rather different cosmopolitan geography (Pollock, Bhabha, Breckenridge, and Chakrabarty 2000).

Bringing experimental practice to Beirut, these musicians create art that is rooted there, that is about the city and about Lebanon. Hence, they create a located cosmopolitanism through an avant-garde form that requires a struggle and commitment to practice, to place, and to building something. Something that is in itself and for itself and that is neither for the West nor intended to prove something to the West. As one of the musicians explained, Beirut "was really the center of new media and new art." It is "a city that accepts new experiences. Other cities in the sixties and seventies in the Arab world don't at all." So many were "conservative, and most of the artists went to Beirut. I want this back for Beirut because I feel better being an artist in Beirut and having all these artists coming and trying to make exchange and also going to exhibit in other Arab cities." You can "make your art so at least you speak the same language as someone who doesn't know anything about you," thus making a "bridge for exchange and for culture and for art." Such a characterization reveals a deep history of experimental practice in the Middle East that is significant for understanding the development of multiple international "scenes" of experimental musical practice (Heffley 2005; Fischlin and Heble 2004; Plourde 2009), as well as a cosmopolitanism that entails connections within the Arab world and beyond it (Meijer 1999).

In this context, the cosmopolitan is localized, with particular meaning in and for the Middle East. In a recent essay published in the online journal *Perfect Sound Forever*, Sharif Sehnaoui argues for the significance of cosmopolitanism for the Middle East, locating the global—as an aspiration expressed in improvisation—in the particular historical and contemporary sociopolitical dynamics of the region:

Our activities help to reach new ground for improvisation, contemporary, free jazz, electronic, experimental kinds of music in our increasingly globalized world. This new tendency is vital to the music world in general and has been a constant in the 20th Century when we see that several new regions have developed possibilities as in South-America, Russia, Eastern Asia, Northern and East Europe among other places. The very survival of these highly underrated and, by nature, non-ethno-centric musics are allowed by this movement. So why not the Arab world as well? This is all the more crucial considering the international spotlight on this part of the world, filled with stories of war, extremism, fanaticism, misery, blood and exploitation. Music is one of the main elements that can be helpful both as an internal factor and as an external one as different voices and ways inch towards global interaction. (Sehnaoui 2007)

A colonial history, civil war, experiences of living in a condition of war, and the call for a located cosmopolitan practice reflect a particularity of place that is political and historical rather than one imbued with an "essentialized culture."

Cosmopolitanisms at Large

The multiple ways in which musical practice and outlooks meld seamlessly with those of cultural diplomacy made the Tabadol Project possible. At the same time, the fissures between a cosmopolitan subject and a nation-state-making apparatus emerge in the particularities of the project, fissures that do not reflect a generalized tension of "local" and "global" inherent to cosmopolitanism but that suggest incompatibilities, limits, and the general lumpiness of meeting points between divergent social spaces and modalities. Though the project's formation was opportunistic, by working through the available categories and requirements with a musical form that fit both neatly and uneasily with cultural diplomacy, it raises questions about what the minimum criteria of national culture are, what its markers are, and when and how it is policed. Hence, specific concerns such as visas and airport security, taste and the limits of the popular, and reified national culture present limits to a totalizing cosmopolitanism, reflecting instead multiple and divergent cosmopolitanisms that were put into play around a range of motivations and commitments.

Cosmopolitanism is worked out in difficult ways in practice. It is about being in the world, not only about relating to others in a particular way. Many things share cosmopolitan aspirations, but the question is how to bring together ideals and practice, practice that is not only toward an ideal, but a livedness, an experience that is cosmopolitan. Such experience might not be easy or gentle, but instead might be based in conditions of war and struggle. Cosmopolitanisms, thus, emerge in multiple modalities, whether American diplomacy that draws on a Kantian cosmopolitanism that aspires to transcend the nation through a particular mode of being national, a musical practice inscribed with and inscribing social potentialities, or an experience of being in the world and being worldly from a place marked as intolerant while carrying a cosmopolitan legacy inflected with domination and conflict.

Notes

1. A complete listing of participants and venues can be found on the organizer's website: http://www.soundfield.org/tabadol.html (accessed December 6, 2010).

2. See Stokes (2007) for a rich and nuanced examination of musical cosmopolitanism and its particular valences in a Middle Eastern context, and Turino (2000) for an exploration of music as caught up in dynamics of nationalism and cosmopolitanism in Zimbabwe.

3. The DiploFoundation is a nonprofit with offices in Malta, Geneva, and Belgrade that supports diplomacy through educational programs, research, and technology.

4. Artists traveling to the U.S. to perform submit a special application describing their "cultural uniqueness" that is vetted by Department of Homeland Security officials. After 9/11, musicians from Muslim countries have been consistently denied visas to travel to festivals (Peterson 2003).

5. Statements by the musicians are drawn from discussions during the course of the project and from video of State Department exit interviews administered by the organizer. Because these statements were not articulated in formal interview contexts and especially due to the private nature of the video, I have chosen to not attribute statements to specific musicians.

6. In 2010 the Cultural Visitors Program focused on bringing artists "particularly from diverse and traditionally underrepresented communities" (John F. Kennedy Center for the Performing Arts 2010).

7. The performance can be viewed online at http://www.kennedy-center.org/explorer/artists/?entity_id=16867&source_type=B (accessed December 6, 2010).

8. For Deleuze and Guattari, only LaMonte Young achieves deterritorialization with his single computer-generated tones (1987, 344).

9. The seeds of the Tabadol Project were planted in July of 2005, when an American composer, bass clarinettist, and concert organizer obtained sponsorship by the State Department as a CultureConnect Envoy (a program that is now defunct) to travel to Lebanon to participate in the Irtijal festival in Beirut. As a CultureConnect Envoy, he also conducted improvisation workshops and gave additional concerts in diplomatic settings. There was criticism at the time by other American musicians, and much discussion about what the relationship with the State Department entailed. He argued that the artistic work and experience were more significant than the source of funding. Drawing on the relationship then established with the State Department representatives (who work primarily in countries with large Muslim populations), he organized the Tabadol Project, which extended the cultural exchange that provided the basis for the funding for the initial trip by bringing Lebanese musicians to the United States. Funding for this project was provided by the U.S. Department of State and the Kennedy Center as part of the State Department's Global Cultural Initiative.

References

Adorno, Theodor. 1967. "Perennial Fashion—Jazz." In *Prisms*, 119–32. Cambridge, MA: MIT Press.

Anderson, Benedict. 2006. *Imagined Communities: Reflections on the Origin and Spread of Nationalism*. London: Verso.

Appiah, Kwame Anthony. 1997. "Cosmopolitan Patriots." *Critical Inquiry* 23 (3): 617–39.

Attali, Jacques. 1999. *Noise: The Political Economy of Music*. Minneapolis: University of Minnesota Press.

Beers, Charlotte. 2002. "U.S. Public Diplomacy in the Arab and Muslim Worlds." Remarks at the Washington Institute for Near East Policy. Washington, DC: Washington Institute for Near East Policy. http://www.state.gov/r/us/10424.htm.

Breckenridge, Carol, Sheldon Pollock, Homi Bhabha, and Dipesh Chakrabarty, eds. 2002. *Cosmopolitanism*. Durham, NC: Duke University Press.

Brown, Wendy. 2006. *Regulating Aversion: Tolerance in the Age of Identity and Empire*. Princeton, NJ: Princeton University Press.

Brubeck, Dave and Iola. 1962. *The Real Ambassadors*. Columbia OL 5850.

Burkhalter, Thomas. 2009. "Challenging the Concept of Cultural Difference—'Locality' and 'Place' in the Music of Contemporary Beirut." PhD diss. University of Bern (Switzerland).

———. 2010. "Tarek Atoui—or: Reflections on the New Musical Avant-Gardes of the 21st Century." In *Indicated by Signs*. Edited by Aleya Hamza and Edit Molnar. Cairo: Bonner Kunstverein, Goethe Institute Kairo.

———. 2011. "Between Art for Art's Sake and Musical Protest: How Musicians from Beirut React to War and Conflict." *Popular Music and Society* 34 (2).

Cheah, Pheng. 1998. Introduction Part II: "The Cosmopolitical—Today." In *Cosmopolitics: Thinking and Feeling beyond the Nation*. Edited by Pheng Cheah and Bruce Robbins, 20–41. Minneapolis: University of Minnesota Press.

Cheah, Pheng, and Bruce Robbins, eds. *Cosmopolitcs: Thinking and Feeling beyond the Nation*. Minneapolis: University of Minnesota Press.

Cotter, Suzanne, ed. 2006. *Out of Beirut*. Oxford: Modern Art Oxford.

Davenport, Lisa. 2009. *Jazz Diplomacy: Promoting America in the Cold War Era*. Jackson: University Press of Mississippi.

Deleuze, Gilles, and Félix Guattari. 1987. *A Thousand Plateaus: Capitalism and Schizophrenia*. Minneapolis: University of Minnesota Press.

Derrida, Jacques. 2005. *Paper Machine*. Palo Alto, CA: Stanford University Press.

DiploFoundation. 2003. *Cultural Diplomacy*. Malta: DiploFoundation. Accessed June 2, 2010, http://textus.diplomacy.edu/textusBin/BViewers/oview/culturaldiplomacy/oview.asp.

Erlmann, Veit. 1999. *Music, Modernity, and the Global Imagination: South Africa and the West*. New York: Oxford University Press.

Fischlin, Daniel, and Ajay Heble, eds. 2004. *The Other Side of Nowhere: Jazz, Improvisation, and Communities in Dialogue*. Middletown, CT: Wesleyan University Press.

Foucault, Michel. 1991. "Governmentality." In *The Foucault Effect: Studies in Governmentality*. Edited by Graham Burchell, Colin Gordon, and Peter Miller, 87–104. Chicago: University of Chicago Press.

Harvey, David. 2000. "Cosmopolitanism and the Banality of Geographic Evils." *Public Culture* 12 (2): 529–64.

Heffley, Mike. 2005. *Northern Sun, Southern Moon: Europe's Reinvention of Jazz*. New Haven: Yale University Press.

Held, David. 2010. *Cosmopolitanism: Ideals, Realities & Deficits*. Cambridge: Polity Press.

John F. Kennedy Center for the Performing Arts. 2010. *Explore the Arts* (Performing Artists Cultural Visitors Program). http://www.kennedy-center .org/explorer/artists/?entity_id=22192&source_type=B.

Kant, Immanuel. 1991. "Idea for a Universal History with a Cosmopolitan Purpose." In *Political Writings*, 54–60. Cambridge: Cambridge University Press.

Kerbaj, Mazen. 2006. "Starry Night." Accessed December 2, 2010, http://muniak .com/mazenkerbaj.html.

Kohut, Andrew. 2003. "American Public Diplomacy in the Islamic World." Hearing of the Senate Committee on Foreign Relations. http://people-press .org/commentary/display.php3?AnalysisID=63.

Lewis, George E. 2004. "Improvised Music after 1950: Afrological and Eurological Perspectives." In *The Other Side of Nowhere: Jazz, Improvisation, and Communities in Dialogue*. Edited by Daniel Fischlin and Ajay Heble, 131–62. Middletown, CT: Wesleyan University Press.

———. 2008. *A Power Stronger than Itself: The AACM and American Experimental Music*. Chicago: University of Chicago Press.

Peterson, Marina. 2003. ""World in a Weekend': Public Concerts and the Emergence of a Transnational Urban Space." *Journal of Popular Music Studies* 15 (2): 121–39.

———. 2010. "Garden, City, World: Los Angeles' Late Twentieth Century Multicultural Arts Festivals." In *The Politics of Cultural Programming in Public Spaces*. Edited by Robert Gehl and Victoria Watts. Cambridge: Cambridge Scholars Publishing.

Plourde, Lorraine. 2009. "Difficult Music: An Ethnography of Listening for the Avant-Garde in Tokyo." PhD diss., Columbia University.

Pollock, Sheldon, Homi Bhabha, Carol Breckenridge, and Dipesh Chakrabarty. 2000. "Cosmopolitanisms." *Public Culture* 12 (3): 577–89.

Prevost, Edwin. 1995. *No Sound Is Innocent*. Essex: Copula.

Radano, Ronald M., and Philip V. Bohlman. 2000. *Music and the Racial Imagination*. Chicago: University of Chicago Press.

Robbins, Bruce. 1998. Introduction Part I: "Actually Existing Cosmopolitanism." In *Cosmopolitics: Thinking and Feeling beyond the Nation*. Edited by Pheng Cheah and Bruce Robbins, 1–19. Minneapolis: University of Minnesota Press.

Scott, James C. 1999. *Seeing Like a State: How Certain Schemes to Improve the Human Condition Have Failed*. New Haven, CT: Yale University Press.

Sehnaoui, Sharif. 2007. "The Lebanese Music Scene: Why Free Improvised Music?" *Perfect Sound Forever*. Accessed May 25, 2007, http://www.furious.com /perfect/lebanonmusic.html.

Stokes, Martin. 2007. "On Musical Cosmopolitanism." Paper presented at the Macalester International Roundtable, Institute for Global Citizenship, Macalester College, St. Paul, Minnesota. Accessed December 2, 2010, http://digitalcommons.macalester.edu/intlrdtable/3.

Turino, Thomas. 2000. *Nationals, Cosmopolitans, and Popular Music in Zimbabwe*. Chicago: University of Chicago Press.

U.S. Department of State. n.d. Cultural Programs Division. Accessed August 16, 2010, http://exchanges.state.gov/cultural/index.html.

U.S. Department of State. n.d. *Diplomacy: The U.S. Department of State at Work*. http://www.state.gov/r/pa/ei/rls/dos/46732.htm.

Vertovec, Steven, and Robin Cohen. 2002. *Conceiving Cosmopolitanism: Theory, Context, and Practice*. Oxford: Oxford University Press.

Von Eschen, Penny M. 2004. *Satchmo Blows Up the World: Jazz Ambassadors Play the Cold War*. Cambridge, MA: Harvard University Press.

Wright, Robin. 2004. "U.S. Struggles to Win Hearts, Minds in the Muslim World: Diplomacy Efforts Lack Funds, Follow-Through." *Washington Post*, August 20: A01.

CHAPTER 8

Activism and Authenticity

Palestinian and Related Hip-Hop
in an International Frame

⌒

CAROLINE ROONEY

> He dreams as I do, as the angel does
> That life is here . . . not over there.
> —Mahmoud Darwish, "Under Siege"[1]

First, a shimmering cymbal sound with two soft beats from the kick drum over a dark screen bearing the film's title: *Local Angel* (2002).[2] The film begins with this pause, and then all of a sudden there is a violent explosion of sound synced to flashing strobe lights. The sound and the images reveal a drummer's body pounding out a fast and relentless 4/4 beat formation with little variation, a near wall of sound, while the drummer's head is covered by an Abu Ghraib/Guantánamo Bay–style hood. What should we make of this strange figure, at once anonymized and silent, depersonalized, and yet energetically animated with a Dionysian drive: a drive that is both exhilarating in its abandon and menacing in its implied blind violence? As the drum solo reaches its climax, the body of the drummer lifts up and is thrown back as if being hit by staccato flying bullets of sound before crumpling and slumping.

The overall effect of this opening scene from Udi Aloni's *Local Angel* is a little like these stanzas from William Blake's "The Tyger":

> What the hammer? What the chain?
> In what furnace was thy brain?
> What the anvil? What dread grasp
> Dare its deadly terrors clasp?

When the stars threw down their spears
And watered heaven with their tears
Did he smile his work to see?
Did he who made the Lamb make thee? (2008, 197)

That is to say, there is the same inexplicably introduced hyperforceful (four-beat) rhythm—"What the hammer? What the chain?"—placed within a context that raises the question of the relation of this energy to the angelic and divine. Udi Aloni's film, announcing itself as *Local Angel*, offers as first "illustration" or juxtaposition the hybrid figure of the terrorist-drummer accompanied by a voiceover that speaks of the creation of angels and the embattled relationship between human nature and the divine. Without further explanation, the film cuts to a New York cityscape (over a jazzy, klezmer-style sound track) of high-rise buildings pasted with huge billboards of aspirational lifestyles and fashions, featuring, in particular, advertisements for Gap clothing. Our attention is then directed to the gap-toothed grimace of the city's skyline, the gaps here being the absence of the Twin Towers in the otherwise stock panning—"Look upon my works, ye Mighty, and despair!" (Shelley 2008, 1079)—of the city's iconic skyscraper horizon.

There are connections to be made, therefore, between these staggered or stuttering "G/gaps." In particular, there is a connection to be made between the sheen of fashionable modernity at its most awesome and the scene of the masked drummer. As the autobiographical musico-political documentary of *Local Angel* unfolds, it may be said that Udi Aloni's reaction to 9/11 broadly resembles the portrayal in a short story entitled "Twilight of the Superheroes," by Deborah Eisenberg: "It was as if there had been a curtain painted with the map of the earth. . . . The planes struck, tearing through the curtain of that blue September morning, exposing the dark world that lay right behind it, of populations ruthlessly exploited, inflamed with hatred, and tired of waiting for change to happen by" (2006, 33).

Or, with a less oppositional schema, it is as if 9/11 served to rend America's taken-for-granted universalism, in the form of American metropolitan civilization constituting the vanguard of modernity, to reveal its actuality as a mythology—in fact, as a blinkered insularity. Furthermore, Aloni understands, more readily than many, that there is a connection to be made between "here" and "there," between the trauma of 9/11 and Israel-Palestine, or as he says in the film: "After the event of September 11, I told myself it all begins over there."

While *Local Angel* deliberately plays with the figure of quasi-monstrous terrorist menace at its start, once the trajectory of Aloni's film takes him back to Israel, his homeland, this mythic figure is unhooded, ironically via the figure of "the hoodie," as we are introduced to Palestinian youth through the hip-hop group DAM, the members of DAM looking and sounding much like their American counterparts. It is as if audiences are presented with an historically concrete anthropological instance of Foucault's following Sphinx-like statement: "Superficially, one might say that knowledge of man, unlike the sciences of nature, is always linked, even in its vaguest form, to ethics or politics; more fundamentally, modern thought is advancing towards that region where man's Other must become the Same as himself" (1982, 328). For now, this statement is important in how it illuminates the point that hip-hop in a Palestinian context is a matter of its interrelated potentialities as regards its protest poetry dimension, its internationalism, its improvisational technologies, and its "keep it real" appeal.

A few general remarks on the avant-garde dimensions of hip-hop may be put forward as a means of contextualization. While the "hop" of "hip-hop" pertains to the music's beat, the "hip" pertains to what is trendy, current, of the moment, clued up, streetwise. Not all hip-hop is avant-garde, of course. Much of it is trendy in the self-commodifying sense. However, Adorno's widespread rejection of popular culture in favor of an elitist avant-garde—one whose difficulty and aloofness constitute its resistance to capitalist instrumen-talization—does not apply to hip-hop. The avant-garde strands of hip-hop remain popular and antielitist. The anti-co-optivist stance of this aspect of hip-hop shares a certain cultural horizon with Arab preoccupations with authenticity (*asala*). However, the authenticity at stake, as regards hip-hop, is not a matter of cultural purity. The "roots" in question may instead be said to reflect a commitment to the affiliative orality of "street" origins, and not filiative tradition. That is, this authenticity is a question of activism.

Although African American in its provenance, hip-hop has become one of the predominant forms of expression of global youth culture. With re-spect to this global youth culture, a travelogue by Jared Cohen, *Children of Jihad*, has some telling observations to offer.[3] *Children of Jihad* chronicles Cohen's travels around the Middle East, where he meets the young people of Iran, Iraq, Syria, and Lebanon and compares lifestyles, viewpoints, and values. On the one hand, Cohen finds that the youth of the Middle East and the youth of America have much in common: they are mutually into similar fast-food joints, trendy fashion, bars, clubs, movies, technology, and popular music. With respect to this discovery, what Cohen finds challenged is the ideological stereotype produced by Western commentators of Islamic cultures as fearful of and resistant to capitalist modernity. On the other hand, Cohen is troubled by what seems to him to be a paradox, this "paradox" being that, while there is a global mutuality or cosmopolitan connectivity amongst youth on a cultural level, youth in the Middle East are often radically critical of America's Middle East foreign policies, especially as regards Israel-Palestine. Cohen writes:

> Technology and unprecedented access to the outside world have given these young people sources of entertainment and means for communication that their parents never enjoyed. They embrace connectivity that transcends politics, religion, and extremism. The young men of Hezbollah were a perfect example. One minute they uttered extremist rhetoric about the American and Israeli governments, the next they went to nightclubs and danced to American music, watched American movies, and talked favorably about the concept of "America," a land as positively mythic for them as for generations of chasers of the American dream.
>
> Technology widened the generation gap, affording these youth the opportunity to communicate in new and liberating ways. I found youth of every political persuasion in the Middle East living multiple lives, separating their social and recreational activities from their ideological enterprises. (2007, 6)

Cohen therefore configures Middle Eastern youth as doppelgängers: doubling as partly liberal Dr. Jekylls and partly terrorizing Mr. Hydes. What he does not reflect on is that this doubling effect could well be a matter of his own projections. In fact, his position may be said to contain a number of questionable assumptions. Firstly, he assumes that it is a contradiction to like American culture but to dislike American ideology, especially as regards U.S. foreign policy. That is, it is as if the diversity of American cultural forms and the positions of American foreign-policy makers are considered to be automatically at one with each other, which would be at odds with the ideal of democratic freedom. Secondly, he assumes that the popular culture of global youth is American by virtue of provenance, as if there were not multiple modernities with exchanges of influence and adaptations that are not just unidirectional. And thirdly, Cohen seems to equate universality with the commodity form, which would constitute a repression of nonstandardized forms of universality.

Ironically, while Cohen presumes some kind of continuity between American popular culture and American international governance, he notices several times that the youth of the Middle East are careful to distinguish between the American people and the American government. He writes: "Middle Eastern youth are far more sophisticated than earlier generations in their ability to distinguish between governments, people and religions. Hardly fans of their own governments and the ruling circles, they themselves bristle at being associated with regimes they don't support. Most know the difference between Americans and the American government and they know the difference between Jews and Israel; they want Americans to know the difference between, say, the supreme leader of the Islamic Republic and Iranians" (2007, 272).

Contradictions abound in Cohen's book because, while he is able to acknowledge differing local particularities, he writes as if ultimately the only possible form of universality would be (American) globalization. It may be proposed that the figure of the terrorist as an uncanny double arises at the very point at which other kinds of universality are rejected and repressed. For one related example, Mohsin Hamid dramatizes the interplay between sociopolitical ostracism and doubling effects in *The Reluctant Fundamentalist* (2007).

Among the popular culture forms that Cohen encounters in the Middle East is hip-hop. For instance, he goes to a party in Beirut at which, he says, young Lebanese are dancing to American hip-hop and Arab dance music (2007, 111). Overall, he seems to assume that modernity is American and that this American modernity constitutes the basis for the universal, implying that there is no significant difference between the commodity form and a politics and culture of modernity (admittedly, more of a modernist consideration than a postmodernist one). What I now wish to explore is how Arab hip-hop, especially Palestinian hip-hop, serves to challenge this globalization model of the universal. A reworked form of hip-hop offers an alternative internationalism marked by a youthful politics of the left, one that is fiercely critical of Israel and Israel's supporters.

We can aptly begin with the Palestinian rap group DAM, actually the first Palestinian rap group, the group that Aloni's *Local Angel* served to draw international attention to. A further film, one inspired by *Local Angel*, Jackie Reem Salloum's documentary *Slingshot Hip Hop* (2008), has also widely disseminated the work of DAM alongside other Palestinian hip-hop groups, including the Gaza-based PR (The Palestinian Rapperz) and Arapeyat (a female duo). While Aloni's film makes use of an experimental musical bricolage to demonstrate the intertwined fates of Israelis and Palestinians, Salloum's film may be said to offer a more empirical study of Palestinian hip-hop from a particularly Palestinian perspective, but also a perspective that is cosmopolitan, as will be evidenced.[4]

As this chapter has begun to indicate, Aloni deliberately sets out to challenge American and Israeli stereotypes in his film, especially of Palestinians as fanatical Islamist terrorists. For this reason, he shows DAM performing its now famous song "Who's the Terrorist?" and, more widely, Aloni's film, by meeting with Palestinians on their own terms, importantly attempts to offset the emotionally charged aggression of identity politics with the possibilities of interaction on a human level.[5] In addition, through merely drawing attention to Palestinian hip-hop, with its stylistic visual, vocal, and musical resemblances to American hip-hop, both *Local Angel* and *Slingshot Hip Hop* serve to complicate ideological assumptions of "us" and "them."

In *Slingshot Hip Hop*, Tamer Nafar, of DAM, speaks of the influences on the artistic formation of DAM, and, of course, American hip-hop is mentioned as a crucial influence here. Yet DAM offers not only an acknowledgment of this cultural source but also singles out the work of African American rapper Tupac Shakur as a key influence, together with the work of several poets and writers from Arab literary and musical cultures. Apart from Tupac, there are a number of rap influences, including Chuck D and Public Enemy, while literary influences include Mahmoud Darwish and Edward Said, as well as women writers such as Hanan al-Shayk (a Lebanese writer), Ahlam Mosteghameni (an Algerian writer), and Nawal El-Sadaawi (an Egyptian writer).[6]

There are two points that can be made in relation to this choice and combination of cultural sources. The first is that while the Palestinian liberation struggle is unavoidably a national struggle, the cultural movement supporting it in the case of DAM as well as other Palestinian groups is not just narrowly nationalist (purely Palestinian) but international in its reach both in terms of influences and audiences. The second point, reinforcing the first, is that the figures that inspire DAM tend to configure an international solidarity amongst the oppressed beyond borders.

So, here, Tupac is a significant influence as one of the first and most widely disseminated rappers to write with a rebellious social conscience of international reach. In "Just a Breath of Freedom," a poem about protest in the context of South Africa, he writes: "Held captive 4 your politics / They wanted 2 break your soul / They ordered the extermination / of all minds they couldn't control."[7] And in "Liberty Needs Glasses," he writes: "justice stubbed her big toe on mandela / and liberty was misquoted by the indians / slavery was just a learning phase / forgotten with out a verdict."[8] The American rap scene is itself far from homogenous, with two dominant tendencies that might be singled out. Drawing here on terminology put forward by Hannah Arendt, who herself draws on Bernard Lazare, as initially applied to European Jews of the nineteenth century and first half of the twentieth century, it may be proposed that there is a parvenu hip-hop scene and a pariah hip-hop scene.[9] According to Arendt, the parvenu is an outsider who seeks to assimilate within the structures of power, to make it up the social ladder and gain acceptance by the elite, while the conscious pariah embraces an outsider status defiantly in solidarity with other pariahs. My contention is that there is a parvenu kind of African American rap or upwardly mobile rap, which is all about seeking wealth, fame, and acceptance (for instance, Jay-Z). Distinct from this is rap that entails a pariah solidarity with all who are oppressed. This can be noted of some of Tupac's work (for instance, as quoted earlier) but is especially characteristic of the radical rap of Peruvian-born Immortal Technique. Immortal Technique's "The War against Us All" (feat. Mumia Abu Jamal) contains these lines, sampled from a speech by Mumia: "It [the Iraq war] is ultimately a war on us all. That's because the billions and billions of U.S. dollars being spent on this war . . . is money that'll never be spent on education, on health care, on the reconstruction of crumbling public housing or to train and place the millions of workers who have lost manufacturing jobs in the past three years alone. This war in reality is a war against the nation's workers and poor. . . . What's next? Iran? Syria? Venezuela?" (2004).[10]

In the song "Dedication" ("Ihda"), DAM offers its dedication to all the oppressed people of the world: "To whoever is caged in a nightmare full of dreams"; "Dedicated to all the people / Walking amongst barbarians but still remaining human."[11] The group may be said to be positioning itself in a similar place to Marxist internationalists of the past, particularly as associated with liberation movements, but there are some significant differences. DAM's embrace of the Palestinian struggle and resistance is not really a militant one: the group is explicit about its commitment to work through words, culture, and education in tandem with rejecting violence and hatred. In *Slingshot Hip Hop*, Tamer Nafar explains: "I don't want to be misunderstood. We reach for peace." In a situation where Palestinian youth have no goals, no facilities, and are demoralized, one rapper maintains: "Rap gives us oxygen." Tamer Nafar is shown working with children in Lyd (commonly known as Lod in the Hebrew), since he wishes to teach them "how they can help their country with music, not violence."[12] And in DAM's song "Change Tomorrow" ("Nghayyir Bukra"), Tamer Nafar raps, as translated from the Arabic: "We want education, we want improvement / To have the ability to change tomorrow." And: "Keep on asking for a life of equality / And if someone asks you to hate say no" (DAM 2006).[13] In "Who's the Terrorist?" ("Min Irhabi") DAM outlines their predicament: "I'm not against peace. Peace is against me."[14] Meanwhile, in *Slingshot Hip Hop*, rapper Mohammed says that after Israeli snipers shot at Palestinians who then threw back rocks, "I started thinking about another way to resist." So rap is construed as the slingshot of the Palestinian David against the Israeli Goliath.

Also different from the Marxist revolutionary position is that while the emphasis is on the oppressed, DAM focuses more on the human element than on a political commitment to class struggle. As Suhell Nafar raps: "The path to equality is a long way to travel / You are not a terrorist / You are not a beast / You're a human being / And what ruins your reputation is something called politics."[15] It is also worth noting that unlike in the case of Marxism, spirituality is given its expression, although not in the form of strict religious adherence. Tupac, for instance, was influenced by a range of spiritual sources, from Zen Buddhism to the Bhagavad Gita to the Christian mysticism of Pierre Teilhard de Chardin (the French thinker who influenced the Senegalese liberation leader Léopold Senghor).[16]

It is also worth mentioning that DAM's members, as '48 Palestinians based in Israel, are committed to maintaining ties with young Palestinians "outside" in the occupied territories, which is the most urgent starting point for their pariah solidarity with the oppressed elsewhere.[17] Joseph Massad, in noting that the appearance of Palestinian Israeli rap groups is to be understood in terms of an attempt to create local unities, writes: "Their songs address not only the horrors of Israeli colonial racism, but also the disunity of the Palestinian population within, especially as regards the religious and class divisions fostered by Israeli policies. While the music borrows from American hip hop, produced by synthesizers and percussion, it is punctuated by Arab musical phrases and rhythms (using hand drums)." He goes on to quote from MWR, which raps in colloquial Palestinian and appeals to an identification with the downtrodden beyond the divisions of class and religion—for instance: "It does not matter who among us is Christian or Muslim" (2005, 193).

The outlook of DAM and MWR is shared, and arguably extended, by other Arab rappers and hip-hop groups on the international scene. One of these is Lowkey, the Iraqi-British rapper whose song "Tears to Laughter" became the anthem for the protest marches in Britain in support of Gaza during the 2008–2009 siege. In "Tears to Laughter," Lowkey raps, "It doesn't matter if you're a Christian or Jew. They're just people living in conditions different to you."[18] So Lowkey challenges identity politics as being blind to questions of a universal humanity. He also says, "I'm not related to the strangers on the TV / But I relate because they could have been me." And, "Imagine how you'd feel if this was your family." And Lowkey sums up: "I view this from a human perspective."

It is significant that in the rerecorded version of "Tears to Laughter," namely "Long Live Palestine," Lowkey is joined by an international gathering of rappers, including women, who are given guest slots. Those featured include DAM, and also The Narcicyst (Canadian-Iraqi), Eslam Jawaad (Syrian-Lebanese), Hich Kas (an Iranian rapper whose name means "nobody"), Reveal (an Iranian-born UK artist), Shadia Mansour (Palestinian-British, known as the First Lady of Arab Hip-Hop), and Hasan Salaam (an African American Muslim). Furthermore, they rap alternately in English and Arabic.[19]

It is perhaps also worth mentioning that there are Jewish and Israeli hip-hop groups that have differing bearings on the internationalism of hip-hop. Tamer Nafar attempted to work with Israeli rapper Subliminal, but this proved impossible due to their considerable political differences, as revealed in the film *Channels of Rage* (2003). Subliminal, who self-identifies with the Israeli right, paradoxically uses rap, traditionally the cultural form of oppressed minorities, in support of the dominant and dominating majority.[20] A website about *Channels of Rage* tackles this paradox, or hypocrisy, as follows:

"'Zionist hip-hop' is patriotic and pro-army. . . . Kobi [Subliminal] explains, 'People always say to me, "Rap is protest music, so what is there for a boy from a good neighbourhood to protest about?" My protest songs aren't about not having enough food, but about my country not having enough pride.'"[21]

While Subliminal's music is influenced by Tupac Shakur (as is DAM's), the eclecticism of his work draws on Hanukkah songs and Jewish hymns combined with the strains of military music such as fanfares. In his song "Divide and Conquer" (the title in itself is significant), he speaks of his sense of persecution and the need for separatist, patriotic militancy when presented with the Palestinian olive branch.[22] Subliminal exhibits here the traits of what I have elsewhere called "pariah elitism": both the sense of being an elite victim and a victimized elite (Rooney 2009). As mentioned earlier, Arendt speaks of the parvenu and the pariah as two discrete alternatives to each other. However, pariah elitism, which we can make into a third category, accounts for elite groups presenting themselves as if they were pariahs as well as accounting for those who seek to make pariahdom an elite condition.

Not all Jewish rap is Zionist, of course. A very different Jewish group, a South American "urban collective" called Hip Hop Hoodios, has a song called "Que Pasa in Israel" that draws attention to similarities between border controls keeping Mexicans in their place and Israelis keeping Palestinians in their place. The song's refrain is "What's going on in Israel?"[23] That is to say, this Jewish group has an international perspective rejected by Subliminal's fiercely elitist patriotism. Similarly, when Lowkey teams up with Immortal Technique on the song "Voices of the Voiceless," they say they speak out for every victim of racist persecution, "from Auschwitz to Hebron."[24]

Returning to Cohen in the light of contemporary Arab hip-hop, as mentioned, his view of the universal seems narrowly restricted to a commodified form of material American culture that gets exported globally. He thinks this gets people to buy into the American dream of self-betterment, but he does not realize that many young people regard American politics as actually preventing access to the modernity that is desired. The new connectivity that has arisen through the international hip-hop movement calls for a new and wider universality than that going by the name of globalization. What is universalized here is the pariah status of African Americans within America, with respect to a constituency that has felt excluded by the experience of racism from the American dream. As such, hip-hop in its very formation (while allowing for its divergent developments) has constituted a critique of American modernity as well as a rallying cry toward a more authentic universalism. Of course, hip-hop has been commodified, but the more radical groups are capable of using it as a new protest form to build an international community of artists who are highly aware of one another's messages and work in shared solidarity: from Tupac to DAM to Lowkey to I-voice (a Palestinian-Beiruti group) to the aspiring female rappers profiled in both *Slingshot Hip Hop* and a recent BBC documentary series called *Syrian School* (dir. Max Baring, 2010). It should be noted that, while some strands of American rap have been criticized for their misogyny, in the Arab rap world young women are often encouraged to make their voices heard and groups like DAM promote feminist messages.

In *Syrian School*, which profiles different forms of schooling and youth experience in contemporary Syria, we are introduced to a Syrian headmistress who is against rap because, according to a pupil, anything Western gets a red line. This same head teacher says the Palestinian cause is not served by music but by "blood sacrifice." However, her young pupils maintain that rap spreads quickly on television and is effective in reaching both Western and Arab audiences (Baring 2010). A similar point is made in *Slingshot Hip Hop* when a Palestinian on a radio phone-in show says, "Soon all Americans will be singing our words" (Salloum 2008).

From this, certain strands of rap emerge as an assertive progressive force: against the anti-Western politics of martyrdom and blood sacrifice upheld by some of the older generation, there is a movement among the younger generation that sees in rap, and related forms of contemporary popular culture, a capacity to create international connectivity against the divisive identity politics of ethnicity and religion without giving up on a radical politics of the left. The importance of this can be registered through the fact that one of the problematic effects of the Bush and Blair response to 9/11 has been the simplistic discursive broadening of the pariah category of "terrorist" through widely disseminated political rhetoric. This is particularly notable in the fate of the terms *radical* and *radicalization*, which by now have come to be uniformly and highly reductively equated with terms such as *terrorist*, *extremism*, and *fanaticism*. Where once *radicalism* was a term used for a liberation politics against oppression, it has now widely come to connote fanaticism. What this entails is a loss of distinction between reactionary extremism and progressive radicalism, and an ignorance of the often cosmopolitan left-wing intellectual and artistic movements in Arab metropolitan centers. The vanguardism at stake here is a question of the attempt to generate, as opposed to reflect, popular support for antiessentialist emancipation movements through aesthetic and cultural forums.

While African American rap has been associated with black nationalism and Palestinian rap with Palestinian nationalism—and, it should be added, with justification—I have aimed in this chapter to stress the ways in which liberation movements and their cultures of protest should not be reduced to such nationalist determinations—that is, ones predicated on race or ethnicity—for this would be to ignore the utopian internationalism that is also importantly at stake. In order to further explain this point, a brief comparative case study will be made of the Zimbabwean liberation struggle. Thomas Turino, in *Nationalists, Cosmopolitans and Popular Music in Zimbabwe*, draws attention to the progressive role played by music in advancing the country's anticolonial movement, and he accurately draws attention to the thoroughly cosmopolitan nature of the preindependence music scene (2000, 165, 189).[25] This is significant because liberation movements in their anticolonial phases serve to challenge the reductive appropriations of the universal on the part of racial nationalisms with a call to a wider, more authentic universality. In the case of Zimbabwe, the reactive and reactionary phase of insistent cultural nationalism, with its appeal to the "authentically Zimbabwean," constituted a postindependence phenomenon, with the new rulers seeking to unify the nation through homogenizing antihybrid, anticosmopolitan rhetoric and policies.

With such considerations in mind, this chapter will now consider how the utopian internationalism of liberationist hip-hop is well matched by the specific aesthetics and techniques of hip-hop as an avant-garde art form. The main question to be entertained here involves the relationship of hip-hop to authenticity. With respect to this question, what needs to be challenged is the stereotypical association of authenticity with purity and essence. It could be maintained that there is really no need to think of authenticity as a question of purity and essentialism, in spite of all the ideological gestures that encourage such a conception, and more than that, it could even be argued that the very move that equates the authentic with the pure is the corrupting or inauthentic turn. In order to explain this, and why this should matter for Palestinian hip-hop and rap, an argument by the Palestinian poet Mourid Barghouti will now be introduced.

In an essay entitled "Verbicide," Barghouti argues Palestinians have to contend with "the pollution of language" on the part of the Israelis and he evidences this pollution as follows: "The Israeli occupation imposes a double, triple, endless redefinition of the Palestinian. Call him militant, outlaw, criminal, terrorist, irrelevant, cancer, cockroach, serpent, virus—the list becomes endless. Be the one who makes the definitions. Define! Classify! Demonize! Misinform! Simplify! Stick on the label! Then send in the tanks!" (Barghouti 2003).

The pollution of language may be said to be a matter of a performative instrumentalization, whereby language is used to produce "realities" in total disregard of what is actually the case. Moreover, it involves the manipulation of language to sanction malpractices, arguably through attempts to essentialize authenticity. Barghouti's argument is fascinatingly similar to one put forward by Zimbabwean poet Chenjerai Hove in his analysis of authoritarianism in Zimbabwe, which he sees as deriving from "the corruption of language." Hove writes: "I believe that corruption begins with the corruption of language. If a senior politician uses vulgar language in public, that is the beginning of corruption. . . . Once language degenerates into a vehicle for untruth, people are engulfed in a form of corruption" (Hove 2002, 5).

In both the cases made by Barghouti and Hove, the pollution/corruption of language empties language of its capacity to be meaningful with respect to given realities. Thus, Barghouti maintains: "There were times when the poetic imagination worked to escape reality. I claim that the poetic imagination now works to confront it."

This emphasis on confronting reality has historically constituted an important formational impulse for hip-hop as an aesthetic movement, with its often repeated motto "keep it real." However, what it means to "keep it real" is often unconvincingly elaborated in clichés of racial and cultural essentialisms, a problematically simplifying interpretation that Paul Gilroy critiques aptly (see Gilroy 2004).[26]

When Barghouti and Hove speak of the "corruption" and "pollution" of language, neither proposes that the antithesis to such would retain something like a "purity" of language or of cultural expression. Indeed, the authenticity at stake is not a matter of purity but rather of refusing the simplifications of language, ideological jargon, or commodified language, in order to address our human sociality, that is, relationality (bearing in mind the Marxist understanding that the commodity form, seeming to appear from nowhere, eclipses the "sociality of labor"). Barghouti writes: "Language is a shared element between the world of the marketplace and that of poetry. The dissimilar language of poetry is our suggestion of a different language for this world. It is our attempt to restore to each word its specificity and resist the process of collective vulgarization and to establish new relations among words to create a fresh perception of things."

Correlated with the "keep it real" desire of certain strands of hip-hop is the significance of its improvisational techniques. Of course, hip-hop is an art of sampling, quoting, collage, bricolage. But what at least partially accompanies this is an aesthetic of deploying what is ready at hand in terms of the needs of the moment. Hip-hop art forms and techniques often respond to a scarcity of resources: no drum kit, you can always beat-box; no band, you can always DJ and make new tracks out of old ones. In this context of scarce resources, an art of the voice can be an art of the basics, but the importance of hip-hop's orality goes beyond this minimalism. It concerns a capacity to speak "reality" to power—to seize the moment using whatever resources are available to contest the jargon of the powerful with the word on the street. In *Slingshot Hip Hop*, Tamer Nafar maintains that while Chuck D has spoken of hip-hop as "our CNN," the same applies to DAM. This is not just a case of the new(s) as content but of "the fresh perspective" as a question of oral and sonic styles.

You can certainly immediately hear the influence of American rap on a group like DAM, as well as other Palestinian rap artists: be this a matter of the beats, the scratching, the flow, the breaks, or whatever else. To make use of a term offered by Maira and Shihade, this could reflect "sonic alliance" (2010, 34),[27] enabling listeners to understand that there is a common purpose between those disadvantaged by America within America and those disadvantaged by Israel (backed by America) within Israel and the occupied territories. That said, Palestinian rap is orally specific to the Palestinian experience, and I would maintain that this remains the case for listeners who may not know either Arabic or how to identify precisely the splices and strains of Arab poetry, texts, and music in the hip-hop (including excerpts from the speeches of Nasser and poetry of Tawfeek Ziad, and the arguable echoes of Mohamed Munir's "Iqrar" in "Ma ili Hurriyya" or those of Kazem al-Sahar's "Wanin" in "Ya Sayidati," alongside the syncretic reggae influences on "Inqilab" and the intriguing use of Delibes's "Lakme" flower duet to introduce "Al-Hurriyya Untha").[28] Let us listen (and it has to be *listen*), for instance, to DAM's hook in the song "Min Ihrabhi." (Here, the reader would ideally need to play a clip, easily located on YouTube.)

Even if a listener does not know what the words mean, it is still possible to hear the powerful tone of indignation with the strongly stressed first syllable and the dip in pitch toward the rising pitch of incredulity. Obviously, knowing that the words translate as "Who's the terrorist?" followed by lines such as "I'm the terrorist? / How am I the terrorist / When you've taken my land?" heightens the effect, for the words are perfectly matched with the "counterheckling" rhythm (the kind of deflecting rhythm you would adopt to contest someone's heckling of you) and with the outraged tone. The direct address of this song is to the Israelis, which is significant because the song challenges the very way in which the Israelis use terms such as *terrorist* to try to screen themselves from the fact that the Palestinians are living, sentient human beings and not a set of nonhuman hate words. It is a Palestinian case of: "If you prick us, will we not bleed?"[29] That is, the authenticity at stake is a matter of rendering undeniable a real human existence with the affects and responses that are entirely appropriate, genuine, for real, in a given situation of abuse and oppression. What you can hear in the sounds of both voice and music in DAM's work is a range of affects that convincingly match their situations: anger and frustration ("I Don't Have Freedom"); tenderness ("Change Tomorrow"); cultural solidarity or *sumud* ("Intro"); lyricism ("Dedication"); mournful yearning ("Stranger in My Own Country"); pride undercut with buffoonish humor ("It's Dam").

Perhaps a "stand tall" ethos is something we can hear across all the songs: a refusal to be crushed, one enhanced by the strong Arab percussion combined with the insistent hip-hop vocal rhythms. The rallying cry of "standing tall" apparently owes itself to Samih al-Qasem's poem "Muntasib al-Qama" ("Standing Tall") (Maira and Shihade 2010, 31), while "Walking Tall" is the title of a Marcel Khalife song and DAM's lyrics contain a number of related references, from "walking tall" ("Dedication") to "Keep walking with your head held up high" ("Stranger in My Own Country"). Interestingly, the root of the word *maqam*, which refers to the modal groupings of Arab melodies, is *q-w-m*, which means "to stand up" or "to rise" (Shiloah 2010, 47). "Stand up" is a gesture related to oratory, to coming forward and assuming a platform, which may further facilitate the notion of taking a stand and "standing tall."

Yet this improvisational alacrity to respond to the urgency of the moment with street-level realities is not pure spontaneity. For instance, a performer has to know what a beat can do, to know how to ride it, to get the right effects. While protest poetry and protest music can easily go the way of jargon and stock gestures, artful protest may be said to require a flexibility of technique (based on practice and good know-how) capable of confronting the "now" and "here," as well as of maintaining a certain freedom of spirit.

The earlier reference in this chapter to William Blake might have seemed questionable precisely as a frame of reference: why allude to English Romantic poetry? However, English Romantic poetry's lyrical preoccupation with spirited human freedom and equal rights is not specific to this tradition of poetry, for it concerns the repeatedly repressed and repeatedly thwarted strivings for those only partially realized and so unrealized Romantic ideals of equality, emancipation, and human relationality (a better term than *brotherhood*). In this respect, there is a contrapuntal temporal tension in much Palestinian writing and art. On the one hand, as already touched on, there is what could be called a modernity of empowerment and opportunity that the Palestinians are trying to break into as they are constantly excluded from it. Here, Tamer Nafar of DAM comments: "We grew up in our Arabic neighbourhood, Arabic ghettos . . . you have a separate wall between both neighbourhoods, between the Arabic poverty neighbourhoods and the Jewish rich Kibbutz."[30]

Darwish, in his poem "Under Siege," makes a similar point in a more spiritual and lyrical way: "A little of this absolute and blue infinity / Would be enough / To lighten the burden of these times."[31] The mere sky appears as a daily reminder of and promise of a freedom that is a real possibility but endlessly unattainable. On the other hand, along with this sense of an historical present that appears within reach as it is simultaneously perpetually denied, there is a sense of the utopian for a certain Palestinian consciousness that is a question of being "the advance guard" or, with respect to cultural expression, the "avant-garde." That is, because of their predicament, the Palestinians are at the forefront of the very question of our repressed, denied, and ignored human connectedness (not the limited connectivity that depends on the privileges of access), and, as Jean Genet recognized and was mesmerized by, this could be seen as a matter of the angelic aura or beauty of the Palestinian freedom fighters: it is as if, for Genet, they were messengers from the future or from utopia (see Genet 1989).[32]

Let us now return to Foucault's statement, quoted earlier, as follows: "Superficially, one might say that knowledge of man, unlike the sciences of nature, is always linked, even in its vaguest form, to ethics or politics; more fundamentally, modern thought is advancing towards that region where man's Other must become the Same as himself." This could be juxtaposed with the words of DAM also quoted earlier: "You are not a beast / You're a human being / And what ruins your reputation is something called politics." It may be proposed that the supposed transcendence of politics and ethics concerns not the naïve idea of somehow leaving politics and ethics behind but rather of not reducing the question of our humanity to political interests and to moral posturing. That said, it could be objected that Foucault's choice of the word *same* (assuming sameness as our trajectory) is a rather unfortunate one. The logic of globalization may be said to be a logic of sameness, commodities being, after all, clones. What is needed instead is an alternative logic to refer to a potential commonality of experience, one that actually plays a large role in hip-hop as an art movement, namely: the structure and poetics of analogy. That is to say, what is at stake is not a case of universal sameness but a case of points of comparison and points of contact, of relationality: a question of finding common ground as a question, it could be proposed, of metaphorical thinking and expression (see Rooney 2011).[33]

My attention has been drawn to the widespread deployment of analogy as a poetic form within and structure of hip-hop by my PhD student Blake Brandes, who is a rapper (DJ Encryption) and music producer. He writes: "Hip-hop has proven itself to be a remarkably versatile medium for adapting external elements to fit localized concerns. Ultimately, analogy and hip-hop are all about relation. Analogy, like hip-hop, opens doors between people and cultures. It expresses similarity, correspondence, and increased understanding."[34]

The importance of analogy in the context of this essay may be explained by a closer look at some lines of Lowkey and DAM.

Lowkey states: "I am not related to the strangers on the TV / But I relate because they could have been me." In this, he does not see himself as the same as Gazan Palestinian "strangers" ("related" as in "family") but analogous to them (able to "relate" in the sense of connect with and so give voice to their suffering). In "Innocent Criminals," DAM raps, "Get into my shoes / And your feet will hurt,"[35] appealing precisely to a comparative imagination. Of course, many different forms of analogy could be entertained, including the musical borrowings already touched on, but I concentrate here on the question of imagining self as other and other as self as a particularly apt instance of understanding the recourse to analogy in the Palestinian context. Moreover, this comparative, analogy-producing consciousness may be said to be understandably quite pervasive in Palestinian writing, due to the double consciousness of "here" and "there," "inside" and "outside." What makes Aloni's film notable in terms of Israeli cultural production is the extent to which it plays with points of juncture, comparison, and crossover: as one example of such, Aloni gets DAM to rap in Hebrew and Jewish Israeli singers to sing in Arabic.

In an opening scene of *Local Angel*, the voiceover claims, "With every blink, God creates countless new angels," but here the English subtitle offers a suggestive error by transcribing *angels* as *angles*: in every instant, God creates many new angles. This not only reverberates with Barghouti's "fresh perspective" but also suggests that it would be possible to see the angel as an angle: that is, as a point of intersection between two lines or two planes. In every instant, there's the creation of many possible new analogies.

In *Local Angel*, one metaphorical moment is especially moving. It concerns Aloni's visit to an Arab Christian cemetery in Tel Aviv that overlooks the sea. In the quiet cemetery, the only movement is of a plastic bag blowing in the wind, which Aloni says "reminds me of the living." The camera focuses on the sculpture of a beautiful angel that dominates the cemetery, the film's iconic cover image. Meanwhile, in the distance, out at sea, one particular wave can be seen repeatedly breaking and, as it does, its white foam fans up in what looks like the two joined wings of the angel. A concatenation of visual analogies is thus set up, suggesting that the plastic bag blowing in the wind is like the angel's wings, which are like the still of a wave of the sea, which "rising up," both the same and different every time, is like a *maqam*. Here is a metaphor of there, there of here, or a point of comparison with, a meeting place. And what of the sacred as secular, secular as sacred? It is worth quoting Gilroy on this: "Historically, black political culture's most powerful notions of agency have been figured through the sacred. They can also get figured through the profane, and there, a different idea of worldly redemption can be observed. Both of these traditions come together for me in the traditions of musical performance that culminate in hip hop. In them, we find what I call the ethics of antiphony—a kind of ideal communicative moment in the relationship between the performer and the crowd that surpasses anything the structure of the family can provide." (2004, 94)

So, let us say that the angel is the figure of figuration, perhaps specifically, figuration of the point at which the secular turns sacred or the sacred secular. And so finally, authenticity cannot be said to inhere. It does not inhere in an identity or essence. It is this that the figure of the (Jekyll and Hyde) double, a figure of finitude, forecloses in a will-to-identity-and-inherence that negates the "over there" as uncanny and terrorizing. In contradistinction to this binary logic of literalization, hip-hop may be understood to posit authenticity as a question of analogy: "that's the joint" as the point is the joint, authenticity as an uncontainable in-between of entities.

While hip-hop is an art form of the oppressed, it also pertains to the culturally repressed, bringing a postmodernist avant-garde into a relation with what postmodernist aesthetics would otherwise repress: the real, for prime example, along with lyricism, orality, and community. Or, as Greg Dimitriades, comments: "Hip hop engages the postmodern present in its stress on the discontinuous and contingent while it nurtures a community building musical tradition rooted in the oral" (2004, 425). Hopefully, it will be understood why this chapter has argued that Palestinian hip-hop, which is like but not the same as American hip-hop, needs to engage with a musico-poetics of authenticity as relationality: a reconception of authenticity that works against the would-be authentications of jargons of identity with their potential for violence.

This chapter was written before the Arab Spring, a fact that emphasizes how the strands of Arab hip-hop we have been considering do indeed have an avant-garde significance. The hip-hop in question may be said to advance a liberationist revolutionary consciousness, constituting a vanguard social movement. In fact, one of the triggering points of the Tunisian uprising was a rap by El Général, "Rais LeBled" ("My President, Your Country" / "Head of State"), one that speaks reality to power and that insists on humane solidarity and dignity against political cynicism and corruption. As argued earlier, the ideological fixation on extremism by the American and British governments, together with accomplices such as deposed Egyptian president Hosni Mubarak, has served to obscure the difference between extremism and radicalism—this being the blind spot that the uprisings exposed. The avant-garde significance of this revolutionary consciousness is that while it is a radicalism that capitalism obviously tries to surpass, its improvisatory agility (hip-hop as such) enables it, as we have seen, to wrong-foot the rigid with rhythm. In the Egyptian film *Microphone*, about the underground arts scene in Alexandria and made in the run-up to the revolution, the hip-hop group Y-Crew raps: "Our music's gonna change you. . . . I'm trying to wake you from your sleep" (Abdalla 2011).

Notes

1. Mahmoud Darwish, "Under Siege," trans. Marjolijn de Jager, http//:www
.palestinechronicle.com/view_article_details.php?id=14055.

2. *Local Angel: Theological Political Fragments,* dir. Udi Aloni (2002; London: ICA, 2004). Aloni is a Jewish Israeli filmmaker, and *Local Angel* may be considered supportive of the Palestinian cause.

3. This chapter substantially reworks some pages of an earlier article that considered Cohen's work at greater length: Caroline Rooney, "Arab Hip Hop in an International Frame." *Orient: German Journal for Politics, Economics and Culture in the Near and Middle East* III (2010).

4. Jackie Reem Salloum, a Palestinian-American, traces the genesis, styles, and uses of Palestinian hip-hop in her film in collaboration with the artists concerned. Amongst other collaborative considerations, the artists were given opportunities to film themselves.

5. At stake here is the notion of a common humanity as a premise for justice, as opposed to sectarian claims made on the basis of religion or ethnicity.

6. *Slingshot Hip Hop,* dir. Jackie Reem Salloum.

7. Tupac Shakur, "Just a Breath of Freedom," http://www.tupac_a_shakur .tripod.com/id139.htm.

8. Tupac Shakur, "Liberty Needs Glasses," http://www.alleyezonme.com/poetry /index.phtml.

9. See Hannah Arendt, *The Jew as Pariah: Jewish Identity and Politics in the Modern Age,* ed. Ron H. Feldman (New York: Grove Press, 1978): 55–56; 67–90. In "The Jews and Society," Arendt writes: "For the formation of a social history of the Jews within nineteenth-century European society, it was, however, decisive that to a certain extent every Jew in every generation had somehow at some time to decide whether he would remain a pariah and stay out of society altogether, or become a parvenu. . . . Jews felt simultaneously the pariah's regret at not having become a parvenu and the parvenu's bad conscience at having betrayed his people and exchanged equal rights for personal privileges." Hannah Arendt, "The Jews in Society," in *The Portable Hannah Arendt,* ed. Peter Baer (London: Penguin Books, 2003), 86–87.

10. Immortal Technique. "The War against Us All" (feat. Mumia Abu Jamal), Bin Laden remix (Bin Laden Pt. 2 EP), Viper Records, 2004.

11. DAM, "Dedication," *Dedication,* Red Circle Music, 2006.

12. *Singshot Hip Hop,* dir. Jackie Reem Salloum.

13. DAM, "Change Tomorrow," *Dedication.*

14. DAM, "Who's the Terrorist?" ("Meen Erhabe" / "Min Irhabi"), 2001. See *Local Angel,* dir. Udi Aloni, for a performance of the song. See also YouTube.

15. DAM, "Change Tomorrow," *Dedication.*

16. Tupac's step-aunt is Assata Shakur, formerly of the Black Panthers and influenced by the liberation theory of Fanon and Senghor. She lives in exile in Cuba and has become an iconic pariah figure amongst the rap community.

17. For a wider discussion of the significance of this, see Sunaina Maira and

Magid Shihade, "Palestinian Hip Hop: Youth, Identity and Nation" in *Orient: German Journal for Politics, Economics and Culture of the Middle East* III (2010), pp. 26–35.

18. Lowkey, "Tears to Laughter," SO Empire Recordings and Mtunes, 2009. The proceeds were donated to the Disasters Emergency Committee (DEC) Gaza appeal.

19. Lowkey et. al., *Long Live Palestine: Parts 1 and 2*, Mesopotamia Records, 2009. The EP broke the hip-hop records on Amazon's download chart.

20. It is interesting to note that his mother is from Iran and his father from Tunisia, and so his sense of a Jewish minority status may derive from this background.

21. See http://www.azm.org/AZM_MovieGuide_ChannelsofRage.pdf.

22. See "Israelis Use Hip Hop to Support Zionist Position," http://pub12 .ezboard.com/fpoliticalpalacefrm17.showMessage?topicID+564.topic.

23. Hip Hop Hoodios, "Que Pasa in Israel," *Carne Masada: Quite Possibly the Very Best of Hip Hop Hoodios*, Jazzheads Records, 2009.

24. Immortal Technique and Lowkey, "Voices of the Voiceless," SO Empire Recordings, 2009.

25. Joseph Massad entertains a similar perspective in "Liberating Songs," referenced earlier, in that he defines the question of nationalism to be a matter of popular sentiment and cosmopolitan expression as opposed to one of essentialized identity.

26. See Paul Gilroy, "It's a Family Affair," in *That's the Joint! The Hip-Hop Studies Reader*, ed. Murray Forman and Mark Anthony Neal (London: Routledge, 2004).

27. Maira and Shihade refer specifically to the sonic alliance amongst Palestinian artists.

28. Of course, DAM also makes use of both Western and Arab instrumentation, with effective use of hip-hop breaks to contrast the textures.

29. William Shakespeare, *The Merchant of Venice* (Act III, Scene 1).

30. Tamer Nafar, interview, *Democracy Now* (November 2008), http://www .democracynow.org/2008/5/15/slingshot_hip_hop_palestinian_rap_group.

31. Mahmoud Darwish, "Under Siege," trans. Marjolijn de Jager, www. poemhunter.com/poem/under-siege/. Other translations of the poem are also posted on the Internet.

32. See Jean Genet, *Prisoner of Love,* trans. Barbara Bray (London: Picador, 1989).

33. See Caroline Rooney, "Utopian Cosmopolitanism and the Conscious Pariah: Harare, Ramallah, Cairo," in *The Journal of Commonwealth Literature* (2011).

34. Blake Brandes, "Form and Flow: The Role of Analogy in American Hip Hop," work in progress.

35. DAM, "Innocent Criminals," video, *Local Angel*.

References

Abdalla, Ahmad. 2011. *Microphone*. United Artists.

Aloni, Udi. 2004. *Local Angel: Theological Political Fragments*. London: ICA.

Barghouti, Mourid. 2003. "Verbicide," *New Internationalist* (August), http:/
findarticles.com/articles/mi_mo3QP/is_359/ai_107480485.

Baring, Max. 2010 (March). *Syrian School*. BBC.

Blake, William. 2008. "The Tyger." In *Romanticism: An Anthology*. 3rd ed. Edited
by Duncan Wu. Oxford: Blackwell Publishing.

Cohen, Jared. 2007. *Children of Jihad: A Young American's Travels among the Youth
of the Middle East*. New York: Gotham Books.

Dimitriades, Greg. 2004. "Hip-Hop: From Live Performance to Mediated
Narrative." In *That's the Joint! The Hip-Hop Studies Reader*. Edited by Murray
Forman and Mark Anthony Neal. London: Routledge.

Eisenberg, Deborah. 2006. "Twilight of the Superheroes." In *Twilight of the
Superheroes*. Basingstoke: Picador.

Foucault, Michel. 1982. *The Order of Things*. London: Tavistock Publications.

Gilroy, Paul. 2004. "It's a Family Affair." In *That's the Joint! The Hip-Hop Studies
Reader*. Edited by Murray Forman and Mark Anthony Neal. London:
Routledge.

Halachmi, Anat. 2003. *Channels of Rage*. Anat Halachmi Productions, Tel Aviv.

Hamid, Mohsin, 2007. *The Reluctant Fundamentalist*. London: Penguin Books.

Hove, Chenjerai. 2002. "Collapse of Law: Collapse of Conscience." In *Palaver
Finish*. Harare: Weaver Press.

Maira, Sunaina, and Magid Shihade. 2010. "Palestinian Hip Hop: Youth, Identity
and Nation." *Orient* 3: 26–35.

Massad, Joseph. 2005. "Liberating Songs: Palestine Put to Music." In *Palestine,
Israel and the Politics of Popular Culture*. Edited by Rebecca L. Stein and Ted
Swedenburg. Durham, NC: Duke University Press.

Rooney, Caroline. 2009. "The Disappointed of the Earth." Special issue on
Psychoanalysis, Fascism, and Fundamentalism, *Psychoanalysis and History* 11.
Edited by Julia Borossa and Ivan Ward.

Salloum, Jackie Reem. 2008. *Slingshot Hip Hop*. Fresh Booza Productions,
Palestine/USA.

Shelley, Percy. 2008. "Ozymandias." In *Romanticism: An Anthology*, 3rd ed. Edited
by Duncan Wu. Oxford: Blackwell Publishing.

Shiloah, Amnon. 2010. "The Concepts Held about Music as Cultural Facts with a
Special Emphasis on the Notion of *Maqam*." *Orient* 3: 43–51.

Turino, Thomas. 2000. *Nationalists, Cosmopolitans and Popular Music in Zimbabwe*.
Chicago: University of Chicago Press.

CHAPTER NINE

Noise and Its Formless Shadows

Egypt's Extreme Metal as Avant-Garde *Nafas Dawsha*

~~~

BENJAMIN J. HARBERT

In January 1997, Egyptian authorities jailed nearly one hundred Egyptian university students, all part of the local metal scene.[1] The event registered briefly in Western newspapers, which portrayed the curiosity of a conflict between young Egyptians a decade late to the heavy metal trend and a bumbling government overly suspicious of Westernisms (Daniszewski 1997; Jehl 1997; Gauch 1997; Goldberg 1997). Yet neither of these descriptions was quite accurate. In fact, Egypt's metal musicians and fans were in lockstep with an underground international extreme metal, which was developed in the wake of the commercial metal wave of the 1980s and had been pushing musical conventions ever since. Meanwhile, far from laughably dismissible, the government's brutal crackdown, informed by its high-stakes wrangling with radical Islamic groups, was a calculated strategy that held up this group of "practicing Satanists" as a straw man against which to redefine its defense of Islam. It also provided a welcome distraction from the radical privatization of the public sector. The practice of persecuting the metal communities then spread across the Arab world to Morocco, Bahrain, and Jordan.

This essay aims to retell this case of music made semi-illegal, as understood by those musicians involved in the arrests and those who have brought back the scene post-arrests. In a way, Egyptians have been engaged in a war of interpretations over metal not in a direct sense of political struggle and resistance but rather in a complex manner that takes place in personal aesthetic worlds as well as political worlds, spread across the pages of Egyptian newsmagazines and sequestered to desert concerts on the outskirts of Cairo and Alexandria. The bulk of research for this project took place in 2006 in Cairo and Alexandria, through attending metal concerts and rehearsals, conducting interviews, and examining related materials housed in the archive at *Al-Ahram*, Egypt's largest circulating daily paper.[2]

The story is one familiar to other manifestations of the Arab avant-garde: a political resistance developed in a space made open through the social cohesion around poetically open aesthetics. In fact, many activists I met during my research in Cairo felt a particular sympathy to and curiosity toward participants in the resurgent metal underground. Some had been witness to the senseless brutality of the 1997 crackdown, citing the event as a memorable instance of human rights violations under Mubarak's watch. Others felt a kinship to a group successfully operating under the radar despite the threat of arrest and prosecution. In fact, the organizational skills of resurgent metal in Cairo resemble those of the 2011 protests in Tahrir Square. Egyptians took stock of their differences to reorganize under a unity of sentiment (Temlali 2011, 49). Ideally, aesthetic space can forcibly open rhetorical space for experimentation, with logics unfettered by associations of imperialism and nationalism. In this sense, the metal scene in Egypt was an organizing node within Egyptian civil society. The recent history of metal hints at the struggle for freedom not enough to argue that metal toppled a regime, but that music has a transgressive modality that carves out possibilities obscured by the official, the quotidian, and the traditional.

In some ways, what transpired in 1997 was a war over what metal is. Through an analysis of the media and the testimony of those who remember the event, I will analyze the way in which the government took advantage of certain aspects of metal's outward appearance, its expressive image. One reading of this media campaign is that the Egyptian government was able to cast metal as a more insidious Western *popular* music—a type of colonial coercion targeted at a vulnerable Egyptian youth. Internationally, metal musicians have always struggled against reductive definitions of metal as popular music, with many championing metal's more transgressive elements. An account of metal in Egypt up to the 1997 arrests will show a double defeat of what we might call the avant-garde contingent of Egyptian metal: dismantling the scene through fear tactics and defining metal as an extreme form of Western popular music.

Following the tragic story of metal's double defeat, I will show how the struggle over metal's meaning took a particular form in the careful resurgence of metal since the crackdown. To do so, I will explore accounts of radical musical experiences both centripetally and centrifugally (in other words, in terms of musical structuring and musical meaning), as championed by Egypt's metal apologists and as framed as an avant-garde practice in the Near East.

I will describe Egyptian metal practice as an existential and political play with noise and music through testimony of members of the metal scene as well as musical analysis and news analysis. What will emerge is a particular metalness—a feeling that is inextricably tied to being in Egypt.

Metal in Egypt

On October 15, 1970, twenty-seven days after the UK release of Black Sabbath's *Paranoid*, Anwar Sadat became president of Egypt. *Paranoid* is widely regarded as the definitive heavy metal album (Cope 2010), while many trace the beginning of Egypt's contemporary woes to Sadat's administration. In 1974, Sadat declared the *infitah* ("openness"), an open-door economic policy that had lasting ramifications for Egypt. The policy marked the final turn away from the USSR during the Cold War. Alongside the corresponding economic alignment with the United States was Sadat's encouragement of conservative Islam, a reversal of his predecessor Gamal Abdel Nasser's religious repression. In a matter of years, Sadat completely reshaped the role of government in Egypt.

One commodity that slipped into the country relatively unnoticed was Black Sabbath's *Paranoid*. This began the development of metal as a genre in Egypt, paralleling its spread in Europe and the United States, albeit on a much smaller scale and without support from the local media industry. Egyptian bands such as the Mass, the Black Coats, and Les Petits Chats drove the early local-rock scene with a sound that led to the development of Egyptian metal. Egypt was also an occasional stopping point for touring Western bands. Led Zeppelin recorded the song "Kashmir" at the studios of Hany Mehanna in Giza. Musicians such as Ritchie Blackmore of Deep Purple sat in with local bands in the late 1970s. The local metal bands helped maintain a demand for bootlegged albums and localized the genres performatively and stylistically through the following decades by playing a mix of covers and original proto-metal songs. Thus, the seeds of the 1997 arrests were all planted in the early 1970s—metal, radical Islam, and pro-U.S. economic policies.

In 1981, Sadat was assassinated by Islamic radicals, ironic given Sadat's initial support of the Muslim Brotherhood. His successor, Hosni Mubarak, extended the state-of-emergency laws put in place at the time of the assassination, while mostly continuing Sadat's economic policies. By the early 1990s, satellite television offered Egyptians MTV, metal concerts, and movies—things that Egyptian television had not featured. Seif El-Din Moussa of Cairo's thrash metal band Wyvern remembers this period: "Back in the years when I was younger, it was very difficult to get an album. . . . There were not enough stores that actually had the albums available, so it was either you were very lucky to find something or you know someone who knows someone who got a copy of the album from another one coming from the States" (2006). In a sense, the small metal scene resembled Theodor Adorno's ideal avant-garde—a free space, relatively detached from market forces (Adorno 2001). For Adorno, the avant-garde has the potential to avoid the reduction to a commodity-fetish. Unlinked from the marketplace, music can become a practice outside of commercial transaction. In Egypt, there was no money to be made from metal. Tape kiosks didn't sell metal. Instead, fans traded tapes and photocopied artwork and lyrics. One fan told me about how his mother made him an Iron Maiden T-shirt because none were to be bought.[3] Nonmetalhead[4] Egyptians sensed no threat as fans walked the corniche of the Nile in black T-shirts and long hair. It was just strange and youthful. Ahmed Samadie of Alexandria's industrial death metal trio Worm explains the indifference with which most Egyptians viewed metalheads before the 1997 arrests: "Maybe people felt that guys with long hair and T-shirts with logos or bands [were] awkward looking. . . . We didn't have this big, known scene in Egypt with heavy metal being a generally accepted kind of music where rockers go in and out and that's normal. So, before, 'Okay, he's weird. The one with the logo T-shirt and long hair? This is a weird guy'" (2006). At this moment, the war over what metal was had not yet begun. The type of threat that metal might be has a different inflection whether seen as "popular" music or as "avant-garde." Popular music, especially that of the West, is thought of as coercive whereas an avant-garde or at least a cosmopolitan project of musical transgression (see Burkhalter in this volume) surpasses the state. For Mubarak's government, the rhetoric of repressing coercive Western popular music would be easier than repressing a cultural anomaly.

By 1992, Egypt's metal scene had begun to thrive. Enough tapes and paraphernalia circulated around Egypt to fuel a large fan base that filled auditoriums. Local bands Terra, Andromeda, Steel Edge, and Sidewinder caught the attention of sponsors and some international labels. Metal albums began to be available for purchase at The Juke Box in the World Trade Centre, an upscale Cairo shopping mall replete with jeans, bikinis, and French china. Slowly, metal was becoming popular music, no longer unlinked from the world of commerce or unnoticed by Egypt-at-large. Ahmed Samadie recalls that promising moment for metal: "The scene was really huge. There were lots of professional bands and musical collaborations. Bands even from here made the word to the outside. People in Europe and the USA knew about bands from Egypt. Many foreigners came to the gigs and they were really big gigs, sponsored by Marlboro and Pepsi" (2006).

On the eve of the arrests, metal was changing on the international stage. An increase in popularity came with a radical diversification of metal styles.

In the shadows of the growing popularity of metal in Egypt lurked more obscure and transgressive forms of metal. By the mid-1990s, global metal had begun to fragment as did the scene in Egypt. It was the Internet of the late 1990s that had the greatest impact, granting fans the ability to explore relatively obscure and extreme underground acts on their own time. Deena Weinstein attributes metal's genre fragmentation to the global spread of metal outside the United States, where certain musical elements were intensified to such a point that they warranted definition as different genres (2000, 285–90). This stylistic change ushered in a new era of metal marked by diverse extremism. Some bands distinguished themselves by tempo, some by pitch, some by form, some by timbre. In many cases, formal aspects of the music went under the knife to be resurrected as the defining characteristic of metal subgenres—stoner metal, Viking metal, grindcore, folk metal, black metal, and funeral doom, to name but a few. In so doing, metal dove underground, again relatively unhinged from the marketplace and from the public eye.

While metal had largely been the domain of upper-middle class college students in Egypt, the scene spread to an isolated group that identified around doom metal. The soon-to-be-infamous Khaled Madani and his Doom Club came from Shubra, a poorer Cairo neighborhood with a high concentration of Coptic Christians—not a place likely to cultivate a cosmopolitan avant-garde practice. His Doom Club began to operate independently around doom metal—an extreme genre characterized by slow rhythms, down-tuned guitars, and lyrical content about impending destruction, ruin, and death.[5] The "old guard" of the metal scene gradually left. Members of pre-extreme bands like Terra, Andromeda, and Sidewinder grew older and began to devote time to their young families and careers. Groups of metalheads hung out in the abandoned Qasr al-Barun ("The Baron's Palace") in Heliopolis, a Euro-Orientalist concrete villa inspired by Angkor Wat and Orissian temples and built by French architect Alexandre Marcel. Heliopolis is a distinct enough section of Cairo, its twentieth-century wealth represented by its clear urban planning, Italianate architecture, and chain restaurants. Qasr al-Barun is a site of rumors and superstitions.

As metal continued to flourish in ever-stranger forms, Egypt-at-large began to take notice. A 1996 concert called Crack of Doom brought uninvited guests. One musician recalls someone videotaping sporting a yellow jacket and a typically Egyptian mustache, not often worn by fans at metal concerts. Most thought that authorities were filming drug and alcohol use. Little did they know that the footage would be used to identify accused Satanists.

In November 1996, an anonymous fax came into the offices of *Ruz al-Yusuf*, a sensationalist tabloid weekly. The fax detailed supposed Satanic rituals taking place at metal concerts on the outskirts of Cairo and Alexandria. Journalist Abdullah Kamal published excerpts of the fax even though he could not contact its author (Khattab 1997). What Kamal claims to have intended to be a story alerting parents and communities to "social problems" ended up in a media echo chamber. The more other papers wrote about the supposed Satanic practices, the more faxes, phone calls, and letters the presses received about the scourge of metal. Other periodicals began accusing local metal bands Black Rose, Opacity, Steel Edge, and others of encouraging Satanic worship. The linking of anti-Islamic practice, exemplified as Satanism, to popular music described a type of poison injected into Egypt through the vehicle of non-Egyptian culture. The openness of metal and its links to the avant-garde certainly had no room in this metaphor.

Metal fans wrote open letters in student newspapers to deny the accusations. In fact, the graphic images of metalheads worshipping Satan, accompanied by cat murdering, mass orgies, and illicit drug use came from sources abroad and did not depict anyone actually in Egypt. Yet, as the stories developed over the next several weeks, metal began to represent a dangerous force imported into Egypt via Israeli subterfuge to corrupt Egyptian youth. Newspaper photographs appeared of American youths in metal garb, pills, computers (to represent the Internet and its dangers), provocative women, and metal album art. The papers sold, and metal moved from an obscure and unintelligibly noisy genre of music to a force that might infiltrate and corrupt Egypt and Islam, not to mention endanger communities.

One photograph in particular stood out from the rest. It was taken at an actual Egyptian show with a long-haired metal fan, attired in black, holding a three-foot cross upside down. The photo, mixed with images from abroad, illustrated that the enemy had arrived. On December 9, *Ruz al-Yusuf* ran an indirect call for action suggesting there was a certainty of Satanic homicides given the deluge of faxes and letters that had arrived in their offices. The article did not mention that no evidence actually existed. As a result of this description of metal as dangerously popular, public sentiment was ready for extreme measures.

At around 4 a.m. on January 22, 1997, nearly one hundred metal fans suffered a rude awakening. That morning, terrified mothers of those in the metal scene began calling each other in a flurry, warning that the state security police were forcing their way into homes and taking their children into custody. Within a matter of hours, armed state security police had packed armored police vans with identified metal musicians and fans. According to an informant who wishes to remain anonymous, the arrested faced two weeks of torture, which included being attacked by dogs, sexually abused, beaten to unconsciousness, and extended periods of isolation in dark cold rooms filled with the stench of feces. At one point, jailed Islamic extremists were informed that "the Satanists" had arrived. The ensuing riot aimed at killing the metal fans and musicians resulted in their transfer to another prison. (A full transcript of the interview is in the appendix to illustrate the severity of their treatment.)

Some avoided the arrests, especially those of different or dual citizenship and therefore less susceptible to government harassment. Those who lacked such protections lived in constant fear of the police. Samadie explains, "I was in a band and two of my band mates were arrested. We [went] to sleep full-dressed with shoes and everything because we were expecting cops knocking on the door at any moment and dragging us in just because we play in a metal band. . . . The atmosphere [was] stinking with fear. Just because we play[ed] music, we [were] a target" (2006). For captivated news readers, however, the arrests heightened interest in the story. Photographs of the accused exiting police vans with black lines over their eyes to protect their identity graced the pages of newspapers. Television crews hovered around the jail to get glimpses of the "Satanists" and their families. Television interviews of the accused focused on uncovering details such as the ritual killing of cats in Qasr al-Barun. The identities of the accused were kept hidden, but during a particularly harsh interview on state television, the camera kept "slipping" to reveal the appearance of one traumatized youth (Di Giovanni 1997). The images of what "Satanism" really looked like were no longer presented through photographs from Europe and the United States. The country now had its very own "Satanists" to splash on the covers of newspapers around the country. In a sense, the visual space previously held by images of "Satanists" in Europe and the United States now held Egypt's own. Khaled Madani of the Doom Club was termed by the press *amir al-gama'* ("commander of the group"), a designation usually used to identify leaders of violent Islamic extremists.

Mufti Nasr Farid Wassel, Egypt's top cleric, accused the alleged Satanists of apostasy and publicly advocated the death sentence. Egyptian newspapers continued to publish lurid (as well as uncorroborated and fictitious) accounts of *musiqa mitalik*, for example:

Children had swapped beer and whisky for the blood of cats and pigeons and been tattooed with skulls and other symbols of the occult. . . . Hard rock was played as the fans dug through graves in search of human bones that could be "gifted" to the devil. . . . "We used to dance to heavy metal," says 22-year-old Khalid. . . . "After that we would slaughter a cat or a bird and smear our bodies with the blood. Most of us also got high on drugs or alcohol and each ritual ended with an orgy." . . . Tariq, another suspected Satanist still under interrogation, told police he has done nothing to be ashamed of. "We want to be different, to be unconventional. Satan encourages instant enjoyment and permits what religion forbids. We want to imitate foreigners and live life in our own way." Dr. Ahmed Al Magdoub of Cairo University, says: "This group of youths became victims of alcoholism, drugs, sex, crime and even the devil. The absence of democracy in our country has created an intellectual vacuum that sucks in unacceptable foreign influences." The Imam of the Arab world's most prestigious university, Al Azhar, says . . . "Israel is behind these devil-worshippers and this is part of a Zionist conspiracy aimed at corrupting our youth." An Egyptian MP, Sarwat Abaza, warned: "If they insist on following their wicked ways, we should act according to Islamic law. In this case the punishment for all apostates is execution." (Bhatia 1997)

The official narrative had congealed: Israeli subterfuge was responsible for introducing disturbing anti-Islamic practices into Egypt through morally void upper-class university students. Another article illustrates the echo effect of this reporting:

During these parties, youths dressed in black swayed to the rhythm of "heavy metal" rock music, took drugs, drank alcoholic beverages and dabbed themselves with the blood of cats or birds, said one worshipper, Khaled Rushdi. Rushdi also told investigators that they engaged in illicit sex, tore up the Koran, Islam's holy book, and held up crucifixes upside down to mark their contempt for religions. The parties were usually held in the desert outside Cairo, the Commonwealth cemetery in the Egyptian capital, the up-market neighborhood of Heliopolis or in five-star hotels in restaurants in Cairo and the northern city of Alexandria. (Mekki 1997)

Collages that sometimes accompanied the articles included Stars of David, aloof long-haired boys with black T-shirts, guitars, satellite dishes, and computers, along with the sexually provocative women mentioned earlier. The most pithy headline in the weekly, English-language *Egyptian Gazette* read, "Devil Worship—Made in America and Exported by Israel."

The public debate did include condemnation of the arrests and accusations of media sensationalism. A February 27, 1997, cover story in the weekly *Sabah al-Khayr* urged the students not to abandon metal, ridiculing those who equated nonmainstream music with Satanism. In its March 6 issue, the editor suggested that parents file a lawsuit against the Ministry of Interior to uphold citizens' rights, stating, "Why did the State Security Police overreact and where are the citizens' rights, even if they were suspects?" On March 8, *Akhbar al-Yum* accused the press of exaggerating stories to sell its publications: "The media was hysterical, dying for information day after day. So when we didn't give them any, they reported on rituals performed abroad as if they were taking place in Egypt by the defendants we arrested" (Khattab 1997).

But the damage had been done. Metal practices came to represent evil incarnate in these exaggerated reports because the media characterization touched on particular Egyptian fears and anxieties. In his analysis of the approximately one hundred clippings on the incident housed at the French Research Institute in Cairo, Ted Swedenburg suggests that the "causes" cited by the media for the development of the "Satanic scourge" might be grouped by external and internal factors (Swedenburg 2000). The external include Western political domination via Satanism, the "cultural invasion" of Egypt through Western and Saudi Arabian media, and Zionism. The internal causes are slightly more complex. Children of the morally bereft, indulgent, and absent *awlad al-zawat* (children of the aristocracy) live in a *firagh thaqafi* (cultural vacuum) left by the *infitah* and a lack of democracy due to Mubarak's continuing extension of emergency law. Without strong religious beliefs, jobs, or proper recreation, these youths are victims of institutional failure, particularly a corrupt media and failed university system. This narrative ties directly into historically rooted anxieties of the nonaristocracy, or *awlad al-balad* (children of the country), exploiting a class division that associates the upper class with foreign and corrupting influence. (See Messiri 1978, 84–91; Armbrust 1996; El-Hamamsy 1975). Thus, this small group of metal fans and musicians was primed for transformation into the menacing Other in terms of popular music, though for many the music and practice occupied more of an avant-garde nature—an open aesthetic space that offered a poetic way of refiguring a world filled with contradictions, injustice, and meaninglessness.

After the arrests, most metalheads either left Egypt or cut their hair to disappear into more conventional Egyptian lives. Those who did not still live in fear of misinformed vigilante justice, not uncommon in Egypt. Seif El-Din Moussa of Wyvern remembers his unease as Egyptians were swallowing the sensationalist stories whole, believing metalheads to be enemies of Egypt and Islam. In Moussa's words, "Imagine this. In 1997, you walk on the street, you see every single guy on the street, he's holding a newspaper or a magazine that is talking about the arrests and after he reads the article, he says, 'These guys are Satanists and should be executed.' Everybody who is wearing black and long hair is being harassed on the streets and insulted on the streets" (2006). The reporting had certainly gotten out of hand. As suggested earlier, the journalist Abdullah Kamal, who broke the story for *Ruz al-Yusuf*, claimed afterward that he originally "published the story as a social problem that families and schools should notice and remedy. . . . The coverage severely lacked precision and investigation. All papers felt obliged to write about it as the issue of the moment, and most of them put no effort into checking the information" (Khattab 1997). The Egyptian government, however, played a large role in elevating the hysteria, seizing an opportunity to redefine the noise of metal as a signifier of deviance. It was a political strategy that had nothing to do with metal or even Satanism directly. The government needed a distraction from two issues: the rapid privatization of the public sector (initiated by Mubarak's sweeping cabinet changes) and the intensifying criticism from exiled and imprisoned Islamic extremists accusing Egypt of being anti-Islam. Interior Minister Hassan El Alfy became a national hero through his involvement with this crackdown on metal, though none of those arrested were ever convicted of a crime.

Eventually, all media coverage stopped and the story went away. The detainees themselves were all released in a matter of weeks. News articles on *musiqa mitalik* entered the archives in thick black binders—material memory of one of the most dangerous cultural battles ever fought over Egypt's youth. But metal does not accept defeat. It rises above defeat, in this case by rejecting that the battle was cultural.

Resurgent Egyptian Extreme Metal

By 2006, most Egyptians remembered the case and were still wary of metal. In fact, when returning to my car after interviewing the metal bands Worm and Mascara in Alexandria, the driver and photographer who had stayed behind expressed relief that we had returned safely. They said that images of Satanic rituals involving blood and orgies ran through their heads. That was nine years after the arrests. The war over what "metal" was had shifted to two places. For the metal fan, metal's meaning was emergent, developing out of discussions with friends, going to concerts, finding groups on the Internet, and engaging with the music itself. For the nonfan, metal had a stigma. While mistrust of the media and the government kept metal from representing Satan incarnate, many Egyptians knew that metal was something that might attract the unwanted scrutiny of the state security police. Several Egyptian friends asked me not to mention their names while doing this research out of fear of association. (My only friends interested were journalist-activists, many of whom had some association to the 1990s scene.) As a result of this cold war over metal's meaning, few outside the fan community took part in the discussions that revolved around defining the practice. This was a marked difference from when Marlboro, Virgin Megastore, concert producers, and other people in the wider music industry had a part in the conversation.

Over the years, the metal scene had quietly reemerged in Egypt in a space that was relatively separate from daily Egyptian life. If Egyptian "culture" is understood in terms of the tourist industry and the growing religiosity of segments of the country, metal fans could step outside the ubiquitous papyrus, hieroglyphs, and crescents to either escape or reconfigure the signs of being Egyptian. At the same time, many fans also criticized the images of metal that came from the 1997 media coverage—alcohol, upside-down crosses, and violence. In its resurgent form, metal was dislodged from popular music to become experimental once again. The more ubiquitous Internet (at least for this demographic) provided a clandestine forum for organizing shows and distributing e-flyers. Three competing concert promoters were vying for popularity. Fans arrived at all-night concerts in the outlying desert via a series of microbuses, some shedding their *galalib* to reveal black T-shirts with an array of band logos: Iron Maiden, Sepultura, Children of Bodum, Slipnot, Metallica, Amon Amarth, and so on. The stage backdrops were once again walls of amplifiers, doubling as dark canvases for light shows and pyrotechnics, all powered by rented generators.

In the summer of 2006, I attended Metal Accord, a concert in the desert outside Cairo. From a commercial standpoint, the event had all the markings of a public fair one might see in the upmarket neighborhood of Zamalek—an admission fee at the door, food stalls, groups of young men greeting each other warmly. Behind the stage, the Giza pyramids loomed as one of the only visual reminders that we were still in Egypt. Members of bands passed around self-produced "demos," replete with original artwork and track listings in English.[6] No music was for sale. Rather, the complimentary recordings were meant to expose audiences to their music. The original tracks shuffle in between non-Egyptian tracks and become points of debate among fans: Is this band derivative? Is that band more professional than the other? Is adding Egyptian "color" to an international metal sound a legitimate means of anchoring metal to Egypt? As the bands sound-checked, I stumbled across several of these debates after being introduced to various members of the scene. In a sense, the musical practice engendered critical debates about cosmopolitanism, nationalism, musical innovation, consumerism, and musical purism—all discussions shared by rock and avant-garde worlds.

The music began. My attention shifted to four hundred young people clad in metal shirts who head-banged to Megadeth covers and a sprinkling of originals. The scene here looked so familiar, seemingly another example of globalized popular music used to forge a cosmopolitan youth identity aimed at challenging the status quo. But was that all the brutal crackdown had been about eight years earlier, disaffected youth rallying the defiant flag of metal while the government had rallied the public against it?

As the night progressed, something began to puzzle me. The rebellion typically associated with metal was muted. The fans self-policed one another. When the mosh pits got too violent, the fans broke people up and calmed them down. It was a challenge to spot a bottle of Stella or Heineken. No-where was there a whiff of hashish. Occasionally, a contingent of fans would go behind a building to pray. I wondered: was the reemergent metal under-ground going to remain soft in the shadow of the 1997 arrests?

To my surprise, front man and drummer Seif El-Din Moussa of Cairo's Wyvern praised the well-behaved fans in a later interview: "We thanked the crowds and fans so much because if it wasn't for their discipline and follow-ing the rules, this concert would have been a big failure." In fact, the idea of provocation—the supposed raison d'être of metal—is anathema to El-Din. He states, "Back in the late nineties, [fans] used to imitate. For example, they saw a metal video where a band was holding an inverted cross, for example, or breaking a cross, or setting fire to a cross, so they start imitating them. But these days, the organizers are smarter. They have more control over the crowds. The crowd is smarter. They know that this is stupid, that this shouldn't be done, and these actions provoke lots of people" (2006). Mohammed Omran, the guitarist for Cairo's progressive death metal band Stigma, says that fans are more aware of the dangers of associating themselves with metal. "Rather than people just listening to the music and not caring about what the government thinks they are doing, now they are aware that the government might misinterpret certain things" (2006). The 1997 ar-rests are old news, but there remains an association of metal with menacing deviance—at its worst, metal is still rendered as the Satanist weapon of the Mossad,[7] and at its least, it is seen as a foreign indulgence. Tarek Shehata of Worm confirms that the vilification of metalheads persists: "Two years ago, I was wearing a T-shirt with a band from Germany, a band called Immortal, on it. We were just in this café and there was this guy, a friend of ours actually, and he had one of his friends at the table, and I remember hearing something like, 'Oh yeah, there's another Satanist'" (2006). When interviewing the Cairene progressive death metal band Stigma, I asked them if the danger of being arrested makes metal in Egypt exciting. Unanimously, the band answered with a resounding "No!" citing the horrific conditions in Egyptian prisons as an obvious deterrent. Tarek Shehata later put it simply, "No one dares to fuck with the government here" (2006). Egyptian prisons do not make for exciting stories, only tragic ones. I wondered why anyone post-arrests risks so much to play metal.

A stumbling block toward answering these questions is that the literature on metal often treats the genre as a popular and rebellious music. Understand-ing metal from the perspective of the avant-garde is illuminating as, overall, the literature untangles critical issues of aesthetic experiences of challenging musics.

Discussion: Extreme Metal as an Avant-Garde

While often thought of as a popular genre, metal has largely operated underground, resisting trends, mass dissemination, and, to a degree, commodification itself. Interest in the practice by the Egyptian government also belies the idea that the debates within the community are politically figured. Analysis of extreme metal is better engaged with the literature on the avant-garde than the popular for three reasons.[8] First of all, this critical literature suits the particular aesthetic efficacy of Egyptian metal. Much scholarly discussion of metal has focused on issues of power and expressivity from the standpoint of popular music (Walser 1993; Wallach 2005; LeVine 2008). Metal in Egypt, however, fulfills another role for its practitioners given that, in part, the stakes of rebellion are not worth the risks that playful rebellion might bring. There is a consensus that metal provides a critical medium through which its insiders play with existential and political issues reflected in Egyptian metalhead distinctions between "real" fans and "posers." While these distinctions exist worldwide among an array of rock offshoots, the control over what metal means among Egyptian youth intensifies the politics of who "gets" metal. Framing metal as an avant-garde practice adds to the critical attention to nonrebellious aesthetic efficacy found in metal scholarship (Berger 1999; Weinstein 2000; Kahn-Harris 2007).

The second reason for analyzing Egyptian metal as an avant-garde is that in Egypt-at-large, metal does not have the same wider references that it does in the West. Especially before the 1997 media campaign, metal was mostly unheard of in Egypt. Instead of signifying lower class white male "barbarism" as it does in the West, it was fairly free from cultural references in Egypt. Still today, it sounds more alien to Egyptians, much in the way that Debussy's incorporation of Indonesian music might have been for the majority of late nineteenth-century French listeners. To most Egyptians, especially pre-arrests, extreme metal is a curious noise.

The third justification for viewing Egyptian metal as an avant-garde is that its musicians embrace a radical approach to certain formal musical elements; for example, they isolate fast drumming, growled vocal production, and distorted guitar tones and push these elements to the limit. This extreme compositional play recalls what music critic Paul Griffiths uses to identify "avant-garde music." Griffiths's criterial definition includes aesthetic newness, the shirking of traditional norms, the "abandonment of traditional tonality, the development of new rhythmic complexity, the recognition of colour as an essential, the creation of a quite new form for each work, the exploration of deeper mental processes" (1978, 13). Such a definition resonates with the kind of radical musical approaches that metal musicians develop, especially in the case of Egypt.

Popular musicians and producers in the West have a long-standing tradition of refreshing their practice by dipping into the avant-garde, be it the Beatles with *Sgt. Pepper's Lonely Hearts Club Band* (1967) or Radiohead's *Kid A* (2000). Arguably, music transgression has played a cat-and-mouse game with mainstream pop since the birth of punk in the late 1970s. As Keir Keightley argues, the modernist mode in rock has often informed judgments of authenticity (2001, 135–36). From this ideological perspective, the "rock genius" breaks with traditional forms to save music from the specter of commercial crystallization. While that archetypal musician is part of the narrative embraced by the Western music industry, not so in Egypt. Risk-aversion, quick turnover of product in pace with piracy practices, and a lack of market feedback have all contributed to a commercial music market that produces single hits that sell quickly (Frishkopf 2010, 17–18). The economic model in Arab popular music has shifted from "masterpiece" to "fast-food." Metal and its transgressive nature built upon principles of complex virtuosity place Egyptian metal in a space outside the supposed timeless practice of *turath* ("heritage") of *musiqa 'arabiyya* and disposable popular music. In its marginalization, metal sidesteps the polemics of nostalgia for an unmediated past and consumption of the highly mediated and suspicious realm of state-influenced or profit-oriented media industries. In essence, metal provides a new cultural logic that emerges from practice—concerts and acquisition of music serve as primary activities that engender discussions in private spaces, be they bedrooms, Internet forums, or in a crowd. The openness of metal—its resistance to definitive readings—is what gave it its efficacy in Egypt, not its particular expressive modality but its open logic.

Many cultural theories on the avant-garde identify direct political strategy in a way similar to how Egyptian media described the dangers of metal—the noise of metal representing a direct attack on religion and the state. First, consider the notion that music can embed antiestablishment power. Robert Adlington suggests that intersections between the political and the avant-garde exist outside the "artistic avant-garde," manifested as the "psychedelia" of psychedelic rock, the "prog" of progressive rock, the "free" of free jazz, and the radical commentaries of folk and soul (2009). Contrary to Adorno's insistence on an avant-garde autonomous from popular musics, radical political force can be embedded in commodities—a Trojan horse of sorts.

Second, consider the notion of cultural coded "readings" of music. Susan McClary suggests that the Western avant-garde covertly maintains a class status quo, housed and supported in academic, cultural, and broadcast institutions (1989). Deliberate unintelligibility can be used to maintain socioeconomic divisions. This Bourdieuian echo posits an economy of code passing as "taste" that legitimates power dynamics between those who "get" the avant-garde and those who don't (see Bourdieu 1984).

Both Adlington's and McClary's assessments of the political efficacy of avant-garde privilege the expressive (whether conscious or not) role of music in a matrix of social struggle. The account just given of metal's extremism as a contemplative practice is at odds with these assessments. In fact, both of these accounts reify radical musical experience—a particular play with noise—as community-defining indicators, messages to be sent and interpreted. In a sense, the Egyptian government made a similar argument, reifying the out-ward appearances of noise into symbols that, in this case, read as deviance, threat, and moral decline.

A deliberate play with noise was a serious liability for those practicing in Egypt in 1997. Outside forces reified metal's ambiguities into concrete things to fear, referentially linking technology, the Internet, and outside influence to a seeming conspiracy against Egypt and Islam. Through media representation and state action, the metalheads' experiential play with ambiguity stood for a serious expression of deviance.

The Efficacy of Resurgent Egyptian Extreme Metal

To a metalhead, the experience of unintelligibility is not nihilistic, though it might be construed that way to an outsider. Metal can be revealing in much the same way that Theodor Adorno describes his avant-gardists: "The terror which Schoenberg and Webern spread, today as in the past, comes not from their incomprehensibility but from the fact that they are all too correctly un-derstood. Their music gives form to that anxiety, that terror, that insight into the catastrophic situation which others merely evade by regressing. They are called individualists, and yet their work is nothing but a single dialogue with the powers which destroy individuality—powers whose 'formless shadows' fall gigantically on their music" (2001, 60). Adorno's suggestion of dialogue implies that we are mistaken if we look for one-way musical expression, but rather, we should interpret the music as a metaphoric dialogue with and contemplation of critical issues. Formless shadows also fall gigantically on Egyptian extreme metal. To reveal what casts these shadows, we must examine the efficacy of metal through Egyptian metalhead experiences by connecting their "terrors and fears" to musical phenomena. At the heart of my analysis is this: there is a means of understanding that relies on accepting practices of unintelligibility.

Cairene guitarist and tattoo artist Timur Reda reflects on what metal must seem like to an Egyptian nonmetalhead: "I'm sure they're like, 'Who are these kids? Jumping around. Making a lot of noise? If you just scratch the surface, then that's it. They don't ask why, they're not interested in why" (2006). The surface interpretation as addressed earlier is that metal is a simple form of youth rebellion. Going beyond the surface requires asking three questions: First, who are these kids? Second, why do they make a lot of noise? This second question requires some untangling, because noise is not a thing as much as it is an experience. So third, what is this noise?

Q: Who are these kids?
A: Young Egyptians who don't necessarily feel Egyptian.

As mentioned earlier, the demographic of Egypt's metal scene is fairly uniform. Most members are from relatively wealthy families, but not the ultrarich business class.[9] They are educated and have a cosmopolitan world-view shaped by access to international media. They are feeling more and more detached from the growing religious conservatives and uneducated Egyptians. With an eye to the world through cable television and the Internet, most Egyptian youths of *awlad al-zawat* can envision a life beyond Egypt while being conscripted to living with its lack of opportunities, corruption, and—at least until 2011—political stagnation.

Many of the Egyptian metal musicians I met would leave Egypt if given the chance. By the time this book is in print, several will have immigrated to the United States, Canada, and Germany. Leaving Egypt, however, does not relieve the feeling of alienation, for even if relocated, they are still Egyptians, just Egyptians living abroad. For these young people, Egyptian metal engages the problem shared by many young, educated, cosmopolitan Egyptians: being Egyptian.

This next question is more complicated than the first and requires a two-part answer.

Q: Why do they make a lot of noise?
A: First, radical critique.

For metal fans, music allows a contemplation of everyday alienation by pulling the listener into a simultaneously strange and familiar fantastical world. I suggest the term *empathetic aporia* to refer to an irresolvable internal conflict between a capacity and an incapacity to relate to another. I choose to differentiate this quandary from alienation—which is an experience of isolation—because it describes better an experience of internal discord of the phenomenon itself. The empathetic aporia festers between the familiar and the unfamiliar, challenging the distinction between the self and the other, and can be illuminated, albeit not resolved, through metal experiences. Concert promoter Tarek Morsy says that metal is "telling you what is really going on in the world" (2006). Certainly, metal fans worldwide attest to the music's ability to violently disrupt the quotidian to illuminate the realities of death, war, anger, alienation, and anxiety—topics often ignored by the mainstream.

Keith Kahn-Harris identifies a primary discourse in extreme metal that develops Sarah Thornton's Bourdieuian notion of "subcultural capital" into two types of prestige acquisition: mundane cultural capital and transgressive cultural capital (2007, 129–31). The former involves fluency with bands, styles, genres, and other subcultural content, whereas the latter employs a strategy of exclusion and transgression that embraces change and looks outside the canon. In essence, a politics of truth gains dimensionality through a relationship between *doxa* and *praxa* in metal, both resisting the coercion of trends through an interplay between solidarity of a metal community and a critical individualism (Kahn-Harris 2007, 130). The modality of this discourse begins with the acknowledgment of horror.

Focusing on negative themes, metal reveals truths that culture (in this sense: norms, rules, or interpretive traditions) provincially hides. As Seif El-Din Moussa of Wyvern explains, metal is political but not expressively so; rather, its politics derives from its commitment to look unflinchingly at horrifying realities of the world: "Heavy metal music and heavy metal lyrics are very profound. They usually discuss unusual matters. They talk about politics, they talk about chaos, they talk about anger, they talk about emotions. . . . They talk about these issues from a darker side. They don't talk about peace, they talk about the tragedy of war. They don't talk about love, they talk about the negative side of hate. So, yes, they tend to be political, not to sell, but this is how they think. This is why they play music. This is their own perspective" (2006).

Rhetorician Kenneth Burke associates this type of symbolic play with negativity. He suggests that the impossibility of presenting a negative image relegates the representation of negativity to the domain of signs. In his words, "The negative is properly shown by a sign, not by an image. For a 'negative image' would be a contradiction in terms" (1966, 430). He argues that in language, and by extension other forms of artistic expression, there is a dramatic culmination of negativity in the theme of Hell, which "is, to perfection, a function of the negative. . . . The notion of Hell involves a scenic reinforcement of the negative as a principle, the total or ultimate thou-shalt-not" (474–75). Herein lies the contemplative efficacy of horrifying imagery—in our case a representation of an empathetic aporia visible through gaps in comprehension.

A sign, however, is not necessarily a decipherable direct communication.

Promoter Tarek Morsy attests to metal's openness when saying that the meaning of metal does not read as would a newspaper; rather, it provides people who are already conscious of world problems a means of dealing with them. Morsy says that, as opposed to the love themes that predominate within Arab popular music, "metal describes how I feel" (2006). He acknowledges that not all fans engage with metal in this way. In his words, "They are not intellectual enough to understand what this music is really about. They just take it as a lifestyle. . . . Most of the fans are like, 'I like this weird environment. I am a heavy metal fan, so I am weird to the society.' Most of them are teenagers who think in this way. That's why they know a lot of bands by heart, 'I know this band, this band, this band . . ?' What do they know?" (2006). A deeper engagement of metal recalls what Krzysztof Ziarek calls radical critique. Within this community in Egypt, extreme metal music and its accoutrements offer open radical critique, something quite different from political resistance, pointed struggle, or dissent. In his examination of avant-garde poetry, Ziarek suggests that art's efficacy reveals "the possibility of thinking not only beyond the currently existing forms of power but also . . . beyond the very idea of being as power" (2004, 6). Ziarek's argument is helpful because he identifies in art a transformative force that contains a capacity to critique on a deeper level—in our case, a radical critique of empathy that involves disassembly and possibility. Metal experiences—whether visual, musical, or lyrical—enable critical capacities to play with the experience of the empathetic.

During a series of interviews with bassist Khaled Sallam of Konzaross, a psychedelic melodic dark metal one-man project, the ways in which metal offers contemplation emerged. During our first meeting, he relayed dozens of stories about his violent past. When harassed for his long hair and distinct attire, Khaled fought back against everyone from peers to police. Now in his thirties, Khaled is a devout Muslim and still an active, though somewhat reclusive, member of the metal community. At a later meeting, I asked Khaled if he saw connections between his violent youth and the metal aesthetic. He explained that whenever he tried to talk to someone about his frustration, anxiety, alienation, and depression, that person would say, "No, Khaled, don't fixate on those things; life is not that bad" (2006). Playing and listening to metal, he said, allows him a means of holding violence at arm's length and looking it over—a way of playing with subjects that everyone else ignores.

Sallam is primarily a bedroom musician, fiercely independent within Cairo's metal scene. His music barely has an audience, and his subgenre specificity hints at exclusion more than belonging to a certain scene. In fact, he credits himself as the founder of the genre. Herein lies an instance of Kahn-Harris's transgressive subcultural capital: a valuation of metal's critical capacity enacted through rising above the mundane. Metal, then, is marked by a communal practice of individual awakening by means of shock. Berger quotes an American fan, who says that death metal "is intended to break the listener free from the comforting clichés of any party line and to inspire critical thinking and self-determination" (1999, 66).

When Khaled composes music, his intent is for the listeners to "live inside the track and think." Rather than hoping to induce violent head-banging, he hopes his music will feed the imagination and that the listeners will participate and "create the mode themselves" (2006), allowing them a parallel contemplation of violence through radical critique.

Q: Why do they make a lot of noise?
A: Second, it might not be a lot of noise to them. It might be just right.

An interview with the Cairo-based progressive death metal band Stigma touched on these issues during a discussion about stylistic differences in the Egyptian metal subscenes. The band members said that certain feelings engender an appetite for more extreme music—in particular, black metal.[10]

MOHAMMED OMRAN: People say that the Alexandria scene is mostly extreme black metal.
TIMUR REDA: Not trying to overanalyze it, but for someone who has a lot of issues to deal with, might be feeling depressed, or outcast, they would probably turn to something more extreme, as opposed to pop music. [Pop music] doesn't really give the tension. (2006)

What Omran refers to as "the tension" that exists musically in metal relates to an existential tension endemic to many in the demographic of the metalheads described thus far. But what exactly is it about extreme metal that allows upper-middle class, educated, cosmopolitan youth to explore issues of depression and alienation bred of their empathetic aporia?

Metal comprises repeated riffs, mostly listened to as songs, played over and over. For this reason, examining the radicalism in metal is difficult. Champions of the avant-garde have suggested that popular music's repeatability often renders art into toothless commodity (Benjamin 1986; Adorno 2001). From this view, repeated familiarity breeds a type of contented lethargy based in a regression to simple gratification. For example, hearing the opening riff from Black Sabbath's "Iron Man" over and over resolves the anticipation of the feeling. Some have suggested, however, that popular music can be revolutionary, as experimental songs are commodity repurposed for revolutionary ends (Pratt 1994; Adlington 2009). The problem with this argument is that it focuses on a song or piece. Instead, a focus on an individual's listening history shows that extreme metal listeners often pass through a repertoire that changes radically. This is important for any committed metal fan. Seif El-Din Moussa describes his pathway into and through metal: "I started listening to disco and then pop music but there was something missing. Then I was introduced accidentally to an album by Scorpions. . . . It was hard rock. I liked that kind of music. Then, I took it from there. I started listening to Europe, Bon Jovi. Then, a little bit of Savatage, Metallica, and then I got involved in my own band" (2006). Shifting our focus diachronically—from the "work of art" to the experience of a repertoire through a listener's lifetime—we see, in fact, that many metal listeners seek to maintain radical musical experience by searching out a newer, more challenging repertoire after an existing album collection becomes too predictable. In essence, metal offers a graduated repertoire that can become a pathway to musical extremism. Some extreme metal listeners describe the experience as akin to a drug addiction (Berger 1999, 59).

This individual phenomenon for a listener mirrors the general development of metal since its beginnings and especially as manifested since the 1990s (Weinstein 2000, 287). Metal originated in exotic representation. Proto-metal bands such as Black Sabbath, Blue Cheer, and Budgie began pulling apart the blues genre, extending the practice of hard rock bands such as the Rolling Stones and Led Zeppelin. Andrew Cope suggests that the birth of heavy metal can be located in the genre transgressions initiated by Black Sabbath (2010). While hard rock musicians referenced blues tropes, metal musicians began deconstructing existing musical syntax and aesthetic coding. Metal aesthetics continued to develop in constant retreat from everyday music. The genre eventually became referentially untethered as its musical criteria became exaggerated beyond recognition. Specific amplifications and distortions of metal stylings shook the references of the blues. During the late 1970s and 1980s, metal musicians smoothed over the intonation of the sharpened minor "blues" third and swung rhythmic syncopations, abandoned twelve-bar form, and privileged an operatic vocal style over a blues mimicry. Musicians pushed certain stylistic envelopes in favor of referential play with the African American Other.

For an example of how targeted musical and lyrical exaggeration happens at the expense of cultural reference, consider the connection of Pat Hare's 1954 "I'm Gonna Murder My Baby," with its blunt lyrical focus on lethal domestic violence and early distorted guitar, to Slayer's 1986 "Angel of Death," in which screams about the horror of Josef Mengele's atrocities at Auschwitz are accompanied by thrashing metal guitars. The latter is a mutated variation of an originally disturbing bad-man ballad. Between Hare and Slayer is a genealogy of exaggeration of both a lyrical theme and timbral orientation—from Hare and Howlin' Wolf to the Rolling Stones to Black Sabbath to Iron Maiden to Slayer. In exchange for its lost demographic references, after forty years of retreat from the familiar, metal now employs extremely distorted and down-tuned guitars, machine-gun-like bass drumming, and guttural vocals punctuated by shrieks. For a seasoned metal practitioner, noise operates in productive relation to what it disturbs.[11] To an outsider, it can all be noise.

Reports of mistaken contraband in the 1997 Egyptian press include a Chicago Bulls hat, a black Bugs Bunny T-shirt, a black Statue of Liberty T-shirt, and Beethoven CDs. To a metalhead, the errors that authorities made in identifying contraband are comical. Newspaper and magazine articles preceding and following the arrests depict a similar swath of supposed "Satanic" paraphernalia that would strike a European or American as off target. To the larger Egyptian audience at the time of the arrests, however, metal imagery was largely unknown; outside meanings of metal had not yet been described and codified. Newspapers were doing the work of identifying a noise: generating imagery that destabilized their notions of their community by giving form to anxieties.

But for the metalhead, much of metal's structural operation relies on unintelligibility—a noise that provides a desired feeling of instability. Metal produces material that is pointedly difficult to decipher—lyrics, sound, imagery, and behavior. There is a premium placed on noise, but noise must be specifically targeted toward what it disturbs. Listeners poise themselves on the edge of intelligibility, progressing through harder, weirder, darker, more complex, or more disturbing music for a certain effect. For this reason, some experiential goals of listening to and participating in metal can retreat into oblivion rather than remain on a fixed traditional canon.

The problem with noise is that upon repeated listening, noisy things become less noisy. Repeatability normalizes irregularity as patterns become apparent upon successive listening, especially in recorded media. For this reason, noise in the listener's ear is difficult to pinpoint. Egypt's relatively small scene provides an excellent field in which to examine this. Following the conversations among fans about what is music and what is noise reveals a dynamic sense of noise that, in part, depends on how seasoned a particular listener is to metal. The variety of metal styles among bands at a single concert provides plenty of controversy centered on what seems to be taste for things like "heaviness," "darkness," and "brutality."

Egyptian concert organizers curate a wide assortment of metal bands that play with noise to varying degrees. Concert flyers often indicate stylistic differences using references to more widely known American and European bands. One Metal Accord flyer lists the billing as such:

Enraged (Evanescence, Nightwish)

Sirens (Savatage)

Eyesore (Sepultura, Soulfly, Hatebreed, Stone Sour)

Wyvern (Metallica, Megadeth, Sepultura, Slayer)

Viper

Hatesuffocation (Demo ["Infectus"], Morbid Angel, Amon Amarth, Nile)

Worm (Demo ["Blood Lust"], Morbid Angel, Behemoth, Torture Killer, Kataklysm)

In the top right of the flyer is a qualifier: "All Bands Play Originals." The designation "demo" means that the band has a recording, usually distributed for free on CDs or available for free download on the Internet. At shows, styles range from pop-inflected grunge rock to black metal. Much of my conversation with fans at Metal Accord revolved around two questions often put to me: "Do you think this is music?" and "Don't you think that this isn't hard enough?" As I took in our conversations, I looked back at the older Egyptian gentleman selling food and wondered about his thoughts. Certainly he heard (and saw) more noise than music.

Noise is in the ear of the beholder. After Metal Accord, the topic of what metal sounds like to an Egyptian nonmetalhead came up in a conversation with Worm, the industrial death metal trio from Alexandria. Sitting in the group's rehearsal studio, the bass player brought up an instance in which an Egyptian not exposed to metal was confused by the music:

> TAREK SHEHATA: We had this painter over at my place a couple of years ago—we were renovating—and I was just playing the guitar with distortion and all that stuff. He asked me, "What's that sound? What is that?" He couldn't interpret it. Some sort of hissing or something like that.
>
> AHMED SAMADIE: The guitar is malfunctioning!
>
> SHEHATA: Yeah. Like, "Listen, you're not supposed to do that with your guitar!"
>
> SAMADIE: Ninety percent of the people are into Oriental music or Eastern beats. So, to them, heavy metal music is like a disaster. For example, they listen to Metallica and they can't tell the difference between the songs. It's just noise that goes from play to stop. They're not used to this kind of music. (2006)

In another conversation with Mohammed Omran, the issue of metal's sound to the uninitiated arose. Omran describes the experience of hearing metal for most Egyptians: "To them it's just some kind of incoherent noise. . . . It's pretty much the case for everyone who doesn't listen to metal with the first time trying to get into it. It's really hard to discern the notes and instruments from each other" (2006). The point is not simply recognition, but understanding a self-positioning between the noise and music. A savvy listener can distinguish levels of noise within the music. Omran accounts for friends who don't listen enough to position themselves within the din on metal: "It's interesting to see when I give a friend a metal song and ask him or her to listen to it. They don't get it. Until you're in it, you can't distinguish between it. Even rock and metal, to some people there is no distinction between rock and metal. Anything with loud guitars is just noise, period" (2006).

For the seasoned listener, what once was noise becomes recognizable because of a history of listening to the music to a point where the jarring unfamiliarity becomes predictable, acceptable, and less intense. The natural reaction is then to seek harder, less intelligible styles.

The counterbalance to this is nostalgic association. Much of the metal repertoire in Egypt involves covers of other bands (primarily American or European bands with widely known albums). Metal bands in general often "pay homage" to earlier bands through covering and, in some cases, updating classic repertoire.[12] In addition, the original riffs, drumbeats, lyrical content, and such draw from a pool of stock material. The degrees of noisiness in a diverse collection of metal styles provide for a gradation in which a new listener might find an entry point. In 2006, when the noise of metal had become associated with illegality, rock bands with slight metal tinges helped provide an access point to the wary. Sherine Amr of Alexandria's all-female metal group Mascara describes this phenomenon: "There are more and more who listen to metal than before. Now there are these bands who are something in between metal and rock. Rock is 'legal' [whereas] metal is 'illegal.' So this mixture makes people like, 'Okay, if I listen to this, maybe I can listen to this too'" (2006). That said, the motor behind listening trends in metal lies in experiences of unintelligibility—listening with an aim to sit on the border between noise and music. Central to this practice is intent to engage with noise. Robert Walser identifies one of the key moments in the development of metal as being intent to distort (as opposed to understanding distortion as mechanical failure) as a semiotic means of iconically representing power overflowing its channels (1993, 42). But while noise is somewhat measurable in Fourier analysis, tolerance for noise is not.

Once a taste for unintelligibility develops, a path through more challenging metal develops, not unlike a fixation for spicy foods. This, for many, is the point of metal: a moving target of experiencing the border between form and noise. And as a metaphor, metal offers motion through practice versus stagnation through acquisition. One of the main criticisms that veteran metal fans will make toward post-high-speed-Internet listeners is that younger fans aim at collecting albums without getting to know albums well.[13] Getting to know an album well amounts to experiencing the noise—the unintelligibility, the inhumanness—and reckoning with it. The following provides an analysis of noise as grotesque in metal, with particular emphasis on timbral phenomena in guitar.

Q: What is noise?

A: Grotesque dismemberment.

When he was young, bassist Khaled Sallam said he was drawn to horror movies and images of skulls on satellite TV. In fact, the imagery and lyrical content of metal draws heavily from the horror genre, which, in turn, has inherited the fantastical images of early colonial travel writing—for example, of James Bruce, Vivant Denon, John Lewis Burckhardt, and Lady Anne Blunt. In metal imagery, album art and lyrics exploit the image of the monster. By "monster," I mean the unified and incomprehensible combination of the self and the other; the exaggerated, the unfamiliar, and the alien (Frankenstein, demons, mummies, and zombies). Monsters are imaginary representations of the self and other taken to an extreme. Throughout the forty-year history of metal, monster images abound—for example, the exotic birdman on a horse from Budgie's debut album and the winged cyborg on Judas Priest's debut album.

Now recall the curious metal "contraband" confiscated by Egyptian authorities. That Bugs Bunny was suspect is plausible from the perspective of metal as an instance of Western cultural encroachment. To a Westerner, the recognizable Warner Brothers cartoon represents a comic character. While it is hard to imagine that Bugs Bunny's ubiquity has not seeped into every mind in the world, consider the anthropomorphism without the cultural references. As a part-human, part-rabbit being, he is in league with classical monsters: the centaur, sphinx, and minotaur.

What separates Bugs Bunny from metal imagery is his lack of grotesque features. Through conspicuous dismemberment of the human body and incorporation of nonhuman characteristics, the grotesque body maintains permeable boundaries through open, gaping orifices (Salem 2001, 215). The openness is poetic, allowing a violent coupling of human and nonhuman, aborting the classical with the grotesque. The monster image unsettles the viewer not because it is ugly but because the classical is aborted, the beautiful is aborted, the human is aborted. These grotesque images of the monster provide a visual foil for normality, revealing through the instability of the metal monster (and thus the crisis of empathy—is it man or creature?) but also the aborted as manifested.

Among Egypt's discontented metal fans, the image of the monster illuminates the empathetic aporia. Metal's radical critique occurs through the monster that offers an experience of empathetic challenge—an extreme feeling of simultaneous affinity and revulsion. Metal is an experience that potentially offers radical critique of the empathetic aporia, formally through acoustical, musical, visual, and performative redundancies of the grotesque monster.

Q: What is noise?
A: *Nafas dawsha*, an ecstatic experience of delocalization.

Mascara's violinist, Nancy Mounir, and front woman, Sherine Amr, recount their initial apprehension with the outside appearances of metal crowds—I would argue: an apprehension that, for them, now plays with the empathetic aporia.

NANCY MOUNIR: The first time I went to a Metal Accord concert, I was a little bit scared. It was really dark there. I didn't know how I got there because someone was driving me there. I was like, "Okay, where am I? Just somewhere in the middle of the desert?" People are drunk . . .

SHERINE AMR: Throwing up on the floor because they took an overdose . . .

MOUNIR: But nobody harms anybody there. It's very safe. It looks very scary but it's safe after all. They are so peaceful.

AMR: They just look like freaks and monsters. . . .

MOUNIR: Monsters or freaks or something.

AMR: But they're so peaceful. They don't do anything. Actually, they're friendly. (2006)

Overcoming outside appearances to discover metalhead friendliness is a theme among fan testimonials. Many speak of the juxtaposition of the intimidating outward look and inward amiability of metalheads, including reflexive discussions of dress, behavior, and personality. The juxtaposition is located throughout metal practice. Berger locates this tension in the deliberate performance of violence and order in the metal event (1999, 71). Metal experience, then, can be seen as play with the idea of violence through diverse modes of performance that include dress, attitude, interpersonal interaction, dancing, and storytelling.

Instability also comes to stand in metal aesthetics through its delocalizing force. In his discussion of *tarab*—an ecstatic feeling achievable with Arab music—Ali Jihad Racy describes the experience of *nafas sharqi*, an essence of the East (2003, 126). Extreme metal is in retreat from these references. While metal can also induce ecstatic experiences, it achieves something more akin to what I will term *nafas dawsha*, loosely meaning the "essence of destabilization of location," a transcendent experience that moves in an alternate direction to that of *tarab*.

Many Egyptian bands play with local musical references; but this is serious play, not parody. What constitutes the familiar may be culturally specific, but the grotesque monster image may retain its efficacy when crossing borders. Consider Egyptian metalhead reception of a European band using Egyptian monster imagery: Iron Maiden's 1984 *Powerslave*.[14] The album art and title track draw from Orientalist images of the Sphinx, mummies, cobras, pyramids, and despotic Pharaohs, evoking the grotesque of the Orient. Iron Maiden's "mascot," Eddie, assumes the face of the Sphinx. For Iron Maiden fans, Eddie himself is the identifiable monster, familiar and otherworldly, human and nonhuman, powerful and merciless. The title track of *Powerslave* even includes an "Oriental" guitar riff complete with the requisite augmented second—a clear suggestion of the Orient in movies, mimicking the obvious exoticism of *maqam hijaz*.[15]

In general, Egyptians are hyperaware and -critical of Orientalist representation. While they balk at the representational absurdity of the Bangles' 1986 hit "Walk Like an Egyptian," the *Powerslave* album is dear to Egyptian metal fans' hearts. As was explained to me, the album confirmed Egypt's place on the metal map. But a finer analysis from the standpoint of play with the empathetic aporia reveals how European and Egyptian perspectives of the *Powerslave* album can do the same work for the metal fan. In both cases, the imagery juxtaposes the alien and the familiar, revealing the grotesque. Egyptian imagery for the Western listener plays off of pharaonic-themed horror movies: Western explorers supernaturally awakening mummies that, in turn, resurrect an ancient and exotic despotism. This horror subgenre itself is a late incarnation of Orientalism. While self-Orientalization occurs, the poetics of *Powerslave* to an Egyptian plays with the everyday theater of ancient Egypt, from papyrus dealers stalking tourists near five-star hotels to Egyptian nationalist imagery on the Egyptian pound. The alien pharaonic imagery and augmented second interval for British Iron Maiden is the familiar for the Egyptian fan. As Eddie inhabits the imagery of the Sphinx, sarcophagi, and mummies, he animates what is familiar to an Egyptian, making it a grotesque representation of the empathetic aporia. Testifying to the seriousness of Egyptian adoption of *Powerslave*, Wyvern opened a set at the El-Sawi Culture Wheel venue in Cairo with the title track. The band performed with no sense of self-Orientalizing irony that would reveal a critique of Orientalist representation.

Communally, the noise of the grotesque comes out at a concert. Many fans come to a concert in traditional white *galabiyya* with a black T-shirt and jeans underneath. A band logo peeks out from the collar of the Egyptian garb, which is soon shed. Long hair, tattoos, and boots dominate the field of vision, and plenty of fans smile when talking about how the scene might be mistaken for a European show. Seif El-Din Moussa, Wyvern's front man, says, "We have videos of concerts. If we showed them to people and said, 'This is an Ozzfest concert,' they would totally buy it" (2006). Dress, however, does not have its power in imitating the West; rather, imitation in dress produces a noise of the grotesque that unites with other combinations of self and other, transgressing additional boundaries of gender appearance, class appearance, and representation of a "savage–civilized" spectrum.

Though the heavier grotesque musical moments dominate in extreme metal by way of loud targeted distortions, delicate moments of classical-esque sections act as contrast. Remarkably, given the international spread of metal, many bands localize metal by adding regional musics in the delicate sections. The Basque metal band Adhur adds Basque folk music, Israel's Orphaned Land adds what it calls "pan-Oriental" sections in an attempt to defeat existing political regionalisms (see Hecker 2005, 61–63), France's Blut Aus Nord includes cathedral choirs. I posit that this is not identity-making local branding but referential play that bears on the empathetic aporia—an inclusion of the familiar with the raw destructive distorted grotesque of the heavier sections. It is a gesture of delicate normative familiarity to make the musical monster more familiar and, in the end, more effective as a monster. In the next example, the band Odious from Alexandria juxtaposes sections of *'ud* and tabla with brutal black metal. The synthesizer plays both roles, adding a familiar Arab pop style to the black metal style. The result is a unified juxtaposition of the classical and the grotesque—a familiar style dismembered by the violent severity of black metal. Such musical work with pastiche pervades art music, especially in the avant-garde, and popular music alike. Particular to extreme metal is the starkness of the juxtaposition—another representation of the empathetic aporia.

In a subtler vein, guitarist Mohamed Khalifa of Viper found that the stylistic incorporation emerged in the course of composing. In his words, "Once the band started getting going and we were jamming regularly together, all this Arabic-sounding stuff kept coming out, especially in the lead guitar harmonies. It was minimal at first, but became more and more pronounced. Toward the end, early 1997 that is, it really was becoming a central part of our music. It was no longer just an influence. We were contemplating adding a keyboard player with one of those keyboards they sell over there with all the Arabic instruments. I played tabla and wanted to include that in the music" (2010).

Metal guitar timbres do not simply disturb the system. The sound itself is a combination of noise and identifiable tone. This aspect of metal is perhaps its most definitive: the particular musical play found in metal. Understanding metal in this way helps demonstrate deliberate use of noise and the importance of overtones. The social noise as constructed by the reports of accused Satanism is an exegetic mistake in defining what, in fact, the noise of metal is disturbing. Noise exists in many genres of music as a productive element of musical experience.

Being awash in overtones is also part of *tarab* in *musiqa 'arabiyya*. Racy documents this phenomenon in his investigation of effective *tarab*, which, as an event, "becomes potent as an experiential complex, or as a sensory-visual 'feast'" (2003, 195). Racy accounts for timbral complexity in *musiqa 'arabiyya* in musicians' preferences for slackening strings. Not only does the lowered tension make the *'ud* easier to play, it more importantly results in enhanced overtone effects, much like the formants that Harris Berger and Cornelia Fales describe in their analysis of vernacular descriptions of guitar timbres (2005). What Arab musicians might call "sweeter," a metal guitarist might call "heavier." In both cases, the complexity of sound in the upper registers gives what in *tarab* is the creative ecstatic experience of *sultannah* (Racy 2003, 136). The "sensory-visual feast" of metal also extends beyond timbre.

Patterns of cognitive play with noise and form manifest themselves across all other aspects of metal practice. Redundancy reinforces its particular work. These other manifestations of this cognitive play include references, singing styles, rhythms, band logos, and dress.

Lyrically, a listener may experience the grotesque space between recognition and noise in the extremely growled vocal timbres of the singers—a sound known as "brutal vocals." Contorting the voice in this style does the same acoustical work as guitar distortion; it increases harmonic information in the upper register that manifests itself as noise. The harsh roar can be augmented with distortion pedals, referentially producing a humanoid sound—either animalistic or mechanical or both. Knowing the lyrics aids in this play with recognition.

Rhythmic extremism can produce powerful juxtapositions of noise and form beyond the referential tensions between black metal "blast beats" and typical Egyptian 4/4 dance rhythms *baladi* and *malfuf*. Drumming in Worm's "Codex" is programmed, pushing the boundary of human possibility with its mechanical precision. While an accomplished drummer could come close to the programmed tracks, the imagery of man-machine would be lost. This is not the extreme drum programming found in Netherlands-based experimentation in metal and grind musics; rather, it borders what sounds human and mechanical in the same way that virtuosic death metal drummers push

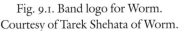

Fig. 9.1. Band logo for Worm.
Courtesy of Tarek Shehata of Worm.

Fig. 9.2. Band logo for Mascara
(Mass Scar Era). Courtesy of Sherine
Amr of Mascara.

the limits of speed beyond seemingly human possibility. The result is the grotesque—a noise of inhumanity mixed with the musical normalcy of a danceable rhythm. While Racy suggests that slowness is preferred in *tarab*, it is possible that extreme speed provides an inverse exaggeration of measured time that produces an alternate experienced time in the same way a fast-paced video game requires a restricted perceptual attention.

Metal band logos, especially those of extreme bands, also play with noise and form. Worm's logo (Fig. 9.1) is in a tradition of semidecipherable logos—a further redundancy of the grotesque. As Weinstein describes, metal logos developed in the 1970s, when LP covers offered an aesthetic experience beyond their use for marketing identification (2000, 28–29). As the genre developed, the distinct angular typefaces that gave early logos an ominous, threatening feel gave way to a style marked by a high degree of unintelligibility. Berger notes the difficulty of deciphering death metal band names by the end of the century (1999, 263). In many cases, the more extreme the music, the more obscured the band name in the iconography of the logo. As seen in Figure 9.1, the word is semilegible—and that only when one knows the name of the band. The pointy bladelike lines set in symmetry give the impression of a mechanical weapon or insect. The simultaneity of these connotations and the word *worm* recapitulate the noise between text and image.

Play with band logos can also be more semantic. Mascara is itself a semi-acronym of "Massive Scar Era," juxtaposing brutality with the feminine in the imagery of makeup covering the surface of mass disfigurement. As seen in Figure 9.2, the band's logo sets the English title and stylized electric guitar in a script that resembles Arabic.

Together, these redundancies as a "sensory-visual feast" nourish the empathetic crisis by offering a dynamic world of judgment. The excess of noise across the spectrum of metal genres, sounds, fans, and references offers alienated contemplation of critical issues for Egyptian metalheads. Experiencing measured disorientation stands at the heart of metal, around which a community develops replete with the rhetorics of who "gets" metal and who doesn't. The assessment offered here is by no means definitive. Metal as rebellion, metal as Western imitation, and metal as intimidation also exist but, as stated, the stakes of these embodiments of metal are high.

This revelatory deep play through the borders of recognition might have remained an autonomous musical practice on the outskirts of town, but the Egyptian government rechanneled and repurposed the noise of this practice. Mohammed Omran explains, "Metal bands were a very easy target because anything that could be seen as going against general religious trends would very easily rile up the general public. . . . [The government] would have the public on their side, the media on their side as well, who just look for a juicy story" (2006). Harnessing an effective media campaign, description of sound, dress, and behavior reified the practice into an anti-Muslim influence making its way across the borders, aimed at Egyptian youths. Given this interpretation of noise, students appeared as Satanists—in league with terrorists and drug dealers—and were subjected to interrogation and detainment.

Epilogue: Noise Relocates!

Ten years following the arrests, at a Mascara concert in Alexandria, the band performed its original "Satan Never Loves" with a slide show of "posers" depicted in cartoons. When asked about the song's message, Sherine Amr was direct: "People act like zombies. . . . Seriously. I saw this guy. His hair is as long as mine. It was all curly and it was all over his face. You cannot see his face and he walks like this" (2006). The radical critique that metal offers is not against those who do not belong to "the club," but rather against those who accept their worlds at face value. This core theme in metal resonates beyond musical practice.

It is no surprise that many who avoided metal as a result of the 1997 arrests found other venues for destabilizing the status quo. Two examples stand out. Award-winning journalist, political activist, and prolific blogger Wa'l Abbas was about to start learning the drum set before the 1997 arrests. His vigilant commentary on political injustice and human rights abuse in Egypt (through his website, misrdigital.com) made him a key player in the takeover of Tahrir Square in 2011.

Artist Nader Sadek relocated to New York after the arrests and now explores the monster in his artwork—unlikely juxtapositions of extremely devout Muslim women in hijab and extreme metal imagery. His work destabilizes on many levels both in Egypt and the United States, where he works with well-known extreme metal musicians.

The noise of metal extends the feeling of *nafas dawsha*, casting rippling shadows on the quotidian. The closing lyrics from Wyvern's "Kingdom of Gold" dwell in the empathetic aporia, calling into question the façade of pharaonic national identity in the frustrating present of a futureless possibility before the Arab Spring:

> You've been cursed by your own deeds; you've ruined it all to history.
> "Pharaoh's descendants," that's all you say.
> But what have you left before you die?
> Surrounded by your failures, waiting for the magic,
> Accusing your master for your misery.
> And still you cry on and still you lean on and still you pry on
> The kingdom of gold.

But the aporia is not resolved. By nature, such resolution is impossible and therein lies its continued critical capacity for Egypt. Rather than celebrate and embrace a new Egyptian nationalism, Sherine Amr of Mascara keeps a watchful eye over revolutionary posers: "I think Egyptians became more popular after the revolution. Now it's just like, if I make a movie that's shit that's about this revolution, I'll be really famous" (Amr 2011, 119). Metal does not celebrate its victories. It rises above them.

Appendix

TRANSCRIPT OF THE ACCOUNT OF THE ARRESTS BY AN ANONYMOUS METAL FAN [OMAR].

The arrests took place on Wednesday night. It was Ramadan. The government, or ministry, chose Ramadan because God told Muslims that in Ramadan, Satan and all his descendants are being chained. So, to arrest the devil worshippers, Ramadan was the best time. That Thursday or Friday was police day. And every year in the police day, the ministry prepares a nice surprise of propaganda . . . by arresting a group, which is usually a terrorist group. It was half past five o'clock in the morning. I was sleeping and my father woke me up.

"Hey, Papa, Papa."

"Are you doing something wrong?"

"Papa, no, I'm sleeping here. What's wrong with you?"

"Nothing, nothing. Are you sure you did nothing wrong?"

"Dad, what's wrong?"

"There are people who want you."

The first idea that popped into my mind was one of my friends might have gotten into trouble. I woke up and ran to check, I thought it was a friend. Then I realized: people in black, guns, in my house. What? Is this in a dream? I was pinching myself. "I'm still sleeping. No, it's a funny dream, yeah."

And then, "Hi. So you are [Omar]?"

"Yes."

"We need you. About . . . you know."

"Know what?"

"The Satanist thing that people are talking about."

"Satanist thing?!"

"Yes, but we need you for further interrogations. Please come with us now and you will be back early in the morning."

"Okay, why don't I come back in the morning if you're returning me early in the morning and you can interrogate me at that time?"

"No, no, we need you. You can't imagine. It's a huge thing."

My father was paralyzed.

"What's happening?"

I looked to him and he said, "I think you should go."

Then one of the officers said, "We know that [Omar] is a good boy and he will show us his room and his CDs."

I remembered that *Ruz al-Yusuf* started to do these stupid articles about Satanism in Egypt and stuff like that and in the university's paper. We published a letter saying that these people are stupid and they should not affect our interest in music. It's definitely not related to heavy metal.

"Aren't you old enough to stop exchanging CDs with a kid like me?"

I paid for that. I went to my room and they followed me and came into my room and they started to check my CDs, my tapes, my videos, my books beside my bed. I can't sleep without reading, so I have lots of books on different subjects. One of them was a book on espionage or something like that. They were so interested in the book on espionage. On the other side of the bed was my collection of stamps and they started to check the back of each stamp, searching for drugs! And they confiscated a black T-shirt with a skull playing guitar drawing and, under it, "Death by Metal." It's a T-shirt that you can buy anywhere. And from a combination of about two hundred tapes and CDs, they confiscated Pink Floyd's *Dark Side of the Moon*, Savatage's *Dead Winter Dead*, and the album of Black Sabbath where Glenn Hughes was the lead vocalist. They left some tracks of Omen, lots of things, Candlemass, Slayer, lots of things that they could have interrogated me [for having], if they wanted. They just took such stupid stuff.

"Mr. [Omar], we need you with us."

"Ok."

So I put on another black T-shirt and blue jeans and my Texas boots and had my [long] hair and then he looked at me and said, "[Omar], you look like a decent person and your family looks like a decent family. Please try to change the black look."

"What do you mean?"

"Put on something white or something like that."

How stupid was he? So, I said, "Fine, I'll do that."

So I put on a white shirt and I left with them.

I realized five or six police vehicles were downstairs. In them were lots of people that I knew and two or three of my friends. They didn't look at me in my eyes. We left and picked up another two on our way to the police station. There, I realized that no less than eighty people were there that I knew, people from the Roxy. I thought, "The *Ruz al-Yusuf* articles! It's like a conviction. Oh my God! This cannot be true. This should not be true. This cannot happen to us!"

If you put eighty persons in one room and each one started to hiss, you would find noise. From time to time, an officer enters into our room and it started to increase gradually.

"Please, please, try to lower down the voice!"

Hissing again, and then, oops, the voices are up. The third and fourth escalate every time and then, suddenly, the door opens and an attack happens. Ten, seven, maybe eight, officers enter the room and they go crazy. They start hitting everybody that they see in front of them. I was hit in between my legs, in my nose, in my chest, a kick in my ass. They put me in the ground and someone put their foot into me. It's happening to everyone in the room.

Then, they started to take us into the big corridor and throw us into the corridor with insults that I've never heard in my life. From the insults, it was obvious that they already had [made] a decision. We are Satanists and we are beaten accordingly.

They undressed us and asked us to stand, starting from eight until four. It was so tiring. Whenever you'd move, there would be someone there to punch you in the back, to hit you. Me and six or seven of the persons had long hair and, thus, we attracted more.

It's not only being beaten, but it's also a psychological war. You are blindfolded and cuffed and your hands are up to the sky and you hear footsteps behind you. We were all facing the walls. From time to time, you hear footsteps and then the walkie-talkies start to give sounds and it's right behind you. If you shake, someone—you don't know who, when, what—will hit you with something. In an offensive way, in a humiliating way. They humiliate you on your first day so that you lose your dignity. You are humiliated. You are afraid by the end of the day.

Some of our parents who had connections were able to sneak in some food.

We tried to complain to them, believing that they could help us out of this. So we complained and it, obviously, seemed in vain. The top officers were there in the morning, they were not there at night, so it was a bit peaceful. But we were eighty persons, lying on the ground in a relatively small corridor. We were eighty persons, so it was too much.

At dawn, they came again. They kept [acting] as if they were preparing for the interrogation, preparing each one of our files to be sent to the prosecutor.

The second night at midnight, they sent us to the compound where the prosecutor of state security [is]. You should know the significance of the state security in this country. It's almost a military code. It's not human. It denies you lots of your rights. You're not standing [in front of] your natural judge. They usually deal with drug dealers and terrorists.

We went there and obviously the media was following like crazy. Huge cars transferred us. We were eighty people packed into two huge cars which had small holes, and it was so dark. Lots of prisoners before us, obviously, used it as restrooms. It was lousy, it was lousy. But we went there and journalists and media were waiting for us and it was a scene. We were all handcuffed, blindfolded. We went to the dungeons of the place. It's a strange place. They keep people there until they're freed by the prosecutor.

I stayed with the [prosecutor] for an hour. The guy said, "Ok, we have to remand you because we confiscated stuff in your house." A Pink Floyd tape, a tape of Black Sabbath, and the movie *The Sound of Music*.

"I am not the person for you guys!"

He felt that I was lying and he decided to remand me for fourteen days. I was shocked. I didn't believe it.

We returned to the same police station. They emptied that police station to take care of that case only for these couple of days. We spent the night there and then returned [to the state security office] at four or five. We slept until dusk and then at dusk my father came with food and then he left for a couple of hours. And then (that was the third night), he came with a person into the police station, he is a barber.

"Excuse me? You would pay a bribe to get a barber in? Why would you do that?"

"To shave your hair."

"Papa, I am not shaving my hair. A seventeen- or eighteen-year-old kid, I mean that's . . ."

It was an asset to me, yeah.

"No, no, you are getting it shaved."

"Papa! Impossible!"

"[Omar], you do not know, and do not tell anybody, [that] you—all of you—are being transferred to the Tora Prison."

"What?!"

(The Tora Prison is like Alcatraz. The reputation of Alcatraz is like the Tora Prison.)

"Papa, are you speaking the truth?"

"Yes, I am speaking the truth. I got inside information."

He said, "Do you know what they would do to you if they see such hair?" It was that long back then. "Okay, please, go ahead, shave."

So, I know I was the only one who knew that we were going to Tora and that was hellish, so I had my only good friend with me. One thing you should know is that we were the only two from the American University in Cairo and anything in this country that is related to a youth problem, the AUC should be involved as the promoter of apostasy and bad things like that, drugs, naked women. If you ride the taxi and you pass in front of the university, [the driver] will tell you nice rumors that he was once there and he saw the swimming pool and women were topless inside, he will tell you crazy things.

It was January, it was cold, it was so cold, it was crazy cold in there. It was freezing. Anyway, [he got me] something to change into and a huge copy of the Qur'an and he put on the top, as if he knew that they were going to search it.

There were eighty persons arrested the very first night, about thirty of them were released—the funny thing is that one of the remaining members who stayed around for three weeks, he does nothing, he's a forty-two-year-old carpenter or something like that and he was arrested because he was taped on the last concert in M'adi and why did he go to the concert? Because he saw an ad that said tickets for ten pounds, plus one beer, and saw pretty women and followed them getting into there. He thought, I have ten pounds, and I will get a nice beer and I will go and mingle and touch an ass here and there. That's what he thought. So, he was a victim of his stupidity and a victim of the stupidity of the system as well. They wouldn't believe him. Look at him! He shouldn't be there! And he was.

My father, he is so funny. He sent with the car [to Tora Prison] a barrel of KFC. It was a huge door for the prison and then a small door, which was about that high, and then you enter the prison like that. Suddenly, in front of me, hell broke lose. It was bad. It was so bad. I was first hit on the back of my neck. I [lost] my glasses, they disappear, evaporated, and my barrel of KFC, of course, I lost it. They are hitting you everywhere and they are pushing you in every direction and they had dogs to increase the terrorist atmosphere. So they terrorized us like crazy and I was handcuffed to another one of our colleagues—he was a guitarist in a nice band. Anyway, some officers were hitting me and pushing me into this direction, and the others were pushing me in the other direction. So that's another pain, extra pain. People started to faint and I thought it to be wise to throw yourself under a pile of fainting people—I mean, that's an honest solution! Play dead! Play dead!

After maybe an hour, suddenly, the boss of the prison, as if he just arrived, "What's happening here? What's going on? Oh my God! What about human rights! Stop, you stupid officer here and there!" Then he slapped a couple of them and then I thought, "What? Another angel?"

Then he told us to file up here and there in a row and, "Sorry for that, I didn't know it was happening."

We got used to that.

Then they started to remove the handcuffs and they asked each one of us to collect our stuff, which was all over the place. There was a door into, I don't know, a dark area—and they formed a couple of rows in which you should run in between into this room. After five or six persons, you gain the experience that you should close your eyes, you should try to minimize your size, and you run as crazy as possible, as fast as possible, to receive the minimum amount of hits. It's a tradition. Then you enter into this dark area and you realize that it's cold, it's a refrigerator. Very frigid. They keep us there for about an hour. The refrigerator is like a hangar, very dark, I can't see my hands and it stinks like crazy. And they kept us there. It was the end of January, it was about 10 degrees Celsius and inside this fridge.

They started to call our names, one by one, to be searched.

"Welcome to the prison. To make sure you are the person, what does your father do?"

Stuff like that.

Since I was the first person to get in there, I was the last to get out of there. Most of them, they got searched and then presented to the head of the prison and some of the generals, who would check you, check your information, and then they send you to your cell. I was the last, almost, and I was getting searched and three ugly assistants were searching me and they sexually harassed me.

I had a pack of cigarettes in my pocket and [one of the assistants] checked it and took half of it for himself. And then the other officers said, "No," so he gave them back to me. I wanted to embarrass him, so I said, "Why don't you take it all?"

Then they started searching under my balls. Why would you search under my balls? And then he started to squeeze them. "Ah, you are homosexual, you are happy now, eh?"

"Satanist," to them, equals homosexuality; one of the [supposed] rituals is homosexuality, killing cats, and drinking their blood.

I was the last to enter the room with the general and head of the prison. I entered and they asked me about my name and where I live.

"Your father?"

"Engineer."

"Your mother?"

"Pharmacist."

"[Omar], you seem different from the other people, you seem like you come from a decent family. Why do you do that? Why would you be a homosexual?"

"Sir, I'm not a homosexual."

"Why are you a Satanist?"

"Sir, I'm not a Satanist."

"Come with me, [Omar], you can spend the night in my office."

Then on our way out of this room, they were unpacking my bag and the huge Qur'an fell out of my bag.

"Mmm . . . proportionate of size. Is that to dance on it?"

So, I took that time to say, "Please, sir, there is nothing satanic in Egypt. There are no Satanists in Egypt. It cannot happen. Trust me."

"But they said that they had videos of you."

"Did you see it, sir?"

"No."

"Why do you believe it?"

"Because they said so."

It was nice to see the cell. We slept. The second day in the morning, they woke us up at eleven and they told us that we should clean ourselves, clean our cells, and afterward we clean the bathrooms for the other prisoners. Then we return to the cells and started to get used to the thing and started to sing even at night. We started singing Savatage, Metallica, whatever we can sing together. Visits were not allowed in prison. Maybe because parents did not know that the kids are there.

The third day in the morning, they woke us up in a rising manner as well and they asked us to look to the wall, hands up, blindfolded, and I felt almost sure that they were filming us, maybe to show it to the leadership? "This is how they look and this is what they look [like]." Then they left. It wasn't more than ten minutes.

At night, the head of the prison, he asked for me. He said, "Hi."

"I'm fine."

"Do you need anything?"

"No, thank you, sir."

In Tora, they didn't feed us for three days. We had the water and that's it. I got a fever on the third night, a heavy fever, and I called for the doctor. Nobody answered me until the next morning. They sent a doctor and he looked at me. "Ok, take this." I started to [think], "They hate us like crazy and so maybe they would kill us and say that we committed suicide. Maybe that would support their case." So, I didn't take the pill and I kept it because my mom is a pharmacist and I tried hard [to think] that one day I would be back and I'd show it to her.

The last night, we were singing and it was nice and we got used to the place, and then we started to hear shouts from far away. Shouts, screams, from a faraway place and we didn't know what was that. Four hours later, about seven o'clock in the morning, the doors opened suddenly and a farewell reception took place. Very terrorizing, very bad, very painful. I remember [my friend], he was handcuffed to me that day and after we got hit enough for an hour, an officer was walking with his walkie-talkie and he said, "I don't like the way you look," and then, "wshah!" hit him with the back of the walkie-talkie and started a blood stream here. And he couldn't say a word. And the stupid people, they are so stupid and they kept hitting us and yelling at us.

"You son of a bitch, you don't know where you are going, you are coming to my prison!"

"Oh my God, we are going to another prison? Why?"

Later on, we realized that the sounds of the screams of the night were because the Islamists of the same prison were told that the Satanists were in the same prison as them, and they decided to revolt and they wanted to kill us. So they crushed them. That's why they had to quickly transfer us to another prison.

Anyway, the stupid people who were hitting us and terrorizing us, they were forcing us to sign on documents. They [had] confiscated everything we had with us: food, cigarettes, money.

And at the end of the stay in Tora, after two or three nights, they hit us hard to make us sign documents saying that we received our money and stuff back.

We left the Tora Prison and we were packed in two cars to the al-Marg Prison. Al-Marg is inside an agricultural compound and there is a food booth and a water stream and ponds and the cells we had were nice. It looked like a cheap camp. It was nice, I liked it, I liked it. Anyway, we went there and it was a heavy reception party. They gave us lessons about discipline and how we should be treated like animals here if we do not listen to officers and stuff like that. But they put us away, that was the nice thing, they put us away from the other prisoners. This also happened in the Tora Prison, but in al-Marg Prison, they had special cells far away at the end of the detention facility for people like us, particular prisoners with different needs, stuff like that. So we had this compound just for us. But the cells were so tight. I had to sleep by putting my legs on the wall, like this, because it was not enough for me and they put three persons in one cell.

They gave us about ten minutes every morning to walk in the sun and to clean ourselves, stuff like that. If we had problems, for example, if one night I had problems with the plumbing inside the small cell, and I woke up to find myself in debris, they sent us a plumber who was in prison to come and clean and do the thing for us. The visits from our parents were more common and every day they sent us food, good food, and they prevented the other prisoners from taking anything from us.

Anyway, so I stayed there for about nine more days. We even got used to the officers and they got used to us. They started to tell us jokes and stuff like that. One of them even asked an officer if we could play football in the field. We were not afraid at that time.

It was the problem of the last two days. Obviously, throughout the past two weeks, the coverage of the case was high, high, high, and then it started to settle and then the public opinion and intellects started to find that most of the prisoners are sons of their friends and that it should not be true whatever they read in the papers. Pressures started to come from outside Egypt. So, obviously, it seemed that the case was getting away from their hands. They cannot make a case out of it.

So they wanted us, in the last two days, each one of us was called on his own, separately, and blindfolded and handcuffed, and they started to beat us individually to try to force us to admit something that we didn't do, stuff like that. Tell other names, keep their case alive, stuff like that. But, I guess by then, we were much stronger. Nobody gave them the right answer. We gave them assurance that "It's over, guys. Let's end this." Of course, they tried to scare us and tell us, "Ok, ok, if you don't want to talk, you stay here for another month," stuff like that. But they failed, they failed to keep it going.

There were only ten or twelve people who stayed for an additional two weeks and another two for three weeks, but the rest of us were released after a few days, the remand was over. And then, they sent us back to the prosecution.

They got us to [be] interrogated alone in a separate floor. Unfortunately, on that floor, there was an interrogation for four, or five, or six leaders for the Islamic Jamaat and they had these huge beards and they gave us this dirty look.

"So these are the worshippers of the shit?"

"Yes, they are."

In a half hour, there was a strange movement in the building and obviously one of them had shaved his beard in the bathroom and changed clothes with his lawyer and he escaped. We were so scared. These people had been standing in front of us and a few meters away and know us very well from the past half an hour. God save us. It's never going to end.

But, however, we entered into the prosecution room. In passing [the prosecutor said], "Ah, I see you gained weight in prison. It seems good for your health. Don't be sad for the experience. Did anybody hit you?"

"Hit me? They killed me inside."

"I'm sorry for that. Do you want to say any other thing?"

"No, but I want to return home. I want to be with my family."

And then the best of luck. And that was it. And I returned and then, the second day, they called my name.

[Omar] and another eight names and, "Ok, you are released."

"Hallelujah!" and "Happiness" and stuff like that.

Some people cried. This was noon and then, at seven, they called our names again and they put us into a huge car and they transferred us to Nazughli, where the headquarters of the Ministry of Interior and the state security police [is].

I didn't tell you that [at] the very first interrogation of the prosecution, he told me to sign under whatever I said during the interrogation. I told him, so this is what I said? I have to sign for it? And he said yes, and the first paper, there was a huge paper filled in black, and I said, "What does it include?" And he said,

"These are the charges against you." You should have seen the charges. It was wonderful. It would hang me. It was true that the Grand Jurist—I heard after we were home—he, in a public statement, said that "All devil worshippers should be hanged in a public place." The accusations included homosexuality (why would that be an accusation anyway?), drinking blood of cats, forming an organization to topple the regime—this was one of the charges for [someone] of my age—topple the regime with heavy metal!?

Twenty accusations, they accused me of lots of things. And at the end of the day, nothing. But they got us to Nazughli and they called my dad and he received me and I'm now free, according to the law. They put me there, they handcuffed us again, they blindfolded us again. They kept us moving in stupid patterns. And I know! I stood in the same area up to the stairs, in the room, back, back, back, down the stairs again—as if we are terrorists [and] that we are going to memorize the map of the location. "They will be back to blow us away!" You are dealing with terrorists and I'm fine with that, but not with us! We are kids! One [girl] was thirteen years old, and she stayed for six days while we were there. She was not beaten, but she was emotionally terrorized. Thirteen years! She is still a baby. Calling her a bitch, a prostitute. Why would you do that?

Notes

1. The exact number of people arrested varies from account to account. While the official records of the event may never be found, newspapers and firsthand reports range from the high seventies to more than one hundred.

2. The research for this essay was supported by the UCLA Graduate Division's Graduate Summer Research Mentorship Program under the guidance of Dr. Ali Jihad Racy. The bulk of research took place during the summer of 2006, and follow-up research, including more media analysis, took place over the following four years. Parts of this essay have been presented by the author at the 2007 Society for Ethnomusicology Annual Meeting in Columbus, Ohio; the 2007 International Association for the Study of Popular Music Annual Conference in Mexico City; the 2007 International Association for the Study of Popular Music (U.S. Branch) Annual Conference in Boston; and the 2007 Society for Ethnomusicology (Southern California Chapter) Annual Meeting in Riverside, California. In addition to the support of the interviewees cited in this paper, I am particularly grateful for the conversations about this research with Nagwa Hassaan, Jailan Zayan, Ali Jihad Racy, Roger Savage, Mina Girgis, and Mohamed Khalifa.

3. Today, given the ability to download MP3s, the metal scene is even more detached from a local market economy, though it is perhaps connected to an economy of information technology—computers, Internet, software, hard drives, and MP3 players, including cell phones.

4. For the purposes of this paper, *metalhead* will refer to musical insiders—

musicians and fans who have a demonstrated fluency with bands, histories, performance, and dress. The *nonmetalhead* is one for whom metal music and performance makes no sense or represents something that a metalhead would disagree with. Since this is an ascriptive designation, metalheadness is something to be understood through practice and confirmed socially, be that through local communities or international communities and mediated through television, Internet, magazines, or sound recordings.

5. Candlemass (Sweden), Witchfinder General (UK), and Saint Vitus (USA) came to define the doom metal genre in the 1980s, though it had only a modest following until the 1990s.

6. Care should be taken to understand self-production in Egypt as a practice related to but distinct from do-it-yourself production in the West. Egypt's cassette industry that developed in the 1980s was a semiformal economy in which cassette kiosks ran duplication equipment in the back of the shop.

7. The Mossad is the Israeli intelligence and special operations organization. In Egypt, it is often suspected of covert paramilitary operations beyond the Israeli border in a wide range of conspiracy theories.

8. I am not arguing that metal is an avant-garde tradition but, rather, that it shares common traits and implications.

9. I was told that the ultra-elite in Egypt maintain a punk scene.

10. The black metal genre is associated with a series of murders and church burnings in Norway that took place in the late 1990s. Many in the metal community view the Norwegian bands as having misinterpreted the dark imagery of metal to a degree that a few of the scene's members adopted a violent, xenophobic mission to return Norway to its pre-Christian "roots." See Moynihan and Søderlind (1998).

11. Musical uses for noise have been characterized as disturbances by several theorists. Of note, Jacques Attali characterizes noise in relation to organized systems, often simulacra themselves. Drawing from information theory, he suggests that noise disrupts resonance (1985, 26–27). Amiri Baraka treats noise similarly in his valorization of antiassimilative "honking" by jazz saxophonists— noise as political protest in the context of mainstream music (1999, 172).

12. A good example of this is Iron Maiden's "Aces High," recorded in 1984. By the time bands such as Arch Enemy and Children of Bodom recorded the songs twenty years later, the key dropped due to down-tuned guitars, the tempo increased, and the vocal style became much harsher.

13. Such criticism is in line with Adorno's critique of the popular music collector. See Adorno (2001).

14. Other instances of this phenomenon include Slayer's filming of its "Seasons in the Abyss" video at the Giza pyramids and the pharaonic death metal band, Nile, from Greenville, South Carolina.

15. The scale degrees of a minor second and major third are found in this Arab

tetrachord and often mimicked in European music to signify Arabness musically. For more on this device in other settings, see Rasmussen (1992) and Locke (1991).

References

Adlington, Robert. 2009. "Introduction: Avant-Garde Music and the Sixties." In *Sound Commitments: Avant-Garde Music and the Sixties*, 3–14. New York: Oxford University Press.

Adorno, Theodor W. 2001. "On the Fetish Character in Music and the Regression of Listening." In *The Culture Industry: Selected Essays on Mass Culture*. Edited by J. M. Bernstein, 29–60. New York: Routledge.

Amr, Sherine, et al. 2011. "Massive Scar Era Confessional." *Bidoun* 25: 119–21.

Armbrust, Walter. 1996. *Mass Culture and Modernism in Egypt*. Cambridge: Cambridge University Press.

Attali, Jacques. 1985. *Noise: The Political Economy of Music*. Vol. 16 of *Theory and History of Literature*. Minneapolis: University of Minnesota Press.

Baraka, Imamu Amiri. 1999. *Blues People: Negro Music in White America*. 1st Quill ed. New York: William Morrow.

Benjamin, Walter. 1986. "The Work of Art in the Age of Mechanical Reproduction." In *Illuminations*, 217–51. New York: Schocken Books.

Berger, Harris M. 1999. *Metal, Rock, and Jazz: Perception and the Phenomenology of Musical Experience*. Hanover, NH: University Press of New England.

Berger, Harris M., and Cornelia Fales. 2005. "The Match of Perceptual and Acoustic Features of Timbre over Time: 'Heaviness' in the Perception of Heavy Metal Guitar Textures." In *Wired for Sound: Engineering and Technologies in Sonic Cultures*. Edited by P. D. Greene and T. Porcello, 181–97. Middletown, CT: Wesleyan University Press.

Bhatia, Shyam. 1997. "Egypt's Youth Plunder British Graves for Skulls to the Sound of Heavy Metal: Only Rock 'n' Roll?" *The Observer*, February 9, 14.

Burke, Kenneth. 1966. *Language as Symbolic Action: Essays on Life, Literature, and Method*. Berkeley: University of California Press.

Cope, Andrew L. 2010. *Black Sabbath and the Rise of Heavy Metal Music*. Ashgate Popular and Folk Music Series. Burlington, VT: Ashgate.

Daniszewski, John. 1997. "Signs of Satanic Rituals Rock Rich Egyptian Parents." *Calgary Herald*, February 15, C3.

Di Giovanni, Janine. 1997. "A Deadly Divide." *The Guardian*, October 4, T20.

El-Hamamsy, Laila. 1975. "The Assertion of Egyptian Identity." In *Ethnic Identity: Cultural Continuities and Change*. Edited by George Deffos and Lola Romanucci-Ross, 276–306. Palo Alto, CA: Mayfield.

Frishkopf, Michael. 2010. "Introduction: Music and Media in the Arab World and *Music and Media in the Arab World* as Music and Media in the Arab World:

A Metadiscourse." In *Music and Media in the Arab World*. Edited by Michael Frishkopf, 1–66. Cairo: American University in Cairo Press.

Gauch, Sarah. 1997. "Egypt's Police See Satan in Teens' Western Ways." *Christian Science Monitor*, February 10, 5.

Goldberg, Nicholas. 1997. "'Satanic Cult' Provokes Egyptian Soul Searching." *The Guardian*, February 6, 13.

Griffiths, Paul. 1978. *A Concise History of Avant-Garde Music: From Debussy to Boulez*. New York: Oxford University Press.

Hecker, Pierre. 2005. "Taking a Trip to the Middle Eastern Metal Scene: Transnational Social Spaces and Identity Formations on a Non-National Level." *NORD-SÜD aktuell* 19 (1): 57–66.

Jehl, Douglas. 1997. "It's Heavy Going for Sex, Satan and Heavy Metal." Cairo Journal. *New York Times*, February 10, 4.

Kahn-Harris, Keith. 2002. "'I Hate This Fucking Country': Dealing with the Global and the Local in the Israeli Extreme Metal Scene." *Critical Studies* 19: 133–51.

——. 2007. *Extreme Metal: Music and Culture on the Edge*. New York: Berg Publishers.

Keightley, Keir. 2001. "Reconsidering Rock." In *The Cambridge Companion to Pop and Rock*. Cambridge Companions to Music. Edited by Simon Frith, Will Straw, and John Street, 109–42. New York: Cambridge University Press.

Khattab, Azza. 1997. "The Devil They Know." *Egypt Today*, May 1.

LeVine, Mark. 2008. *Heavy Metal Islam: Rock, Resistance, and the Struggle for the Soul of Islam*. New York: Three Rivers Press.

Locke, Ralph P. 1991. "Constructing the Oriental 'Other': Saint-Saëns's 'Samson et Dalila.'" *Cambridge Opera Journal* 3 (3): 261–302.

Mekki, Hassan. 1997. "Egypt Declares War on Satan Worshippers." Agence France-Presse, January 27.

Messiri, Sawsan. 1978. "Ibn al-Balad: A Concept of Egyptian Identity." *Social, Economic and Political Studies of the Middle East* 24. Leiden: Brill.

Moynihan, Michael, and Didrik Søderlind. 1998. *Lords of Chaos: The Bloody Rise of the Satanic Metal Underground*. Venice, CA: Feral House.

Pratt, Ray. 1994. *Rhythm and Resistance: The Political Uses of American Popular Music*. Washington, DC: Smithsonian Institution Press.

Racy, Ali Jihad. 2003. *Making Music in the Arab World: The Culture and Artistry of Tarab*. Cambridge: Cambridge University Press.

Rasmussen, Anne. 1992. "'An Evening in the Orient': The Middle Eastern Nightclub in America." *Asian Music* 23 (2): 63–88.

Swedenburg, Ted. 2000. "Satanic Heavy Metal in Egypt." Paper presented at the Ninety-Ninth Annual Meeting of the American Anthropological Association, San Francisco, December 15–19.

Temlali, Yassine. 2011. "The 'Arab Spring': Rebirth or Final Throes of Pan-Arabism?" Special issue, *Perspectives* (*People's Power: The Arab World in Revolt*) 2: 46–49.

Wallach, Jeremy. 2005. "Underground Rock Music and Democratization in Indonesia." *World Literature Today* 79 (3–4): 16–20.

Walser, Robert. 1993. *Running with the Devil: Power, Gender, and Madness in Heavy Metal Music*. Hanover, NH: University Press of New England.

Weinstein, Deena. *Heavy Metal: The Music and Its Culture*. Rev. ed. New York: Da Capo Press, 2000.

Ziarek, Krzysztof. 2004. *The Force of Art (Cultural Memory in the Present)*. Stanford, CA: Stanford University Press.

Cited Interviews by the Author

Khaled Sallam of Konzaross 7/13/2006

Mohammed Omran and Timur Reda of Stigma 7/16/2006, 7/25/2006

Tarek Morsy 7/21/2006

Seif El-Din Moussa of Wyvern 7/22/2006

Wa'l Abbas 7/24/2006

Sherine Amr and Nancy Mounir of Mascara 7/26/2006

Ahmed Samadie and Tarek Shehata of Worm 7/26/2006

"Omar" 7/27/2006

Mohamed Khalifa of Viper 12/22/2010

Selected Discography

‿‿

"A" Trio. *Music to Our Ears*. Al-Maslakh. *2011*: Lebanon

Atoui, Tarek. *Mort aux Vaches*. Staalplaat. *2008*: Netherlands

DAM. *Ihda / Dedication*. Red Circle Music. *2006*: UK

El-Dabh, Halim. *Columbia-Princeton Electronic Music Center*. Columbia Records. *1964*: United States

El-Dabh, Halim. *Crossing into the Electric Magnetic*. Without Fear Recordings. *2000*: United States

El-Dabh, Halim. *Here History Began*. Ministry of Culture and National Guidance. *1961*: Egypt

El-Dabh, Halim. *Ptahmose and the Magic Spell, Part One: The Osiris Ritual*. Hawthorne Records. *1972*: United States

El-Dabh, Halim. *Sounds of New Music*. Folkways Records. *1957*: United States

Elsaffar, Amir. *Inana*. Pi Recordings. *2011*: United States

Elsaffar, Amir. *Two Rivers*. Pi Recordings. *2007*: United States

Elsaffar, Amir, and Hafez Modirzadeh. *Radif Suite*. Pi Recordings. *2010*: United States

Jubran, Kamilya, and Werner Hasler. *Wameedd*. Unit Records W&K 001. *2005*: Switzerland

Kerbaj, Mazen, and Franz Hautzinger. *Abu Tarek*. Creative Sources Recordings 025. *2005*: Portugal

Kerbaj, Mazen. *BRT VRT ZRT KRT*. Al Maslakh MSLKH 01. *2005*: Lebanon

Mascara. *Unfamiliar Territory*. Self-released. *2010*: Egypt

Moultaka, Zad. *Zajal*. L'Empreinte Digitale. *2010*: France

Muslimgauze. *Infidel*. Extreme XEP 026. *1994*: Germany

Nadeem, Aida. *Beyond Destruction*. Uruk Records. *2010*: Denmark

Nadeem, Aida. *Out of Baghdad*. Uruk Records. *2005*: Denmark

Odious. *Mirror of Vibrations*. Sleaszy Rider Records. *2007*: Greece

Osman Arabi. *Beat Mutation Rituals*. Kalpamantra. *2011*: UK

Praed. *Made in Japan*. Annihaya Records. *2011*: Lebanon

Praed. *Muesli Man*. Creative Source Recordings. *2008*: Lebanon

Rahbani, Ziad. *Ana Moush Kafer*. Relax-In Internation. *2008 (Remaster)*: Lebanon

Rahbani, Ziad. *Bi-ma Innu*. Voix de l'Orient. *1995*: Lebanon

Rahbani, Ziad. *Bilafrah*. Voix de l'Orient. *1977*: Lebanon

Scarab. *Valley of the Sandwalkers*. Self-released. *2007*: Egypt

Scrambled Eggs and "A" Trio. *Beach Party at Mirna el Chalouhi*. Johnny Kafta. *2010*: Lebanon

Scrambled Eggs. *Peace Is Overrated & War Misunderstood*. Ruptured. *2010*: Lebanon

Scrambled Eggs. *Scrambled Eggs and Friends*. Johnny Kafta. *2010*: Lebanon

Sehnaoui, Sharif. *Old & New Acoustics*. Al-Maslakh *2010*: Lebanon

Turkmani, Mahmoud. *Ya Sharr Mout*. Enja Records ENJ-9530. *2008*: Germany

Turkmani, Mahmoud. *Zakira*. Enja 9475. *2004*: Germany

Various Artists. *The Ruptured Sessions (Vols. 1–4)*. Ruptured. *2009–2012*: Lebanon

Various Artists. *Waking Up Scheherazade*. Grey Past Records ABA 001. *2007*: Netherlands

Worm. *The Armageddon Codex*. Self-released. *2004*: Egypt

Wyvern. *The Clown*. Self-released. *2009*: Egypt

Yassin, Raed. *The New Album*. Annihaya. *2009*: Lebanon

Yassin, Raed, and Gene Coleman. *The Adventures of Nabil Fawzi*. Al Maslakh Recordings 04. *2006:* Lebanon

A Note on Sayyed Darwish's Recordings

According to Saed Muhssin: "Historic sources suggest that most of [Sayyed] Darwish's recordings (perhaps with the exception of one song on record) were done at Setrak Mechian's studio in Cairo in the late 1910s and early 1920s. However, no accurate documentation of which songs were recorded is available. In fact, it is because some of those songs were later dubbed on tape and are circulating that we know they were recorded in the first place."

Contributors

⌒

SAMI W. ASMAR is a NASA physicist specializing in research in the fields of planetary gravity and atmospheres. He has authored a book on techniques of Radio Science and is a recipient of several NASA medals and awards. A director of the UCLA Near East Ensemble, he is also the founder of the Turath.org web resource on world music and has published numerous articles on Arab musicology.

THOMAS BURKHALTER, an ethnomusicologist, music journalist, and cultural producer from Bern, Switzerland, runs the research project *Global Niches—Music in a Transnational World* at the Zurich University of the Arts. He is the founder and editor-in-chief of *Norient—Network for Local and Global Sounds and Media Culture*. He produced and tours with the audiovisual performances *Sonic Traces: From the Arab World* and *Sonic Traces: From Switzerland* and codirected the documentary film *Buy More Incense* (2002) about second- and third-generation Indian and Pakistani musicians in the UK. His first book, *Local Music Scenes and Globalization: Transnational Platforms in Beirut*, is published by Routledge (2013).

KAY DICKINSON is an associate professor at Concordia University, Montreal. She is the editor of *Movie Music* (Routledge, 2002) and the author of *Off Key: When Film and Music Won't Work Together* (Oxford University Press, 2008). Her research into Arab culture has appeared in *Screen*, *Camera Obscura*, *Framework* and *Screening the Past*, and includes editorship of an "In Focus" section of the *Cinema Journal* on the Arab revolutions. Her monograph *Arab Cinema Travels: Syria, Palestine, Dubai and Beyond* is forthcoming.

BENJAMIN J. HARBERT is an assistant professor of music at Georgetown University. He has published peer-reviewed articles in the *International Journal of Community Music* and *Pacific Review of Ethnomusicology* and is currently working on a monograph about the history of music at Angola Prison. Before returning to academia, he directed the guitar, percussion, and music theory programs at Chicago's Old Town School of Folk Music. Harbert is a concert-level performer on guitar, Near Eastern 'ud, and Indian tabla. He has led a number of performance groups, including the Los Angeles Electric 8 and extended rock ensemble arrangements of Erik Satie's *musique d'ameublement.*

MICHAEL KHOURY is a Detroit-based violinist, bassist, and economist who is the author of several publications on economics and music. As a musician, he has recorded as a bass player in several psychedelic and garage rock bands. In the realm of the avant-garde, Khoury performs as a violinist, often in duet or ensemble with Ben Hall, Hans Buetow, Christopher Riggs, Will Soderberg, and Leyya Tawil. He has worked with Faruq Z. Bey, Wolfgang Fuchs, The Northwoods Improvisers, The Graveyards, Maury Coles, and Dennis Gonzalez. Khoury is also the proprietor of the Entropy Stereo record label, as well as the micro Detroit Improvisation label.

SAED MUHSSIN is a performer of traditional and modern Arab art music, Turkish music, Arab folk music, and free improvisation. In addition to his solo work, Muhssin currently directs and performs with the Arab Orchestra of San Francisco and the Saed Muhssin Trio. He teaches 'ud, Arab music theory, and ear training. His research interests include twentieth-century Arab musical forms and performance practice.

MARINA PETERSON is an associate professor of performance studies in the School of Interdisciplinary Arts at Ohio University. An anthropologist, she is the author of *Sound, Space, and the City: Civic Performance in Downtown Los Angeles* (University of Pennsylvania Press, 2010) and coeditor of *Global Downtowns* (University of Pennsylvania Press, 2012).

KAMRAN RASTEGAR is an assistant professor of Arabic literature and teaches in the International Letters and Visual Studies program at Tufts University, where he also directs the Arabic program. His first monograph, *Literary Modernity between the Middle East and Europe* (Routledge, 2007), was the first book-length comparative study of modern Arabic and Persian literatures, and his second monograph, *Surviving Images: Cinema, War, and Cultural Memory in the Middle East and North Africa*, is forthcoming.

CAROLINE ROONEY is a professor of African and Middle Eastern Studies at the University of Kent. From 2009 to 2012, she held an ESRC/AHRC Global Uncertainties fellowship with a research program entitled *Radical Distrust.* She is currently a Global Uncertainties Leadership fellow, conducting a program that examines the roles played by utopian thinking and arts activism in the imagining of a common ground. Her books include *African Literature, Animism and Politics* (Routledge, 2000) and *Decolonising Gender: Literature and a Poetics of the Real* (Routledge, 2007). With Ayman El De-souky, she coedited a special issue of the *Journal of Postcolonial Writing* on Egyptian Literary Culture and Egyptian Modernity (September 2011) and, with Blake Brandes, coedited a special issue of *Wasafiri* on Global Youth Cultures (December 2012).

SHAYNA SILVERSTEIN currently holds an Andrew W. Mellon postdoctoral fellowship at the University of Pennsylvania and is due to take up an assistant professorship in ethnomusicology at the University of Maryland at College Park in 2014. Her current research examines Syrian popular dance music with a focus on *dabka*. She has received substantial support from Fulbright-IIE, the University of Chicago, and the U.S. Department of Education, and her work has been published in the fields of anthropology, ethnomusicology, and Middle East studies.

Index

〜

Abboushi, Tarek, 76
'Abd al-Wahhab, Muhammad, 17, 121, 130, 131,
    135, 136, 137, 139, 147, 149, 150, 156, 169
Abdelnour, Christine, 106, 185
Abdel-Rahim, Gamal, 179–180
Abdul-Malik, Ahmed, 80
abstract music, 195
activism (social and political), 28, 211, 230;
    anticolonialism, 63; antielitist hip-hop,
    211; anti-imperialism, 24, 63, 64; anti-
    Westernism, 64, 218; black politics, 224
Adonis (poet), 15, 16, 17, 21, 23, 25–26, 62
Adorno, Theodor, 15–16, 211, 232, 242, 243
adwar, 122, 124, 127
Afash, Kinan Abo, 46
Africa: music from, 89–92, 100, 111, 165, 177
African American music: performers, 12, 80,
    215, 216, 217; heritage, 76, 91, 211, 218, 248
Afro-Futurism, 90–91
agriculture, 165, 169–170, 172
Ahmad, Zakariyya, 130, 131, 139
airports (and security), 190, 204
al-Afghani, Jamal al-Din, 7
al-Assad, Bashar, 39, 63
al-Assad, Hafez, 39, 64
al-Atrash, Farid, 147
al-Bakkar, Muhammad, 102
al-Basha, Tawfiq, 148
Aleppo, 51, 84
Alexandria, 238, 247
al-Hazima ("the defeat" in the Arab Israeli war
    of 1967), 96
'Ali Lu'a, Muhammad, 131
'Ali Muhammad, Farida, 85
al-Nakba ("the catastrophe" of the creation of
    the State of Israel), 96, 174
al-Qasabgi, Mohammad, 130, 136, 139
al-Qasem, Samih, 222
al-Rumi, Halim, 148
al-Safi, Wadi', 96, 148
al-Shayk, Hanan, 214
al-Sunbati, Riyadh, 81, 130, 131
al-Tahtawi, Rifa'a, 7

al-Wadi, Solhi, 37–38, 40, 41, 42
aleatoric music, 54, 55, 56, 59, 62, 94
ambassadors: cultural, 192–193
American University of Cairo, 98, 175
Amin, M. C., 13
Amin, Qasim, 7
Amr, Sherine, 251, 253, 258, 259
Andromeda, 232, 233
aporia, 244–245
"Arab" (the term), 13–14
Arabian Knightz, 13, 20, 98
Arab music: standardizing of, 7. *See also adwar;
    dawr;* Eastern music *(musiqa sharqiyya);
    mawwal (mawawil); muwashshahat; qafla;
    qasida; radif; taqasim; sama'i, taqsim; wasla;
    taqtuqa* songs
Arab world. *See under individual place-names*
Arabness: in music, 27, 270
Arab Spring, 13, 20, 24, 27, 63, 64, 98, 99, 225,
    230, 259
Arapeyat, 213
Armstrong, Louis, 78, 192–193
art: autonomy of, 26, 50
art music: European, 37–38, 50, 149; Western,
    40, 42, 50, 51, 62; orchestration, 47
art schools: l'Académie Libanaise des Beaux-
    Arts (ALBA), 93
Asia, 4, 25, 90–91, 111
'ataba, 148, 154
atonalism, 44, 50, 60, 165
Atoui, Tarek, 95, 100
authenticity (asala), 13, 17, 43, 50, 102, 211, 219,
    221, 225
avant-garde: as a concept, 4–5, 50, 74–76, 168;
    history, 2, 3–4, 25, 92, 166; metal as, 241–242
Azmeh, Kinan, 56
Azzawi, Wissam, 85

Bach, Johann Sebastian, 45, 47
Badreddin, Shafi, 38, 40–41, 56–62
Baghboudarian, Missak, 40
Baghdad, 8, 66, 86
baile funk, 91, 106

MUSIC / CULTURE
A series from Wesleyan University Press
Edited by Harris M. Berger and Annie J. Randall
Originating editors: George Lipsitz, Susan McClary, and Robert Walser

Listening to Salsa:
Gender, Latin Popular Music, and
Puerto Rican Cultures
by Frances Aparicio

Jazz Consciousness:
Music, Race, and Humanity
by Paul Austerlitz

Metal, Rock, and Jazz:
Perception and the Phenomenology
of Musical Experience
by Harris M. Berger

Identity and Everyday Life:
Essays in the Study of Folklore, Music,
and Popular Culture
by Harris M. Berger and
Giovanna P. Del Negro

Stance: Ideas about Emotion,
Style, and Meaning for the Study
of Expressive Culture
by Harris M. Berger

Monument Eternal:
The Music of Alice Coltrane
by Franya J. Berkman

Bright Balkan Morning:
Romani Lives and the Power of
Music in Greek Macedonia
by Dick Blau and Charles
and Angeliki Keil

Musical Childhoods and
the Cultures of Youth
edited by Susan Boynton
and Roe-Min Kok

Music and Cinema
edited by James Buhler, Caryl
Flinn, and David Neumeyer

The Arab Avant-Garde: Music,
Politics, Modernity
edited by
Thomas Burkhalter,
Kay Dickinson, and
Benjamin J. Harbert

Music and Cyberliberties
by Patrick Burkart

Listening and Longing:
Music Lovers in the Age of Barnum
By Daniel Cavicchi

My Music
by Susan D. Crafts,
Daniel Cavicchi, Charles Keil,
and the Music
in Daily Life Project

Born in the USA:
Bruce Springsteen and the American
Tradition
by Jim Cullen

Presence and Pleasure:
The Funk Grooves of James Brown
and Parliament
by Anne Danielsen

Echo and Reverb:
Fabricating Space in
Popular Music Recording,
1900–1960
by Peter Doyle

Phat Beats, Dope Rhymes:Hip Hop
Down Under Comin' Upper
by Ian Maxwell

Some Liked It Hot: Jazz Women in
Film and Television, 1928–1959
By Kristin A. McGee

Carriacou String Band Serenade:
Performing Identity in the Eastern
Caribbean
by Rebecca S. Miller

Global Noise:
Rap and Hip-Hop outside the USA
edited by Tony Mitchell

Popular Music in Theory:
An Introduction
by Keith Negus

Upside Your Head!
Rhythm and Blues on Central
Avenue
by Johnny Otis

Coming to You Wherever You Are:
MuchMusic, MTV, *and*
Youth Identities
by Kip Pegley

Musicking Bodies:
Gesture and Voice in Hindustani
Music
by Matthew Rahaim

Singing Archaeology:
Philip Glass's Akhnaten
by John Richardson

Black Noise:
Rap Music and Black Culture in
Contemporary America
by Tricia Rose

The Book of Music and Nature:
An Anthology of Sounds, Words, Thoughts
edited by David Rothenberg
and Marta Ulvaeus

Angora Matta: Fatal Acts
of North-South Translation
by Marta Elena Savigliano

Making Beats:
The Art of Sample-Based Hip-Hop
by Joseph G. Schloss

Dissonant Identities:The Rock 'n' Roll
Scene in Austin, Texas
by Barry Shank

Among the Jasmine Trees: Music and
Modernity in Contemporary Syria
by Jonathan Holt Shannon

Banda: Mexican Musical Life
across Borders
by Helena Simonett

Global Soundtracks:
Worlds of Film Music
edited by Mark Slobin

Subcultural Sounds:
Micromusics of the West
by Mark Slobin

Music, Society, Education
by Christopher Small

Musicking: The Meanings
of Performing and Listening
by Christopher Small

Music of the Common Tongue:
Survival and Celebration in African
American Music
by Christopher Small